W9-BSA-587

TARGETS

of

HATRED

Anti-Abortion Terrorism

Patricia Baird-Windle

and

Eleanor J. Bader

palgrave

for St. Martin's Press

TARGETS OF HATRED

Copyright © Patricia Baird-Windle and Eleanor J. Bader, 2001. All rights reserved. No part of this book may be used or reproduced in any manner whatsoever without written permission except in the case of brief quotations embodied in critical articles or reviews.

First published 2001 by
PALGRAVE™
175 Fifth Avenue, New York, N.Y. 10010.
Companies and representatives throughout the world.

PALGRAVE is the new global publishing imprint of St. Martin's Press LLC
Scholarly and Reference Division and Palgrave Publishers Ltd. (formerly Macmillan Press Ltd.).

ISBN 0-312-23925-4 hardback

Library of Congress Cataloging-in-Publication Data available from the Library of Congress.

Excerpt on p. **256** from "Dirge Without Music," by Edna St. Vincent Millay, *Collected Poems* by Edna St. Vincent Millay and Norma Millay Ellis (HarperCollins, 1928, 1955). Reprinted by permission of Elizabeth Barnett, Literary Executor.

Designed by Acme Art, Inc.

First edition: May 2001
10 9 8 7 6 5 4 3 2 1

Printed in the United States of America.

DEDICATION

FROM PATRICIA BAIRD-WINDLE

For Six Generations of Indomitable Women
So that you will always know my love

For
Brooke Laine Beshears and Lexee Windle, my granddaughters
Roni Laine Windle, my daughter
Jean White Perro and Iris Elaine Baird, my sisters
And
In Memory of
Eusinee "Noonie" White Baird, my beloved mother
Emmie Johnson White, my indomitable grandmother
And
Mary Cooper Johnson (Hora-Hogan), my career-woman
exemplar great-grandmother

FROM ELEANOR J. BADER

In Memory of
Helen Freudenheim
And
Esther T. Rand,
Women who inspired me to believe in the possibility of social justice
and women's equality

CONTENTS

Acknowledgments...vi

Preface: Patricia Baird-Windle................................. x

Introduction: Patricia Baird-Windle xiii

Authors' Note.. xix

1. The State of the Union: Abortion in North America.............. 1

2. The Way We Were: America before the
   1973 *Roe v. Wade* Decision................................. 19

3. From *Roe* to Reagan: 1973–1980 39

4. Bombing (and Kidnapping) in the Name of the Lord: 1980–1985 .. 61

5. Writing the Book on Coercion: 1985–1990 87

6. From Mayhem to Murder: 1990–1995...................... 139

7. Rx for Safety: 1995 to the Present......................... 251

8. Of Champions and Challenges 323

   Appendix A. Interviews: July 1998 to May 2000............... 333

   Appendix B. Cities Experiencing Blockades: 1988–1993......... 341

   Appendix C. Pro-Choice Organizations in the
   United States and Canada................................. 345

   Appendix D. Abortion in the United States and Canada:
   A Time Line of Major Events 348

   Notes 355

   Index... 383

ACKNOWLEDGMENTS

PATRICIA

This book has been in progress since 1993, when I increasingly realized that the media were getting less than three percent of the story. And naturally, many people have aided me in bringing out the full story. First, Ted Windle is my rock, the live-in professional doter who so generously enables all of my life. Ted is a male feminist who is simply a fine person first. I learned courage and tenacity from Ted and my late mentor, Dr. Judith M. Levy.

Much of the book represents the reflections and experiences of my golden daughter, Roni Laine Windle. She was roundly abused by anti behavior and still has triumphed. Roni and my colleague Susan Hill gave me great guidance and encouragement. Reid, my oldest son, gave the clinics his every Saturday for years as our first security videographer. His garbage was stolen many times, his credit cards tampered with. Edward W. "Tod" Windle, III, middle son, was administrator of the Port St. Lucie and West Palm clinics when the antis were the most fractious. Tod's wit and sarcasm helped keep everyone going. Thanks to my youngest son, Joseph, for his radio band monitoring; it foiled an anti stunt of disabling their bus in the Melbourne clinic drive. How surprised they were!

An unsung group of people known as trackers and defenders kept clinics open across the United States and Canada. I thank all of them but particularly Anne and Richard Bower, Ann Baker, Cathy Dillon, Phyllis Erwin, Phyllis Rinaldo, Jon Luckey, Lisa Sergi, Margaret Thomas and Michael and Roberta Sampere. Special thanks go to Susan A. England, the attorney on our Supreme Court team who also serves as defender, tracker and doctor transporter extraordinaire. Many had their garbage stolen, their tires flattened, were stalked and much more, and still they came. Debi Johnson saw her home picketed and had to stare down the barrel of a frightened cop's gun.

The volunteers—and many others—confronted danger even after James Barrett was shot in Pensacola. Fred Hobbs and Sam Maddox were the only police who believed, and said so. I also thank the visionary team from the group Refuse & Resist!, including Mary Lou Greenberg, Tracy Stein and

Debra Sweet. Anne Bower of *Body Politic* magazine fought to give the public more than sound bites, and crafted the indexes for this book. Ann Baker of the National Center for the Pro Choice Majority gathered important records and facts for the appendices. Merle Hoffman, Dallas Blanchard, Ph.D., D.J. Webb, Tracy Sefl, Ph.D., Jean Peterman, Ph.D., and Carla Eckhardt and gave their professionalism to the Domestic Terrorism: Guerrilla War Against Abortion Providers survey, providing underpinnings of proof and interview profiles for the book. Dr. Frank Snydle died at 48, just a few months after the exorbitant pressures against him stopped. You decide if his untimely death was partly attributable to domestic terrorism. There are too many doctors to name who continue to serve women regardless of the extortionate aggression foisted on them. Bravo! There are too many staff members and clinic principals in the United States and Canada to name, but for whose valiant contributions I am grateful. Agreeing to tell their stories to Eleanor and me should not have to be an act of courage, but it is. Telling the truth put our faces back on the targets of the unbalanced.

I have some negative acknowledgments, as well. James Reynolds, Chief of the Domestic Terrorism office of the Department of Justice; Rick Jancha, Assistant U.S. Attorney for the Middle District of Florida, Orlando office; and Janet Reno, Attorney General of the United States, are public servants charged with protecting equally the rights of all citizens. The white marble face above the columns of the Supreme Court promises equality under the law. Just where does that leave everyone at clinics, including millions of women whose right to privacy, right to work, right to unimpeded medical care and right to simply be left alone have been trampled? To paraphrase Harriet Tubman, Ain't I a Citizen?

With Peg Yorkin, Eleanor Smeal, Kathryn Spillar, Talbot "Sandy" D'Alemberte, Esq., now president of Florida State University, and Stephen Gey, Esq., FSU constitutional law scholar, with Susan England Esq., and Kathy Patrick, Esq., we had the life-altering experience of going to the Supreme Court.

Eleanor J. Bader gave strong young legs, talent and tenacity to my dream. There would be no *Targets of Hatred* without her. Sheree B., ace agent, took a chance on us. Karen Wolny, senior editor at Palgrave-USA, valiantly shouldered our hefty banner. And a mensch named Henry, like a nurse named Eileen, apologized that we had to live through such awful stuff. Carole and Lyle stood with me far longer than seemed reasonable. Mike Doughney and Lauren Sabina Kneisley told me how important this book was when I was too whipped by anti abuse to write it. They believed. They understood with the gift of compassion for the bloody warrior.

Finally, I want to thank all the women who, with their families, defied the antis, turned a deaf ear to screamers on the sidewalks, stepped over the bodies of demonstrators blocking the doors, and in essence, thumbed their noses at those they loudly proclaimed to be busybodies. You gave, and continue to give, us strength.

Patricia Baird-Windle
December 1, 2000

ELEANOR

Thanks are due to an enormous number of friends, colleagues and associates who provided me with emotional support and friendship during the nearly three years it took to write and research this book. Some have also given their time—reading draft after draft of the manuscript. Others provided money, food and housing to help ease the way during the long periods spent on the road gathering the materials on which *Targets of Hatred* is based.

Blessings to all; I owe you big time!

[Initials are being used to protect the safety of these compañeros and compañeras, since the antis often go after identifiable supporters of choice and women's autonomy.]

Eternal gratitude to: Ellen A., Francine A., Joyce A., Judy A., Michael A., Nathan A., Robert A., Sidney A., Ann B., Anne B., Junior B., Peggy B., Gary C., Bobby D., Doreen D., Dr. Mary D., Susan D., Hillary E., Judy E., Trish E., Ben F., Julia F., Ron F., Amy G., Mary Lou G., Monica G., Jean H., Stephen H., Betsy I., Donald J., Andrew K., Ernece K., Gittel K., Beverly L., Claudia L., Gary L., Sharon L., Chiara M., Christopher M., Laura M., Miriam M., Suzanne M., Victor M., Fraidy N., Shelley O-K., Eric P., Holly P., Stephanie P., Chloe R., Donna R., Linda R., Stanley R., Ann S., Debra S., Rachel S., Tracy S., Gregory T., Maria T., Raysa V., Barbara W., Diane W., Laura W., Lecia W. and Barbara Z.

Special praises to: Jack A., whose unwavering devotion to me, and support for this project, helped get me through many tough moments. He is a true partner, and I am more grateful than I can ever express. I am also forever indebted to the National Center for the Pro Choice Majority, an amazing archive, and the National Abortion Federation. Both are staffed by incredibly knowledgeable and helpful people who came through for this project in countless ways.

I also bestow my thanks on co-author Patricia Baird-Windle, one of the toughest and most creative warriors on the planet. Mil gracias, woman!

Additionally, the intrepid editors and staff at Palgrave, who helped mold hundreds of pages into a coherent, readable text—Alan B., Meredith H., Amy M., Ella P., Karen W., and Meg W.—deserve bountiful praise. Henry K., a libel lawyer extraordinaire, put Patricia and me through some intense paces, but led us to write a more precise and thorough book. Hearty commendations.

Lastly, I want to offer my personal thanks to the thousands of women and men who work in reproductive health clinics throughout North America. I don't know how you do it, but I respect your dedication, tenacity and fearlessness. Because of your compassion, the struggle continues.

Eleanor J. Bader
December 1, 2000

PREFACE

PATRICIA BAIRD-WINDLE

I am an abortion provider. This is the proud term our medical service field uses for everyone who works in or with a clinic. In 1977 my first small clinic, The Aware Woman Center for Choice, was the thirty-fourth to open in Florida and the first in the state to be substantially targeted by organized anti-abortionists. The picketing in the 1970s was initially peaceful, with candlelight vigils and quiet demonstrations. At the same time, there were glimmers of things to come, indicators of the shadowy coercion tactics and threats that would eventually become standard practice for the anti-abortion movement.

Indeed, in the twenty-four years since I opened Aware Woman, I have continually experienced opposition. But although the constant torment—blockades, break-ins, crank calls, glued locks, picket lines, and the taunting and belittling of patients and staff—have been difficult to weather, it is the disbelief of people, the looks that tell me that what I am describing cannot possibly be real, that has been most bothersome. Strangely, few skeptics have been straightforward in asking me to prove my assertions. More often I simply hear or see doubt in the voices or eyes of people I am trying to educate about the terrors inflicted on my staff, my doctors, our families, and those associated with us.

My experience is not unique. In fact, the history of abortion is filled with stories of vilification and misunderstanding. In the late 1960s, as abortion laws were loosened around the nation, Catholic bishops formed a giant propaganda machine. The arcane rhetoric they used harkened back to the 1860s when medical associations first sought to bring healthcare, including abortion, into a standardized mainstream. A century later, as the likelihood of legalization loomed, their books and articles adopted a language that can best be described as distorted. A one-ounce fetus became "a living child" or "baby." A pregnant woman became a "mother."

In addition, our opponents have continually manipulated language to defame providers. Rather than presenting us as dedicated caregivers intent on serving women, they routinely demean our motives and sense of mission, alleging that we are "butchers" or "murderers" whose "blood lust" demands the "sacrifice of unborn children." While rational thought renders these descriptions ridiculous, the image of providers as less than noble has seeped into the North American psyche, increasing ambivalence about the process.

Meanwhile, the propaganda machine styles the anti-abortion movement as well-meaning, devoted Christians who peacefully picket and exercise their rights of free speech and assembly. Lost in the haze is the truth about the anger, the screaming, the accusatory and menacing words that are shrieked at patients and staff by protesters.

Still, why has it taken the public so many years to glimpse the face of anti-abortion violence?

The short answer is that providers have a complex job to do inside their clinics. We simply cannot interrupt working on the inside to pay attention to the complex melee on the outside, nor do we have the time, energy or money to build a competing propaganda machine.

I learned this firsthand in 1977, when my first clinic opened after major travail. Then, in 1989, my three clinics became the targets of more concentrated anti-abortion activism than we had previously experienced, far surpassing the harassment of everyone entering or leaving the facilities. Then, in 1993, the IMPACT Team, a national project of Operation Rescue, stepped up its attacks on Central Florida clinics, primarily mine, even further. Media from across the United States and from Australia, England, Finland, France, Germany and Sweden arrived. I naively assumed that placing a press spotlight on the horrors would help us. Unfortunately, the journalists reported only the most overt actions, generally ignoring the long-term subversive maneuvers that were nearly paralyzing us. Worse, we were unable to get help from the police, other law enforcement agencies, or our communities. In desperation, we begged the United States Attorney's Office for help. They slammed the doors rudely. During one particularly awful meeting, an FBI agent actually fell asleep as I outlined what we were experiencing.

As *Targets of Hatred: Anti-Abortion Terrorism* unfolds, you will see that anti-abortion lawlessness has been noted in location after location since the mid-1970s. You will also see that the press and media's reluctance to report these ongoing attacks, in conjunction with collateral harassment, has squelched the efforts of those who might otherwise have assisted us. For example, when more than 570 objections were received by my local newspaper to protest a story about me and what I do, the paper became extremely cautious and ended up indulging the other side. We call it the BOB syndrome. They Bend Over Backward to be "fair" even when they see the protesters' vile or illegal behavior with their own eyes. Cops BOB. Judges BOB. Journalists and legislators BOB. Needless to say, this behavior adversely affects providers and undermines our confidence and our commitment.

I finally gave in when I decided, in the summer of 1999, to retire. I just couldn't take it anymore. I was physically ill and exhausted and had spent the bulk of my retirement savings on litigation to stifle the antis. But rest assured: I have neither given up nor been silenced. Since retiring, I have worked tirelessly to inform anyone and everyone about the extent of anti-abortion fury. I have also dedicated myself to rectifying the omission of providers' experiences from North American history and to making sure that our stories are told, analyzed and listened to.

Targets of Hatred recounts the experiences of more than 190 providers throughout the United States and Canada, along the way touching on women's history, religious history, legal history, and law enforcement history. As you delve into our narrative of anti-abortion transgression—despite the heft of this volume we have presented fewer than ten percent of the incidents at targeted locations—we hope you will agree that justice has been derailed. In addition, please note that although the right to privacy still protects freedom of choice, if there are no providers left, choice becomes a hollow phrase and access a moot point.

INTRODUCTION

PATRICIA BAIRD-WINDLE

MARCH 1993: NATIONWIDE

Storms were brewing in the Atlantic. Mother Nature seemed to be outdoing herself, building up thunderheads along the eastern seaboard. But bad weather was not the nation's only problem. Violence against abortion providers—clinic owners, doctors, nurses, counselors and lab technicians—was escalating, and had begun to deter the hundreds of thousands of women who relied on clinics for their reproductive care.

Toxic butyric acid attacks were fouling frightening numbers of health centers, causing medical problems for personnel, patients and police; arsons and bombings were also becoming more frequent. One fire, in Corpus Christi, Texas, destroyed an entire office complex as well as its intended target, Reproductive Health Services. Mass sit-ins, called "blockades" by clinics and "rescues" by anti-abortion groups, were closing centers nationwide, delaying scheduled surgeries for hours and sometimes days. Police forces dealt, in an oft-maddeningly and suspiciously dilatory fashion, by slowly prying limp protesters from clinic doors. Providers understood that the hauling of demonstrators was not a routine part of police work. Nonetheless, clinic employees knew that law enforcement's reluctance to make arrests and clear entrances was increasing stress levels and fear among patients and workers. The hatred on the faces of blockaders, and the mashing, punching, pinching and biting of clinic volunteers, all pointed to a palpable increase in animosity against us. Indeed, it looked as if the protesting mobs would spin out of control. The vitriol was combustible.

The volatility increased in early 1993 when anti-abortion leaders announced their major efforts for that spring and summer. One project, a four-month "boot camp" called the IMPACT Team, was organized to train a national cadre of Christian activists in anti-abortion tactics. IMPACT was scheduled to take place in central Florida and would be followed by the intensive targeting of health centers in Minneapolis/St. Paul. The major and longest campaign, however, was to be directed at the Aware Woman Centers for Choice in Melbourne, Port St. Lucie and West Palm Beach, Florida, small clinics on the central coast that my husband and I owned.

Kathy Spillar, head of the Clinic Defense Project of the Feminist Majority Foundation (FMF), came to Melbourne in November 1992. After seeing the anti-abortion activity in central Florida, she told FMF president Eleanor (Ellie) Smeal that although dozens of volunteers were being trained to shield patients from view, far more needed to be done.

Smeal, a seasoned organizer, made immediate plans for a press conference at the National Press Club in Washington, D.C., to describe the ever-more-intense threat. The conference was held on Friday, March 6, 1993. Marilyn Chrisman Eldridge, director of a group of nonprofit clinics in Texas and Oklahoma, was asked to describe the devastation wrought by arson at her Corpus Christi clinic. That fire had destroyed not just the health center but seven nearby businesses. I also spoke, telling the media about the IMPACT Team's efforts to close my clinics. My testimony outlined, in vivid terms, the way anti-abortion leaders taught team participants to engage in borderline-legal activities, from "street preaching," to researching doctors to ascertain weaknesses, to blanketing communities with menacing posters denouncing my doctors and me as "murderers" and "baby killers." I spoke of how they had harassed me, my family and my employees—going so far as to block one of my doctors from leaving both his home and private office—and detailed other methods used to sabotage clinic functioning.

About thirty reporters, including representatives from the *New York Times,* ABC TV News, the *Houston Chronicle* and Cox Broadcasting, attended the conference. Smeal opened with commentary about the frightening and intimidating climate the anti-abortion movement had created. Eldridge, a pioneer in abortion provision, then spoke about the butyric acid attack she had experienced in San Antonio and detailed the shocking Corpus Christi fire. Her final remarks were uttered in a low, compelling voice: "I cannot close without telling you that whenever I turn the key in the ignition of my car, I worry that a bomb may go off. The hatred of the antis is such that I fear I will be murdered. That is how bad it is getting."

I concluded with a plea: "You must not think that these protestors are all peaceful, religious people who are a bit misguided and rude, perhaps, but harmless. The hardcore group arrayed against us is paid. Domestic terrorism is their job. They are extortionists pure and simple."

The first question came from a tall, red-headed reporter from the *New York Times,* Felicity Barringer. From the back of the room she shouted to me, "What proof do you offer that they are paid?" I am rarely at a loss for words, but I was so worn out from the targeting in Florida that I went blank. Years later I still regret that moment and wish that I had pointed out the vast number of people who are at clinics eight to ten hours a day, five to six days a week, but have no visible means of support. I wish I had prodded *her* to investigate since there are ample court transcripts, sworn depositions and prior interviews to substantiate my claim.

After thirty minutes spent answering questions, the press conference waned. None of the reporters asked Chrisman or me about the implied violence or the difficulties of trying to provide reproductive healthcare while simultaneously fighting a low-grade guerrilla war. In fact, they seemed oddly disengaged, missing the prophesy of impending violence that we had handed them.

Hours later Chrisman returned to Texas and Smeal and I headed to Florida. That night we spoke to a group of clinic defenders who were being trained at the Unitarian church in Melbourne. Smeal and I explained what was likely to happen the next day, once Operation Rescue (OR) founder and "rescue" movement leader Randall Terry arrived. We tried to be upbeat and convey our resolve to keep the clinic open.

Saturday morning was gray, chilly, with winds gusting up to fifty-five miles an hour. When about one hundred antis swarmed onto the narrow two-lane highway that follows the Atlantic Ocean, they realized that the picketing they had planned at my oceanfront condominium was not to be. Sign after sign was ripped from their hands by the same storm that two days earlier had made it difficult for my plane to land at Washington National Airport. After reconnoitering for a few minutes, OR leaders announced that they would hold an outdoor prayer vigil in front of the building I lived in.

Police told my husband, Ted, and me to stay inside until the demonstrators were gone. Spillar also begged us to stay away from the dwelling's large windows. She was outside, talking to media and police and trading occasional jibes with the antis when a *Newsweek* reporter asked if it was possible to speak to us. Spillar escorted him through the protestors and got him in. His first, all-too obvious question was, "Do you feel trapped inside like this?" The answer, of course, was yes.

At 10:00 A.M., the crowd that had hog-tied traffic on the area's two-lane artery for four hours got into their vehicles and proceeded north to the Aware Woman Center for Choice in Melbourne, twelve miles away. After a short wait, we followed, dreading what the rest of the day would bring us. As we turned a curve about a half mile from the clinic, we could see the profusion of police, anti-abortion activists, media and clinic defenders who had gathered. The side of the highway was full, the small access street crammed. Six or seven media vans and satellite trucks had paid neighbors to let them park on their lawns. As Ted and I approached the clinic, cheers and applause swelled from the pro-choice side. The fanatics on the south side glared. Some hissed and booed. Dozens moved as if they were going to block the car, a defiant though routine gesture. In the main driveway, as more than sixty antis moved apart when cops blew whistles, we wondered if we were going to be able to get inside the clinic. We stopped on the far side of the parking lot and slowly got out of the vehicle, protectively accompanied by pro-choice volunteers. Immediately, four or five anti-abortionists perched on ladders behind a ten-foot privacy fence began screaming at us: "Please, please stop this baby-killing. You don't need the money anymore. Aren't you ashamed, Patricia? Ted, what is it like to have your paycheck signed by a woman?"

As usual, I did my best to ignore them and greet the crowd of media who had assembled for interviews. Inside the building, Ellie Smeal gave a short motivational talk, trying to lift staff spirits by reminding them how important their work is to women who need gynecological and abortion services. I moved from waiting rooms to counseling rooms to talk with patients and the people who were with them. I explained what was happening outside and answered questions. One by one the women told me how angry they were at the protesters; a few admitted fear. Many asked me why they had to endure these conditions. Several women made reference to a patient who could not stop crying because the hordes of antis had scared her so badly. Her surgery had to be postponed because the protesters had made her claustrophobic when they pressed in on her car. The presence of police and media had further exacerbated her terror. At the time, this woman had no way of knowing that her doctor's testimony about the antis' impact on her would eventually reach the Supreme Court of the United States.

As the patients and I spoke, the screams of a teenage girl standing on an A-frame ladder could be heard: "Mommy, Mommy, I had blue eyes. Why did you rip me apart? Mommy, why did you kill me?"

Once our doctor arrived and navigated through the temporary garage set up to hide and protect him from prying cameras and potential violence, Ellie Smeal and I went back outside. Press interviews were held in the clinic's garden so that we could watch for the arrival of Randall Terry, the founder of Operation Rescue.

Cheers started from across the street, alerting us that Terry was approaching. He slowly made his way through his fans like a rock star, shaking hands and greeting his adoring minions, and headed toward the clinic driveway. I hung back from the throng that was picketing on the sidewalk and clogging the street. I had never spoken to Terry, despite his three prior visits to Brevard County. Now, as I saw him behaving as if he owned the area, I went down to the front walkway.

Terry immediately launched into a showy, preachy harangue as the media crowded in, satellite dishes and microphones swaying in the constant, punishing wind. The police tried to separate people but did not succeed; they were out-trumped by the crush of Terry's admirers. Ellie crowded in on Terry, asking him why he brought people to harass women and clinics. She signaled to me to show Terry the list of illegal and smarmy anti-abortion activities that I had compiled for the press. Terry grabbed the papers, tore the thick stack into pieces, and ground it with his foot. "Why don't you stop killing babies, Patricia?" he thundered. "Ellie, it will not do any good for you to be here. She is going to have to stop. We are going to see to it that she and her doctors have no place to hide. We will run them to ground. It will be fun."

I found my voice and responded: "Randy, why are you doing these things to us?" Terry, a solid foot taller than I and two decades younger, bent to respond. The crowd, noisy until a minute before, became silent. As Terry leaned forward, he made a thumb and index finger gesture of accusation. Without realizing it, I made exactly the same gesture back, modeling him. Since I had never before taken a stance that looked combative, I hated the apparent implication. Nonetheless, our confrontation led both local and national news that evening; the photograph of our stand-off continues to be used to illustrate the abortion conflict.

Meanwhile, Kathy Patrick, an attorney whom Ellie Smeal had flown to Melbourne to help us get legal protection, found that her flight home to Houston had been grounded by what was being called "the windstorm of the century." As the winds continued to howl and the clinic's shingle roof began to peel away, she sat at the computer and hammered out a request for an injunction to ban the antis from blocking our doors and harassing patients. Patrick's petition eventually went to the highest court in Florida; appeals later took it—and our clinic—to the United States Supreme Court.

Over a late lunch, I continued to outline the litany of tactics that had been used against the Aware Woman Centers for Choice. I told both Smeal and Patrick that in February 1992 a mysterious package had been found at the clinic during a midnight security review of the building. The security guard had called me from a nearby service station. I advised him to move away and call the police. A full bomb team and thirteen emergency vehicles from three law enforcement groups responded, as did Ted and I. The package was exploded by remote control. It turned out to be nothing but was an example of how, once again, we were called out in the middle of the night to assist the police. Over the twenty-two years we ran the clinics, the antis caused the authorities to call us dozens of times. Hours of sleep were interrupted because of their antics.

I spent the next day, March 8, composing a summary of the things I felt needed to be done to protect clinics, providers and patients and make me feel less alone. The memo stated my worst fear, that one of us was going to be killed. Two days later, in the Florida Gulf coast town of Pensacola, Dr. David Gunn was executed by an anti-abortion zealot. Sixteen months later Dr. John Bayard Britton and his escort, James Barrett, were shot to death at another Pensacola clinic. Unfortunately, the murders had just begun.

Eleanor Smeal had announced the increasing violence on March 6; Marilyn Chrisman Eldridge had told the press in no uncertain terms that she was afraid she would be assassinated because of her involvement in providing abortion services. Two days later I had echoed her. A skeptical media thought we were exaggerating—even lying—and perpetuated the social denial that had long accompanied the anti-abortion threat. Then, still unable to accept the fact that an allegedly Christian political movement had turned deadly, they began to focus on the pathology of individual fanatics. Repeatedly we were told that the killings were "isolated incidents," the work of a "lone gunman." It was a mistake that would have hideous long-term consequences for both abortion providers and women who desire reproductive health services. It was a mistake that would literally kill.

Targets of Hatred is the by-product of the disbelief that abortion providers in the United States and Canada face each and every day. After the 1993 and 1994 murders, I began to obsess about how we could force media and legislators and, most important, law enforcement to believe us when we described anti-abortionists as domestic terrorists. I soon realized that my individual story, however dramatic, would not be enough to sway them. In the face of sound-bite journalism, it became clear that a full-length book was essential if providers' experiences were to be understood.

Unfortunately, when this realization dawned I was totally immersed in trying to keep my clinics open in the face of heavy targeting, so I knew that I could not write the book alone. Journalist Eleanor J. Bader agreed to be my co-writer after penning a feature article about me for a now-defunct feminist magazine. Eleanor quickly grasped the scorn providers endure when her editor slashed large sections of the article. The editor thought my story preposterous and refused to believe that the things I described had really happened. Eleanor heard this reaction again and again as she interviewed clinic staff in thirty-nine states and several Canadian provinces. Indeed, as the research mounted, she and I came to see that cultural denial has made anti-abortion lawlessness one of the least understood subjects of the late twentieth and early twenty-first centuries.

The story speaks for itself. It is high time to correct the record.

AUTHORS' NOTE

Targets of Hatred is a social history. It chronicles the movements leading up to *Roe v. Wade*, the 1973 Supreme Court decision that legalized abortion, and looks at what has happened since the decision was issued nearly thirty years ago. Alongside a chronological account of the violence and harassment that have long plagued clinic workers, *Targets of Hatred* presents the human side of the "abortion wars," the observations and reactions of front-line workers who describe, in their own words, being taunted, stalked and threatened by anti-choice extremists. Since these stories have been lost in discussions of abortion politics, our goal is to rectify that oversight.

The book is organized in five-year increments, with chapters that are wildly divergent in length. This is because some five-year periods saw minimal anti-abortion activity, while other periods saw a great deal. In addition, the book relies upon short, vignette-like entries to show the pattern of developing violence and its geographic spread. Some clinics and clinic workers appear repeatedly. Others appear only once. Regardless, we hope that by the time you reach the end of this book, you will have a new appreciation for their efforts and commitment.

That said, *Targets of Hatred* is not easy reading, and we fear that you will become overwhelmed by so many stories of arson, blockades, bombings, invasions and acts of vandalism. It is undeniably upsetting stuff. Nonetheless, we believe that the events described show a clear trajectory, one that moves from vandalism and harassment to torment and torture. We also believe that the book offers proof of a national and international conspiracy. But judge for yourself. Watch as tactics accumulate, exhausting and frightening providers and patients. Note the changes in anti-abortion rhetoric. See how verbal incitement opens the door to murder and mayhem. Monitor the intersections—and the divergences—among "right to life" organizations, the evangelical right wing, the Catholic church, and the Republican and Democratic parties.

Last, understand the impact that the violence has had on abortion availability in both Canada and the United States. As you do so, please bear in mind that without providers, there is no choice.

Many of you may believe that the people carrying out tactics against abortion providers are simply peaceful, well-meaning Christians. Police and others often say this, as you will see. This erroneous assumption frequently brings later apologies as torment, torture and murder play out across the United States and Canada. We chose to put an explanation of the antis' psychopathology early in the book so that you could follow the increase in violence and understand what kinds of people do these things, and why. We promise to prove the pathology presented here long before you finish the book.

CHAPTER ONE

The State of the Union: Abortion in North America

When the Supreme Court decided *Roe v. Wade* on January 22, 1973, most Americans believed the abortion issue was finally settled. Women who desired to terminate unwanted pregnancies could do so; likewise, those who wanted to reproduce could have as many children as they felt capable of rearing.

Women's clinics began to proliferate, and it was the dream of entrepreneurs, many of them feminists, to make abortion as accessible as dental or optical care and as supportive, caring and nonjudgmental as possible. Unfortunately, their dream has been deferred. Although clinics did open in all fifty states, early opposition made it obvious that abortion was different from other medical services. By the late 1970s, well-organized foes had demonstrated that they would do everything within their means to close clinics or limit the availability of care. While their efforts to ban abortion have fallen flat, the gradual, incremental winnowing away of the right to choose has been extremely successful.

At the start of the twenty-first century, abortion services are available in only sixteen percent of U.S. counties. South Dakota has just one provider for the entire state; North Dakota has two; West Virginia has four. Between 1992 and 1996 the number of providers fell by fourteen percent, from 2,380 to 2,042, leaving nearly one-third of American cities without a reproductive health center.[1] Rural areas are even worse off and would-be patients are often forced to travel hundreds of miles to see a physician.[2]

A 1998 study by the New York–based Alan Guttmacher Institute attributes the drop in services to both anti-abortion terrorism and legislative successes in curtailing access. Take Medicaid, the federally funded health insurance program for the indigent. At the present time, Medicaid pays for abortions in extremely limited circumstances: if completing the pregnancy would endanger the life of the woman or if she became pregnant as a result of rape or incest. Only fourteen states—California, Connecticut, Hawaii, Maryland, Massachusetts, Minnesota, Montana, New Jersey, New Mexico, New York, Oregon, Vermont, Washington and West Virginia—voluntarily pay for the abortions of all Medicaid-eligible women who want one.[3] In the rest of the country, the poor have to borrow money, or scrimp on food or household supplies, to pay for their surgeries. Predictably, many bear children they do not want or believe they can adequately care for.

Teenagers, twenty percent of whom will get pregnant at least once before their twentieth birthday, also face roadblocks in exercising their freedom of choice.[4] Thirty states currently enforce laws that require a minor to get the consent of or notify an adult, typically a parent, prior to an abortion. Of those, only Delaware, Maryland and West Virginia allow a medical professional to waive the requirement if he or she feels it is in the young woman's best interest to do so. In addition, with the exception of Idaho and Utah, all states with parental consent or notification laws have judicial bypass programs that force minors to go before a judge if they believe parental involvement to be ill-advised. Although eight states allow young women to confide in an adult other than a parent, "pro-family" activists have lobbied hard—and made inroads—to give parents sole reproductive authority over their daughters. At their behest, the Child Custody Protection Act, currently before the U.S. Congress, would make it a crime punishable by up to a year in jail for a nonparent or guardian to transport a minor from a state with parental consent/notification laws to a state without them for the purpose of having an abortion.

Opponents of such strictures charge that those young women who can, already do confide in their parents; they further argue that good familial relationships cannot be legislated. According to a joint statement issued by the American Academy of Pediatrics, the American College of Obstetricians and Gynecologists, the American Public Health Association and the Society for Adolescent Medicine: "Adolescents should be strongly encouraged to involve their parents and other trusted adults in decisions regarding pregnancy termination, and the majority voluntarily do so. Legislation mandating parental involvement does not achieve the intended benefit of promoting family communication, but does increase the risk of harm to the adolescent by delaying access to appropriate medical care."[5] Nonetheless, politicians continue to pander to "pro-family" constituents by campaigning on "I'm pro-choice, but . . . " platforms.

While teenagers and poor women have been targeted for access restrictions, they are not the only ones to be threatened. For more than a decade Congress has barred military hospitals from offering abortion services, even if the servicewoman or the dependent of a serviceman is willing to pay for the procedure out of pocket; similarly, federal workers can use their health insurance to pay for abortions only in cases of life endangerment, rape or incest. Intact dilation and evacuation (the falsely named "partial-birth") abortions, many of them requested following the detection of fetal abnormalities in the second- or third-trimester, are prohibited in eight states: Indiana, Kansas, Mississippi, Oklahoma, South Carolina, South Dakota, Tennessee and Utah.[6] Nineteen states impose mandatory waiting periods—usually eighteen to twenty-four hours—that keep women from having abortions until they have received a state-mandated lecture on abortion risks, fetal development, childbearing and adoption.[7]

A 1998 study of Mississippi's waiting period, conducted one year after "informed consent" went into effect, revealed that the percentage of women seeking abortions who traveled out of state rose from 18.6 to 25.4. In addition, the percentage of procedures performed after twelve weeks' gestation rose from 10.4 to 14.5, a scary trend since the later the abortion, the greater the risk.[8]

Yet the threat to access from legal requirements that limit availability are but part of the problem; coupled with the fact that the majority of abortions in the United States are performed by two percent of the country's obstetrician-gynecologists, two-thirds of whom are sixty-five years of age or older, the country is facing a critical shortage of providers. On top of this, since only twelve percent of ob-gyn residency programs require training in first-trimester procedures, young doctors eager to go into reproductive health have to go out of their way to study techniques. Additionally, doctor-only laws in forty-four states keep physician's assistants, nurse practitioners and midwives from offering services. Despite evidence of their competence in offering safe abortions, they are barred from doing so.[9]

Hospitals present another obstacle to access. A 1996 study by the Alan Guttmacher Institute found just 703 hospital providers in the fifty states. Most, 58 percent, performed fewer than 30 procedures annually; only twelve facilities provided 1,000 or more.[10] Worse, between 1988 and 1992, eighteen percent of American hospitals stopped providing abortions altogether.[11] Much of the blame for this reduction falls on mergers. In the past several years, forty percent of the nation's 5,200 nonfederal hospitals have either merged or entered into an agreement to do so; the vast majority have joined with Catholic institutions.[12] While about half have maintained their reproductive health services, the remainder have eliminated abortions, vasectomies and tubal ligations in accordance with Catholic dictate. Distribution of contraceptives, including the morning-after pill and condoms for the prevention of pregnancy, AIDS and sexually transmitted diseases (STDs), has also ceased. In many rural areas, this effectively denies care to thousands of people. Equally appalling, write prochoice activists Rosemary Candelario and Catherine Rich, "if fewer hospitals perform fewer abortions, fewer providers are trained."[13]

Small wonder, then, that the number of abortions in the United States has declined steadily since the first years after *Roe v. Wade* and now total between 1.2 and 1.4 million annually. While better access to contraception and the availability of the morning-after pill account for some of the reduction, antiabortion violence, harassment and propaganda are also partly responsible.

"In 1977 it was almost a party when women came for their abortions," says Eileen Schnitger, director of Public Affairs at Women's Health Care Specialists (formerly called the Feminist Women's Health Centers), a nonprofit four-clinic chain in California. "The women would feel joy because they were in a pro-woman place. Now we see women who want to have smiles on their faces, want to show their relief, but who feel guilty. I blame that on the anti-abortion movement. The shame thing has been brought out by them. Today when women feel genuinely good about having an abortion, they act as if it's a feeling they should not have."[14] Still, despite the shrinking numbers of procedures and providers, the fact remains that forty-three percent of American women will have at least one abortion in their lifetime.[15] Furthermore, women have shown that they will jump through rings of fire to get them. But as tenacious as abortion patients have proven themselves to be, anti-abortion extremists are equally intrepid.

WHO, WHAT, WHEN AND WHERE:
THE ANTI-ABORTION MOVEMENT

Hundreds of anti-abortion groups, many of them church- or community-based, currently exist; all want to reverse *Roe v. Wade* and recriminalize abortion. While most engage in legal protest—lobbying legislators, pro-choice lawmakers and feminist organizations—many of those remaining at clinics have tested or crossed the line into illegal activities. Quiet, peaceful pickets are largely a thing of the past, say providers, because most moderates have left the field due to increasing violence. The extremists who remain employ actions spanning a broad continuum, from the increasingly nasty pestering of patients as they enter and leave reproductive health centers, to harassing clinic workers and their families; from tampering with or destroying medical equipment, to brutal violence against clinic property or personnel. Arson, chemical attacks, firebombings, kidnappings, stabbings, shootings, vandalism and murder—all have occurred because some extreme anti-abortionists are frustrated that legal efforts to outlaw abortion have so far failed.

Who are these anti-abortion groups? What distinguishes those who do and do not engage in terrorism, violence or other illegal actions? The following roster, beginning with the most moderate group and ending with what many consider the most extreme, is meant to introduce the major anti-choice organizations operating in the United States and Canada:

- The Washington, D.C.-based **National Right to Life Committee** (NRTLC; www.nrlc.org) is the oldest and most staid anti-abortion organization in the United States. Its goal is to end abortion; its strategy is to chip away at the right to choose. Toward that end, it supports legislation and does extensive lobbying to curtail abortion access. The NRTLC's current agenda? State-by-state passage of bans on dilation and evacuation (NRTLC erroneously calls them "partial-birth") abortions and human embryo research. It has also launched a campaign in favor of the Women and Children Resources Act, an $85 million federal appropriation bill that seeks to fund services for women seeking "abortion alternatives." The act would finance virulently anti-abortion crisis pregnancy centers, maternity homes and adoption agencies. In addition, the NRTLC is lobbying hard in support of the Child Custody Prevention Act, the bill that would make it a crime for a nonparent or guardian to transport a minor across state lines for an abortion.

  Right to Life leaders argue that *Roe v. Wade* brought with it an ethos of disrespect for human life that is exemplified by efforts to legalize assisted suicide and euthanasia. Opponents of both, they have initiated a national campaign for passage of the Pain Relief Promotion Act. The act would bar controlled substances from being used to "kill patients" and would mandate palliative care in all instances, regardless of what the patient desires.

  While individual members of the NRTLC have participated in actions sponsored by organizations including the more radical Lambs of Christ and Operation Rescue/Operation Save America, NRTLC publicly denounces violence directed at abortion providers and plans neither clinic invasions nor "rescues." At the same time, the group has done precious little to dissuade violent extremists or decry the use of inflammatory rhetoric.

- The **American Life League** (ALL; www.all.org) "exists to serve God by helping to build a society that respects and protects innocent human life from fertilization to natural death without compromise, without exception, without apology."[16] Founded in the late 1970s by disgruntled former NRTLC staffers Judie and Paul Brown, the group relies on "biblical principles" and, unlike the NRTLC, has a wide political agenda. According to its statement of purpose, ALL opposes "all abortion, contraceptive methods that cause abortion, and other threats to the human person and the family."[17] Their platform forbids abortion in cases of rape, incest, fetal deformity or life endangerment, even if the life of the woman is in danger, and opposes eugenics, human embryo research, population control and reproductive technologies. ALL literature also explicitly denounces violence and the notion that it is "justifiable homicide" to kill abortion providers.

  The American Life League does not confine its work to an adult membership and several ALL offshoots attempt to reach youth. Among them: Crossroads, a college outreach group based at Steubenville University in Ohio; Rock for Life, an international organization that distributes anti-abortion leaflets at concerts and shows; and Why Life?, an outreach effort aimed at junior high and high school students.

  Stop Planned Parenthood (STOPP), another outreach effort, exists to denounce the reproductive health organization. Despite the fact that only 72 of the 132 Planned Parenthood affiliates in the United States provide abortions, ALL continues to portray the group as the nation's primary provider. In fact, says Ron Fitzsimmons of the National Coalition of Abortion Providers (NCAP), independent clinics and doctors terminate more than three-quarters of America's unwanted pregnancies. This does not faze STOPP founder Jim Sedlak. "Even if Planned Parenthood stopped doing abortions tomorrow we'd still oppose them because they support a free-sex lifestyle among youth," he says. "We don't believe kids have to have sex. We talk about all the problems that occur when you have sex and we send out a pro-chastity message."[18]

- The **Pro-Life Action League** (PLAL; www.prolifeaction.org) was founded in 1980 by former Roman Catholic (Benedictine) seminarian and journalist Joseph Scheidler. Eager for tangible victories, Scheidler opted to bypass the NRTLC and has, for twenty years, organized in-your-face demonstrations, sit-ins and blockades. His 1985 book, *Closed: 99 Ways to Stop Abortion,* is a classic text for anti-choice zealots and would-be saboteurs. Aggressive "sidewalk counseling" meant to stop women from ending unwanted pregnancies; amplified demonstrations, often using bullhorns, outside operating rooms; "rescue" missions, the precursors of blockades, at clinics; confrontations with doctors at their homes, offices, churches and at restaurants, funerals and social functions; the taunting of pro-choice politicians and organizational representatives—these are the stock-in-trade of PLAL.

The group purports to engage in only aboveboard activities; none-theless, it was found liable for extortion, a violation of the Racketeer Influenced Corrupt Organizations (RICO) Act, in 1998 and has been ordered to pay damages to two clinics represented by the National Organization for Women (NOW) and the National Women's Health Organization (NWHO). PLAL is currently appealing the decision.

- **Operation Rescue/Operation Rescue National/Operation Save America** (OR or OSA; www.operationsaveamerica.org; www.orn.org), a group founded by fundamentalist preacher Randall Terry in 1986, changed its name from Operation Rescue National to Operation Save America in the spring of 1999, presumably to reflect its growing interest in denouncing not just abortion but family planning, homosexuality, pornography and the lack of prayer in public school classrooms. (Most pro-choice activists believe that the change had a more sinister motive: to confuse the courts and dodge attempts to trace the organization's financial assets and potential liabilities. Patricia Baird-Windle states that "the name change fits the Operation Rescue pattern of making public threats, overtly or covertly carrying out these threats, then denying that they did anything. OR members distance themselves from their actions by frequent name changing and denials, maintaining the pretense that they were never involved in illegal activities."[19])

The OR/OSA Web page states its purported—if ambiguous—purpose: "OR unashamedly takes up the cause of pre-born children in the name of Jesus Christ. We employ only Biblical principles. The Bible is our foundation; the cross of Christ is our strategy; the repentance of the church of Jesus Christ is our ultimate goal."[20])

During its brief heyday, 1988 to 1994, OR/OSA's sole focus was on "ending the slaughter of innocent babies" by blocking clinic doors. Terry says that this was a tactical decision. "From the beginning when I founded

OR, the vision was not only to end child killing; the vision was to recapture the power bases of America, for child killing to be the first domino, if you will, to fall. Once we mobilize the momentum, the manpower, the money and all that goes with that to make child killing illegal, we will have sufficient moral authority and moral force and momentum to get the homosexual movement back in the closet, to get the condom pushers in our schools to go back to the fringes of society where they belong."[21]

OR/OSA is currently headed by the Reverend Philip "Flip" Benham, a former bar owner who was "saved" in 1976. Under his leadership, the group has continued to protest at abortion clinics and leads a "God is Going to School" project to promote daily prayer and the posting of the Ten Commandments in educational settings. OR/OSA has also demonstrated against the sale of "pornographic" books by Barnes & Noble Booksellers. In addition, in 1998 and 1999 the group picketed the annual June Gay Days gathering at Disney theme parks and has assailed the diversity and tolerance that Gay Days celebrates.

Although OR/OSA has pursued only minor efforts against contraception, Randall Terry has repeatedly exhorted his followers to oppose human interference with God's reproductive plan. "We should trust God with how many children we should have," he wrote in an article reprinted in *Life Advocate Magazine*. "At its core birth control is anti-child. When we use birth control we are saying, 'No, I don't want children.' If you are on the pill or using an IUD, stop immediately. They are abortifacients. . . . Leave the number of children you have in God's hands. . . . Our children are the only eternal possession we have except our souls."[22]

While OR-sponsored "rescues" often involve low-level violence, the group publicly condemns the concept of "justifiable homicide" against providers.

- **Missionaries to the Pre-Born** (MTP; www.execpc.com/~restore/mtp/mtp) was founded in 1990 by fundamentalist Matt Trewhella, a former Detroit gang member. An avid supporter of armed resistance and Christian militias, Trewhella has great contempt for reformist groups such as the National Right to Life Committee. MTP castigates the incremental approach to ending abortion demonstrated by the push to ban so-called partial-birth abortions and sees the campaign as a move from "a half-measure to a minuscule-measure strategy."[23] It further opposes the gradual winnowing away of reproductive options. For the Missionaries, it is all or nothing.

- **The Lambs of Christ** (www.thelambsofchrist.com) are best known for organizing mass sit-ins at clinics and pushing junker cars into entryways to prevent ingress and egress and then encouraging participants not to divulge their names to arresting police officers. Once incarcerated, Lambs often show their "oneness with the unborn" by refusing to bathe and defecating and urinating on themselves. Lambs founder Father Norman Weslin, a retired military officer, was married and raised two adopted children before being called to the ministry as a middle-age adult.

    A member of the Roman Catholic Oblates of Wisdom, Weslin was ordained in the late 1980s. Since founding the Lambs, he has been arrested between sixty and seventy times for anti-abortion protests. He is rumored to support himself—and at least partially finance the Lambs— through donations supplemented by a substantial military pension.

    The Lambs' Web page, complete with funereal music, includes articles about abortion, morality and political doctrine. "One Nation Under Satan," for example, advises readers that "all the severe problems which the administration of our beloved country is now experiencing are not so much because of the sexual abuse of young women, perjury, obstruction of justice or tampering with witnesses, but the reason for evil that prevails in the United States is because our president kills Jesus Christ's babies. This is no longer 'One Nation Under God.' This is now 'One Nation Under Satan.'"[24] Another piece depicts "unborn babies" as "America's most despised minority."[25]

- *Life Advocate Magazine/*Advocates for Life Ministries** (ALM; http:// spiritone.com/~lifeadvo/) was one of the most extreme groups and publications in the United States before it dissolved in late 1999. Multnomah Bible College graduate Andrew Burnett started the Portland, Oregon–based Advocates for Life Ministries in 1985. ALM's initial publication, *The Advocate,* evolved into the slick, full color, bimonthly *Life Advocate Magazine* a decade later. In 1994 Burnett started the American Coalition of Life Activists (ACLA) to explicitly foster a pro-violence ethos.

    ACLA also published The Nuremberg Files, a Web page that continues to urge readers to "visualize abortionists on trial." They name more than three hundred health workers, clinic owners and pro-choice activists, many of whom have no direct connection with the provision of abortion, and label them murderers, criminals and child killers. The pro-choice community calls it a hit list. ALM calls it First Amendment privilege. Former ACLA director David Crane told the press at the time of the Files' 1997 posting that the page was organized as a forum for the gathering "of information on abortionists and their accomplices for the day when they may be formally charged and tried at Nuremberg-type trials for their crimes."[26] He makes no bones about ACLA's beliefs; for members of the group, *Roe v. Wade* should be overturned, abortion should be recriminalized and capital punishment should be made the appropriate penalty for everyone engaged in reproductive health work. The Web page is currently bouncing between several Internet service providers.

The Files became contested terrain following a Planned Parenthood lawsuit in which several doctors identified on them sued ALM for threatening and menacing behavior. In February 1999 a jury ruled in the doctors' favor. In the case the Nuremberg Files were found to pose an explicit threat and to incite violence, illegal activities under the 1994 Freedom of Access to Clinic Entrances (FACE) Act. The jury hearing the case also awarded Planned Parenthood monetary damages of $107 million, money that, to date, has gone uncollected.

ACLA officially disbanded in 1997; *Life Advocate Magazine* ceased publication in late 1999.

Andrew Burnett and David Crane are part of a cadre of people who articulate a virulently anti-choice/pro-violence position. The Office of International Criminal Justice, Inc., a nonprofit organization located in Chicago, Illinois, and Huntsville, Texas, that monitors crime-related and law enforcement activities, has collected the names of individuals in the United States and Canada whose message, it believes, represents a threat to purveyors of reproductive freedom. Among them are Jeffrey Baker, a leader of the Constitution Party; Bowie, Maryland, activist Jayne Bray and her husband, the Reverend Michael Bray; convicted firebomber John Brockhoeft; former Klansman and Pensacola, Florida, activist John Burt; Joseph Lapsley Foreman, cofounder of the American Coalition of Life Activists with Andrew Burnett and an active member of Missionaries to the Pre-Born; Roy McMillan, a friend of assassin Paul Hill and leader of the Christian Action Group; Joseph Scheidler; Donald Spitz, a former OR regional director from Chesapeake, Virginia; Randall Terry; Donald Treshman, an early student of Joseph Scheidler who became national director of Rescue America; Matt Trewhella, founder of Missionaries to the Pre-Born; Father David Trosch, a Catholic priest who supports executing abortion doctors; Gordon Watson, a Canadian "justifiable homicide" advocate; and Jeff White, a California leader of Operation Save America/Operation Rescue.[27]

GOD'S WARRIORS:
SOME THOUGHTS ON WHY THE ANTIS DO THE THINGS THEY DO

When Theodor Wiesengrund Adorno, director of Germany's Frankfort Institute for Social Research from 1958 to 1969, studied burgeoning fascist
movements in mid-twentieth-century Europe, he identified several personality
traits that seem applicable to individuals within the pro-violence sector of the
anti-abortion movement. In analyzing the "authoritarian personality," people
who attempt to exert power over others in an attempt to control their behavior,
he discovered profound feelings of dependency, inadequacy and hostility.
"Because of their feelings of worthlessness," he wrote, "they tend to displace their
anger and hate towards themselves onto another group. The bigot is simply
transferring his [sic] own sense of low self-esteem and his own self-hatred to
another racial, cultural or religious group."[28]

Social psychologist and sociologist Erich Fromm, studying the same
historical period, noted the appearance of both sadistic and masochistic drives
within the authoritarian character. "Sadism," he wrote in *Escape from Freedom*,
"was understood as aiming at unrestricted power over another person more or
less mixed with destructiveness; masochism as aiming at dissolving oneself in an
overwhelmingly strong power. Both the sadistic and masochistic trends are
caused by the inability of the isolated individual to stand alone and his [sic] need
for a symbiotic relationship that overcomes this aloneness."[29] Fromm concluded
that people often escaped feelings of detachment and loneliness by submerging
themselves in relationships with "a person, an institution, God, the nation,
conscience, or a psychic compulsion."[30]

Today's anti-abortionists, even those who appear to act as lone aggressors, take
power from their relationship to a God they believe speaks directly to them. In
concert with churches and political organizations, they take pride in bucking liberal
social initiatives and believe they and their colleagues are conveying God's immu-
table law to North American women. The rules as they know them are ironclad:
terminating a pregnancy is always wrong, and no pregnancy is either ill-timed or
mistaken. A sworn 1998 deposition in which attorney Roy Lucas questioned full-
time Melbourne, Florida activist Meredith T. Raney Jr. is illustrative. Raney
testified that his goal in protesting in front of the Aware Woman Center for Choice,
and frequently trespassing, was to tell women the truth. "That's the truth as you
see it, right?" asked Lucas. "It's the truth," Raney answered.

Groups of like-minded people—be they the Lambs of Christ, Missionaries
to the Pre-Born or members of Operation Save America—reinforce this rigid,

black-and-white thinking and act to ground the individual in something important. "By becoming part of a power which is felt as unshakably strong, eternal and glamorous, one participates in its strength and glory," Fromm wrote.[31] While participants surrender many of their freedoms and give up what Fromm calls the integrity of the individual when they join restrictive mass organizations, they gain a sense of community cohesion, a solidarity born of having a common intellectual and spiritual game plan.

For anti-abortion activists intent on "saving America" and imposing "biblical authority" on its people, surrendering autonomy and the power of individual decision making are small costs for perceived salvation. Similarly, submission to a judgmental and punishing God, and accepting one's social impotence, conform to a worldview in which self-sacrifice, obedience and self-denial are the highest virtues. In addition, the promise of heaven as the reward for earthly suffering further sweetens the pot. Until ascension into the next life, however, male anti-choice leaders must submit to God; this schema requires women to submit to their spouses, ministers, organizational leaders and the Divine.

Beyond the safety of the tight-knit group, several additional factors contribute to the making of contemporary anti-abortion zealots. Anyone who has been to a "rescue" or conversed with an "anti" knows that one of the most common retorts is, "What if your mother had aborted you?" Most of us respond simply: "Then we wouldn't be having this conversation, would we?"

Anti-abortionists' feelings of inadequacy, of having only a tenuous hold on the universe, are enormous, says pro-choice psychologist Dr. John Beery. "Abortion is an existential crisis for them. It represents their fear of non-being. Every abortion re-enacts their core feeling of non-existence. Their way of dealing with that feeling is to act out. People like Randall Terry are really bright and narcissistic as all get out. Their need to have power and control reflects their insecurity. Rather than focus on the fear and anxiety, they build themselves up. If you look at the leaders and reverse what you see, you'll learn what is really going on. They're afraid. They're intimidated by women. They're scared they are non-entities. The rules give their lives meaning. They'd have to confront their own fears if their world was less rigid."[32]

Add the male desire to control and subordinate women (and the concomitant female desire for male domination), and you have a mix that is potentially explosive. "It doesn't surprise me that male anti-abortionists leaders tend to represent two poles. They are either married men with lots of children or isolated, single men with few social relationships," says Beery. "Both extremes are equally misogynist. These men see abortion as a threat to traditional Judeo-Christian cultural assumptions about women's place. On one level they know that abortion takes women out of a subservient role. If a woman has a load of kids she's not going anywhere. On another level, it is a way for men to tell women that they don't get to be in control, they don't get a choice about their lives."[33]

Dr. Phyllis Chesler, a psychologist who has authored numerous books, including *About Men, Mothers on Trial* and *Letters to a Young Feminist,* further explains that "if men have been humiliated by their fathers, or have been abandoned or ruled by tyrannical males, they tend to scapegoat women. Somehow, many of them skip over the helplessness of their mothers and project onto women the crimes of men as they have known them."[34] For those who find comfort in fundamentalism or other dogmatic religions, there is the added danger, she adds, that they will attempt to prove their worth to the "Good Father, the Father they never had," by engaging in acts of extremism.[35]

"Fundamentalism encourages the loose screws, the most disturbed, to act on what they believe," Chesler concludes.[36] Indeed, convicted clinic bombers Matthew Goldsby, Kaye Wiggins and James and Kathren Simmons, fundamentalists all, told authorities that they torched a Pensacola, Florida, clinic as a birthday present to Jesus. Others claim that they are motivated by a desire to quell the Satanic influences they believe are rampant in our culture. Their acts of anti-abortion terrorism, they charge, are meant as selfless, redemptive gestures.

Flip Benham, Randall Terry, Matt Trewhella, Keith Tucci and Norman Weslin are just a few of the anti-abortion leaders who admit to seeking forgiveness for past sins, including, for several, prolonged periods of alcohol or substance abuse. While it is beyond the scope of this book to psychoanalyze individual opponents of choice, one cannot help but wonder if the political adrenaline derived from conservative theological activism has replaced alcohol or drugs for the recovering user. Has one addiction supplanted another? And does the addict's need to continually up the dose explain the circuit that moves some folks from picketing, to blockading, to large-scale violence?

Theodor W. Adorno found the right-wing devotees he studied to be closed-minded and intolerant of ambiguity; the same characteristics define North American anti-abortionists. Tirelessly dedicated, their efforts have had a discernibly negative impact on clinics and the workers they employ.

RELUCTANT COMBATANTS:
CLINIC WORKERS AND THEIR PATIENTS UNDER ATTACK

Susan Hill, founder of the National Women's Health Organization (NWHO), has been in the reproductive health field since 1973. Media seek her out whenever there is an especially violent incident, and she has testified before Congress on innumerable occasions. Cool, calm and centered, Susan exudes professional competence and managerial know-how. Fast-moving and articulate, there is no ignoring that she is a woman in charge.

Yet even the supremely adept have their breaking point, and Hill's came at a dinner with the authors of this book. After reeling off a litany of anti-choice incidents at eight NWHO locations, her voice broke and she got to the point: "Do you have any idea what we could have accomplished if we had not had to waste so much of our time dealing with the antis?" she asked.[37] Instead of days spent filing police reports and negotiating with insurance companies in the aftermath of arsons, bombings and break-ins, more clinics could have expanded their self-help and sexuality education programs. They could have developed better well-woman care and learned more about reproductive technologies. Perhaps most important, clinics could have functioned as centers of female empowerment, places where women of all races, classes and sexual orientations could have learned about their bodies and received the emotional support they need to live fulfilling, independent lives.

Back in the 1970s many foresaw just such a future. "When we first opened, we started the health center as a political statement," says Shauna Heckert, executive director of Women's Health Specialists (formerly called Feminist Women's Health Centers), a nonprofit, four-clinic chain in California.[38] "We believed in women's liberation and a key to liberation was controlling our reproduction, getting to know our bodies. Our goal was much loftier than abortion per se. We did advocacy. We wrote books. We traveled around the world teaching self-help techniques. Then, in 1980, the biggest, baddest anti-abortion president in the whole wide world, Reagan, got elected and we knew how hard it was going to be. Our focus had to shift from the lofty goal of women's liberation to protecting our buildings, protecting our staffs and protecting our clients. Before this, we were critical of the American Medical Association, the American College of Obstetricians and Gynecologists and Planned Parenthood. We wanted women to control their reproductive systems, not have them controlled by doctors. But after Reagan won and the violence escalated, we had to jump into bed with Planned Parenthood and stop building a liberation movement. We had to focus on staying open since the antis were doing things every single day to close us down and recriminalize abortion."[39]

For many clinic workers—exact numbers or percentages are not available— the daily toll of anti-abortion efforts has been so great that they have either left the women's health movement or moved far from the front lines. Who can blame them? Clinic director Jude Hanzo left her job at a Portland, Oregon, clinic in

1997 because screaming picketers outside her home made her feel as if she could never get away from work. Although she remains on the board of a California clinic, she felt that resigning was the only way she could restore balance to her life. She had worked in abortion facilities for twenty years. Cathy Conner, a Delaware clinic director, quit after demonstrations outside her residence traumatized her two young children. Similarly, Michelle Farley left the Alabama clinic she had directed because she could not heal from the acute trauma—the murder of a security guard and the maiming of a nurse—without doing so. Others—doctors, counselors, nurses, medical assistants, administrators and technicians—have moved to other work sites because of family pressure or because they could no longer live with the stress of continual harassment, violence or threats. Still others have been forced to quit for health reasons provoked by prolonged physical and psychological strain.

What is surprising is how many have stayed. While researching *Targets of Hatred* we discovered a nearly universal tendency among long-term providers: the refusal to let other people tell them what they can and cannot do. But determination alone cannot deflect the impact of anti-abortion terrorism, and most targeted providers suffer from stress disorders of one kind or another. According to Dr. Paul Mullen, professor of psychiatry at Monash University in Australia, seventy percent of people who have been stalked—a common experience among abortion workers—show signs of post-traumatic stress disorder (PTSD) marked by chronic anxiety, depression and/or disturbed sleep.[40] Florida provider Sandy Sheldon reports that for almost a year after winning a legal battle against an anti who had stalked her, both she and her elementary school–age daughter were afraid to invite friends to their home. Similarly, clinic owner Lorraine Maguire says that her daughter did not run a wedding announcement in the newspapers for fear that the anti who had been stalking the family would disrupt the nuptials.

Furthermore, since October 1998, when Dr. Barnett Slepian was shot to death while standing in his curtainless, Amherst, New York, kitchen, some clinic workers have lived in cavelike darkness to deter would-be assailants from peering into their homes. Others drape their windows heavily. Dr. Susan Wicklund goes nowhere without a large, well-trained attack dog. Dr. Damon Stutes keeps a loaded, licensed gun within constant reach. Many targeted providers have bulletproof vests and have installed motion detectors outside their homes. Hypervigilance is the order of the day.

To a large extent, how people cope is dependent on the severity of the extremism directed at them. In places where violence or harassment is rare or episodic, people react as they do when confronting any other stressor: they grow depressed, manic or less functional, and overeat, overspend, drink, take drugs, or act out against their co-workers, friends and family. Typically, as long as the incidents are few and far between and of short duration, long-term damage is minimal; a significant number of staffers, however, experience such recurrent symptoms as irregular or bounding heartbeat, excessive sweating, muscle tension and pain, dizziness, faintness, indigestion or diarrhea at the first sign of trauma.[41]

In more prolonged assaults—daily demonstrations, ongoing sabotage or confrontations at the clinic; intimidating home picketing accompanied by screaming protestors carrying gory signs; sustained periods of "rescue" or blockading; or following a murder, shooting, arson, bombing or serious vandalism—clinic staffers are likely to experience intense fear and feelings of helplessness, rage or frustration. People with full-blown post-traumatic stress disorder often have difficulty falling or staying asleep, and experience difficulty concentrating or remembering aspects of the traumatic event or period. Some are irritable and have inexplicable bursts of anger or exaggerated startle responses. Nightmares, flashbacks, intrusive memories and serious depression are also common. Indeed, in conducting the interviews for this book, we were stunned by how many providers told us about bad dreams, eating disorders and panic reactions.

Treatment, of course, varies depending on symptoms and the person's history of victimization. Some clinic workers have needed to take time off—ranging from a few days, to a few weeks, to several years—to recover from anti-abortion aggression. Others have found diving back into work to be the best therapy. For many clinic workers, the desire to stand up to the antis and defy their bullying has inspired renewed perseverance.

Still, how and why people cling to their high ideals and continue to provide abortion care remains a mystery best explained by the human desire to do the right thing. Everyone we asked had the same response: the satisfaction derived from helping women end unwanted or problem pregnancies is tremendous.

Nonetheless, clinic workers have needs that other workers do not and require frequent time-outs to assess what they are doing and how they are coping with anxiety and stress. Some health centers have retreats where mediated discussions are held and staff are pampered with massage, aromatherapy and other alternative treatments. Others hold weekly meetings with ample time for workers to blow off steam and formulate solutions for everything from dealing with difficult patients to dealing with obstreperous antis. Humor is also a mighty balm; those clinics that have devised ways to use laughter fare better than those that don't.

Ultimately, though, the decision to work in a clinic rests with the individual. For those electing to stay, what one clinic owner calls "snatching normal" is key.

Whether that means going to a movie, taking a trip, shopping or talking to a friend about something other than abortion is their prerogative. Carye Ortman, executive director of the Lovejoy SurgiCenter in Portland, Oregon, believes that as long as providers engage the world, serving on the PTA, singing in a choir or participating in an organization, they can avert the feelings of isolation that often accompany clinic employment. Everyone, however, agrees that until the stigma is lifted from abortion services, and until the political climate that tolerates woman-hating and anti-abortion lawlessness is eradicated, clinic workers will continue to face a slew of challenges that test their convictions.

"Everything we touch is clouded by the fact that we do abortions," says Eileen Schnitger, director of Public Affairs at Women's Health Specialists in northern California, "whether it's hiring a doctor, renting a car, hiring staff, renting an office, or getting malpractice insurance. Abortion is treated differently from other business activities. When people ask you what you do, and you tell them, a negative reaction is often felt."[42]

Changing that reaction—and reclaiming abortion as an essential and routine health service for all women of reproductive age—is one of the major tasks facing reproductive rights activists and clinic workers. "Abortion should not be something embarrassing or shameful," says Mary Lou Greenberg, a pro-choice activist who lives and works in New York City. "It is a fact of life. Women will have abortions whether they are legal or not. Our job is to help people understand abortion as a normal procedure for heterosexually active women. It's one of several ways that we take control of our destinies. We've lost a lot of ground to the right-wing since 1973: Medicaid, waiting periods, parental consent and notification, and a diminished number of providers. Part of the reason 'pro-family' movements have won so many victories is because we've acted as if abortion is a tragedy, something to regret forever. We've got to stop letting people make us feel bad about not carrying every pregnancy to term. Abortion should be cause for relief and reflection, not breast-beating and shame. We need to reinvigorate the women's movement to recapture this spirit. That's the only way we'll be able to push the anti-abortionists to the margins where they belong."[43]

CHAPTER TWO

The Way We Were: America before the 1973 Roe v. Wade Decision

When the nine Justices of the United States Supreme Court issued the *Roe v. Wade* decision on January 22, 1973, they did far more than strike down state anti-abortion laws. They demonstrated the interconnection between mass movements and legislative change, the symbiotic link between public policy and public opinion. Clearly, *Roe v. Wade* did not spring up out of nowhere, nor was it decided in a political vacuum. Indeed, as the repressive 1950s gave way to the increasingly open-minded 1960s, the United States ushered in a host of political and social movements that influenced the thinking of lawmakers, judges and the population at large.

The Civil Rights struggle was one of the most portentous of these movements. Although it had begun to reach into mainstream communities earlier in the decade, the August 1963 March on Washington, organized by the Reverend Martin Luther King Jr., inspired hundreds of thousands of caring Americans to have a dream. As they sang along with Joan Baez, Richie Havens and Peter, Paul and Mary, they truly believed that they could overcome oppression and make the country fulfill its promise of freedom and opportunity for all who dwelled within its borders. Thousands of young people headed South to register African American voters, participate in sit-ins at "whites-only" businesses and publicize boycotts to contest segregation; the majority were radicalized by the staggering oppression that greeted their efforts.

Betty Friedan's book, *The Feminine Mystique,* published the same year as the March on Washington, added to the mix by including a previously ignored constituency, the middle-class housewife. She, too, could be a force for progress, said Friedan, if only she threw off the shackles that bound her to home and hearth and entered the foreground of American politics.

Not surprisingly, open discussion of race and gender led people to question the rules that determined how they lived. Americans from every part of the country and of every race and class debated the rationale for rigid hierarchies and began to experiment with alternative lifestyles. As conversations exploded, organizations and institutions began to spring up, galvanizing the previously passive to consider their lives and the political institutions that governed them.

Even before the March on Washington and Betty Friedan, college students, frustrated by America's growing role in Vietnam and excited by the possibilities of expanded civil rights, had formed Students for a Democratic Society (SDS). The National Organization for Women (NOW) followed in 1966; *Rolling Stone Magazine,* a "new voice" for a "new culture," printed its inaugural issue in 1967.

While reality knocked in April 1968 when the Reverend Martin Luther King Jr. was assassinated, making clear that there would be significant backlash against progressive movements, his murder did not end people's efforts to disrupt business as usual. Indeed, King's death was met by massive rioting in more than one hundred cities across the country. So shaken were the powers-that-be by the disruptions that they called out 21,000 federal and 34,000 state troops to keep peace. But despite the government's armed response, much of the populace would not be quieted and people continued to develop outlets to express their commitment to social activism. That summer women protested their objectification at the 1968 Miss America Pageant in Atlantic City, New Jersey. That same year thousands flocked to Broadway to see *Hair,* a musical celebrating at least some aspects of the "hippie" ethos. The following August youth from around the world traveled to Bethel, New York, for the drug-saturated, free-love–celebrating Woodstock Festival.

Music, pop culture, activism—by the mid to late 1960s, all were glued together by a vision of a better world promulgated by the Vietnam War and the movements that erupted to oppose it. Throughout the country, protestors marched, burned draft cards and engaged in civil disobedience to try to push the government to consider strategies other than aggression and battle. Organizations opposed to the East Asian conflict existed on virtually all college campuses and in towns, cities and suburbs everywhere. From Women Strike for Peace to Vietnam Veterans Against the War, from Black Veterans for Social Justice to Youth Against War and Fascism, a wide array of constituencies repulsed by America's international policies were offering a biting challenge to the status quo. "Give Peace a Chance" became a catchall slogan for the political outlook that many activists began to adhere to.

The brutal 1970 shooting of student protestors at Kent State and Jackson State universities further incited antiwar outrage, a spirit captured by Neil Young's musical anthem, "Ohio," and a poster, popular among teenagers, that simply stated, "They shoot students, don't they?" Likewise, Marvin Gaye's "What's Going On?" asked the question on many people's minds—how could we participate in a brutal war against a country we knew nearly nothing about? Activists took to the streets, joined organizations and consciousness-raising groups, and continued to create alternative institutions, from publishing houses like The Feminist Press, to journals like *Feminist Studies, In These Times* and *Ms. Magazine.*

But while race, poverty, hunger and war were groundbreaking issues for most activists, rigid gender categories and sexual propriety were also capturing a fair amount of attention. The 1965 Supreme Court decision legalizing the sale of contraceptives to married people *(Griswold v. Connecticut)* and the 1972 extension of that right to unmarried adults *(Baird v. Eisenstadt)* seem tame in light of other changes taking place; nonetheless, they represented the loosening of a moral stranglehold that signaled the expansion of personal rights. It is not an overstatement to say that these decisions—and the Food and Drug Administration's approval of the birth control pill in 1960—revolutionized family life by giving heterosexually active people, particularly women, the tools to control their lives.

A year after announcing *Baird v. Eisenstadt,* the Justices went even further and issued the *Roe v. Wade* decision. *Roe* gave women the right to terminate first-trimester pregnancies and provided a framework for regulating second- and third-trimester procedures. In doing so, the Justices took an enormous step in making women and men equal: for the first time, women had what men had—the right to walk away from an unplanned pregnancy.

Is it any wonder that once the magnitude of *Roe* sank in, those uncomfortable with the idea of women's equality and sexual freedom would vigorously oppose the purveyors of legalized abortion? Scientists remind us that for every action there is an equal or greater reaction, and America post-*Roe* perfectly illustrates that reality.

By the early 1960s, people were beginning to open up about issues previously considered too personal for public discourse. Topics such as abortion, contraceptive availability, sex and sexuality were slowly working their way onto the agendas of policymakers, medical associations, religious groups and concerned individuals. In addition, several incidents served as lightning rods, forcing people to break their silence on these subjects.

1962

GROVE, OKLAHOMA

Dr. William Jennings Bryan Henries was jailed for performing abortions in the tiny farming community of Grove, Oklahoma. According to journalist/activist Lawrence Lader, prior to Henries's incarceration, half the town showed up at a dinner to honor him. "It was the first time a community, in fact, a good part of the state, had to examine its feelings about abortion and decide whether to support or repudiate a doctor who had put his reputation on the line," Lader wrote.[1]

Prison, Lader added, radicalized Henries, and the physician issued statements challenging the unjust prohibition on abortion from his jail cell. Two years later, when he was released, he was no longer licensed to practice medicine; Henries spent the rest of his life campaigning for abortion legalization. In 1965 he addressed America's first conference on the subject, an event organized by Californian Patricia Maginnis.[2]

Henries died in 1972 at the age of seventy-six. He is credited with performing approximately 5,000 abortions during the twenty-three years he practiced medicine.[3]

WASHINGTON, D.C.

A model penal code, drafted by the American Law Institute (ALI) and passed at its annual meeting, included—for the first time—the legal concept of justifiable abortion. The code was a suggestion for legislative change and required passage by each state's legislature.

Under the proposed code, a pregnant woman could ask her physician to end a pregnancy. The doctor could consent, as long as the abortion was performed in a hospital, had the approval of at least two other doctors and was deemed necessary to preserve the woman's mental or physical health.[4]

SUMMER: PHOENIX, ARIZONA

Phoenix TV personality Sherri Finkbine became a national symbol for loosening the strictures on abortion. Already a mother of four, Finkbine had taken approximately three dozen tranquilizers during the first weeks of pregnancy with what she and her husband had hoped would be their fifth child. She later learned that the pills contained Thalidomide, a drug known to cause birth defects.

In 1962, Arizona law allowed abortion only to save a woman's life, and everyone agreed that the pills Finkbine had ingested posed no danger to her. Nonetheless, her local prominence was such that strings were pulled and she was able to schedule an abortion. But Finkbine was not the kind of person to settle her own score and forget about everyone else. Fearing that other pregnant women might take the tranquilizers she had obtained, she contacted the *Arizona Republic* newspaper to publicize the danger. After the *Republic* ran a cautionary news story, hospital attorneys balked and Finkbine's abortion was canceled. Although she was able to travel to Sweden for the surgery, Finkbine's was the first case to bring the abortion controversy into the open; her dilemma made abortion a topic of national concern.[5]

A rubella epidemic, which began in 1963 and lasted until 1965, pushed the conversation still further; like Thalidomide, German measles can cause severe health problems in the offspring of women who contract the virus in the first months of pregnancy.

1965

JUNE 7: WASHINGTON, D.C.

The Supreme Court of the United States overturned the convictions of Estelle Griswold and Dr. C. Lee Buxton, staffers at the Planned Parenthood League of Connecticut, who had been arrested in 1961 for illegally dispensing a contraceptive device to a married woman. At the time the decision was issued, it was a crime in Connecticut to use or prescribe a "drug or article" to prevent conception. While some states had begun to liberalize their policies on the distribution of birth control as early as 1936, when the Supreme Court ruled that contraception was not obscene and could no longer be barred from the mails, many still had archaic laws on the books.

In *Griswold v. Connecticut* the Justices ruled that the convictions of Buxton and Griswold were a violation of the right to privacy. The decision opened the door to the sale of contraceptives to legally married couples in every state in the country.[6]

1966

NATIONWIDE

In response to a growing movement to repeal state laws restricting abortion, the U.S. Catholic Conference's Family Life Bureau, headed by the Reverend James

McHugh, created the National Right to Life Committee (NRTLC). The committee's first work was to study, and later monitor, laws affecting women's reproductive choices. While the NRTLC would subsequently attempt to shed its connection to the Catholic church in favor of a more ecumenical public face, the impetus and initial funding of the NRTLC can be directly linked to McHugh's efforts.[7]

JULY 23: SAN FRANCISCO, CALIFORNIA

Patricia Maginnis, president of the Society for Humane Abortion, was arrested for distributing "lewd and obscene literature." Maginnis had been handing out mimeographed rosters of abortion providers operating in Tijuana, Mexico, while standing on a San Francisco street corner.[8] On August 17, 1966, Municipal Court Judge Leo Friedman found that the arrest had violated Maginnis's right to free speech.[9]

Seven months later, in February 1967, Maginnis and an associate were arrested and held in jail for eighteen hours for teaching women how to self-abort. Defense attorneys argued that the arrest violated the women's First Amendment rights. The judge agreed and exonerated them.[10]

1967

APRIL 6: BOSTON, MASSACHUSETTS

By the time Bill Baird was arrested on April 6, 1967, for "indecent exposure of obscene objects," he was already known throughout the country as a birth control and abortion crusader. His education had begun in 1957 when, fresh out of the army, he took a job with Sandoz Pharmaceuticals selling products that induced labor and controlled bleeding after childbirth. "I took the job seriously," he says, "and could see that women were not being adequately treated by the medical profession."[11]

By 1963 Baird was clinical director of Emko Pharmaceuticals, a firm that manufactured an inexpensive contraceptive foam. He had taken the job following a one-year stint as a medical student—he was forced to drop out when his wife became pregnant with the couple's third child in three years—and immediately confronted a thorny legal dilemma. With few exceptions, doctors in New York state, where Baird lived, would not recommend the foam for fear of breaking a law that made it a crime to give out information or show a device or a drug intended to prevent conception or describe where a person could purchase such products.[12]

"I suggested to the company that we go directly to women," says Baird. "I would go to department stores and ask them to let me spend a day selling a feminine product for $3.00. I didn't tell them it was birth control. One day a priest came into the store I was visiting and banged on my table, told me to leave and screamed that the company should not allow such filth. The manager then ordered me out. I'd had problems in other stores, too, so I bought a van which I called the 'Plan Van,' a mobile way for me to dispense birth control information. Women would come up to me and say that they didn't need birth control, that after intercourse they put Pepsi Cola in their vaginas. I heard women talk about using bleach, Lysol and turpentine for douches, and about using a nail or pencils, bobby pins or knitting needles in an effort to abort. As I talked to more and more women, I realized the enormous need for birth control and abortion."[13] Baird used the self-purchased Plan Van at night and on weekends, when he was not at Emko.

"One day I was in Manhattan, at Harlem Hospital. I heard a woman scream and went into the hallway and saw this woman staggering," he says. "I caught her as she fell to the ground. She had tried to abort herself with a coat hanger and had hit an artery. I saw her die. I was so outraged I didn't know what to do first. I went to the Board of Health and said that we had to get birth control out to poor communities. I went to the head of New York City Social Services. Both said that birth control was against the law. This was nuts. I started to have a dream that nurses and social workers would dispense prescription contraceptives and I wanted nonprescription items sold in supermarkets and delis. I wanted to reach women at every level. At the same time, I began to develop a network of doctors who did abortions. My boss found out about this and said that if I kept this up I would be fired. I was let go on May 7, 1965,"[14] a month before the historic *Griswold v. Connecticut* decision was handed down by the Supreme Court.

A week after losing his job, Baird was arrested for the "indecent exposure of an obscene object" in Hempstead, New York, and found himself facing a one-year jail term. "All of a sudden, people came to my side," Baird says, "New York City Mayor John Lindsay, United States Senator Ernest Gruening of Alaska, Manhattan Borough President Percy Sutton. Activist writer Paul Krassner heard about me and mailed me some money. So did antiwar and Yippie organizer Abbie Hoffman. The day after the 1965 election the district attorney announced that he would not prosecute me."[15]

While Baird was pleased with this pronouncement, it was clearly not the sweeping legal change he was pushing for, and he continued to spend as much time as he could in the Plan Van, teaching women about birth control. An April 1966 arrest in Freehold, New Jersey, led to twenty days in jail. "I had just gotten out when I got a letter from a student at Boston University (BU), inviting me to challenge a 'Crimes Against Chastity, Morality, Decency and Good Order' law which said that anyone who prints, publishes, exhibits, gives information, or writes about birth control or abortion was guilty of a felony and subject to five years in prison for each violation. I said no at first but then decided, okay, I'd challenge the law."[16] Despite the federal court ruling in *Griswold v. Connecticut,* similar prohibitions were on the books in twenty-five states.

The BU students secured an auditorium for the presentation and publicized the event. On April 6, 1967, "the students who had planned the event met me and 2,500 people, including some cops, showed up for my talk. The thrust of my speech was that women must be free. I spoke for forty minutes and then announced that I would challenge the law. Before I'd come to BU I stopped at Zayre's Department Store and purchased a condom and one can of Emko Foam. I had arranged this with a nineteen-year-old woman beforehand. I chose her deliberately since she was a minor and handed both items to her; the police then arrested me. As they did, I held up a receipt for $3.09, showing that the state of Massachusetts had collected nine cents tax on the sale of the two items. I was dragged off the stage in handcuffs and tossed in jail for a few hours and released. I was indicted on illegally exhibiting an obscene object, a diaphragm, and illegally distributing medicine, the condom and the foam. On October 17, 1967 the case went to trial. Judge Donald McCauley found me guilty, but said he would not sentence me until the Massachusetts Supreme Court ruled on my appeal."[17]

The state Supreme Court found Baird guilty of illegally dispensing contraceptives, and in early 1970 McCauley sentenced Baird to three months in prison. He served thirty-six days.

Follow-up note: *Baird v. Eisenstadt* (Eisenstadt was the sheriff who imprisoned Baird) eventually found its way to the United States Supreme Court. On March 22, 1972, the Court issued a landmark 6 to 1 opinion affirming the correctness of Baird's mission. "If the right to privacy means anything," the Justices wrote, "it is the right of the individual, married or single, to be free from unwarranted governmental intrusion into matters so fundamentally affecting a person as the decision whether to bear or beget a child."[18]

MAY 27: NEW YORK CITY

The headline in the *New York Times* was audacious: "Clergymen Offer Abortion Advice: 21 Ministers and Rabbis Form New Group." Their "Clergy

Statement on Abortion Law and Consultation Service on Abortion" expressed their philosophy and intention:

> The present abortion laws require over a million women in the United States each year to seek illegal abortions which often cause severe mental anguish, physical suffering, and unnecessary death of women. These laws also compel the birth of unwanted, unloved, and often deformed children; yet a truly human society is one in which the birth of a child is an occasion for genuine celebration, not the imposition of a penalty or punishment upon the mother. These laws brand as criminals wives and mothers who are often driven as helpless victims to desperate acts. The largest percentage of abortion deaths are found among 35-to-39-year-old married women who have five or six children. The present abortion law in New York is most oppressive of the poor and minority groups. . . .
>
> We affirm that there is a period during gestation when although there may be *embryo* life in the fetus, there is no living *child* upon whom the crime of murder can be committed. . . .
>
> We are mindful that there are duly licensed and reputable physicians who in their wisdom perform therapeutic abortions which some may regard as illegal. When a doctor performs such an operation motivated by compassion and concern for the patient, and not simply for monetary gain, we do not regard him [*sic*] as a criminal, but as living by the highest standards of religion and of the Hippocratic Oath.
>
> We believe that it is our pastoral responsibility and religious duty to give aid and assistance to all women with problem pregnancies. To that end we are establishing a Clergymen's Consultation Service on Abortion which will include referral to the best medical advice and aid to women in need.[19]

In the six years it existed, the Clergymen's Consultation Service on Abortion (CCSA) grew into a network of 1,400 ministers and rabbis in cities across the United States. Founder Howard Moody, a Texas-born Baptist minister employed by Judson Memorial Church in New York's Greenwich Village, got the idea for the service from Lawrence Lader. But the former marine turned minister had also had plenty of personal experience, as an urban pastor, in assisting those women who turned to him for help in dealing with unplanned pregnancies. His experience went back to 1957 when, as a newly ordained preacher, he met a woman who had taken a train from Florida to New York looking for an abortionist. His efforts to assist her opened his eyes to both the problem of unwanted pregnancy and the hypocrisy that made abortions available, albeit difficult to access, for women with the economic resources to purchase them.[20]

Immediately after the CCSA announced its formation, it was inundated with calls from women seeking advice and the phone numbers and addresses of reputable abortionists. The referral list the CCSA used was carefully crafted, and each provider was personally checked out. Posing as a patient, Arlene Carmen, a program associate at the Judson Church, made sure that hygienic conditions were maintained and that offices operated professionally. Her visit also insured that the CCSA did not refer patients to "doctors" who expected sex as a condition of surgery, or who upped their fees once the woman was naked, common pre–*Roe* conditions.

CCSA volunteers offered free, in-person counseling and made referrals to providers operating outside New York state; they had decided before opening that prosecution would be more difficult, and thus less likely, if they sent women to abortionists doing business across state lines. This policy proved prescient; when police raided a Bronx provider in May 1969, the arrests did not impact CCSA or the women they counseled and referred. The group also did telephone consultations for women unable to travel to the city for face-to-face advice.

"Cardinal Cooke, the Catholic Cardinal of New York at the time the Clergy Service began, knew what we were doing, but because the law was on the church's side, nothing happened," says Moody. "The church may have expected we'd be stopped by the District Attorney, Frank Hogan. But Hogan took no action against us. I think that part of it was that the timing of what we did was right. There was no enthusiasm for prosecution. There also must have been some knowledge that the women we were seeing included the mothers, wives, daughters and sisters of police captains, district attorneys and judges. It would have been very difficult for them to make arrests. They would have had to go into a church or synagogue to get us. We were not underground. We did private, individual counseling with women in need and we did it openly."[21]

Once New York liberalized its abortion law in March 1970, the state's CCSA shifted gears and began to organize a campaign to lift restrictions on nonhospital procedures; they simultaneously began to organize New York's first freestanding clinic. By the time the Center for Reproductive and Sexual Health (CRASH) opened its doors in 1971, the need for services was so great that they were treating one hundred women a day, six days a week. "CRASH became a model. We charged $125. Every fourth person was indigent so they had their abortions for free," Moody recalls.[22]

The shift from the days of hush-hush, back-alley procedures to open medical care undoubtedly rankled the Catholic church and the newly created National

Right to Life Committee, and they wasted no time in fomenting a strategy for forcing New York state legislators to overturn the permissive abortion policy. "Since the law passed by only one vote they were confident that they would win repeal," says Moody. "But they also began to target the clinic. I remember an invasion sometime in 1972. The invaders were a group of ten young people, students, one of whom later went into Operation Rescue. I told them they had five minutes to leave or I would call the police. They did not leave, the police came, and they were arrested."[23]

Follow-up note: Despite Catholic church and Right to Life efforts, New York state never repealed its liberal abortion policy.

The Reverend Howard Moody continues to engage in activist work, championing a host of social justice issues; he is minister emeritus at Judson Church and was the 1998 recipient of the Margaret Sanger Award from the Planned Parenthood Federation of America. Arlene Carmen died in the early 1990s.

OCTOBER 19: MONTREAL, CANADA

"In 1967 I was involved in the humanist movement," says activist doctor Henry Morgentaler, leader of the campaign to bring legalized abortion to Canada. "I was president of the Humanist Fellowship of Montreal, part of an international movement of atheists, agnostics, and people who are not reliant on the Bible but who are interested in creating a good life based on love and reason. We wanted to fight for quality of life issues so we opposed government funding for Protestant and Catholic schools and pushed for a change in abortion laws."[24]

Britain had inspired the humanists by liberalizing its abortion laws in early 1967. They were further encouraged in October, when Canada's Federal Standing Committee on Health and Welfare announced that it was considering proposed amendments to the Criminal Code relating to abortion. Morgentaler submitted a brief and testified before the Committee on behalf of the Humanist Fellowship. "I was there for about two hours, taking questions from members of Parliament," he says. "As a result I was on the front pages and on TV and radio. Right away, women started to come to my office for abortions. I would say, 'I sympathize with you, but it is a criminal procedure so I cannot do it.' At first, I saw about three women a week. After a few months of turning them away I realized that these women could not wait. I felt like a hypocrite. I would publicly say that these women needed help and then I would not help them when they came to see me. After a lot of soul-searching, stress and anxiety, I eventually decided to defy the law. I was caught in my own rhetoric and made to do something."[25]

Morgentaler had previously done routine dilation and curettage procedures on women who had miscarried, but he had little knowledge about how to perform in-office abortions. He therefore set out to learn all he could about available techniques; to become proficient, he read countless articles in medical journals, spoke to colleagues and discovered a method, mentioned by a British physician, using a vacuum aspirator. "It seemed better than scraping the uterus," Morgentaler says, "so I wrote to Britain and ordered the equipment. It passed through Customs and I started to perform abortions in my office. It was great. Women were getting abortions in an aboveboard office with a nurse in attendance. At first it started slowly, one or two a day, but it quickly grew since doctors heard about me and began making referrals from all over the United States and eastern Canada. Within a year we had so many patients we started a full-time abortion practice. That was 1969."[26]

Shortly thereafter Morgentaler began to train other physicians in Montreal. Things continued to move along until June 1, 1970. "I had been in practice and on panel discussions on TV and radio defending a woman's right to abortion, but after a snitch from the United States told police that his girlfriend was going to Canada for an abortion, my practice was raided," Morgentaler says. "I was arrested with all three of my nurses. We were released on bail and my lawyer dragged the case out until October 1973. Meanwhile, I continued to do abortions since there was no directive ordering me to stop."[27]

1969

ASHLAND, PENNSYLVANIA

Eighty-year-old physician Robert Spencer died. Spencer was the premier illegal abortionist in the eastern United States. He reportedly performed 30,000 procedures during his forty-year career, many of them for free and most costing between $10 and $50.

Spencer became a legend, wrote Lawrence Lader, "not by challenging the law, but by ignoring it. The community protected him. He treated unwanted pregnancies as well as pneumonia because the community wanted it that way."[28]

LOS ANGELES, CALIFORNIA

When lawyer Carol Downer first joined the Abortion Committee of the Los Angeles chapter of the National Organization for Women (NOW) in 1969, she had no idea that she would go on to make feminist history. Already a mother of four, she simply knew that access to abortion was essential for women's autonomy and liberation.

"In those days finding an abortion was the biggest part of the job," she says. "You had to ask someone to ask someone to ask someone. It took time. At that point I had had one abortion. On a scale of one to ten, with ten being the worst, mine was a three or four. It was excruciatingly painful and very scary, done in an area of L.A. I was not familiar with, without anesthesia."[29]

Although California had legalized "therapeutic abortion" in 1967, women had to go before a panel of doctors and plead their cases in order to have legally sanctioned, in-hospital procedures. "They had to say they'd commit suicide unless they had an abortion," Downer says. "It was so humiliating, so degrading. And that record was always there. What if you later wanted to run for public office? It made every woman who went before the committee feel as if she had a guilty secret."[30] Not surprisingly, only the most desperate went before Therapeutic Abortion Committees; the majority, like Downer, sought illegal practitioners.

Downer had joined the newly formed NOW Abortion Committee as a way to voice her concerns about the status of abortion, the memory of her own experience still fresh in her mind. From the start, she and her colleagues organized on several simultaneous fronts: they defended illegal abortionists when they were arrested and planned the creation of their own, women-run, abortion service.

The committee learned to do abortions from a provider who ran an illegal clinic. "He would let us go into the procedure rooms and watch, the three or four of us, none with any prior medical training. We were very small, very collective. We called ourselves the West Coast Sisters. During my training with the illegal provider, I was shown a woman getting an intrauterine device, an IUD. It was the first time I saw a cervix. It was very illuminating to learn that the cervix was accessible; it was like turning on a light for me."[31]

Within months of beginning their work with the NOW Abortion Committee, the West Coast Sisters decided that their energies would be better spent teaching women across the United States about their bodies and how they worked than in opening a health center. "We still wanted to have a clinic," Downer says, "but it ceased to be a specific goal."[32] In early 1970, the thirty to forty women who were part of the committee began to raise money for the purchase of speculums and started to train women to do self-examinations. Committee members also learned to do menstrual extractions; that summer they attended the annual NOW conference with the explicit goal of sharing what they had learned about female anatomy and reproduction.

"We had photos of women doing self-exams which was shocking to some of the women at the convention," says Downer. "They didn't approve. But the word was out. We had signs up with our room numbers and held long self-help sessions. Women were lined up and down the hall. When it was over we gave each woman her own speculum. We met women from around the country that weekend and from that experience got the idea to travel. Two of us, housewives who barely knew how to tip in a restaurant, spent six weeks in the summer of 1970 touring on Greyhound buses and teaching women in Cedar Rapids, Wichita, Kansas City, Des Moines, Ames, Chicago, Detroit, New York and Pennsylvania about abortion history and about how policymakers had been manipulating women. We also showed them how to do self-help exams. We wanted women to think about the political issues—the population policy and moral issues—as well as about the physical examinations."[33]

When the pair returned to California, they decided to contact a local hospital since medical institutions across the state had become much looser about approving "therapeutic abortions." Downer and her Abortion Committee colleagues found a physician who was willing to perform the procedure; they then told the hospital that they would screen prospective patients and do all the paperwork so that women would no longer have to appear before the Therapeutic Abortion Committee in person. The hospital agreed to the plan.

Downer and a committee colleague were arrested in September 1972 for practicing medicine without a license. "The other woman pled guilty in a plea bargain and was given probation," Downer recalls. "We took my case to trial. I got a lot of support from all over the country and my case became a national event. It was a wonderful victory when I was acquitted in November 1972."[34]

Between Downer's arrest and her eventual acquittal, hospitals—including several Catholic facilities—continued to cooperate with the NOW Abortion Committee. Women were pouring into California, says Downer, and she and her associates continued to travel, demonstrating self-help methods to eager students along the West Coast. "We'd see NOW members, college students and others, and it was very exciting to show women how to provide care and start clinics," she says. "By the time Roe was decided, about fifty groups were running women's health projects across the United States and we were busy sharing the technology we had learned from the illegal practitioners we'd visited."[35]

Post Roe, many members of the Abortion Committee, including Carol Downer, decided that the time was finally right for them to open a health center of their own. "We went back into history and found a term that was popularized by Elizabeth Cady Stanton: feminism," says Downer. "We were a women's health clinic but we also wanted to be known as a feminist health center. We eventually became the L.A. Feminist Women's Health Center (FWHC). Then other people decided to start a Feminist Women's Health Center in Oakland; another opened in Orange County, and soon groups all over the country began to take the name."[36]

"The first five years after Roe were burgeoning times for women's health clinics," Downer continues, "but while abortion was an important issue, it was not the only issue. Self-help also had to do with using alternative remedies, getting to know our bodies and understanding childbirth and sexuality."[37] The emergence of the anti-abortion movement forced the movement to shift its focus, she concludes. As a result, women's health activists now concentrate almost exclusively on defending choice and have all but abandoned their earlier, more holistic concerns.

FEBRUARY 14–16: CHICAGO, ILLINOIS

The first national conference on state abortion restrictions resulted in the creation of the National Association for the Repeal of Abortion Laws (NARAL).[38] More than 350 people attended the meeting, including representatives of twenty-one organizations.[39]

SEPTEMBER 5: CALIFORNIA

The California Supreme Court declared its state law banning abortion unconstitutional. California was the first state in the country to do so. Although this did not satisfy feminist health advocates because abortions still had to be performed in a hospital, by 1972 California was performing 135,000 legal procedures a year.[40]

NOVEMBER 10: WASHINGTON, D.C.

United States District Court Judge Arnold Gessell exonerated Dr. Milan Vuitch, a surgeon who had been arrested for performing an abortion a year earlier. He also declared the D.C. law barring abortion unconstitutional, the first time that a federal court invalidated an abortion statute.[41] The ruling allowed physicians licensed in Washington, D.C., to perform any abortions deemed necessary; unlike California, the decision did not mandate that surgery be performed in a hospital, a good thing since the city's leading voluntary hospitals rejected most women who sought procedures. D.C. General, reports Lawrence Lader, "maintained its longstanding virtual blockade and in the first two months of 1970 took only 10 abortion cases."[42] On May 23, 1970, the Appeals Court ruled that public hospitals had to terminate unwanted pregnancies.[43]

The Sons of Thunder, militant Catholics who dressed in khaki, carried rosaries and wore red berets, protested the decision.[44] In retrospect, they were an ominous portent of things to come.

1970

CALIFORNIA

The Central Committee of California's Republican Party decided to test the waters to see if the abortion issue could be used to lure disgruntled Catholics from the Democratic Party. According to former GOP fund raiser Tanya Melich, author of *The Republican War Against Women: An Insider's Report from Behind the Lines,* Republican registrars gathered outside Catholic churches to assist those parishioners who wanted to switch their political affiliation to protest the California Democratic Party's support of legal abortion.[45]

One church alone reportedly registered 530 Party changes.[46]

FEBRUARY 20: MASSACHUSETTS

Bill Baird began serving a three-month jail sentence in Massachusetts' Suffolk County Jail for providing contraception to an unmarried minor and violating the state's decency laws, charges stemming from his April 1967 speech at Boston University. The following is an excerpt from his diary:

> Going to jail I worry about [my wife] Evie. She has been getting sick phone calls and crank letters. . . . In Sheriff Eisenstadt's office, the sheriff expresses personal concern for my welfare. . . . I tell him of the anonymous callers who inform me that the minute I land in jail I am marked for assault, a helpless victim of gang rape. He assures me; neither gang rape nor beatings by guards will take place. . . .
>
> The sheriff decides to place me in a cell, second story near the chaplain's office. Unfortunately, I have to do what is called "hard time." That is, I must stay in my cell 24 hours out of 24. My cell is the size of a large closet. Yellow paint flakes from the walls, the floor is blood red. The ceiling exhibits a network of cracks. The bed has an olive-drab frame and a two-inch cotton mattress dark with rusty brown stains. The mattress, I discover, swarms with lice.[47]

FEBRUARY 21: MASSACHUSETTS

"I am learning that in jail you keep nothing to yourself, not even your body," wrote Bill Baird on day two of his incarceration.

> In any case, I must perform all the functions of my body in open view. I am disturbed by a feeling of being watched. You can't imagine how filthy the beds are. I have a sink, oval-shaped, about 10 inches in diameter. A button on the wall controls the water. No warm water for washing; the jet is ice-cold. The reek of the cellblock is fantastic.[48]

FEBRUARY 22: MASSACHUSETTS

Baird's journal, day three:

> I am almost panic-stricken about Eve and the children. They have been receiving further death threats. Do I have the right to expose my family to violent abuse and depravity?
>
> The food is abominable. I pick insects from my food. It's a treat to get fresh milk with coffee and the usual breakfast quota of six slices of bread; but they serve the milk in a paper bowl, and you have to drink just like a cat—all part of the dehumanizing process.[49]

MARCH 1: NEW YORK STATE

New York state legalized abortions performed by licensed medical doctors before the twenty- fourth week of pregnancy, making its policy the most liberal in the country. The law went into effect on July 1. Within the first year, 55,347 New York residents and 83,975 out-of-staters had abortions in the Empire State.[50] Two weeks later Hawaii Governor John A. Burns gave his thumbs-up to an abortion liberalization bill that had been passed by state legislators. The bill required that abortions be performed before viability—the point at which the fetus can function outside the womb, usually between twenty-four and twenty-eight weeks. Surgery had to be done in a hospital and women also had to be residents of the state for ninety days before undergoing the procedure.[51]

MARCH 27: MASSACHUSETTS

On his last day in Suffolk County Jail, Bill Baird wrote:

I have never advocated overthrow of the system. I believe we have the best system in the world, provided it is run for people and is responsive to human needs. A society that sustains itself by a mass of regulations that have no basis in actual social morality is, however, ailing.[52]

1971

AUGUST 6: HUNTINGTON, NEW YORK

Bill Baird and Nancy Manfredonia, a woman he met that night at a political meeting, were charged with endangering the welfare of Manfredonia's fourteen-month-old daughter, Kathryn. According to *Newsday*, a Long Island newspaper, Manfredonia had gone to hear Baird address the Huntington Women's Liberation Group; when police interrupted the lecture they charged the pair with harming the child by exposing her to birth control and abortion devices.[53] Both Baird and Manfredonia were held in jail overnight pending arraignment on misdemeanor charges.[54]

The day after the arrest, Baird's own daughter received an anonymous letter saying, "Your father's a devil, a child molester and a pervert."[55] The Bairds moved shortly after receiving the note.

1972

WASHINGTON, D.C.

President Richard Nixon rejected the recommendations of the Commission on Population Growth, a committee he had established, that urged states to make abortion accessible. He also wrote to New York's Terence Cardinal Cooke and associated himself with Cooke's efforts to reverse New York's recently liberalized abortion law. This was Nixon's first public effort to influence the abortion politics of an individual state.[56]

JULY 7: NEW YORK STATE

Fordham University law professor Robert Byrn, a Right to Life Committee activist, asked the court to make him the guardian of "Infant Roe," a fictitious fetus symbolizing all "unborn children" between the ages of four- and twenty-four weeks' gestation who were scheduled for abortion in New York state. He also petitioned for an injunction to halt all abortions in municipal hospitals while his guardianship application was pending. Judge Francis Xavier Smith granted Byrn both the injunction and the guardianship petition "on the grounds that a fetus constituted a human person."[57]

The Court of Appeals disagreed. "In the first decision of a higher court on this crucial point," wrote Lawrence Lader, "it ruled that the unborn fetus was not a 'legal' person, and upheld the constitutionality of the state abortion law."[58]

1973

JANUARY 22: WASHINGTON, D.C.

The Supreme Court decided *Roe v. Wade,* finding that state laws which made abortion illegal violated the due process clause of the Fourteenth Amendment by infringing on a woman's right to privacy. The ruling put all decisions about first-trimester abortion in the hands of women and their physicians but allowed state governments to restrict abortions performed in subsequent months to those needed to protect women's health. The Justices also found that abortions performed after fetal viability should be available only if a woman's life or health were at risk; states could otherwise prohibit late-term abortion surgery.[59]

CHAPTER THREE

From Roe to Reagan: 1973–1980

For a large chunk of America, the mid- to late 1960s and early 1970s represented a time in which change seemed inevitable. Bob Dylan sang about revolution, the Beatles imagined world peace and David Bowie, a married father, declared his homosexuality. Indeed, a new social order seemed right around the corner. Yet for a significant portion of the country, long-haired men wearing love beads, authority-snubbing youth, mouthy women and increasingly public gay and lesbian alliances portended a future they wanted no part of. Eager to quash the "hippie culture" they saw everywhere, the disaffected began sowing the seeds of what would, by the late 1970s, be called the New Right or Reagan Revolution.

Part of the impetus for the conservative backlash to sexual liberation rested with the Catholic church, and local parishes took direction from a hierarchy bent on restoring the ban on abortion. Pop culture also came in for the church's drubbing. Shortly after *Roe,* in 1973, the United States Catholic Conference sent a directive to parish priests exhorting them to pressure CBS to protest two episodes of the sitcom *Maude* that presented abortion as an option. Although *Maude* producer Norman Lear decried the campaign as censorship, twenty-five CBS affiliates agreed to stop showing reruns of the offending program.[1]

The next year, 1974, the United States Catholic Conference sent four prominent cardinals to Washington, D.C., to testify before Congress in support of a national prohibition on abortion. Their failure to sway lawmakers led the National Conference of Catholic Bishops to develop a Pastoral Plan for Pro-Life

Activities. The plan, unveiled in 1975, presented a long-term program for the 180,000 parishes in the United States to address abortion at the grass-roots level.[2]

The Catholic church's highly precise organization was simply an extension of earlier "right to life" efforts. In fact, within months of *Roe* hundreds of bills to restrict abortion, most written in consultation with church leadership, were introduced into municipal councils and state legislatures across the country. While most anti-abortion activists, Catholic and not, understood that an outright ban on the procedure would not pass legal muster, they were content to work incrementally. Their strategy required the slow winnowing away of the right to choose, a strategy still in place at the start of the twenty-first century.

Thanks to Catholic efforts, states considered an array of restrictions beginning in 1973: spousal and parental consent laws; requirements that second- and third-trimester procedures be performed in hospitals; twenty-four-hour waiting periods; conscience clauses to allow hospital personnel or medical students to opt out of performing or assisting with the procedure if they found it morally objectionable; and bans on the use of saline solution to induce late-term abortions.

Missouri was one of the most legislatively active states. Within six weeks of *Roe,* seven separate anti-abortion bills were introduced into the General Assembly; five were written with the help of the United States Catholic Conference.[3] During that same period an Illinois bill proposed that doctors tell women considering abortion that "the child she was killing was a human being whose life should be preserved."[4]

But despite these efforts, not everyone opposed to abortion was thrilled with the Catholic church's plan of action. Fundamentalist Christians, for one, were addled by what they felt were inconsistencies in the church's politics, from Catholic opposition to the death penalty, to support for economic justice initiatives. Far more conservative in outlook and worldview, previously apolitical evangelicals decided that the time had come to grapple with the here-and-now of American politics.

Their cause got at least some of its momentum from Rus Walton, whose 1974 book, *One Nation Under God,* presented a political agenda that would become a near mantra for Christian conservatives for decades to come: the desire for less government, lower taxes, a balanced budget, increased military spending and withdrawal from the United Nations. Walton was straightforward in his assessment of what needed to be done. In order to achieve the political spoils they desired, fundamentalist Christians needed to elect other fundamentalist Christians to public office.

Third Century Publishers, the company responsible for printing Walton's tract, called a meeting in June 1974 to discuss how best to do this. Richard

DeVos of the Amway Corporation, Bill Bright of the Campus Crusade for Christ, Art De Moss, Ed McAteer and the Reverend Robert Billings, men who would later be prominent players in the New Right, attended the meeting. Surprisingly, abortion was not on the agenda.[5]

Conservatives credit right-wing heavyweights Richard Viguerie and Paul Weyrich with recognizing the role that abortion could play in mobilizing a counterrevolution against feminist and liberation movements, including the more radical New Left. It was they who argued that abortion, like forced busing, higher taxes and sex education in the schools, could lure thousands of disgruntled but patriotic Americans—people who felt out of sync with the social changes that were swirling around them—to the right-wing cause. "The abortion issue is the door through which many people come into conservative politics, but they don't stop there," Viguerie explained. "Their convictions against abortion are like the first in a series of dominoes. Then we lead them to concern about sexual ethics and standards among young people. This leads to opposition to secular humanism. . . . We point out that secular humanism is identified with both the godfather and the royal road to socialism and communism."[6]

Well-funded groups—money came from the Coors Foundation and Mellon heir Richard Mellon Scaife, among others—formed to push the multi-issue agenda Viguerie and his colleagues favored. A counter to progressive groups like Students for a Democratic Society (SDS), NOW and the American Civil Liberties Union, by the late 1970s the New Right had created the Heritage Foundation, the Committee for Survival of a Free Congress, the Conservative Caucus and the Life Amendment Political Action Committee to elect rightist, anti-choice candidates to every level of government.

Conservatives clearly felt that their moment had arrived. Despite some obvious progressive gains—by 1973, forty-five percent of American women were in the workforce; homosexuality had been removed from the American Psychiatric Association's list of mental disorders; and eleven women had been ordained as Episcopal priests—the 1979 formation of the Moral Majority and Ronald Reagan's campaign for the United States presidency made conservatives feel that the tide had turned in their favor. When Reagan was elected in November 1980, they declared their ascension.

In retrospect, by the late 1970s schisms were already beginning to form within conservative ranks. In the area of abortion, for example, some activists favored adding a Human Life Amendment (HLA) to the United States Constitution. Such an amendment would have declared that life began at the moment of conception and given all rights of personhood to the fetus. Other activists supported a state's right approach, preferring to let each locality decide reproductive policy for itself. Still others, fed up with in-fighting over strategy, tactics and politics, took matters into their own hands and began protesting at zoning and health department hearings to stop clinics from opening. Since their efforts were largely unsuccessful, many radical anti-abortionists decided that the time was right for direct action, and they began storming into clinic waiting and operating rooms. Their protests were the precursors of more violent and disruptive demonstrations that would, by the early 1980s, be organized to contest the efficacy of abortion.

1973

JANUARY 24: NATIONWIDE

Two days after the U.S. Supreme Court stunned America by making first-trimester abortion legal, Catholic bishops, organized into the Committee for Pro-Life Affairs, issued a statement opposing the decision. "This is bad morality, bad medicine and bad public policy, and it cannot be harmonized with basic moral principles. . . . We have no choice but to urge that the court's judgment be opposed and rejected," they wrote.[7]

MARCH 6: SAN ANTONIO, TEXAS

Planned Parenthood opened the first freestanding abortion clinic in Texas. "In 1972 Planned Parenthood convened a task force to see if abortion services could be brought to Texas if and when *Roe* was decided in our favor," says clinic administrator Marilyn Chrisman Eldridge. "I was the chair and six of us met, worked on it and found that we could do this. There was no real mystery in providing abortion services; for us it was such a clear-cut medical issue that we assumed that services would be incorporated into every ob/gyn office. We opened an abortion clinic less than two months after *Roe,* and immediately some people on the Planned Parenthood board said they thought running an abortion clinic would be bad for the community and bad for fund raising, that major donors were not interested in abortion. Remember, this is a hugely Catholic city. Many Planned Parenthood staff, including executive director Myron 'Chris' Chrisman, a Disciples of Christ minister who had been active with the Clergy Consultation Service on Abortion, quit over this. We later incorporated as a private, nonaffiliated, not-for-profit clinic called Reproductive Services."[8]

Follow-up note: By 1999 Reproductive Services had nonprofit clinics with companion adoption agencies in five locations: Tulsa, Oklahoma, and Austin,

El Paso, Harlingen and San Antonio, Texas. All were run by parent company Nova Health Systems.

APRIL: NATIONWIDE

The National Conference of Catholic Bishops issued Pastoral Guidelines for the Catholic Hospital and Catholic Health Care Personnel Ad Hoc Committee on Prolife Activities. The guidelines stated that none of the six hundred Catholic hospitals then operating in the United States could provide abortion services.[9]

MAY 13: MONTREAL, CANADA

Despite his arrest in June 1970, Dr. Henry Morgentaler, the humanist who had begun performing abortions in 1967, continued serving the women who came to his office and continued organizing to change the archaic laws governing the procedure in Canada. "On May 13, 1973, I decided to do a TV program which showed an abortion being performed at my clinic," he says. "*Roe v. Wade* gave me the stimulus, and I was eager to convince Parliament that abortion should be an outpatient procedure. In 1969 the Canadian law had changed to allow women to have abortions in hospitals if a panel of three doctors, called a Therapeutic Abortion Committee, approved. I wanted to show the government that it was possible to do an abortion safely in a clinic setting. Canadian TV showed the abortion, coincidentally, on Mother's Day. After this there was a big anti-abortion campaign, protests in front of my clinic and letters to the editor against me. On August 15, 1973, there was a demonstration and I was arrested for the second time."[10]

Two months later, in October 1973, Morgentaler's trial began. "Lo and behold," he says, "the jury acquitted me on November 13, 1973, after a four-week trial. Lots of doctors testified on my behalf; even the president of the Canadian College of Physicians and Surgeons, a practicing Catholic, testified for me. Women who could not pay, but whose abortions I'd done, spoke favorably. It was a great victory and it meant a great deal to me personally. Here I was, a Jew, an atheist, from a socialist family, an immigrant with a Polish accent, and they voted for justice. It gave me more faith in humankind."[11]

Morgentaler thought that his battle was over. "I thought I'd created some kind of jurisprudence and that there would be no more prosecution of doctors," he admits. "I did not know that a Court of Appeals could overturn a jury decision. But the Court of Appeals in Quebec, which was composed of five conservative Catholic judges, declared me guilty in April 1974."[12]

Although Morgentaler appealed the case to the Supreme Court of Canada, he lost, and on March 27, 1975, the Court sentenced him to a year and a half in the Bordeaux Jail near Montreal. He served ten months and was released in January 1976. In November of that year, the newly elected Parti Quebecois announced that it was dropping outstanding charges against the doctor. In addition, the province's attorney general declared that they had no intention of prosecuting other providers.

"Meanwhile," Morgentaler says, "once I got back to my clinic, a community health center financed by the government of Quebec asked me to train their doctors to perform abortions. I taught about thirty of them over the next few years."[13]

JUNE: FAIRFAX, VIRGINIA

Gail Frances, a registered nurse who had been active in the movement to repeal abortion restrictions since 1969, opened the first clinic in the state of Virginia in June 1973. She was one of the many women, then in their twenties, who became providers of abortion services in the immediate aftermath of the *Roe v. Wade* decision.

Frances still remembers the euphoric shock she and her friends felt when they heard about the Supreme Court's pronouncement. "We were all thrown for a loop," she laughs. "No one I knew expected the Court to rule in our favor. When it did, my friends and I spent the next two days on the phone wondering what it meant."[14]

For Frances, it meant starting a clinic. Immediately after announcing her intentions, however, a Commonwealth of Virginia attorney told her that he was looking for a loophole to close the facility. "Although he never found a technicality to use to do this, the threat was there from day one," she says. "Within six or seven months of opening, local church people were picketing us. The police stopped responding to our calls after a judge told us that he would not prosecute the demonstrators because they were acting out of necessity."[15]

Within a year Frances filed suit to curtail illegal anti-abortion activism. The case, *Northern Virginia Women's Medical Center v. County of Fairfax*, yielded the first injunction in the country and barred protestors from coming onto clinic property or blocking doorways. Demonstrators were, however, allowed to freely picket on sidewalks. Unfortunately, law enforcement rarely monitored activists at Frances's clinic, or in other parts of the country. By the mid-1970s the antis were using increasingly abusive and sometimes threatening language, with words intended to incite. Clinic staff noticed the escalation and worried about the impact the increasingly hateful and potentially violent demonstrations would have on them and their patients.

1974

SUMMER: MARLBORO, MASSACHUSETTS

Activist Catholic priest Joseph Francis O'Rourke defied church law by baptizing the three-month-old son of Carol Morreale, a pro-choice advocate. After Morreale's parish priest refused to baptize the boy, O'Rourke flew to Massachusetts and performed the ceremony on the steps of the church. He was subsequently expelled from the Jesuit order.[16] After his dismissal, O'Rourke became president of Catholics for a Free Choice, a D.C.-based group that challenges church policy on gender and sexual choice issues. He served in this capacity until 1979.

NOVEMBER: CHICO, CALIFORNIA

Dido Hasper was a young, idealistic feminist in 1973, a part-time volunteer at Your Clinic, a health center providing free care to residents of Chico, California. One night a week the clinic performed pregnancy tests and dispensed birth control. It also made referrals to the Feminist Women's Health Center in Oakland for women needing abortions. "The Oakland people eventually called us and said, 'You're referring enough women to us to start your own abortion clinic. Why don't you do it?' They organized a meeting, taught us about self-help, and described what they did. About nine of us later decided to open a locally based facility.[17]

"We all had other jobs," Hasper continues. "Before we opened we met a few times a week and struggled around a bunch of policy issues. Would we be women owned and controlled or doctor controlled? We decided to tax ourselves to get the project off the ground and started to search for a suitable space. We eventually found an office on the top floor of the original Enloe Hospital. It was a really old building but the landlord did a lot of work to get it ready. Right around the time that we found this space, the People's Medical Center in the Bay Area announced that it was closing and gave us their exam table and other supplies. Some students at Chico State donated $2,500 and someone else gave us $500. That's what we started on. By early 1975 we had all quit our jobs and were paying ourselves $100 a week to work at the center. Our first clinic was in February 1975. It grew from there."[18]

The Chico Feminist Women's Health Center (CFWHC) performed seven abortions on opening day; it performed fifteen on the next. Yet in the clinic's first years, staff wanted to do more than help women terminate unwanted pregnancies. "Our real focus was on well-woman services, giving women information and control over their bodies to try and prevent future abortions," says Hasper.[19]

This philosophy separated the CFWHC from their medical colleagues; indeed, their first opponents were not anti-abortion protestors but local doctors and the medical society. "We were health workers who thought women should participate directly in their own care," says Hasper. "This posed a challenge to the doctors in Chico. They complained to the Board of Medical Quality Assurance, which is now the California Medical Board, and we had our first investigation before we opened our doors. They wanted to make sure we weren't practicing medicine without a license. Since we've been open we've always used doctors for abortions. But our well-woman care—pap smears, uterine size checks, breast exams—were initially done by lay health workers."[20] Since 1984, however, all well-woman functions have been performed by licensed nurse practitioners.

That change came on the heels of litigation in which the CFWHC challenged eight local doctors, one nurse, the NorCal Mutual Insurance Company, the Butte/Glen County Medical Society and Enloe Memorial Hospital. The clinic argued that the defendants had violated the Sherman Anti-Trust Act by blacklisting doctors and medical workers associated with the center. The clinic further charged that it had been denied both membership in the medical society and staff privileges at local hospitals.[21]

The CFWHC won a favorable settlement of its case in May 1983. Although they admitted to no wrongdoing, eight of the defendants, including the medical society and the insurance company, agreed to stop discriminating against clinic staff and agreed to pay an undisclosed amount. The financial settlement was reportedly enough to enable the clinic to open a second facility in nearby Redding, California, on August 6, 1983.[22]

1975

WASHINGTON, D.C.

The United States Supreme Court invalidated a Virginia statute that prohibited the advertising of abortion services.[23]

Follow-up note: For years many newspapers skirted the law by insisting that only nonprofit clinics could advertise. Clinics scrambled for a solution to this policy, and many established nonprofit arms to dispense—and advertise—birth control.

SUMMER: ROCKVILLE, MARYLAND

Six women were arrested at the first post-*Roe* abortion-related sit-in in United States history. They were sentenced to six months of unsupervised probation for disrupting clinic services.[24]

1976

WASHINGTON, D.C.

In its second ruling on abortion in a year, the United States Supreme Court struck down a Missouri law that mandated that a wife get her husband's consent before having an abortion, that required doctors to "preserve the life and health of a fetus at every stage of pregnancy" and that prohibited saline abortions. In the same ruling, the Justices approved a requirement that patients complete a consent form before having surgery.[25]

SUMMER: KANSAS CITY, MISSOURI

Convention delegates at the 1976 Republican Party conference developed and approved a platform that supported a constitutional amendment to ban abortion, opposed "forced" busing and federal aid to schools, and supported mandatory school prayer and opposition to gun control. The party also dropped its support for the Equal Rights Amendment.[26]

1977

JUNE: MELBOURNE, FLORIDA

Patricia Baird-Windle: "The road I traveled to establish and maintain the Aware Woman Center for Choice has been circuitous and full of potholes. Years before becoming an abortion provider, I had been a director and producer of USO tours and revues for military service clubs. I'd also owned a jewelry store, worked for an airline and raised four children, two of whom had a life-threatening blood disorder. Our fifth child died from the disease. I also raised my nephew part time.

"Then, in May 1976, two things happened that spurred me to become a clinic owner. I was a consumer member of the Central Florida Health Planning Council, the group responsible for approving the purchase of medical equipment that would cost hospitals more than $150,000. The head of the Council, Dr. Sam Barr, was the owner of the EPOC [Every Person's Own Choice] Clinic in Orlando. Sam called in May and asked me if I would work on a federally funded study of contraceptive availability and use. I contacted the Melbourne Women's Center—I had helped found the center in 1973 but had not stayed active— about the project. Shortly thereafter I began volunteering at the center, doing the survey and assisting with abused-spouse counseling and abortion referrals. We also did pregnancy tests, using kits purchased from Dr. Barr, and we referred patients who wanted an abortion to his clinic. At around the same time, my sixteen-year-old son's seventeen-year-old girlfriend got pregnant, and I took her to Orlando for an abortion. I told the staff at the clinic that I was from the Melbourne Women's Center and said that I wanted to tour the facility. I realized at that moment that there was no mystique about doing this work. It was pretty straightforward for anyone with counseling skills, medical knowledge and business experience.

"By summer's end, I was told that the Women's Center would close unless I stepped forward to fill the slot of executive director. The previous director was burned out, sick of the constant fund raising that forced the center to scramble for cash. Although I was reluctant to take the position, I convinced a friend to act as codirector, and together we began to raise money to make the center viable. We also began to publicize our work. I said the 'A' word— abortion—to the press, and right away *Florida Today* sent a reporter to do a story about our referral service. One of our clients agreed to talk to the paper about her situation, and the reporter wrote a full-length feature about the center. At the same time, we started running paid ads explaining our services and began charging $3.00 per pregnancy test since the shabby building we were in needed new floor tile and we had to raise the money.

"As the agency flourished, I discovered that we'd sent Dr. Barr $58,000 worth of abortion referrals in one year. I realized that we were building his business for him. I asked him if we could talk, and he said we'd go out for a drink after the next Health Planning Council meeting. I was hoping he'd give us $300 per month to subsidize the small nonprofit center. My bottom line was free pregnancy tests, since we'd been buying the test kits from him. The night of the meeting he no-showed me. I was pretty annoyed since I don't like to be taken for granted. This was the last week of October 1976. The first week of November I was scheduled to attend a weeklong workshop for women reentering the workforce. I went with the goal of making up my mind about what to do next in terms of paid work. By the end of the week I'd decided to open my own clinic; it was something I had to do. I met with twelve friends from NOW, and they each agreed to put up $1,000. That was enough for us to get started. The doctor I asked to work for me had a brother who was closing a clinic in Pearl River, New York. My husband and oldest son drove up there and bought his equipment. That was our first activity in establishing the Aware Woman Center for Choice.

"My next step was to contact a Melbourne woman who ran a medical lab and who owned a great deal of real estate. I took her to lunch and asked her advice on finding space for a clinic. She told me she could scarcely believe I was bringing this up, that she owned a medical office that was eighty percent furnished and already had dilators and gyn tables. I went to see it and it was perfect. We took possession in April 1977.

"I got my hands on every book on abortion I could find and began touring clinics in Florida and South Carolina to learn as much as possible before the clinic's scheduled opening on June 21. I also began to hire and train staff. On May 20 I got a call from a reporter at *Florida Today.* He said, 'You're opening an abortion clinic and I am going to print a story about it.' He said the news was all over town. I begged him not to write the article until closer to opening day because, in going around for the Women's Center, I had come into contact with organized opposition to abortion and had met people who were violently opposed to birth control. The reporter didn't listen and ran the announcement of Aware Woman's opening on Friday, June 4, with a banner headline, on the front page. By 4:00 P.M. we had a busload of picketers screaming that we were murderers. The entire staff, six of us, were inside working to get the clinic ready when the protestors arrived; we were all really scared. I later learned that during the weekend following the protest, two churches, Grace Baptist and a local Catholic parish, called 570 households and preached against us from the pulpit. When I got to the clinic on Monday, the sidewalk was impenetrable. I had thought the Friday protest would be a one-time thing and was shocked to see so many people. Later that day I got a call from our landlord, asking me to meet her.

"When I got to the meeting, the building owner informed me that officials from the Medical Society had visited her over the weekend and warned that they would stop referring lab work to her if she allowed the clinic to open. To underscore the point, she had not seen a single patient that day. She begged me not to hold her to the lease. I told her that I would not, but asked her to let us stay in the space until I found another location. I also said that in lieu of a financial settlement I wanted to keep all of the furniture and medical supplies that had been left in the building. She agreed to give us everything.

"The newspapers got wind of what had happened, and for the next month the clinic remained on page 1. Two of the Melbourne Realtors I approached were threatened by anti-abortion activists, told that they would be put out of business if they found a location for the beleaguered health center. Finally, in late June, a Realtor from a neighboring town contacted me. He had found a really run-down building for sale in Cocoa Beach, eighteen miles north of Melbourne, that might be suitable. It had been a medical building but had been empty for years. I looked at it, then called one of our investors and asked her to front for me on the contract since I knew that I could not buy a building in my own name. The space cost $42,000 and I took it on faith that I'd somehow raise the money. I never doubted the decision. If a lease could get pulled as easily and quickly as ours had been, we had no choice but to buy. We moved in under cover of darkness, with no air conditioning, and began to clear the years of dust and paint the offices."[27]

JULY: COCOA BEACH, FLORIDA

Patricia Baird-Windle: "Once we found a new space for Aware Woman, I faced the arduous task of converting a long-empty, mildewed office into a medical center. While staff scrubbed, scraped and polished, Dr. Randall [Randy] Whitney and another staff member went to city hall to apply for the clinic's occupation license. I knew that the facility would need to be inspected and have a license in place before we could open. The first inkling that this would not be a simple process came when the woman behind the desk at the licensing office yelled, 'Oh my God, you're not those abortion people, are you?' The next thing I knew, the city called an emergency city council meeting for the next Tuesday. When I got there the room was full and I was told that they were not letting anyone else in. I told the policeman at the door that the meeting was about me, so I was going to enter. One of our volunteers squeezed me and Dr. Whitney into seats. A Cocoa Beach orthopedic surgeon testified that Dr. Whitney was a quack, which made Randy so mad he was ready to fly. I finally got up to speak and they started to drill me from the dais. The question that strikes me still came from a woman with a heavy middle European accent, wearing a nurse's uniform, sitting in the back of the room. She kept screaming, 'What about the fetuses?' I said that one hundred percent of our fetal tissue would be sent to a certified laboratory. I must have repeated the answer five times. Council members also asked the same questions over and over. When I was finished another woman got up and said that there was no need for abortion in Cocoa Beach because there was no airport in town. The inference was that abortion was only provided in great big cities that women could fly into. It was bizarre. The council finally deconvened the meeting and I left, completely shell-shocked. The next day I hired a lawyer. We went to court to force the city to give us our occupation license and won. Four days later I was told I could get the license.

"Unfortunately, the story does not end here. When I went to pick up the authorization, I was shocked to see that it said that Aware Woman could perform reproductive counseling and dispense prescription contraceptives but could not perform abortions. My lawyer had gone on vacation the day after we won the license and had referred me to his junior partner in case of problems. The judge, Clarence T. Johnson Jr., actually came off his vacation to rehear the case. We went into a chamber meeting with the lawyer for the city of Cocoa Beach and the judge said that he would force the city to pay $1,000 a day for each day they withheld the full license. The city lawyer heard this and reached into his briefcase and handed the license to us.

"Simultaneously, however, the city council convened several emergency meetings to decide what to do about Aware Woman. On July 21 they passed a nineteen-part Healthcare Standards Ordinance."[28] Among other things, the ordinance mandated biased pre- and post-abortion counseling; required the clinic to maintain a blood supply sufficient for immediate emergency transfusions for every patient; ordered bacteriological testing of clinics every three months; and imposed a five-day wait between abortion counseling and surgery.[29]

"The intent to close us down was all too obvious and exposed the hysterical attitudes about abortion that were then common. We had expected to open the clinic on August 1. When the regulations came out we attracted the attention of providers all over the United States," says Baird-Windle. "Several of them referred me to lawyer Roy Lucas. I called Roy at his office in D.C., and two days later he sent his private detective to speak to the city attorney. Meanwhile, we did our first well-woman clinic on August 17, using the occupation license we'd been issued. Roy arrived in Florida on August 23. I called a press conference for that day and spoke about my plans for the clinic. Roy told the reporters that the ordinance discriminated against abortion clinics since it held them to a higher standard than other outpatient health centers and was therefore illegal. He cited the blood supply demand, and pointed out that it exceeded what was required of hospitals. On August 24 we went into federal court. The judge was sarcastic to both sides but gave us a temporary restraining order and said that we could open our abortion clinic as soon as we filed a $1,000 bond with the courts. He later ruled that the ordinance was overly broad, discriminatory, vague and ultimately unconstitutional.

"The same night that we got the temporary order one of the TV stations ran a story on us which said that we were having financial troubles. The story implied that despite the decision, the fight might be over. I admitted to reporters that we were out of money and confessed that we needed support from the community if we were going to exist. We raised $900 in one day, and Randy Whitney loaned us $3,000 to keep us running. But we opened and did our first abortion on September 1. From then on, between one and thirty people picketed us on weekdays. On Saturdays we often had 150 protestors. We also got hundreds of obscene and threatening phone calls. They came in cycles, twenty or thirty at a time, then nothing. The police took a long time to do anything about it, but they eventually traced the calls. They came from a man who made them from his job, on his breaks and lunch hour, using an automatic redialer. The detective asked me if I wanted to go to court against this man or if I just wanted him to stop. I said I wanted the calls to end. I have no idea if anything happened to the guy, but he never called us again.

"We also had a lot of vandalism. Someone wrote 'butcher bin' and 'helter skelter' on our door and painted 'die, die, die' on the walls of the building. Our windows were also constantly broken until we put plasticized screens over them. This continued until 1982, when we decided to move to Melbourne, the central point of our patient territory. The Cocoa Beach building also needed so much work it would have cost us $50,000 to stay there. I had proved that there was a need for abortion in Brevard County and that a clinic could be both financially and politically successful. Full of big plans, I bought a building in secrecy and moved Aware Woman to the Melbourne site in October 1982."[30]

LATE SUMMER: COCOA BEACH, FLORIDA

Shortly after the Aware Woman Center for Choice opened in Cocoa Beach in 1977, Birthright, an anti-abortion group that claims to provide material assistance to pregnant women, announced that it was operating from the same office complex.

Patricia Baird-Windle: "Right away we started to hear rumors about what they told patients about us. People were always coming in and saying that when they'd had their pregnancy test, Birthright staff had told them that Aware Woman was filthy and that we were cruel. One story that really blew me away was that we buried bodies in the backyard where there was some disturbed dirt. I tried to get reporters interested in exposing them, but I never found anyone to investigate the story. Birthright's lies simply became something else for us to deal with."[31]

OCTOBER 3: MCALLEN, TEXAS

Rosaura (Rosie) Jimenez, a twenty-seven-year-old single mother of a five-year-old daughter, died of septicemia (blood poisoning) in a McAllen, Texas, hospital following an illegal abortion obtained in a Mexican border town. At the time of her death, Jimenez was one semester away from completing her college degree.

Jimenez and her child relied on Medicaid to pay for their medical care; acquaintances told reporters that Jimenez sought the illegal abortion after learning that her health insurance would not pay for the procedure. She is the first known casualty of the Hyde Amendment, a 1976 law—still in place—that bans the use of Medicaid for the abortions of most low-income women.[32]

As of December 2000, only fourteen states fund Medicaid abortions.

1978

FT. WAYNE, INDIANA

Shortly after the Ft. Wayne Women's Health Organization opened in 1978, a group called Nurses Concerned for Life began harassing incoming patients. "They followed people," says National Women's Health Organization (NWHO) president Susan Hill. "In one case they called the mother of a twelve-year-old girl who had come to the clinic with her fifteen-year-old sister. The younger girl wanted a pregnancy test. They intercepted her on her way into our facility and took her three blocks away to a McDonald's. They did a pregnancy test on her in the bathroom of the restaurant and told her she was not pregnant. When the girl's mother called us to tell us what had happened, we went into federal court and sued the group for interfering with our patients. It turns out that the girl's mother had told the fifteen-year-old to take her sister for the test because she had to work. She knew what was going on. The twelve-year-old finally did come to see us. She was pregnant and had the abortion. The Nurses eventually entered into a consent decree with us."[33]

Unfortunately, the decree did not quiet things at the clinic. Huge numbers of picketers, coupled with near-constant bomb scares, made life at the Ft. Wayne clinic hellish until the mid-1990s. "We'd evacuate whenever there was a bomb threat and the protestors would scream at the patients—some of whom were thirteen or fourteen years old and all of whom were dressed in medical gowns—that they were baby killers," says Hill. "At first we evacuated to a park near the clinic, but we finally had to rent a townhouse two doors down as a safe space for patients and for ourselves. We paid $350 a month for sixteen years, from 1980 until 1996—more than $67,000—so that our patients and staff would have a warm, quiet space to wait while the clinic was checked for explosive devices."[34]

Although no actual bombs were ever found in the Ft. Wayne Women's Health Organization, the clinic has had three suspicious fires since opening in 1977. The first, in the early 1980s, caused minimal damage; the second required $25,000 worth of repairs and closed the center for nearly a month. The third fire shut the facility for ten days.

"Whenever we're there, protestors are there," says Hill. "Even though we haven't had a bomb threat in more than ten years, the potential for danger is there. It's always something: picketers, fires, invasions, vandalism. Red paint was thrown on both the receptionist and patients in one incident. While individual police officers have been wonderful, overall the police force has been antagonistic and uncooperative. For the ten years we got bomb threats, from 1978 to 1988 or '89, I'd call and ask them to send the bomb squad and they'd tell us to check the building ourselves. When OR [Operation Rescue] started up, they'd meet with the group's leaders and agree on a particular length of time to allow the protest to continue before they'd clear our doorways. They basically told us that if we didn't like what they were doing, we should pack up and leave. Two different police chiefs told me that they would not enforce injunctions against the antis. When I met with local federal officials, I was told that if I didn't put the clinic's address in our ads, we wouldn't have a problem. Almost every law enforcer was clear; we were on our own and should close, leave town."[35]

FEBRUARY 18: CLEVELAND, OHIO

A man posing as a delivery person walked into the Concerned Women's Clinic, threw a bag of flammable liquid into a receptionist's face and then set fire to the clinic interior. The room was filled with patients at the time of the incident, and the receptionist was temporarily blinded by the substance thrown at her. Police arson investigators told staff that the culprit appeared to have been "some guy who just went off his rocker."[36]

"The anti-abortion movement got a lot of bad publicity from this," says Ann Baker, president of the National Center for the Pro Choice Majority. "From that point on, until Eric Rudolph planted a bomb in 1998, all clinic bombings were done at night. To me, this suggests that someone was coordinating these things. Someone decided that they would only damage empty buildings and not hurt people."[37]

FEBRUARY 20: CLEVELAND, OHIO

After the Concerned Women's Clinic was firebombed, local pro-choice activists asked advocate Bill Baird to help them organize a campaign against violence. Accepting their request, Baird immediately held a press conference where he told reporters that inflammatory rhetoric was fueling "the winds of hatred." He also called upon Cleveland area Bishop James A. Hickey "to condemn violence against abortion clinics and their personnel and patients."[38]

The next day the Cleveland Diocese issued a statement urging anti-abortion activists to avoid inflammatory rhetoric and be respectful of life.[39] The diocese also supported Baird's call for a meeting between people on both sides of the issue to deescalate tensions.

Unfortunately, Baird's efforts to involve the Federal Bureau of Investigation (FBI) were less successful. A letter dated April 6, 1978, rebuffed his request that the FBI investigate the fire and stated that, "The facts in this matter indicate a possible violation of Title 18, section 844i (the use of an incendiary device to damage property affecting interstate commerce) which is investigated by the Bureau of Alcohol, Tobacco and Firearms (BATF). The facts as provided showed no evidence of a conspiracy and did not warrant federal investigation but rather should be handled by local authorities. There is no basis for an FBI investigation in this matter under the Federal Bombing Statute."[40] Three months later the Civil Rights Division of the Department of Justice advised the FBI that it wanted no further investigation of the incident.[41]

According to Patricia Baird-Windle, "After this incident Bill railed and begged his provider colleagues to recognize the dangers and develop strategies to protect themselves. He was most often ignored and even decried. It is important to recognize that his prophesies have all come true. Indeed, he is a prophet without honor."[42]

SEPTEMBER 13: ALLENTOWN, PENNSYLVANIA

Two weeks before the scheduled opening of the Allentown Women's Center, anti-abortion protestors led by the Reverend Stephen T. Forish of the Pro-Life Office, Catholic Diocese of Allentown, attended the Hanover Township Council meeting to protest the facility. They demanded that the council rescind a zoning permit that had been issued to the women's center the previous July. The permit allowed the clinic to locate in the city's commercial district.

Echoing the Bishop's Committee for Pro-Life Affairs, Forish told the council that "it's bad medicine, bad ethics, bad everything. . . . They are literally getting away with murder." The priest then switched gears, arguing that it was the outpatient nature of the facility that rankled him. "When it's done in a hospital you can be sure it's under legitimate medical guidelines. Even a pro-abortion person should not be for this kind of establishment," he said.[43]

After the contentious hearing, both sides were on pins and needles waiting for the council's decision. On September 28 the clinic received word that Zoning had decided not to revoke its permit. Two weeks later inspections by the Department of Health and Welfare and the Department of Labor led to a second victory for the women's center. It was licensed as a freestanding ambulatory care facility providing first-trimester abortions. The clinic performed its first procedure on October 21. Staff were jubilant, sure that the worst was behind them; they were consequently shocked to discover, four days later, that two people, including a member of the Township Planning Commission, had filed a formal appeal to revoke the zoning permit of the now-functioning health center. Two more people subsequently signed onto the appeal.[44]

A town Zoning Board meeting on December 5 pitted clinic director Solveig "Rusty" Stengle and building owner Erna Arenz against Forish and other vocal antis. Anti-abortion lobbying—which included a telephone and letter-writing campaign as well as personal appearances at hearings and meetings—apparently paid off. On March 22 the board announced that it was reversing its earlier decision and, effective immediately, was voiding the clinic's license. The board also mandated a $500-a-day fine for each day that the clinic operated past the cease-and-desist order posted that evening.[45] Legal machinations allowed the clinic to stay in business until May 11, when another cease-and-desist order was issued. Upon receiving this second order, the center closed its doors.

Finally, on May 17, the clinic was given the green light to resume operations. A new building permit was authorized after inspections by the Department of Environmental Resources and township sewage officials found the clinic to be in compliance with all local building codes and health and safety regulations.

Follow-up note: Since their nightmarish first year, the Allentown Women's Center has been picketed, blockaded and invaded, but harsh prison terms meted out to protestors in the late 1980s and early 1990s have greatly reduced the number of illegal activities. The lesson is obvious: when police act to enforce the law against disruptions, anti-abortion activists move to more hospitable and tolerant venues.

1979

STAFFORD, VIRGINIA

Judie and Paul Brown, former staffers at the National Right to Life Committee (NRTLC), formed the American Life League (ALL) to work on a host of moral issues they believed were intertwined with abortion. Frustrated by the NRTLC's single-issue focus, ALL was organized to address abortion, homosexuality, birth control and gender roles within both the family and in society in general. ALL's *Pro-Life Activist's Encyclopedia,* a 140-chapter tome authored by ex–Green Beret Brian Clowes, lays out the group's ideology. Chapter headings from the book include: "The American Media: Pro-Abortion and It Shows"; "Homosexuals: A Clear and Present Danger to Our Children"; "Homosexual Practices: Self-Loathing in Action"; "Atheists: Anti-Life to the Core"; "The Equal Rights Amendment: Institutionalizing Abortion"; and "Life Under Communism: Hell on Earth."[46]

FEBRUARY 15: HEMPSTEAD, NEW YORK

Twenty-one-year-old Peter Burkin burst into the waiting room of a nonprofit abortion clinic headed by Bill Baird with a flaming two-foot torch in one hand and a can of gasoline in the other. "Nobody move; this place is going up. In the name of God I'm going to cleanse Bill Baird's soul by fire," he screamed. Fifty people, more than half of them patients, were inside the facility when Burkin ignited the gasoline. While staff got everyone safely evacuated, Burkin was treated with kid gloves by District Attorney Denis Dillon. He received a sentence of two years in a psychiatric facility. Dillon subsequently ran a losing gubernatorial campaign on the Right to Life line.[47]

According to Patricia Baird-Windle, "Florida newspapers generally did not carry regional news in the late 1970s and early 1980s, but the fire at Bill Baird's clinic was reported. Because I had already seen a substantial amount of ugly stuff locally, I started keeping close watch on the media, as did my oldest son, Reid. Before long we were checking seven newspapers a day and constantly patrolling the networks. At this point both the National Abortion Federation and the National Organization for Women subscribed to news clipping services, but neither paid much attention to clinic violence."[48]

APRIL: TAMPA, FLORIDA

Margaret Alvis Gifford, owner and executive director of Alternatives of Tampa, has seen far less anti-abortion violence and harassment than other clinic workers in Florida. Still, when she was setting up the facility in 1979, "little things" proved to be extremely vexing. "When we first moved in we could not get our phones hooked up," says Gifford. "I got all these reasons for why there were problems, why it took two weeks to get service. One day during this period I saw a man up on a phone pole in front of our building. I thought he was finally fixing the lines. When I approached him, he said, 'If you'd get right with God you'd have had phone service earlier.' I couldn't prove that the lines were intentionally sabotaged, but two weeks is a very long time to be without service."[49]

Follow-up note: A few years later, in 1983, the clinic's water was inexplicably turned off. When Alvis Gifford went to investigate the curtailment, she discovered that Alternatives had not been receiving its bills. "They had been buried," she reports. "These are the kinds of things you can't prove are anti-abortion harassment, but they increase your level of frustration. We often don't get mail. Is the mail carrier not delivering it or is something else going on?" she wonders.[50]

Current annoyances include having to warn patients against using a particular Tampa pharmacy because the owner refuses to fill prescriptions issued by the health center. Like most clinics, Alternatives has also learned to keep an extra can of paint around so that graffiti can be covered over.

1980

CHICAGO, ILLINOIS

Former journalism professor, reporter and Benedictine seminarian Joseph Scheidler founded the Pro-Life Action League (PLAL). A devout Catholic and father of seven, Scheidler formed the group as an outlet for his belief in direct action and confrontation. "PLAL tries to make it difficult for those who profit from abortion to exercise their lethal trade," he admits on his Web page. "The League stages demonstrations and pickets at abortion facilities and at the offices of pro-abortion organizations as well as the homes of 'doctors' who perform abortions. These activities alert the community to the fact that abortion is a death-dealing activity."[51]

JUNE: WASHINGTON, D.C.

The Supreme Court ruled that Medicaid did not need to pay for the abortions of poor women. *Harris v. McRae* found that the due process clause of the

Fourteenth Amendment did "not confer an entitlement to such funds as may be necessary to realize all the advantages" provided by *Roe v. Wade*. The Justices further ruled that while poverty might be an impediment to access, the government had no obligation to ensure that all women who desired abortions had the means to get them.[52] By the time this ruling was issued, Rosaura Jimenez had been dead for nearly three years.

SUMMER: DETROIT, MICHIGAN

During their summer nominating conference, conferees at the Republican National Convention listened with rapt attention to Virginia delegate Guy Farley Jr., a Moral Majority adherent who proposed that the party support Supreme Court Justices who believe in "traditional family values" and eschew abortion.[53] The platform committee used Farley's words as a blueprint, voting to support a plank that said, "We will work for the appointment of judges at all levels of the judiciary who respect traditional family values and the sanctity of innocent human life."[54] The platform also affirmed GOP support of a constitutional amendment banning abortion and opposing the use of "taxpayer's dollars" for abortion.[55]

That same year Moral Majority founder Jerry Falwell told the press that he had registered four million new voters, all of whom were committed to "unseating liberal candidates who support abortion and homosexuality and reject the Moral Majority's interpretation of family values."[56]

Follow-up note: anti-abortion activists and Christian right-wingers were rewarded when Ronald Reagan moved into the White House. Former Moral Majority executive director, the Reverend Robert Billings, was named assistant Secretary of Education; Dee Jepsen, an anti-ERA, anti-abortion Christian fundamentalist, was named liaison to women's groups; and Donald Devine, Reagan's campaign coordinator for right to life policies, was appointed head of the Office of Personnel Management. His first deeds? According to ex-Republican Tanya Melich, he immediately tried to eliminate reimbursement for abortions from the health insurance plans of federal employees and removed Planned Parenthood from the list of charities that federal employees could contribute to directly from their paychecks.[57]

FALL: WASHINGTON, D.C.

New Right mastermind Bob Bauman, the congressman credited with writing the Hyde Amendment, was arrested for soliciting sex from a sixteen-year-old boy in downtown Washington, D.C. The charges against him were eventually dropped after he pleaded "acute alcoholism" and agreed to enter a court-supervised rehabilitation program. He subsequently divorced his wife and organized the gay Republican movement.[58]

CHAPTER FOUR

Bombing (and Kidnapping) in the Name of the Lord: 1980–1985

When evangelical Christians Dr. C. Everett Koop and Francis Schaeffer began touring the country with their book and film, *What Ever Happened to the Human Race?*, they warned the thousands who came to see them that *Roe v. Wade* symbolized the triumph of evil over good. It was 1979. Virtue could surely trump sin, they added, but only if Christian activists committed themselves to selfless organizing and relentless activism. Luckily for them, the Moral Majority had just formed and founder Jerry Falwell promised that he would register at least four million conservative Christian voters before the 1980 elections. Pundits everywhere declared the first rumblings of a culture war and anticipated many heady moments for born-again right-wingers.

Indeed, Ronald Reagan's 1980 victory over Jimmy Carter was attributed to the influx of evangelical voters.[1] While nonfundamentalist constituencies panicked at the number of religious traditionalists who had gained power on both the federal and local levels, Protestant conservatives recognized that for the first time in nearly a decade, reversing *Roe v. Wade*—and undoing other gains of the 1960s and 1970s—were real possibilities. Joseph Scheidler had a public, photographed meeting with the president in the first months of the Reagan administration. Furthermore, the appointment of C. Everett Koop as surgeon general invigorated the movement. It seemed only a matter of time before the law shifted in a right-wing direction.

But the euphoria—at least as far as abortion was concerned—was short-lived. In 1981 two different bills came before Congress, and disagreement over which to support led to splits between pro-life forces. On one side, Catholic bishops were endorsing a Human Life Amendment that would have nullified *Roe*. Conversely, the New Right was putting its energy into a Human Life Bill (HLB). Convinced that the amendment was a pie-in-the-sky effort, a panoply of newly organized groups felt that the HLB was more realistic since it would permanently prohibit taxpayer-funded abortions and remove federal court jurisdiction in overturning state anti-abortion measures. Despite its more incremental approach, when the HLB came up for a vote it was defeated; shortly thereafter, Senator Orrin Hatch [R-UT], sponsor of the HLA, withdrew the bill from consideration, presumably to avoid a second loss.[2]

Conservatives were perplexed by the bills' thwarting. In addition, they had other cause for concern. Reagan's appointment of Sandra Day O'Connor to the United States Supreme Court in September 1981 shocked anti-abortionists who believed that her opposition to reproductive choice was insufficiently ironclad.

There was also the issue of culture. Music Television (MTV) debuted in 1981, attracting scores of teenagers and young adults to the irreverent words and music of The Cure, Madonna, NWA, Public Enemy and REM. U2's "Sunday Bloody Sunday" had become an antiwar anthem in 1983, and Bruce Springsteen's "Born in the USA," a Vietnam veteran's lament that was released in 1984, was keeping America's aggressive foreign policy in public view. Even pop star Michael Jackson, whose "Thriller" topped the charts during the early 1980s, seemed to celebrate androgyny and bend definitions of male and female.

While the United States poured millions of dollars into support for international right-wing movements and made some headway in defeating progressive movements in Africa and Central America, the domestic agenda that had originally attracted so many people to the conservative cause was floundering. Paul Laxalt's [R-NV] "Family Protection Act," a thirty-five-point conservative wish list for domestic policy, never made it to the floor of Congress, deemed too much too soon by even the most ideologically supportive. Meanwhile, Gay Pride parades were becoming annual events and queer and feminist publications were proliferating throughout North America.

Small wonder, then, that many zealous ideologues felt betrayed. After years of quiet fortitude, they began formulating direct-action strategies for ending abortion, affirmative action, pornography and lesbian and gay equality. According to reporters James Risen and Judy L. Thomas, between January 1983 and

March 1985 at least 319 acts of violence were committed against 238 reproductive health centers.[3] (This estimate is undoubtedly low; clinics are often loath to burden themselves with reporting anti-abortion incidents since police rarely do anything to help them.) In fact, as early as 1982, clinic firebombings, picket lines and equipment sabotage were regularly featured on the evening news.

Still, when three men calling themselves the Army of God kidnapped clinic owner Dr. Hector Zevallos and his wife, Rosalee Jean, in August 1982, both providers and the pro-choice community understood that the terrain had shifted. A new era in which activists would stop at nothing to win the fight against abortion—and by extension attempt to limit women's autonomy—had begun.

1981

SEPTEMBER 21: COCOA BEACH, FLORIDA

The Aware Woman Center for Choice was awarded $75,000 by the city of Cocoa Beach to compensate for the improper denial of its operation license in 1977.[4] The clinic had tallied more than $152,000 in legal bills to secure the license.

OCTOBER 1: FARGO, NORTH DAKOTA

After months of wrangling with state and city regulatory agencies over permits and licenses, the Fargo Women's Health Organization opened for its first full day of business. Partners in Vision, a group headed by Darold Larson, a "trust officer" for Jerry Falwell's Old Time Gospel Hour, vowed to close the health center and pledged daily pickets until it folded.[5]

1982

JANUARY 23: GRANITE CITY, ILLINOIS

The day after the ninth anniversary of *Roe v. Wade,* the Hope Clinic for Women was gutted by fire. "It happened late on a Saturday night so no one was hurt, but one-third of the building was destroyed," says Allison Hile, on staff since 1979. "Nobody was caught. In 1982 you didn't call BATF or the FBI. You called the local police; when we did, they told us they didn't deal with abortion clinics."[6]

Police recalcitrance notwithstanding, the staff decided that their collective elbow grease and dedication would be enough to get the clinic back in operation.

e night of the fire the executive director got a phone tree going to the staff. We got a generator in for light and the whole staff spent Sunday and Monday cleaning up," says Hile. "On Tuesday we saw patients. The building we were in was owned by Dr. Hector Zevallos. He had his private practice in one part of the building and the clinic took up the other part. We used the waiting area of his private practice to see patients for the six weeks it took us to rebuild."[7]

Hile credits the fire with changing the behavior of local anti-abortionists who had been tormenting the clinic since it opened in 1974. "Some of the regulars were embarrassed by the people in their movement who would try to burn a building," she says. "That feeling has lasted to this day."[8] In addition, a well-enforced injunction bars the blockading of clinic doors and has been an effective deterrent during vigils and demonstrations.

AUGUST 12: EDWARDSVILLE, ILLINOIS

Dr. Hector Zevallos had owned the Hope Clinic for Women for eight years when he and his wife, Rosalee Jean, were kidnapped from their home in the summer of 1982. The evening had started out fairly typically. Mrs. Zevallos was watching TV and her husband was puttering in another part of the house when three men knocked on the door and asked to see a piece of property that the Zevalloses were selling. When Hector went outside to show them the lot, one of the kidnappers pulled a gun on him. The men then got Rosalee Jean, blindfolded the pair, and threw them into a car.

"This happened on a Thursday," says Allison Hile, at that time a clinic counselor. "Friday morning, the thirteenth, it looked like Hector was late for work. It was odd since he always arrived promptly to get ready."[9] When Hector had not shown up by midmorning, clinic workers called his home. Since no one answered, they called a neighbor and had her check on him. "His door was open, the TV was on, and the bowl of popcorn was on the table. She said it was really eerie," says Hile. "We called the police because we knew he was missing. We had other doctors, but by Saturday we were getting more and more concerned. To make matters worse, the executive director, Laura Moody, was also suddenly gone from the clinic, dealing with the police and the FBI. She was stationed at the Zevallos's home, which became police headquarters during the search."[10]

When the Zevallos's eight-day ordeal was over, Hile, other staff, and a concerned public learned what had happened. The kidnappers, mastermind Don Benny Anderson and teenage brothers Matthew and Wayne Moore, had ordered Dr. Zevallos to make an audiotape intended to convince then-President Reagan to make abortion illegal. Both Hector and Rosalee remained blindfolded during their entire captivity; their kidnappers also made them sleep on the frigid cement floor of an abandoned National Guard munitions bunker, fed them cold sandwiches, and did not allow them to bathe or use conventional toilet facilities.[11]

"Hector finally made the anti-abortion tape at gunpoint," says Hile. But the three, calling themselves the Army of God, were still not satisfied and began to pester the doctor to close his clinic. "For seven days and nights he discussed the issue with them, but he would not agree to close the office. The last night things got a lot worse, and he and Rosalee were treated more harshly than they had been treated before," says Hile. "Dr. Zevallos asked them why this was and one of the Moore brothers said he'd been up all night trying to formulate a plan to kill the doctor but still didn't know how to do it. That night Mrs. Zevallos was grabbed, physically assaulted for the first time. At that point Hector said he would close the clinic but needed to go free so that he could talk to his partners about the decision. The kidnappers agreed to let them go and drove Dr. and Mrs. Zevallos to a hill near their home. When they walked into their house, a million people were there and they were confused, disoriented."[12]

"I remember being scared at two particular points," recalls Hile. "When the receiving doorbell at the clinic would ring, if it was a small package being delivered, we were terrified. We imagined Hector's hand or a finger being sent by the kidnappers. The other time I got scared I was at home, in the yard with my husband. I didn't know what was going on and it all caught up with me."[13]

During Dr. Zevallos's absence and for several weeks after his return, the clinic's counseling director brought therapists in to run support groups for those workers desiring help. "We'd sit in the recovery room at the end of each day sharing our worst fears and digging our heels in," says Hile.[14]

While everyone connected with the Hope Clinic was tremendously shaken by the kidnapping, providers across the country were also adversely impacted by it. "I remember hearing about the kidnapping and thinking it was a bad joke," says Susan Hill, president of the National Women's Health Organization. "None of us had ever heard of the Army of God, and none of us had expected things to move from damaging property to hurting us personally. The kidnapping was the first time providers as a group understood the personal threat we faced. The doctors who worked for the National Women's Health Organization started to call and would ask me to reassure them and their families that they were safe. We had ten clinics at that point and I tried to assure people, but I couldn't promise them that they'd be okay. In retrospect, the kidnapping represents the first attack on the supply of doctors. Because the Reagan administration didn't talk to us, in most places we were on our own. We had to add security ourselves. In cities like Fargo and Ft. Wayne—where the antis had been very visible and disruptive—we had to convince doctors to fly in from four states away. It was like a ripple effect. Dr. Zevallos was kidnapped, then there was a fire someplace, and then a bombing. You could not relax since there was always a reminder that they—the antis—were out there. The kidnapping, 1982, marks the time when all providers started to be on twenty-four-hour alert."[15]

Follow-up note: Police caught Anderson and the Moore brothers after Dr. Zevallos provided police with a detailed account of the route they had driven to get to the abandoned concrete ammunition bunker where he and Rosalee were detained. Surprisingly, despite being blindfolded, Zevallos was able to recall the turns the car had taken. This provided the police with the data they needed to apprehend the kidnappers.

Don Benny Anderson was sentenced to two thirty-year terms in prison. Matthew and Wayne Moore each received extended prison terms. Although Dr. Zevallos retired in 1986, at the age of fifty-seven, he still owns the Hope Clinic for Women. He and Rosalee Jean divorced a year after the incident.

OCTOBER: MELBOURNE, FLORIDA

Patricia Baird-Windle: "By the last months of Aware Woman's time in Cocoa Beach, the protests had dwindled. They were constant but small and mostly quiet. The move to Melbourne in October stirred the antis up, and the first true unpleasantness was a one-day protest which occurred a week or two after we reopened. That day a woman from Fort Lauderdale came to the clinic and street-preached at the top of her lungs from morning to night. She was so loud I genuinely feared that she would hemorrhage her throat. I went to the Melbourne cops, who at that time had a very young, very liberal police chief, and said that it was ridiculous that they were letting her scream like that and upset the patients. The police officers told me that there was nothing they could do, that one woman shrieking was not enough for them to be involved. From then on I had NOW people at the clinic as patient escorts.

"Meanwhile, from 1982 to 1986 we had continual bomb threats and repeatedly had to take patients outside, wearing hospital gowns, right after surgery. In addition, different churches took turns picketing, and every Wednesday during 1985 and 1986 we had baby buggy brigades, women pushing baby carriages and strollers near the clinic entrance. As you can imagine, hours in the torrid Florida sun were not good for these small children."[16]

DECEMBER 2: WORCESTER, MASSACHUSETTS

After a three-year battle with anti-abortionists who had challenged the clinic's licensing applications, including the determination of need that had been presented to the Public Health Council and Department of Public Health, the Worcester office of the Planned Parenthood League of Massachusetts (PPLM) opened for service. During their first week in the building they noticed that another company, PP Inc., was also setting up shop. The two groups' logos appeared identical, but that was the only thing they had in common. PP Inc. turned out to be an anti-abortion group called Problem Pregnancy, Inc., that had been established by Massachusetts Citizens for Life to lure patients away from the abortion and reproductive health provider.

"People had to go by their doors to get to the Planned Parenthood clinic, and from the first day we encountered enormous difficulties from the presence of that office," says Alice Verhoeven, vice president of Planned Parenthood/Preterm. "They would picket right in the hallway. Patients would often go into their offices and say, 'I'm here for my appointment.' The people inside would never actually tell patients they were Planned Parenthood, but they led people on. They would take urine for pregnancy tests, and almost every woman was told that the tests were inconclusive. This was a stall tactic. They would delay the women so that by the time they realized they were not at Planned Parenthood they would have missed their appointments with us."[17]

Worse, by the time patients realized their error and entered the real clinic, they were often extremely frazzled. Some women had been forced to watch lurid slides of dismembered fetuses while waiting for the results of their pregnancy tests; others had been yelled at for considering "killing their babies."

"I used to spend more time in the hallways running interference than I did in the clinic," Verhoeven says. "While most patients understood that Planned Parenthood was not to blame, they were still furious about the unsettling intrusion they had experienced."[18]

PPLM knew that they had to mount an aggressive campaign to stop PP Inc. Volunteers were mobilized to escort patients through the gauntlet of people in the hallway and litigation was initiated to keep PP Inc. from representing itself as a reproductive health facility. In May 1983 the clinic also sued its landlord for breach of contract, charging that a clause in their lease guaranteeing tenants the quiet enjoyment of the space they had rented was being violated. The case went all the way to the Supreme Judicial Court of Massachusetts; in June 1983

PPLM won an injunction ordering their landlord to prevent conduct "which impedes or intrudes on access."[19]

Another lawsuit, this one charging PP Inc. with trademark violation, resulted in a second victory for the abortion provider. On June 29, 1984, Middlesex Superior Court Judge Elbert Tuttle ruled that "the intent of Problem Pregnancy in utilizing the initials PP on the door of its offices was to confuse women into entering the PP office in order to give PP counselors an opportunity to persuade these women not to have abortions." The judge ordered the group to remove the logo from its door and enjoined it from using PP Inc. on its advertising or literature. The judge further stated that "Problem Pregnancy's use of the PP initials was an intentional infringement of the Planned Parenthood Federation's registered service mark and was an unfair and deceptive act and practice in violation of Massachusetts law."[20]

In June 1983, after seven months of PP Inc.'s shenanigans, PPLM got an additional injunction to keep the antis from "corridor counseling" inside the building. They also forced the imposter organization to move to another floor, which Verhoeven says reduced the assault on patients and made it possible for PPLM to function.

Nonetheless, PPLM paid a high price for these victories. Former PPLM president Nicki Nichols Gamble states that the litigation of three cases—the infringement on the use of Planned Parenthood's logo, the violation of their right to the quiet enjoyment of the space they rented, and a case contesting the state's denial of the clinic's application for an operating license in September 1982—cost in excess of $200,000.[21]

DECEMBER 29: MICHIGAN

Sister Agnes Mary Mansour, a Sister of Mercy for thirty years, was appointed by Governor James Blanchard to head the Michigan Department of Social Services (DSS). The former college president had been one of five Democratic contenders in a 1982 congressional primary. Although Mansour lost the race, she and the Reverend Edmund C. Szoka, the Archbishop of Detroit, had gone head to head during the election. Her appointment as DSS director further rankled the archbishop, and in February 1983 he ordered her to resign. "The job requires her to direct spending on Medicaid abortions and abortion is an evil sin," Szoka told a *Detroit Free Press* reporter.[22] Mansour refused to buckle and left the order on May 11, 1983.

1983

WASHINGTON, D.C.

In *City of Akron v. Akron Center for Reproductive Health,* the United States Supreme Court invalidated an ordinance that required doctors to give patients anti-abortion information, including materials that said that "the unborn child is a human life from the moment of conception." The ordinance had initially been passed under the pretext of providing "informed consent" to patients. The Justices also struck down both a twenty-four-hour waiting period for women wishing to terminate pregnancies and a requirement that all second-and third-trimester abortions be done in hospitals.[23]

MAY: CHICO CALIFORNIA

The California Employment Development Department (EDD) charged six employees of the Chico Feminist Women's Health Center (CFWHC) with conspiracy to commit unemployment insurance fraud. According to the charges, the women had laid themselves off when clinic income was low and then volunteered as many as seventy hours a week while drawing benefits. The CFWHC volunteers countered that the allegations were provoked by their governor's anti-choice position and amounted to little more than a politically inspired witch hunt.

For four and a half years the clinic was subject to invasive probes in which confidential patient records, as well as financial data, account ledgers and canceled checks, were scrutinized. Finally, in November 1988, Chico Municipal Court Judge Brian Rix dismissed the charges.

After the decision was issued, State Assemblyman John Vasconcellos [D-San Jose] wrote Assemblywoman Maxine Waters [D-Los Angeles], chair of the Democratic Caucus, about the clinic's ordeal. "EDD has wasted staff time of at least $200,000 in direct assistance on this case, and as much as $500,000 in indirect staff time for an alleged conspiracy involving no more than $30,000 in questionable benefits. It is puzzling to me why a state agency would be expending hundreds of thousands of dollars to help prosecute several volunteers of a women's health center while encouraging other volunteers as a matter of policy."[24]

In early 1989 a second judge confirmed that the state had no case and ordered EDD to drop the charges against the six.[25]

MAY: WINNIPEG, CANADA

It was in 1982, says Dr. Henry Morgentaler, that he decided to take his battle to make abortion available to provinces other than Quebec. "I had a freak accident in New York City. I was in a bathroom and a guy attacked me and choked me from behind. It was not abortion related. Before this happened I had been debating whether to challenge the law in other parts of Canada. After this incident I decided, what the hell? There is no safe place. I decided to open clinics in Winnipeg and Toronto."[26]

The Winnipeg clinic opened in May 1983; the Toronto one in June. A month after the Winnipeg opening, police raided the facility and Dr. Morgentaler, Dr. Robert Scott and seven staff members were charged with conspiracy to provide a miscarriage. The prosecutor subsequently dropped the charges against six of the parties; Morgentaler, Scott and head nurse Lynn Crocker remained under arrest.

The clinic was closed until March 23, 1985. A few days after reopening, another raid resulted in Morgentaler being charged with three more counts of procuring a miscarriage. On March 30 the clinic resumed operations and was once again raided. Morgentaler was subsequently charged with several additional counts of violating the criminal code.

The Toronto clinic suffered a similar fate: raided on July 5, 1983, barely a month after opening, its equipment was seized and Doctors Morgentaler, Scott and Smoling were arrested for conspiring to cause miscarriages in pregnant women. On November 8, 1984, a jury acquitted the three physicians. Although the clinic reopened, Attorney General Roy McMurtry challenged the verdict and the doctors were again arrested. On October 1, 1985, the jury decision was set aside by the Ontario Court of Appeals and a new trial was ordered. Morgentaler appealed to the Supreme Court of Canada, and a hearing was held in October 1986.[27]

Follow-up note: Morgentaler's legal roller-coaster ride finally ended on January 28, 1988, when the Canadian Supreme Court struck down the country's abortion law. The Justices found that the law violated the national Charter of Rights and Freedoms because it infringed upon a woman's right "to life, liberty and security of the person."[28]

"After this decision the antis got very well organized," says Morgentaler, "and started to do what they do in the United States in terms of picketing clinics and writing propaganda. The Toronto clinic was picketed every day, usually by twenty or thirty people, from the day it opened until 1991, when I got an injunction which says they cannot come within five hundred feet of the building.

Then, on May 18, 1992, in the middle of the night, someone poured gasoline through the hole in the door and the clinic blew up. Another Toronto clinic, run by a doctor I'd trained, gave us temporary lodging until we could rebuild. We worked when they did not, including Sundays. Fortunately, we had insurance, and the New Democratic Party helped me look for a new space and build an 8,000-square-foot, state-of-the-art facility. It is a very beautiful clinic. The police never found out who set the fire. It is an unsolved crime."[29]

Morgentaler now runs eight clinics across Canada, in Edmonton, Fredericton, Halifax, Montreal, St. John's, Toronto and Winnipeg. "I've had numerous death threats and was assaulted once. A man ran at me with garden shears. He was convicted for this. In 1992 I was sprayed with ketchup in an airport in Calgary, and I have been screamed at by lynch mobs," the seemingly unfazed Morgentaler explains. "You have to understand: I am a survivor of the Holocaust. I spent four years in concentration camps, Dachau and Auschwitz, and either it makes you or it breaks you. I have a philosophical attitude that what happens, happens. I will not be deterred or discouraged by threats. Other doctors tell me that they value my example. I started medical school in 1947, in Germany, after American troops liberated me from Dachau. I continued in Belgium and graduated from the Catholic University of Montreal in 1953. I believe the concentration camp experience sensitized me to suffering, made me want to do whatever I could, personally, to eliminate injustice. Children who are born into families where they receive love and caring do not build concentration camps. This is my contribution to a better world. This is why I will not flinch or give up."[30]

AUGUST: EVERETT, WASHINGTON

Staff at the Feminist Women's Health Center (FWHC) in Yakima, Washington, open since 1980, were so pleased with the work they were doing that, in late 1982, they decided to expand their services and open a second clinic in Everett, three hours away. They were completely unprepared for the hostile reception that greeted them. "As soon as the antis heard we were opening they came en masse," says staffer Beverly Whipple. "There was a daily onslaught. Something was always happening. We'd get hundreds of phone calls—seven hundred hang-ups in one day—which effectively blocked our phone lines. It was impossible to get any work done."[31]

According to Whipple, the antis would also fill every parking space adjacent to the clinic and cover workers' cars with pictures of dismembered fetuses. Individual demonstrators would then form a gauntlet for patients to walk through. They trespassed, followed staff home at night, and copied down the license numbers of incoming patients. "The building was surrounded by ivy, and they'd crawl through the plants to look into our windows," she adds. "They took still photos and videotapes of patients and on November 19 held a prayer vigil in front of the clinic. The protestors had received permission from the City Council to block the road for this event; they had a flatbed truck and a complete sound system and brought hundreds of people to the facility to pray for us."[32]

Two and a half weeks later, on December 3, a man subsequently identified as Curtis Beseda tossed gasoline into a clinic window and ignited it. "The fire did significant damage, destroying a lot of equipment," says Whipple. "But when the fire inspectors came, they suggested that we'd set it ourselves. They said that since we weren't doing well financially, and were a new business under a lot of pressure, perhaps the fire had been our doing. The fire marshal wanted to investigate the staff. We tried to point out how ludicrous this was, but they would not even speak to the antis until we were investigated and came out clean. They wanted us to take lie detector tests. Our attorney said that he understood our refusal, but that if we wanted the case to move forward we had to do the polygraphs. We all took the test and we all, inexplicably, flunked. They eventually threw the test results out and started to question the antis."[33]

The clinic remained closed for two months, until February 1, 1984. That month, and for most of March, it was picketed every day and received an enormous volume of hate mail. Then, on March 26, a second fire was set. This time the clinic had better security and the fire was quickly extinguished. "The gasoline was poured into a counseling room and lit, but the damage affected only one room so we were able to close it off, clear out the smoke, and open later that day. After this fire the officials started to investigate the antis more seriously. Regional BATF had never been involved in a clinic fire in this state before and they were called in," Whipple says.[34]

At the time of the second fire, the clinic was in court seeking an injunction to stop the antis from trespassing and harassing patients and staff. A trial to address this request began on April 19; on the night of April 20, a third fire broke out at the FWHC and caused extensive damage not only to the clinic but also to the building that housed it.

The Everett FWHC never reopened. Although Whipple says that for years staff held onto the hope that they would be able to resurrect the center, financial pressures coupled with an inhospitable community made this impossible.

According to a history of the clinic written in 1996, "Months after the third fire, local police questioned, but chose not to prosecute, Curtis Beseda. However, federal authorities took the violence more seriously and it paid off. Beseda fled to Canada and federal Marshals arrested him when he tried to re-enter the United States. On the witness stand, Beseda admitted he set the three fires in Everett and another in Bellingham. He was sentenced to 20 years."[35]

Follow-up note: In February 1986 the FWHC filed a federal civil lawsuit charging individual protestors with violating the Racketeer Influenced Corrupt Organizations (RICO) Act. Several of the defendants settled out of court, and their payment made it possible for the Yakima health center to purchase the building they currently occupy. A 1990 trial on the RICO claims resulted in another victory for the FWHC and three defendants, Curtis Beseda, Sharon Codispoti and Dotti Roberts, were ordered to pay more than $300,000 to the clinic. Not surprisingly, they appealed the decision. The case was subsequently assigned to a three-judge panel; FWHC staffers were perplexed that one of the judicial panelists had previously been a National Right to Life Committee board member. In August 1995, nearly five years after the appeal was initiated, the panel reversed the lower court decision and ordered the FWHC to pay $19,058 in defendants' court costs. They had no choice but to do so.[36]

Curtis Beseda was released on October 3, 1996 after serving twelve years in prison.[37]

Over the last two decades, North Dakota and Florida police and BATF officers have repeated the slur first uttered in Everett, suggesting that clinic owners or staff were responsible for fires started at clinics in these states. The evidence reveals the lie embedded in this scurrilous assertion; no owner or worker has ever been found guilty of arson.

NOVEMBER 16: FORT LAUDERDALE, FLORIDA

F. Scott Wilson was furious. A self-described devout Christian who opposed abortion, the divorced father flew into an uncontrolled rage when he discovered a business card from The Women's Center on his fourteen-year-old daughter's desk. According to the *Miami Herald,* Wilson's first move was to interrogate the girl about whether she was pregnant and considering abortion. Although she told him she was not, Wilson decided to visit the clinic and inquire about her condition. When the receptionist told him that she could not give him any information, he jumped through a glass window and began to overturn desks, exam tables and medical equipment.[38]

"In his frenzy," says counselor Joan Linwood (not her real name), "he punctured the drywall and tore the vinyl inlay off the floors. Then he calmly sat down and waited for the police to come and arrest him."[39]

Wilson was charged with disorderly conduct and taken to Broward County Jail, where he was released twelve hours later on $1,000 bond. "He never showed up for trial," says Linwood. "We never saw him again. We assume he fled to another state."[40]

Wilson's rampage occurred just two weeks after the clinic moved into a newly renovated office and presaged a spate of vandalism. During the next two years sabotage at The Women's Center was more or less constant. Roofing nails were placed in the parking lot, shots were fired into the director's office and waiting room, windows were broken, and on three separate occasions quart bottles of sticky piña colada mix were smashed in the clinic entrance area. "We had to use a shovel to get all the shards of glass up and then hose it down over and over," says Linwood.[41]

Another incident involved an oil spill in the clinic doorway. "Someone dumped about a gallon of thick black motor oil, the stuff you take out of your car, on the sidewalk out front. We had to use solvents and then kitty litter to absorb it before we could shovel it up. For those two years [1983 to 1985] I kept big pieces of corrugated cardboard in my car at all times. In case of problems, spillages of one kind or other, we could put the cardboard down, enter the clinic, and then figure out how to get whatever had been dumped cleaned up."[42]

1984

NATIONWIDE

American Portrait Films released *The Silent Scream,* a movie narrated by Dr. Bernard Nathanson. Nathanson had been a founder of the National Abortion Rights Action League (NARAL) in 1969 and had been an abortion surgeon until the late 1970s. Then, a political change of heart led him to the anti-abortion cause, and he has been a spokesman for their efforts ever since.

The Silent Scream relies on sonogram footage for its lurid attack on abortion. In concert with film showing a fetus in utero, inflammatory rhetoric describes the "tearing apart of the child." In one particular scene, viewers are told that the "baby" is uttering a "chilling silent scream" to protest his or her "imminent extinction."

Pro-choice groups continue to criticize the film—it is still shown on cable television and is available on the World Wide Web—and say that it is riddled with fallacies. "The film represents an attempt to shift the focus of the abortion debate to the fetus and away from any concern or compassion for women in need of abortion services," says a Planned Parenthood Federation of America fact sheet. "It is an attempt to deny the desperation that once forced American women into life-threatening, humiliating experiences of unsafe, often lethal abortions."[43]

KNOXVILLE, TENNESSEE

Deborah Walsh was working at the Volunteer Medical Clinic in Knoxville, Tennessee, when she learned that if the clinic wanted to obtain an injunction against illegal anti-abortion protest, it needed to document the trespassers in action. Walsh complied and, whenever possible, took photographs of the antis.

"One guy, a minister, was just rabid. He regularly got in the staff and patients' faces and would call us 'murdering whores' and 'wives of Satan.' One day I went outside to take his picture as he did something—at that time we were using plainclothes police for our security—and he grabbed me and threw me into the street, into traffic. The security guard grabbed him and held him in a police hold until the local officer came to make the arrest. I was okay, but I was also completely shaken up by what might have happened. It was the first violence I'd experienced since I started working at the clinic in February 1982. I was completely freaked out. I was throwing up, couldn't eat and lost fourteen pounds in two weeks. He was charged with assault but I don't know or remember if anything happened to him. I do know that he kept coming back to the clinic."[44]

JANUARY: TOLEDO, OHIO

When Carol Dunn—a passionate advocate of legal abortion since 1964, when abortion complications landed her an extended stay in an Ohio hospital—opened Toledo, Ohio's, Center for Choice in January 1984, she was not surprised when local anti-abortion activists turned their attention toward her clinic. They had been picketing and disrupting one of the city's other facilities, Toledo Medical Services, since it opened in 1974, and several local activists, including Marjorie Reed, had become nationally prominent.

Like other abortion opponents, Toledo's activists had been cheered by the election of Ronald Reagan and had stepped up their organizing accordingly. In 1982 they began blockading Toledo Medical, and owner Carl Armstrong had gone to court to request a restraining order. Armstrong won the order and protestors were barred from trespassing or interfering with patients who were entering or leaving the building.

"The activity shifted from Toledo Medical to the Center for Choice immediately after I opened," Dunn says. "Carl had a restraining order. I had nothing. This was a shoestring operation, and I did not have the money to get a court order so I recruited volunteers from NOW and the universities to escort patients. They came from all over the city to help us keep our doors open. In retrospect this may have escalated things because we now had daily confrontations between the escorts and the antis, but at the time I had no choice if I wanted to run a clinic."[45]

Several times during the center's first year protestors invaded the clinic's waiting room. During their second year, in early 1986, someone broke in and cut the hoses on the machines used in first-trimester vacuum aspiration abortions. "After this we got a motion detector and security system, but we had not even made our first payment when the building was set on fire. It was May 20, 1986, and if it wasn't burned it was smoke damaged," says Dunn.[46]

The clinic owner recalls getting a call from the clinic director, who had been notified by the security company, at 5:00 A.M. on the day of the fire. "At first we thought we could clean it up and get back to work in that space," she says. "For the first few days we continued to run pregnancy tests from a small office in the building that our landlord was letting us use. Then, a couple of days later, the landlord sent me a letter canceling our lease."[47]

The cancellation turned out to be legal, and despite months of courtroom wrangling, the Center for Choice lost its bid to retain the space it had spent between $60,000 and $70,000 to renovate two and a half years earlier. By this point Dunn had received some money from her insurance company and had begun to investigate the feasibility of buying a building. Like Patricia Baird-Windle, she knew that landlords would not rent to her—providing rental space to a clinic was, and is, considered too risky by most property owners—so she decided to check out Toledo's warehouse district, a neighborhood that was considered marginal, but where buildings were both solidly built and reasonably priced. She eventually found a space and proceeded to find people who were willing to buy it in their names because she knew that getting a mortgage as Carol Dunn, owner of the Center for Choice, would be next to impossible. Dunn officially took the building over in 1989.

Despite a Kafkaesque string of problems that confounded the clinic—the fire, the canceling of the clinic's lease, the need to find people to masquerade as buyers so that the center could secure a building—the arson garnered remarkable community support for the clinic. "I live in the old west end, an eclectic area which holds an annual festival during the first week of June. Shortly after we got firebombed we had our festival. The year before, in 1985, the antis had picketed the event with pictures of fetuses, and signs and handbills saying that there was a murderer living in the neighborhood. This year, before the festival, I told people that the antis were probably going to picket again. Our neighbors created 'We love our neighbor, Carol Dunn' badges. When the antis showed up, the president of our neighborhood association told them that they were not welcome, that the community knew what I did and did not object to it. It was wonderful. They have not picketed my home or neighborhood since."[48]

Follow-up note: In October 1990, after years of living underground to evade prosecution, Marjorie Reed was convicted of setting the fire that destroyed the Center for Choice and was sentenced to ten years in jail. She served seven years and was released in the fall of 1997. According to anti-abortion activist Michael Bray, who was present at Reed's sentencing, Judge Nicholas J. Walinski told the court that while he believed the defendant to be "morally correct," she was nonetheless guilty of violating the law.[49]

Her capture followed an arson attempt at a National Women's Health Organization (NWHO) clinic in Fairfield, New Jersey. "Sometime in early 1990 the Ft. Wayne Women's Health Organization got a leaflet from the feds which said that Marjorie Reed was wanted for arson and for assaulting a federal officer," says NWHO president Susan Hill. "This was the first time I was made aware of her. Later that year I was at a NARAL luncheon and I got a call that there had been a fire in our Fairfield facility that had burned a glass wall of the building. We'd had that clinic since 1976. The fire was on a Friday night and BATF agents decided to do a stakeout, thinking that whoever had done this would return later in the weekend to finish the job.

"They were right and when Reed returned, they got her. BATF called me and told me that they had a woman in a holding cell who would not give her name. The agent described her to me and I said, 'That sounds like Marjorie Reed.' He said, 'Who is Marjorie Reed?' I couldn't believe it since it was his agency, BATF, that had sent out the flyer asking us to look for her. They finally did a check and found out that the woman was, in fact, Reed. She was a fugitive and had been living in New Jersey with other antis. No one was ever charged with harboring a wanted criminal despite the fact that Reed had been sought for several years for setting the Ohio fire. All in all we were furious with the way the feds handled the case. We were never contacted about the progress of the trial and we weren't even told when Reed was released from jail. It's been frustrating," Hill says.[50]

The Center for Choice II opened 365 days after the May 1986 fire leveled its predecessor. "For that year we borrowed Toledo Medical's facilities. We met our patients there and used the second floor of our director's house, which she was not using, for our offices," says Dunn. "We kept our autoclave there. We paid Toledo Medical $500 a day to use their space, but being there kept our spirits up. We saw patients every week, twice a week, for the whole year. I felt that if we'd closed we would never have reopened."[51]

The Center for Choice II operated out of the warehouse district until late 2000, when the facility moved to a different location. Like earlier incarnations, Dunn has worked hard to make the health center feel homelike, installing plush rugs, wicker chairs and lots of artwork on the walls.

FEBRUARY: NORFOLK, VIRGINIA

In an attempt to blow up the Hillcrest Clinic, anti-abortionist Michael Bray and two companions placed seven pipe bombs against the window of a bank located on the first floor of the building that housed the healthcare facility. The bombs exploded and destroyed the bank's plate-glass windows. The clinic was not damaged. Bray and his compatriots were arrested eleven months later and received sentences ranging from six to fifteen years for their terrorist acts.[52]

JUNE 25: PENSACOLA, FLORIDA

"John Burt came to Pensacola in the early 1980s, an ex-Klansman, an ex-drunk and an ex-drug addict. It was not long after he arrived that things started to happen at the clinic," says Linda Taggart, administrator of the Community Healthcare Center of Pensacola, Inc. (formerly The Ladies Center). "The story I've heard is that shortly after he got here he went to the bus station to pick someone up and while he was waiting he looked at the newspaper and saw an article that said that for every ten live births in Pensacola, there were seven abortions. He read it, got mad, and decided to do something. He already ran a home for 'wayward' women, and he and this group of women were part of the Brownsville Assembly Church. I was the only clinic in town in the early 1980s and Burt and his group picketed and tried some trespassing, but that was it until June 1984 when we were bombed for the first time."[53]

Taggart got a call from the sheriff's office at 4:00 A.M. on the day of the bombing. "I had to drag my daughter, who was sixteen, out of bed and get to the clinic, but it was so dark we couldn't see the damage to our beautiful new building. We'd just moved there in 1982, less than two years before," she says.[54]

The morning light revealed the enormity of the destruction. "The force of the bomb had lifted the roof off and put it down in a different place; the construction people had to virtually tear the place down and start all over. We knew we couldn't wait since it would take about a year to rebuild, so we started to look for another building. We put the little that was salvageable—all my stuff, my books, diplomas and all the clinic's files and records, were destroyed—into storage. My assistant and I then spent every single day looking for space," she continues. "One day I was sitting around feeling depressed and tired when my pager went off. It was the Realtor, telling me that he thought he'd found something for us. I didn't expect much since after your building is bombed there aren't too many landlords who want you, but I went to see this space. It was a former real estate office and it was better than anything we'd seen so we leased it. We then had to get it together as a clinic because the longer we were out of business the happier the antis were. We were closed for five weeks, from June 25 until July 30, 1984.[55]

Once the clinic was reopened, she says, picketing and blockading were stepped up; locks were repeatedly glued, roofing nails were spread throughout the parking lot, and bomb threats were periodically called in. Then, six months later, on December 25, 1984, the clinic was bombed for the second time.

SUMMER: DALLAS, TEXAS

Republican delegates to the party's electoral convention passed a platform that declared that "the unborn child has a fundamental individual right to life which cannot be infringed." The party also reaffirmed its support for a Human Life Amendment and reiterated its opposition to federal funding for abortions or for those organizations that advocated abortion.[56]

OCTOBER 7: NATIONWIDE

A month before the contentious 1984 presidential election that pitted Walter Mondale and Geraldine Ferraro against Ronald Reagan and George Bush, a paid advertisement ran in the *New York Times.* Called The Catholic Statement on Pluralism and Abortion, it stated that "a diversity of opinion regarding abortion exists among committed Catholics." The Catholics for a Free Choice–sponsored ad was signed by ninety-seven people, including two religious brothers, one Franciscan priest and twenty-six nuns. Predictably, the Vatican immediately retaliated.[57]

The statement was intended to support beleaguered pro-choice Catholic Geraldine Ferraro and was published days before Ferraro was scheduled to march in a Columbus Day parade in Philadelphia. Weeks earlier John Cardinal Krol had threatened to pull Catholic school groups and marching bands out of the parade if the vice-presidential candidate took part.

On November 14, John Quinn, chair of the National Conference of Catholic Bishops' Committee on Doctrine, released a statement charging that the ad "contradicts the clear and constant teaching of the church about abortion."[58] Likewise, the Vatican Congregation for Religious and Secular Institutes ordered the signers to retract the statement. Failure to do so, they warned, could result in dismissal from the "community."[59]

According to Barbara Ferraro and Patricia Hussey, outspoken feminist signers of the ad—and Sisters of Notre Dame—the priest and religious brothers who lent their names to the statement quickly "regularized" their relationships with the Vatican and were never heard from again. Several of the twenty-six nuns who signed issued "clarifications" and were likewise let off the hook. Ferraro and Hussey refused to do this. In fact, they issued a statement in April 1986: "We regret that the male celibate church is ignoring and trivializing the experiences of women. We regret that the official church cannot deal with women as full persons and moral agents in our own right. . . . We regret that the official church is continually repressing dissenting voices and seems to be acknowledging only the view of the religious right within Catholicism. We believe that women are to be affirmed in their reproductive decisions on the basis of individual conscience and personal religious freedom."[60]

On July 13, 1988, Ferraro and Hussey voluntarily resigned from the Sisters of Notre Dame. They currently run a shelter for the homeless in Charleston, West Virginia, and opened the first residence for homeless people with AIDS in that state.[61]

FALL: VESTAL, NEW YORK

When Cindy Terry, former wife of Operation Rescue leader Randall Terry, first showed up at Southern Tier Women's Services, near Binghamton, staff had no idea who she was. "We'd never heard of her or of the fundamentalist Christian presence in the anti-abortion movement," says Alexandra Aitken, assistant administrator of the clinic. "On a nonprocedure day Cindy came in and asked for a pregnancy test but asked if we could talk first. I said, of course. She made it clear that she was very much against abortion so I asked her why she'd come to Southern Tier. She said she wanted to hear what we said to patients. Then she left our offices. A few weeks later she appeared in the parking lot with a sign and tried to get our patients to talk to her. She was very persistent. Randall showed up shortly thereafter. It was a slow start, first Cindy by herself and then with Randy. Larger groups started coming to the clinic in 1985 and would chant, sing, and scream at patients. They'd also approach patients' cars and try to keep them from getting out. They would harass everyone coming in and out of our offices."[62]

"Terry launched his first campaigns against our clinic," adds administrator Peg Johnston. "Everything he took national [when he formed Operation Rescue in 1986] he tried here first," from invasions and blockades, to the harassment of the clinic's landlord and the destruction of medical equipment.[63]

"Finally, at some point in 1987, we did something to make the antis much less threatening to our patients and to ourselves," says Aitken. "The father of one of our staff people was a professional sign painter, and he made up a thirty-foot canvas banner which we hung on our fence. It said, 'Please don't feed the protestors.' We put it up whenever the protestors would appear or when they were particularly obnoxious. The patients would see it and laugh. We found that once you made jokes at the antis' expense, it broke the ice and helped everyone take them less seriously."[64]

Although the clinic's sewer system has since been tampered with, its roof vandalized and a series of bomb and death threats have been received by mail, since the mid-1990s Cindy and Randall Terry have rarely appeared at Southern Tier. "We believe that part of the reason there has been so little anti-abortion activity in Vestal is that Terry is trying to go legitimate, be a Republican, a regular politician," Aitken concludes. "He doesn't want his name tied to bombings, shootings, rescues or trespassing, or to anything linked to that side of the movement."[65]

NOVEMBER: WHEATON, MARYLAND

In November 1984 a clinic owned by Gail Frances was firebombed by Michael Bray, Kenneth Shields and Thomas Spinks, the same trio who had attempted to destroy the Hillcrest Clinic in Norfolk nine months earlier. The ten-year-old clinic had for a decade attracted vehement anti-abortion protests, and it was normal to see three hundred demonstrators on Saturdays.

"A twenty-five-pound canister bomb completely destroyed the clinic and four adjacent offices," says Frances. "It blew a metal door out of the entrance into a residential area one hundred yards away. We were leasing the building and the landlord rebuilt, but we had to find another space while he did this. We moved to Kensington, Maryland, put bombproof glass in our windows, and once again became a target for the antis."[66] In fact, the protests were so disruptive that their new landlord paid the health center to vacate the premises. They got enough, says Frances, to move to another Kensington location, where they have remained ever since.

A decade and a half after the bombing, security remains a nagging concern for staff and patients. Bomb- and bullet-resistant glass; self-locking doors that separate clinic areas; bulletproof vests for doctors; panic buttons; a bulletproof reception cubicle, all are part of the ambiance of the clinic. "Once you have your place of business blown up, you start looking over your shoulder," Frances admits. "All of us have assumed the position of not being in the office alone, not going to our cars alone. At the same time, we live with this threat of violence the same way all women live with the fear of rape. Can a woman be raped? Yes, but she doesn't have to think about it every day. Of course I've changed some things that I do. I'm cautious. But I also don't let the fear get inside me. I know that there is nothing you can do if someone wants to kill you. I know I'm going to die someday, but that doesn't mean I'm not going to live. I consider the work I do holy. It makes me smile. Do the anti-abortionists smile from the joy they get from what they do? I don't know. All I know is that what I do makes me happy."[67]

Follow-up note: Michael Bray was sentenced to six years and served forty-six months in federal prison for his role in ten Washington, D.C., area firebombings, including those in Wheaton and Norfolk, committed between February 1984 and January 1985. Spinks and Shields each received fifteen years and were ordered to pay $55,000 in restitution for the same ten incidents.

DECEMBER: TULSA, OKLAHOMA

When word got out that Reproductive Services of Tulsa, Oklahoma, a nonprofit clinic managed by Nova Health Systems, was moving to a small office building in December 1984, anti-abortion protestors marshaled their troops. On the day of the move they followed the loaded van and taunted the men who worked for the company, bellowing that they were "accomplices to murder."

From that day on, protestors led by Clayton Lewis, a fundamentalist who headed the Biblical Action League (BAL), gave the clinic little peace. According to executive administrator Sherri Finik, "the protestors could not be sure who was coming to us or to the other businesses in the building. Their goal was to make us an unwelcome neighbor by harassing everyone who came in or out. They'd holler, telling anyone walking by that the blood of murdered babies was in the building. They told women coming in that they would be punished for having abortions and said that people who tolerated our presence would also be punished."[68]

Barely a month after moving to the site, the clinic received its first phoned-in bomb scare; as a result the entire building had to be evacuated. Within the next twelve months, four or five more calls interrupted business for everyone located there. "Two months after we moved in, two months after we spent $20,000 to turn an office space into a medical facility, the landlord told me that we had to leave," says Finik. "We had a five-year lease, but he had started to get vacate notices and complaints from the other tenants claiming that they were being denied the peaceful enjoyment of the building because of us. The landlord told me that he could not pay his mortgage without the income from his tenants, that if we stayed he'd lose the building and we'd have to move out anyway when the bank foreclosed. His livelihood really was being threatened."[69]

Finik realized the futility of attempting to rent or lease another space, so she set out to find a building that the clinic could afford to purchase. She eventually succeeded in acquiring a piece of property, but it needed extensive renovations to become suitable for use as a medical office. The clinic moved into this freestanding space in March 1987.

By the time they left, Reproductive Services was the sole occupant of the rental property; their former landlord lost the building a short time later. "You'd think a business that has nothing to do with abortion would be indignant at the protestors," Finik says of the ordeal. "But that is not the case. The other tenants were so intimidated that they just wanted to leave. Instead of standing up to the antis and taking defensive action, their response was to run away."[70]

DECEMBER 4: WASHINGTON, D.C.

FBI director William Webster said that attacks on reproductive health centers did not meet the FBI definition of terrorism. As such, Webster admitted that the agency did not put as many resources into investigating clinic bombings or arsons as it did in cases deemed "true" domestic terrorism.[71]

DECEMBER 12: MINNEAPOLIS, MINNESOTA

After William Webster's assertion about domestic terrorism, the *Minneapolis Star and Tribune* ran an editorial titled "Getting Priorities Straight on Clinic Bombings." The piece informed readers that:

> The nation's leading law enforcement agency seems to be policing the cabbage patch with a blind eye to clinic bombings. . . . [FBI director William] Webster says bombings and arsons at abortion and family planning clinics across the country are not terrorism. . . . He says the FBI gives investigations of these attacks low priority. . . . Webster's words conveyed the wrong message. Another Webster—Noah—defines terrorism as acts of violence or force to intimidate

or coerce. (The) bombings at abortion and family planning clinics this year fit the definition. The apparent motive—to frighten people away—qualifies as intimidation. Because their number is increasing, the chance of injury to patients, clinic workers and passers-by is increasing, too. Every reasonable effort by law-enforcement agencies must be devoted to curbing this violence. If the FBI isn't investigating whether an organized group or conspiracy is involved, it should be. . . . The president has decried terrorism overseas, but he has been silent about the bombings and arson at home. Reagan should speak out against this ugly domestic terrorism. And he should be sure that all federal law enforcement agencies get the message.[72]

DECEMBER 20: PENSACOLA, FLORIDA

A twenty-five-year-old woman entered The Ladies Center dressed as Santa Claus. Once inside she began to read a list of names, then paused and announced that the designated parties would not be receiving gifts this year because they had been "murdered by abortion." The woman, a resident of Our Father's House—a Christian residence for pregnant and troubled women run by anti-abortion activist John Burt—received a sixty-day sentence for trespassing.[73]

An identical stunt by Darold Larson in Fargo, North Dakota, landed the disrupter a two-day jail sentence.

DECEMBER 25: PENSACOLA, FLORIDA

Linda Taggart, administrator of the Community Healthcare Center of Pensacola, Inc. (formerly The Ladies Center), first noticed the feelings of free-floating anxiety on the evening of December 24. Still, it was Christmas Eve, and as always, she took her place with the Trinity Presbyterian Church choir.

"I got to bed around midnight," Taggart recalls. "At 4:00 A.M. the phone rang. No one had to tell me. I knew. I had to wake my daughter up since I didn't want to leave her home alone and we drove five miles an hour through pea-soup thick fog to get to the clinic. The fire truck was there and I wondered why since I'd been told by the police that there had been a break-in. A policeman finally came over to me and said he thought there had been an explosion. We still could not see a thing; I have rarely been in fog that thick even though Pensacola is on the Gulf of Mexico and is frequently fogged-in."[74]

The damage was confined to several rooms at one end of the site; as a result, that section of the building was cordoned off until repairs could be made. The clinic was closed for several days, but was quickly made minimally functional.

Two other Pensacola abortion providers were not as lucky. The bombers, later identified as Matthew Goldsby, James and Kathren Simmons and Kaye Wiggins, had hurled incendiary devices at three facilities in a two-mile radius over a twenty-minute period.[75] Only three walls remained at Dr. William Permenter's office, and windows and cornices were blown out of his building. Dr. Bo Bagenholm's office was also badly damaged.[76] All told, the bombs caused $706,000 in damages at the three locations.[77]

Dr. Permenter never rebuilt and left the field of medicine.[78] Likewise, Dr. Bagenholm ceased providing abortions in July 1985.[79]

Matthew Goldsby, his girlfriend Kaye Wiggins and James and Kathren Simmons belonged to the Assemblies of God, a fundamentalist denomination that researchers say is characterized by the belief that God speaks directly to the believer.[80] "Both [Matt Goldsby and James Simmons] felt God was calling them to end abortion. Since two of them felt this compulsion, they concluded that it must have been a specific direction from God," wrote sociologists Dallas Blanchard and Terry Prewitt in their 1993 book, *Religious Violence and Abortion*.[81] In addition, the men called their activities The Gideon Project because Gideon "had laid low the altars of Baal, on which first born children were sacrificed."[82]

Goldsby, a construction worker, and Simmons, a glass cutter—both in their early twenties—were charged with conspiracy to create firearms or explosive devices to damage or destroy a business engaged in interstate commerce; building three firearm or explosive devices; and using those devices to maliciously destroy three separate buildings. Wiggins and Kathren Simmons were charged with aiding and abetting.[83]

The bombers' defense attorneys opened the case by arguing that the men were suffering from severe psychiatric disorders that fueled their anti-abortion furor. Defense witness Dr. Nancy Mullen told the court that "Goldsby experienced grandiose delusions that led him to identify with God. Jesus to Matt is an imaginary friend." She further testified that James Simmons suffered from borderline personality disorder, an emotional condition characterized by emotional instability and impulsive and unpredictable behavior. In addition, she revealed that in her interview with him, Simmons confessed that he obsessed about abortion between five and eight hours a day. Worse, after viewing the film *Assignment Life*, he told her he felt as if "a piece of me was taken out. A piece of me instead of the kid. Like being stuck with a knife."[84]

Dr. Daniel Dansak countered Mullen, contending that both men were sane, able to hold down jobs and engage in normal social interactions. Dansak held sway, and on April 23 the pair were found competent to stand trial.[85]

Goldsby, Wiggins and the two Simmonses were subsequently found guilty of the bombing charges. United States District Judge Roger Vinson dismissed their indictment for the June 25, 1984, bombing—which the defendants took responsibility for—at the request of federal attorneys. Matthew Goldsby and James Simmons received ten-year sentences at the Florida Correctional Institution in Tallahassee. Nineteen year-old Kaye Wiggins and eighteen-year-old Kathren Simmons were given five years' probation.[86]

Both men served four years and were released in late 1989.

CHAPTER FIVE

Writing the Book on Coercion: 1985–1990

Ronald Reagan's first term ended with a thud for most anti-abortionists. After witnessing dozens of legislative attempts to reverse *Roe* fall by the wayside, they were no longer cocky about the possibility of winning. While some frustrated and possibly demented souls were beginning to toss bombs and set fires, activities that were readily condemned by many, including moderate anti-choice groups like the National Right to Life Committee—even mainstream organizations began relying on rhetoric about murder, murderers and an American holocaust to win support.

In addition, anti-abortionists got renewed vigor from two 1985 publications, Joseph Scheidler's *Closed: 99 Ways to Stop Abortion* and Kevin Sherlock's *The Abortion Buster's Manual.* Both codified an array of tactics, teaching would-be activists everything from how to write a press release to how to research medical personnel. Illegal and near-illegal tactics were featured—even taught—though disclaimers indicated that these activities were not recommended.

The books' concrete, hands-on approach reflected years of experience and aimed to turn neophyte protestors into seasoned professionals. In tandem with the 1981 publication of Francis Schaeffer's *A Christian Manifesto,* a philosophical treatise on the morality of civil disobedience and a call for Christian involvement in everyday politics, those inclined to zealotry now had the practical tools to wreak havoc at clinics across the country.

Randall Terry, a 1981 graduate of the unaccredited Elim Bible College in upstate New York, had been profoundly influenced by Schaeffer, Scheidler and Sherlock and was one of many to heed the call. Although he had initially planned to become a missionary after completing Elim, he says that he believes God called him to work on the abortion issue instead. Alongside his then-wife, Cindy Dean Terry, another Elim graduate, he started slowly. His first act as organizer of the newly created Operation Rescue (OR) was to rouse pastors to become involved in the cause. By reaching them, Terry recognized that he could sway thousands of church-going Americans who had never before acted on their opposition to abortion. With a little pastoral prodding Terry knew that OR could get them actively engaged, not just in letter writing and lobbying, but in direct confrontation at clinic doors. His first "rescue," in Binghamton, New York, in January 1986, was a tentative testing of the waters; it involved just seven people and sent Terry to jail for several days.[1]

"I realized we were losing the war," he told *The Forerunner,* a conservative Christian online magazine and World Wide Web site created by Florida activist Jay Rogers. Inspired by Proverbs 24:11, "Rescue those who are unjustly sentenced to death,"[2] the charismatic, young fire-and-brimstone preacher captured the imagination of people who were tired of more than a decade of anti-abortion promises from do-little politicians, some of them conservative Republicans. "Unless the church repents and rises up to do rescues, which is the fruit of repentance, we will never win," he preached.[3]

Ready to up the ante, anti-abortion activists were moved by Terry's passionate oratory and ready to follow him to clinic entrances and driveways. "If my little girl was about to be murdered, I certainly would not write a letter to the editor," Terry charged. "I would dive in with both hands and feet and do whatever was necessary to save her life."[4] Indeed, the antis were so inspired by the preacher's heartfelt pleas that "rescues" became their tactic of choice, at least until law enforcement began cracking down on them for trespassing and other offenses.

Between 1986 and the early 1990s, tens of thousands blockaded women's health centers, risking arrest and fines to demonstrate their hatred of *Roe* and all that it symbolized. Although Terry did not invent the tactic, he certainly popularized it, and at various points during the latter half of the 1980s the "rescues" he staged were featured on prime-time television. The 1988 Democratic National Convention in Atlanta, for example, gave America a firsthand look at Terry and his entourage, and people across the globe saw the determined defiance that Operation Rescue projected as members crawled long distances on their hands and knees to obstruct clinic doors.

Like a spiritual cheerleader who knew exactly how to inflame his followers, Terry reassured participants across the country that they were doing God's work. He also made inroads in tormenting women who needed—and knew that, as unhappily pregnant females, they would do anything to get—abortions.

"Why should we involve ourselves in any physical pro-life activity at all?" he asked OR enthusiasts. "Why not just pray? Can you imagine if a preacher declared, we aren't going to send missionaries anymore, or finance their work; we aren't going to print gospel literature or preach the gospel. Would we accept such nonsense? . . . God does not wave a magic wand. We are His body—His hands and feet. He uses people who work as if it all depends on them, while praying as if it all depends on God."[5]

Terry's star certainly appeared to be rising. A household name, his popularity served as a counterbalance to the loss of fundamentalist face in other quarters. Revelations about married TV preacher Jim Bakker's steamy 1987 affair with church secretary Jessica Hahn and the Reverend Jimmy Swaggert's 1988 confession of "adulterous sins" had thrown many born-again Christians into an embarrassed tizzy. A year later the Reverend Jerry Falwell's abrupt announcement that the Moral Majority was closing its doors on August 31, 1989, because "our mission is accomplished . . . the religious right is solidly in place,"[6] left many feeling bereft. Were it not for Terry's juxtaposition as the squeaky-clean savior of the unborn—a reputation sullied in 2000 by infidelity, and then divorce—who knows what might have happened within fundamentalist circles?

1985

NATIONWIDE

Kevin Sherlock's *Abortion Busters' Manual,* published by Operation Rescue of California, was released. The book provides step-by-step instructions on doctor harassment. Its main premise revolves around what most antis consider the weakest link in the field, the physicians themselves. Chapter 1 lays out the ideology: "If it becomes too much of a hassle to run an abortion mill, then fewer people will do it and the number of abortions will drop. We might not be able to cut off the enemy's head yet, but we can certainly start making him [*sic*] bleed from a number of wounds. . . . Remember: You are at war against people who make big money cutting live babies into squirming pieces."[7]

Insidious tactics are described: "Call the abortion mill and identify yourself to the receptionist as a science magazine or medical supply salesperson. Tell her you don't want to bother the doctors but would like to send each of them a complimentary magazine or sample of one of your products. Ask her for each doctor's name so you can send the product to each one."[8]

"If she refuses to give you the names, ask her how many doctors work at her facility so you can send the promised items to doctors, then thank her and hang up when she gives you the number of abortionists. In a few days, you can call back, ask the receptionist if the doctors got your packages, and when she says no, get the names 'to protect against lost or misdirected mail.'"[9]

The book also teaches readers how to call insurance companies and probe for data, how to visit clinics pretending to be a patient, and how to get information about the training and professional conduct of a particular physician.

Sherlock's skewed notions about race, class and gender are boldly expressed in a section of the book devoted to surveying the clinics. "One word of caution," he writes. "Look the part. Guys, have a woman with you. Whites, don't go to any inner-city private hospital or a county or state hospital looking well-off or well-groomed. Minorities and whites: Don't go into a hi-rent district looking too scruffy."[10]

KNOXVILLE, TENNESSEE

Clinic administrator Deborah Walsh was in court with the abortion foe who had thrown her into traffic the year before, when she met a prominent local business owner who was litigating a work-related conflict. After hearing her testimony about the protestor's behavior, the business man suggested that she hire a motorcycle gang member to do security for her. "He also suggested that I pay the winos who lived in the park across from the clinic to get the antis to go away," she says.[11]

Walsh did not adopt either tactic; instead she opted to put lawn sprinklers in front of the building and chose Saturdays—the day when the number of protestors was the largest and when other businesses in the building were closed—to water the grass and shrubbery. "The second or third Saturday we did this the security guard came inside the clinic and told me that someone had torn the sprinklers out of the ground. I went outside and saw a man with red hair, plaid polyester pants and eyes that were shifting in rage. The guard pointed him out as the one who had torn out the sprinklers. I approached him and told him that the sprinklers were on my property and were perfectly legal, and if the protestors didn't want to get wet they should move to another spot. When I said this he kept his hands at his side but came at me and hit me with his chest, saying, 'Hit me. I'll have you charged with assault.' I didn't touch him but backed way back and told the guard to call 911. While we were waiting for the police I saw the man turn around. He had a .38 revolver in the back waistband of his pants. When the police got to the clinic and got out of their cars, they said, 'Oh, that guy's a police officer. We can't arrest him.' They had to call the police captain or police chief who told them that the officer was allowed to carry a weapon. The cop was, however, given an interoffice reprimand and told that he could not be at any more protests. I never saw him at the clinic again."[12]

Although the officer stayed away from Volunteer Medical Clinic, he began to stalk Walsh and her family. "Shortly after the incident at the clinic, I was with my youngest daughter when I realized I was being followed by him. He sometimes used his police car and sometimes not. It was such a scary feeling to be followed by the police; it was terrifying and totally isolating. I reported it to the precinct but they told me I needed better documentation, actual pictures of him. I moved and the situation resolved itself."[13]

MARCH 14: PENSACOLA, FLORIDA

Penny Lea, head of a Minnesota-based group called I Believe in Life, wrote to 5,000 individuals and churches in the Pensacola area, urging them to attend a rally on March 14. "You are to proceed as directed in Joshua: 6," she told them. "There will be seven trumpets, seven Christian flags, and seven American flags. Following will be Christian leaders without compromise. The rest of the Army will follow. I believe 7,000 would be God's desire." On the appointed day, 2,000 people marched from Pensacola Junior College to The Ladies Center, making this one of the largest demos in anti-abortion history.[14]

SPRING: DALLAS, TEXAS

As soon as the Routh Street Women's Clinic moved to new offices on the extremely busy Central Expressway, the number of anti-abortion protestors stationed in front of the health center skyrocketed. Demonstrator Oldrich Tomanek carried a sign saying, "Routh Street Clinic will eat your baby." Each morning incoming staff were greeted by Tomanek's taunt that "the blood on your hands is the blood you will shed" as well as the jibes of other protestors.[15]

"The building had six offices with an atrium in the middle," says former executive director Charlotte Taft. "Shortly after we moved in, a vacant space on the second floor was rented to The White Rose, a crisis pregnancy center. The center tried to look like an abortion clinic and advertised as providing abortion informa-tion. At that time the Yellow Pages had no separation between abortion providers and anti-abortion groups. We finally got the phone company to put them under abortion alternatives, but at first The White Rose ad was right next to ours. Their staff would see people in the parking lot or hall and drag them into their offices. They used bullhorns to yell right outside our procedure rooms and broadcast a tape of babies crying that could be heard inside. Some of them would scream crude chants like 'the baby's blood will run down your crotch.' After a while, we started to get the word out. Every patient who called was told about the group, but it took us a while to begin doing this. To try to work with the noise they generated is indescribable. It's impossible to explain how awful it was."[16]

Although the Dallas City Council, at the behest of the city's clinics, eventually passed an ordinance banning the use of amplification devices within five hundred feet of a clinic, hospital or nursing home—a boon to Routh Street and other providers—The White Rose did not close its doors upon passage of the bill. Instead, it put poster-size photographs of dismembered fetuses in its office windows.

"One of the first things we did," says Taft, "was get volunteers to stand in front of the pictures. We soon realized that this took too much volunteer time. We also felt that we were spending too much unproductive time with The White Rose people. We asked the landlord to make them take the posters down. He would not, but he let us spray-paint the outside of their windows. At first it was very cathartic. We'd paint, they'd scrape it off, we'd do it again. After a while we decided that we were still spending too much time on something that was in no way about the woman-centered work we wanted to do. After a number of discussions, we decided to use the pictures. We asked the women coming in if they'd seen the photos. They'd say 'yes.' We'd then transform the experience into a learning and teaching tool for women. It was an opportunity for us to educate them about fetal development and what would happen during the abortion. As we got out of the battle, The White Rose took the pictures down. The battle ended and we became more fully engaged with our patients."[17]

In addition, a series of staff meetings allowed workers to discuss their own squeamishness and discomfort about both the photos and the fetal remains they viewed after each abortion. As their ease with the procedure increased, they developed new policies for patients and became more adept at grief counseling and dealing with ambivalence. For Taft, the focal shift taught her that, "We have to tell the truth, feel our feelings, and provide support for women so that they can talk about things that are difficult to talk about. The way the political terms of abortion have been framed make it appear as if there are two sides, pro-choice and anti-choice. Many life experiences are paradoxical. It is not about choosing one or the other. You can be both relieved and grieve. You can have a death and also celebrate life."[18]

Follow-up note: Oldrich Tomanek was convicted of harassing Dallas physician Norman Tompkins and his wife, Carolyn Tompkins, in 1992.

The National Coalition of Abortion Providers (NCAP) organized a congressional hearing into the fraudulent and sometimes harmful practices of "crisis pregnancy centers" in the early 1990s. The hearing described the confusion fostered by Yellow Page listings that included both "crisis pregnancy" and bona fide abortion clinics and resulted in the separation of abortion alternatives and abortion providers in local phone books. Unfortunately, to this day, clinic staff continue to hear stories about women lured into "crisis centers" only to be pummeled with guilt-inducing anti-abortion information. Save for referrals to state welfare agencies and the provision of secondhand maternity and baby clothes, health workers charge these centers with doing little to help women in need.

APRIL 11–13: APPLETON, WISCONSIN

On April 13, 1985, at "Action for Life II," the second annual Pro-Life Action League (PLAL) convention, Joseph Scheidler announced the publication of his book, *Closed: 99 Ways to Stop Abortion,* by Crossway Press. Antis throughout the United States and Canada were inordinately pleased by this step-by-step primer. The book offers readers an extensive variety of "how-tos," including how to organize raucous, disruptive picket lines and vigils outside clinics; how to "sidewalk counsel" patients into having their babies or putting them up for adoption; how to track motor vehicle information to determine who visits clinics; and how to tie up a clinic's telephone lines. Mother Teresa and Father Bruce Ritter, a Catholic priest later disgraced by his proclivity for pedophilia, wrote the introductory sections of *Closed,* and the book garnered significant attention from both Christian and mainstream media.

Among its more revealing advice:

- On leafleting: "People any age can do it. The handicapped are good helpers. People are less likely to refuse something offered by a person in a wheelchair or on crutches."[19]
- On protesting outside of clinics: "When pro-life people are outside a clinic, complications and confusion inside the clinic increase by as much as 400 percent. . . . From this report we can conclude that if they really cared about the health of the woman, they would refuse to perform abortions on the days that pro-life pickets are present. Obviously, they are so greedy that they will proceed with abortions no matter what the conditions."[20]

- On allowing diversity of opinion: "There are no arguments for abortion except those based on man's [*sic*] fallen nature, his propensity to sin, his baser animal instincts, and his desire for selfish gain."[21]
- On language: "Use inflammatory rhetoric. Use abortuary or death camp to describe the abortion clinic. Use abortifacients for pills and IUDs. Use fornication for sex outside of marriage, adultery for having an affair."[22]
- On violence: "While we do not condone any form of violence, we should not condemn without compassion and understanding those whose strong convictions may lead them to illegal activities. We should comfort them and try to help their families. We should assure them that they have a friend, and while we may not condone their actions, we admire the zeal that these actions manifest."[23]
- "Violence has often been instigated by the abortion industry itself, because the very violence of abortion, the cruel dismembering piece by piece of unborn children, sparks a violent antagonism which, though not excusable, is understandable."[24]

During the course of the PLAL conference, the organization renamed itself the Pro-Life Action Network (PLAN); in addition to celebrating the publication of Scheidler's book, conferees spent the weekend planning a coordinated national campaign against providers. They told reporters that they intended to make 1985–86 "a year of pain and fear" for clinic workers and pro-choice Americans, a threat carried out by their intimidating activities.

MAY: NORFOLK, VIRGINIA

Eight men and one woman invaded the Hillcrest Clinic early on a Saturday morning. Suzette Caton, director of public relations, was inside getting organized for the day when she heard a woman pounding on the door. "She said she wanted a pregnancy test, and I opened the door to tell her that we weren't open yet. The men were hiding around the corner. When they saw me at the door, they knocked me down and got in. They then chained themselves to the equipment in our operating room. I filed assault and trespass charges against them and was successful. They were charged and served three weekends in jail."[25]

Hillcrest got an injunction in 1989 that prohibits trespassing on private property. Protestors have violated the injunction only a handful of times because, says Caton, the police have enforced it. A September 1990 clinic invasion, for example, resulted in thirty-four arrests.[26]

JUNE 15: WILMINGTON, DELAWARE

Another invasion, this time at the Delaware Women's Health Organization (DWHO), led to the arrest of twenty-one people, including Joan Andrews Bell, a woman known among antis as "Saint Joan" for her relentless and daring anti-choice activities. "This was the first really threatening action we'd experienced," says Cathy Conner, the clinic's administrator from 1978 to 1987. "It was a Saturday morning. Most of the staff was there as were a handful of patients. I was in the waiting room when a group started to file in through the [then-unlocked] front doors. They went from the hallway into the waiting area, to the operating and recovery rooms. After what they were doing registered I tried to intercept them, but they pushed through and contaminated instruments and disassembled equipment. The police were wonderful but they had never dealt with anything like this before and weren't sure how to handle it. It took them four and a half hours to clear the clinic."[27]

Nineteen of the twenty-one were convicted (and two were acquitted) of conspiracy and criminal trespass. They were ordered to pay court costs and stay at least two blocks away from the clinic for two years. The pair who were acquitted told the court that they represented a Christian news station and were there as reporters, not participants.

According to Patricia Baird-Windle, the tactic of posing as press was repeated in many locations throughout the country; in this way, the antis were able to get videotaped footage of both blockades and demonstrations at close range.

JULY: DALLAS, TEXAS

Right after the Routh Street Women's Clinic moved to Central Expressway, someone erected a billboard and painted "Abortion is Murder: Take it Personally" next to a drawing of a fetus. Staff were horrified.

"The night after it appeared someone put antennae on the fetus so it looked like an alien, then blackened out some words so it said 'Abortion is Personal,'" says former clinic director Charlotte Taft.[28]

The next day Joseph Scheidler appeared at a rally in the clinic's parking lot. According to Taft, he told his followers that he was going to enter every clinic in Dallas. "The crowd, about three hundred people, was screaming, 'Charlotte Taft: Repent.' I thought to myself, 'Something has got to change here.' I went out to the clinic balcony and something in me shifted. I told myself, 'Everybody here loves you.' I stood there as if I were Evita and started to wave and blow kisses. It was an extraordinary experience. It took three to five minutes for them to stop chanting. The pro-choice people, who were also gathered outside, started to chant, 'We love

Charlotte.' It felt like a miracle. To this day I have no idea why I did this. It didn't change anybody's mind but the conflict dissipated. It was like we took our place back. It was a movement in me, not to be a hostage in my own clinic."[29]

LATE SUMMER/EARLY FALL: WILMINGTON, DELAWARE

The June 1985 arrests at the Delaware Women's Health Organization ruffled the feathers of many anti-abortion protestors. In retaliation, says former clinic administrator Cathy Conner, "They started to picket my home. They used bullhorns and carried signs saying 'Cathy Conner: Baby Killer.' My kids were eight and ten at this time. They'd be outside playing and suddenly scream, 'Mom, they're here.' That upset me because I didn't like the antis knowing who my kids were. My husband died five years ago, but back then he worried that they'd find out where he worked and jeopardize his livelihood."[30]

One particular weekend when the Conners were out of town, a busload of antis staged an exceptionally boisterous demonstration. "That day they put a cross with a baby doll hanging from it on my front lawn. By the time we got home neighbors had removed it," and Conner was informed of the antis' activities. For days, however, the clinic director found leaflets denouncing her scattered throughout the neighborhood.[31]

SEPTEMBER 28: PORTLAND, OREGON

An affidavit prepared for an employee of All Women's Health Services reported that, "As I left work on Saturday, I was surrounded by a group of protestors who shouted loudly at me: 'Murderer.' A boy of about six stepped forward and said, 'I hope you die tonight.' [A protestor] . . . then attempted to follow me to my car, at which point I was joined by a pro-choice escort and accompanied. I felt personally threatened by both the picketers' actions and statements, especially that he hoped I'd die. I was concerned for my personal safety in terms of my ability to reach my car and drive home safely."[32]

OCTOBER 18: BOULDER, COLORADO

A stone from a flower box on the front lawn of the Boulder Abortion Clinic was thrown through the window of the facility's waiting room. Although no one was injured by flying glass, a quick-thinking neighbor noted the perpetrator's license tag and he was later arrested. The damage was estimated at between $250 and $350.[33]

The rock throwing occurred the same day that a newspaper article announced that Joseph Scheidler and his followers were coming to Boulder on October 22. According to the article, Scheidler's group aimed to close the Boulder Abortion Clinic. The clinic's owner, Dr. Warren Hern, a provider since 1973, had long inspired Scheidler to barely controlled rage. The author of a well-received textbook on abortion technique, Hern was a nationally prominent pro-choice spokesman who was frequently quoted in the press. Scheidler assailed Hern's *Abortion Practice* as "Nazi medicine" and likened the health center to a death camp.

Although Scheidler was given a platform at the University of Colorado, where he addressed a student organization, by and large Boulder was not taken with the blustering anti-abortionist. On the day of the demonstration, Hern's clinic was protected by both Boulder police and a private, armed security guard hired by the facility.

The following week the clinic was besieged with harassing phone calls. A 1995 report written by Hern and sent to the director of the Department of Justice's Criminal Division details hundreds of calls from bogus patients scheduling appointments they had no intention of keeping and assailing the staff as "baby-killing monsters." The clinic also noted a slew of hang-ups. Hern further reports dozens of calls to his home, many of them death threats.[34]

DECEMBER 28: BOULDER, COLORADO

Boulder Abortion Clinic owner Dr. Warren Hern told reporters that he blamed anti-abortion activists for a rash of unwanted deliveries to the health center. More than fifty service calls were made to the site over a five-day period, including four separate pizza deliveries and a singing telegram. A towing service, plumber, locksmith, carpet cleaner and exterminating service were also called into the ruse.

No one took responsibility for placing the orders.[35]

This tactic was employed in other cities, including Melbourne, Florida. Staff there cite dozens of bogus deliveries in 1993 and 1994. During that same two-year period, taxis and tow trucks periodically appeared at the behest of phantom callers.

1986

JANUARY: NATIONWIDE

The Campaign Report, a newsletter published by the pro-choice Eighty Percent Majority Campaign (now called the National Center for the Pro Choice Majority), documented a disturbing increase in extreme anti-abortion violence for the previous year. According to the report, sixteen firebombings in eight states occurred between February 1985 and October 1985.[36]

JANUARY 22: PROVIDENCE, RHODE ISLAND

The thirteenth anniversary of *Roe v. Wade* was marked by the usual pro- and anti-abortion rallies and events. But in addition, the Reverend John Randall, a Catholic priest from Rhode Island, boosted the morale of the anti-choice community by telling those tuned in to his cable television program that Mary Ann Sorrentino, the director of a Planned Parenthood affiliate in Providence for the past nine years, had been excommunicated from the church the previous June. This was the first public disclosure of the church's action and was meant to encourage activists frustrated by their failure to pass a Human Life Amendment, Human Life Bill or otherwise reverse *Roe.*

The *New York Daily News* reported that Sorrentino was excommunicated after priests in her local parish demanded to question her fifteen-year-old daughter about abortion before allowing her to receive confirmation, a sacrament.[37] According to Sorrentino's account, two days before the scheduled confirmation, pastors at St. Augustine's parish told her daughter, Luisa Ciullo, that she would have to declare that she did not "believe in abortion" because of the nature of her mother's work.[38] Other press reports state that Luisa told the clerics that while she would not choose an abortion for herself, she could and would not speak for others. Shortly after making this statement, the girl was told that she could be confirmed with her peers, but that her mother would not be allowed to receive communion at the event because she had been officially excommunicated. The diocese's subsequent letter to Sorrentino stated that she was being excommunicated "by reason of the universal law of the church. . . . The remedy for this sad situation is for you to renounce your association with abortion clinics and the procurement of abortions."[39]

Sorrentino subsequently chose to leave Planned Parenthood and now hosts a popular Providence talk-radio program.

WINTER: PORTLAND, OREGON

Mail carriers intercepted four letter bombs addressed to three of the city's abortion providers. "The bombs were designed to maim or kill whoever opened them," says Laura Blue, a staffer at All Women's Health Services. "The day ours came was a snow day and almost every other clinic was closed. Right away, when we got the letter, there were flags. The package looked funky. We called the police after it arrived and they deactivated the letter and stopped the packages that were en route to Lovejoy SurgiCenter and Planned Parenthood. The letters turned out to be from a guy whose girlfriend had ended a pregnancy. BATF and the FBI caught him after he did another bombing that was unrelated to abortion. He blew his hand off in that attack. When law enforcement got to his house, they traced the attempted clinic violence to him."[40]

MARCH 26: PENSACOLA, FLORIDA

Six anti-abortion protestors stormed The Ladies Center, knocking clinic administrator Linda Taggart and staffer Georgia Wilde to the ground. Medical equipment was destroyed and Taggart suffered permanent neck, shoulder and ear damage as a result of the assault. The abortion foes were in Pensacola for a national conference.[41]

Follow-up note: During the period in which protestor Joan Andrews Bell was out on bail for this invasion, she did an encore performance at a Missouri clinic. At her sentencing, she refused probation and was given five years in prison for criminal mischief.

Protestor Joseph Scheidler disappeared the day after the Pensacola incident but was arrested when he checked into his Denver hotel room for the 1986 National Right to Life Committee conference. He was charged with conspiracy to commit a criminal act involving burglary and the destruction of medical equipment.[42]

JUNE: CHICAGO, ILLINOIS

It was in the early 1980s that Susan Hill, president of the eight-clinic National Women's Health Organization (NWHO), began to notice that the tactics used by anti-abortionists to obstruct clinic workers and patients were similar, if not identical, in different venues across the country. "If there had not been a national player we would never have known this," she says. "It would have looked like individual acts of terrorism in individual cities and towns. Most of NWHO's clinics were in places that were easy to target—Fargo, North Dakota; Wilmington, Delaware; Columbus, Georgia; Ft. Wayne, Indiana; Milwaukee, Wisconsin; Jackson, Mississippi—and our mission crossed with the antis. Our goal was to make abortion available; theirs was to deny women access. They wanted to find the easiest marks and knew that if they shut us down, women would have to travel long distances to have their abortions."[43]

According to Hill, the six-foot-five inch Joseph Scheidler often showed up at NWHO clinics with his trademark bullhorn, dressed either entirely in black or entirely in white, with a matching hat. "He'd appear in Wilmington or Ft. Wayne with a group of people and it became clear that the players were always the same. After the Appleton, Wisconsin, PLAL conference in 1985, the antis came to Milwaukee. They were energized by the meeting and came to the Summit Women's Health Organization and announced that they were there to inflict pain and fear on us. Reverend Eleanor Yeo had been the clinic administrator since we opened in 1974. The antis saw her as Satan incarnate, and she and her family experienced constant harassment. The clinic also lost two leases due to the pressure they put on our landlord and other tenants in the buildings."[44]

In June 1986 the NWHO began a thirteen-year legal battle against Scheidler. Filed in a Chicago federal court, *NOW v. Scheidler* charged the Pro-Life Action League, Operation Rescue, Scheidler, OR founder Randall Terry and PLAL staffers Timothy Murphy and Andrew Scholberg with conspiring to shut the abortion field through coordinated acts in violation of the Federal Racketeer Influenced Corrupt Organizations Act and Sherman Anti-Trust Act. (On December 7, 1993, lawyers for the NWHO went before the Supreme Court and successfully argued that the RICO Act could be used against "religiously-inspired" people who do not have an overt financial interest in the extortion they carry out.) The defendants countered that the lawsuit was an attempt to stifle free speech and deny protestors their First Amendment rights. Their position was undercut in January 1998 when Randall Terry, by then a congressional candidate, signed a settlement with NOW. Terry agreed not to participate in illegal actions at abortion facilities and said that he would pay a $15,000 fine if he violated the stipulation. In addition, he acknowledged that clinics have the right to conduct business without illegal interference.[45]

During the more than twelve years it took for the case to go to trial, the charges against the antis were continually amended; by the time the case went before a jury in the spring of 1998, *NOW v. Scheidler* was a class action lawsuit in which the NWHO represented more than 900 women's health centers nationwide. Both patients and providers, including Chico Feminist Women's Health Center founder Dido Hasper, Patricia Baird-Windle, Lynne Randall, Linda Taggart and NWHO staffers Cathy Conner, Susan Hill, Diane Strauss and Jennifer Vriens, testified. Hill described sixteen arsons at her eight clinics and had jurors riveted to their seats by depictions of bomb threats, death threats, invasions, assaults, vandalism and "rescues." She further tapped into people's sense of outrage when she described the absurdity of having to rent an apartment near the Ft. Wayne WHO so that patients would have a safe, warm space to wait during evacuations prompted by bomb threats.

According to Sara Love, one of five pro-choice attorneys who argued the case, patient testimony about the blockades was key in swaying the jury against the defendants. "Four patients testified anonymously," says Love. "One woman had the entire courtroom in tears when she testified about her experience in Los Angeles in February 1989. This woman had had surgery to try and save her reproductive organs the week before she went to the clinic. She was going in to the facility to see her doctor for a postoperative exam. Her minister drove her. She got out of the car—she could still barely move—and as she started to walk up the entryway she was scratched and clawed by people calling her a baby killer. In the process of pushing and shoving her, her sutures ruptured. Clinic volunteers finally got to her and helped her get into the backseat of the minister's car. She was bleeding really badly and had to be rushed to the emergency room. This woman was personally opposed to abortion. Nonetheless, she had to spend time in the hospital to recover from the attack on her. Jurors were enraged at the obvious physical and mental trauma she had endured."[46]

Other testimony, says Love, from a patient who learned that she was carrying a congenitally deformed fetus that would die shortly after birth and who was kept out of a clinic by rabid blockaders, as well as that of clinic workers who described being smashed against clinic doors and repeatedly hit, poked and stepped on during "rescues," further moved jurors and spectators away from "pro-life" support.

"We also repeatedly caught the antis in lies," says Love. "They'd say they had not been in a particular place and we would have pictures or videotapes of them in these places. Keith Tucci lied about having once sold used cars. He denied he'd done this. He was caught, and I think this made the jurors wonder what else he might be lying about."[47]

In addition, hundreds of statements, letters and articles the antis had written cemented the case against them. A Pro-Life Action League brochure which said, "You can try for 50 years to do it the nice, polite way or you can do it next week the nasty way,"[48] and a comment by Scheidler to a Chicago reporter that, "I have yet to shed my first tear when I see a charred abortion clinic. I am not going to condone the violence but that's as far as I go,"[49] led jurors to uphold the claims that the defendants had banded together in a nationwide extortion campaign intended to close clinics. Letters between Scheidler and extremists not named in the case, including Don Benny Anderson, Michael Bray, John Burt and Matthew Goldsby, linked the co-conspirators and sealed the case against those named in the suit.

On April 20, 1998, after a seven and a half week trial, a jury of four women and two men found the defendants guilty of RICO violations and awarded the

Summit Women's Health Organization in Milwaukee and the Delaware WHO in Wilmington $257,780 in damages. The decision also acknowledged the many people—twenty-eight categories in all—who had been victimized by the defendants; in addition to patients and staff, landlords, neighbors, lab couriers, drug company representatives, repair people and bankers had been adversely impacted.

"No citizen in this country is entitled to extort, threaten or deprive others of a Constitutionally protected right," an elated Hill told the press immediately after the verdict was announced. "No healthcare worker or patient should be subjected to the years of pain and fear that Scheidler, Operation Rescue and their foot soldiers have inflicted on us. Americans should be free to go to work without fear, to access healthcare without violence, and to operate businesses free from attacks."[50]

To date, neither WHO clinic has received reparations. In July 1999, however, United States District Court Judge David Coar ordered Scheidler, PLAL, OR and activists Timothy Murphy and Andrew Scholberg to pay the plaintiffs. He further barred them, in a federal injunction, from blocking clinic doors and driveways, damaging clinic property and threatening doctors or patients for the next twelve years. The order can be enforced by any law enforcement official or judge. Violation, Coar warned, can lead to incarceration.[51] The antis are appealing the rulings but were forced to deposit a bond equal to the amount of the damages in order to do so. If they lose on appeal, this money will go directly to the clinics.

JULY 31: WICHITA, KANSAS

At about 11:30 P.M. on a Monday evening, Women's Health Care Services was firebombed. "Before the bombing we were picketed by the Shield of Roses, a Catholic women's group that was always peaceful and nonharassing of patients," says clinic owner Dr. George Tiller. "But there had always been an undercurrent of nonacceptance among certain people. One time they punctured a hole in a window, stuck a hose in, and filled the basement with water. On the night of the bombing one-third of our office was destroyed. We lost all our patient charts, including those of our family-practice patients who had nothing to do with abortion. It cost about $125,000 to repair the building. Our insurance paid but our premiums were quadrupled immediately afterwards."[52]

It took the health center three months to rebuild. In the interim, it used an office that belonged to a friend of Tiller's. "When we got it on Tuesday it had no phone, no gas, no furniture, no drapes, no medical equipment or electricity," he says. "But by Wednesday we had everything we needed and saw seventeen patients. We got gas, electricity, and the phone done in one working day. It was a miracle. You know what it's like to get a phone installed or a utility turned on. It can take weeks. Essentially, the community said that they would not tolerate the violence against us. We rented beds and either made do or did without until we moved back into our regular offices."[53] No one claimed responsibility for the bombing, and no one was apprehended. The clinic has since received approximately half a dozen phony bomb threats.

FALL: BINGHAMTON, NEW YORK

Former used car salesman, musician, drug user and high school dropout turned evangelical Christian Randall Terry founded Operation Rescue (OR). According to journalists James Risen and Judy L. Thomas, Terry first got the call to stop abortion during an October 1983 prayer group at the Church of Pierce Creek in upstate New York.[54] Although his initial foray into activism began when he and his then-wife, Cindy, picketed Southern Tier Women's Services, by October 1984 Terry was staffing a crisis pregnancy center near Binghamton, New York. Within a year he had made contact with Joseph Scheidler and the Pro-Life Action Network.

Scheidler was apparently taken with Terry's verbal acuity and organizing skills and lost no time in bringing him into the inner circle. Yet Risen and Thomas report early strains in their association. "Stark religious differences placed early limits on the Terry-Scheidler relationship," they write. "Terry, like other fundamentalists, believed that Catholics had not found the true path to Christ, and before long he was trying to save Scheidler's soul. . . . For Scheidler, a pragmatist who had rebelled against the restrictions placed on anti-abortion protest by the Catholic church, religious differences were irrelevant to his work with Protestants in a shared cause, but he failed to grasp that religion was everything to Randall Terry."[55]

By 1987 Terry was head over heels into organizing OR, drawing on clergy contacts he had made while a student at Elim Bible College. At the 1987 PLAN convention, Terry announced a "rescue," scheduled for Philadelphia, with a test-run in nearby Cherry Hill, New Jersey, slated for November 1987. Participants in the two "rescues"—Philadelphia and Cherry Hill—found the experiences so exhilarating that Terry soon announced OR's first large-scale event, a May 1988 "rescue" in New York City. Six hundred people, including Catholic auxiliary bishop Austin Vaughan and New York Giant football star Mark Bavaro,[56] went to The Big Apple for a week of clinic disruption. Sixteen hundred disorderly conduct arrests were made; most protestors received small fines.[57] A few weeks later, in early July, the group reconvened in Philadelphia. It was there that evangelical Michael Hirsh—currently an attorney in Atlanta, Georgia, and a key proponent of the theory that it is "justifiable homicide" to kill abortion providers—urged Terry to bring OR to the Democratic National Convention being held later that month in Atlanta.[58] Terry rose to the challenge and within weeks was known in households throughout the United States.

FALL: BOULDER, COLORADO

The City Council passed a weak "buffer zone ordinance" designed to keep anti-abortion protestors from harassing patients. The ordinance required abortion opponents to stay at least eight feet from an approaching woman and/or her escort, but only if the patient or escort put her hand up and ordered the protestors to step back.

The fundamental problem with the ordinance, Dr. Warren Hern of the Boulder Abortion Clinic charged, was that it "placed the burden of prosecution on the patient. It also assumed that anti-abortion demonstrators are reasonable people who respond to reasonable requests and respect the law. Overwhelming experience shows this is not the case."[59]

The citywide ordinance was the first of its kind in the nation.

OCTOBER: TEXAS

Texas Attorney General Steve Gardner charged the Problem Pregnancy Center in Fort Worth with violating the Texas Deceptive Trade Practices Act. Like PP Inc., the bogus clinic that had tormented Planned Parenthood patients in Worcester, Massachusetts, several years earlier, Gardner found the center guilty of giving "Right to Life" information to women lured into visiting their offices through false advertisements. The Yellow Pages responded by promising to list the center under "abortion alternative organizations" in their 1986–87 edition. The 1985 listing allowed the Problem Pregnancy Center to be listed under "abortion information."[60]

OCTOBER: FARGO, NORTH DAKOTA

Penny Lea of I Believe in Life exhorted her North Dakota followers to be "raving idiots for Jesus Christ." The goal of the "idiocy"? Lea told the press that she aimed not only to eliminate abortion but was working "to make North Dakota a Christian state."[61]

NOVEMBER 11: WILMINGTON, DELAWARE

Cathy Conner, former administrator of the Delaware Women's Health Organization (DWHO), was alone in the clinic when Joseph Scheidler barged in with three of his colleagues. Scheidler's organization, the Pro-Life Action Network (PLAN), had announced a series of demonstrations at clinics in Wilmington for Saturday, November 12, and Conner recalls thinking that she had things for the next day under control. She had met with the police and had assurances that they would be on hand to keep the peace. DWHO staff had been primed and knew to expect disruptions.

Clinics across North America were not yet fully aware of the need for heightened security in 1986, and DWHO was no exception. In a scene that sounds preposterous a decade and a half later, Scheidler and associates simply walked into the building. Once there, Scheidler launched into an intimidating diatribe about the evils of abortion. "He told me he planned to close us down," Conner recalls. "He said he planned to make Delaware the first state in the country to be abortion free. He actually said he was there to case the place. While he looked around he put our phone lines on hold for between five and seven minutes. When he was ready to go, on his way out, he told me that I should find myself another job or I'd be in a heap of trouble. My adrenaline was pumping but I called the police as soon as he left."[62]

The police came and took a report from Conner, but the officers told her that they were unwilling to arrest Scheidler until after the next day's demonstration. "They said they were afraid of problems if they acted before the demonstrations were over," she says.[63]

NOVEMBER 12: WILMINGTON, DELAWARE

Scheidler's PLAN protest at the DWHO was relatively peaceful, Cathy Conner recalls, lasting approximately an hour and a half before moving on to Planned Parenthood. DWHO staff thought they were done with the group, at least for the moment.

Not so. At the conclusion of PLAN's rally at Planned Parenthood, police arrested Scheidler for trespassing at DWHO the previous day. "He was shocked," says Conner. "He didn't expect that to happen."[64]

But Scheidler was not the only one to receive a surprise that Saturday. When Conner returned home, she was greeted by a PLAN entourage screaming outside her residence. "I had to walk through them to get inside," she says. "I didn't let my kids out of the house for the rest of that day. None of us went out. I was both furious and fearful. Scheidler knew where I lived. The fear and intimidation is so great because you just don't know what will happen next."[65]

Conner and her family sold their house shortly after the PLAN demonstration and moved clandestinely. Although their new home was never picketed, Conner left the DWHO in 1987. "It was a difficult decision for me to make, leaving. I really liked the job. But when I took it I didn't realize I'd be part of a political hot potato. I was stressed, tired of my privacy being invaded. They knew my kids' names. I finally decided not to put myself, or them, in the firing line any longer."[66]

Follow-up note: Scheidler was found guilty of trespassing and was fined $50 by a municipal court judge.

1987

CHERRY HILL, NEW JERSEY

When protest began outside the Cherry Hill Women's Center, a primary prop was a metal garbage can with the word "sin" painted on it. Demonstrators filled the can with plastic doll parts dripping red paint and several times a week paraded in front of the clinic carrying a sign reading "America's Trash: Dead Babies" while waving an American flag.

The protests also included the direct expression of threats, says Bob Rowell of the South Jersey Clinic Defense Coalition. "One guy would go up to escorts and say things like, 'The only reason you people don't have anything happen to you is because we are Christians. Well, maybe something will happen and I'll ask God to forgive me.'"[67]

Follow-up note: In other sites, plastic dolls dripping with ketchup or barbecue sauce have been placed in front of clinics or at the homes of clinic personnel.

MARCH: TULSA, OKLAHOMA

When Reproductive Services of Tulsa, Oklahoma, was forced to vacate the rental property it had occupied for twenty-six months, staff hoped that the worst anti-abortion harassment was behind them. It was not. Executive administrator Sherri Finik recalls that the freestanding building that the clinic had purchased was immediately hit by protestors. Numerous rallies and blockades were organized, and vandalism became routine.

The clinic's locks were repeatedly filled with Super Glue and their electrical box and air-conditioning units were tampered with. Beginning in early 1987 windows were randomly and regularly broken. One night what Finik calls "stink bait," a foul-smelling substance that may have been butyric acid, was thrown into the clinic through a broken window. This caused the office to open later than usual because the space had to be aired out and checked for possible contamination. On other occasions staff arrived in the morning to find that bullets had been fired into the facility during the night.

People, as well as property, felt the anti-abortionists' sting. "Staff members were followed," reports Finik. "They were tailed. The message was simple: 'You can't hide. We know where you live.' Staff would get home some days and find people who'd been protesting at the clinic sitting in front of their houses."[68] Although Finik states that it was worse in the late 1980s, she acknowledges that family members of clinic employees continue to face the antis' wrath. In fact, since 1987 Finik's three children have been repeatedly accosted and called names. "They've seen people come up to me in the mall and say, 'You murder babies.' Teachers make comments: 'I saw your mother on TV last night.' They can't always tell if the teacher disapproves or admires me, but it makes them uncomfortable to be singled out for attention. Students ask, 'How can your mother kill babies?' At times it's been embarrassing to them, but they're strong, emotionally healthy kids. I started working at the clinic in 1978, when my oldest was three and I was pregnant with the twins. This has been their whole life. They accept that their mother gets a lot of attention, some of it hateful. A few times they've gotten worried and said, 'Are you going to get killed or blown up? We're worried about you.' But since they know I'll never quit, that's all they've ever said."[69]

Not everyone associated with Reproductive Services has exhibited the same stubbornness. Some staff members have resigned and FedEx, UPS, mail carriers and repair people often complain about the abuse they confront when they arrive at the clinic. Being told that you are helping to kill babies does not sit well with many people, says Finik, and those who can choose where to work are likely to avoid doing business with a site that is known to be volatile.

"The antis try to make people ashamed or afraid to do business with us," she adds. One of their most tangible successes resulted from a court proceeding in which the city prosecutor was charging protestors with trespassing during a blockade. During the proceedings, Finik was questioned by the protestors' attorney and was asked to identify the company that handled the clinic's fetal remains. Although the question was irrelevant to the case, the judge ordered Finik to answer. "That afternoon the company started getting harassing phone calls and they quickly dropped us as a client. I had to find someone else to perform this service, and in a community the size of Tulsa there are only two or three. I finally found a replacement but I worry about the same thing happening to them," she says.[70]

APRIL 30–MAY 2: ATLANTA, GEORGIA

The fourth annual Pro-Life Action Network conference elected Andrew Burnett, Joseph Scheidler and Randall Terry to a Leadership Council. The council was created to formulate a national agenda for the movement.[71]

OCTOBER 3: PORTLAND, OREGON

A daily incident report states that protestors outside All Women's Health Services taunted patients by screaming: "They cut babies up into little pieces in there. . . . They sacrifice children on an altar as part of devil worship. They drink the blood of aborted fetuses in there."[72]

1988

NATIONWIDE

Operation Rescue released its inaugural brochure:

> It would be a tremendous testimony to millions of Americans and their political representatives, that people still exist who are willing to stand for their fellow human beings, even at personal risk. If 1,500 people spend a day in jail together, it would be an inspiration to multitudes of Christians to take a stronger stand for the children. . . . In the civil rights movement the sight of hundreds and hundreds of blacks [sic] jailed together for peaceful protest against the injustice of segregation helped win the sympathy of the nation to their cause. . . . Whether for good or bad, political change comes after a group of Americans bring enough tension in the nation and pressure on politicians that the laws are changed.

The brochure listed several organizational cosponsors for OR's activities: Advocates for Life, the American Life League and the Pro-Life Action Network.[73]

FEBRUARY 2: NATIONWIDE

The Department of Health and Human Services promulgated regulations prohibiting 4,200 federally funded health and family planning clinics—none of which provided abortion services—from doing abortion counseling or making referrals to providers.[74]

More than four million women were affected by the rule. "I am disappointed that the president does not trust women to make sound decisions about their own healthcare after receiving all the information about the legal medical options at their disposal," said Majority Leader George Mitchell [D-ME].[75] The "gag rule" remained in effect until February 1993, when it was repealed by newly inaugurated President Bill Clinton.

FEBRUARY 4: FARGO, NORTH DAKOTA

The Cass County District Court found the Fargo-Moorhead Women's Help and Caring Connection—an anti-abortion "crisis pregnancy" counseling group that had been forced to change its name from the Fargo Women's Help Organization in 1984 after workers from the Fargo Women's Health Organization proved that numerous women had been temporarily diverted by the center—guilty of false and misleading advertising. The group had run newspaper and Yellow Page ads with the word "abortion" in red letters on one line, followed by "advisory services, pregnancy tests, confidential" on the next. The court found the ads to be deceptive since the group was virulently anti-abortion and berated any woman who came to its offices seeking full-options counseling.[76] The court mandated that Women's Help and Caring Connection state that it advocates "abortion alternatives" in future advertisements.

FEBRUARY 6: BOULDER, COLORADO

Although regular picketing and "sidewalk counseling" at the Boulder Abortion Clinic was something of a given, during the first week of February things took an ugly turn. According to clinic owner Dr. Warren Hern, "Immediately following several anti-abortion statements by President Reagan and [Republican presidential hopeful] Pat Robertson, there were five shots fired through the front windows of my waiting room by the front entrance. I had just walked through the area and had left the building. The lights were on and there were cars in the parking lot. One of my staff members was almost struck by two of the bullets after he heard the noise from the first three and went to investigate." Damage was estimated at $1,000.[77]

Police investigated the shooting but no one was apprehended. Hern subsequently spent more than $30,000 to install bulletproof windows and steel code-operated doors at the facility.[78]

Follow-up note: Data about drive-by shootings into clinics are sparse, but similar incidents occurred in Fort Lauderdale, Hollywood and Orlando, Florida. It is likely that other sites have experienced similar late-night gunfire.

MAY 1: PORTLAND, OREGON

Affidavit of KLM, a patient at All Women's Health Services:

> I received a phone call at my sister's residence the morning of my abortion procedure at 6:00 A.M. The woman on the other end of the line asked for me by name and stated "I understand you are having an abortion this morning. I would like to read to you a Scripture from the Bible in the hopes that I may save a life." As I understand, this was all to be kept confidential. My right to privacy has been invaded. I realize the severity of the action I find it right for myself to take, and don't feel anyone has the right to come back at me with their religious beliefs or opinions.[79]

MAY 7: PENSACOLA, FLORIDA

Following a tip phoned in to BATF by his father-in-law, Vietnam veteran John Brockhoeft was charged with possession of an unregistered destructive device and put in Escambia County Jail. Brockhoeft had first gone to Pensacola in 1986 to protest Joan Andrews Bell's incarceration and was headed back to that city to bomb The Ladies Center when he was apprehended.[80]

After receiving the call, BATF went to Brockhoeft's Kentucky home and interviewed his wife, Jody. They also searched the premises and found nitro and glycerine; although the chemicals had not been mixed, BATF decided to track Brockhoeft to his Pensacola destination.[81]

According to BATF agent Robert Hofer, Brockhoeft spent the evening of May 6, the day before the intended bombing of The Ladies Center, with John Burt at Our Father's House. During their visit, Burt drove Brockhoeft to a parking lot across from the clinic where they sat and watched the building. Around midnight BATF agents followed Brockhoeft from Burt's facility; they arrested him en route to the clinic after determining that his vehicle was filled with explosives.[82]

Brockhoeft was sentenced to twenty-six months for possession of fulgurous materials. He was subsequently arrested for setting a 1985 fire at the Margaret Sanger Center in Cincinnati and was given an additional seven years in prison. Brockhoeft was released in January 1995.[83]

Wife Jody divorced Brockhoeft and entered the federal witness protection program after confiding to BATF agents that she was "deathly afraid" of her spouse.[84] John Brockhoeft has since remarried. Burt was given two years of house arrest for his role in the potentially deadly incident. He told prosecutors that he took Brockhoeft to the parking lot to look at an anti-abortion billboard and did not know anything about plans to blow up the clinic.[85]

SUMMER: NEW ORLEANS, LOUISIANA

According to Tanya Melich, author of *The Republican War Against Women: An Insider's Report from Behind the Lines,* two-thirds of the delegates attending the 1988 Republican National Convention were "white Protestant men, and almost three quarters had incomes over $50,000 a year. There were fewer women, fewer Jews and fewer minorities than in 1984."[86] The 1988 abortion plank was identical to the one passed in 1984, Melich wrote, and explicitly praised religious and private organizations that offered alternatives to abortion.[87]

SUMMER: PITTSBURGH, PENNSYLVANIA

By the late 1980s, "rescues" had become the tactic of choice for most anti-abortion protestors; few cities with clinics escaped unscathed. Pittsburgh, however, was one of the hardest hit. The three abortion providers located there were near-constant targets of sit-ins and blockades. Starting in the summer of 1988, boisterous, well-orchestrated, and precisely choreographed six hundred to eight hundred person protests occurred almost every Saturday at at least one facility.

While the city was initially lenient toward the protestors, by the fall of 1989 law enforcers and elected officials were furious at the resources being expended to handle illegal anti-abortion activities. After tallying up the arrests—1,600 between August 1988 and August 1989—the City Law Department announced that it was prepared to file liens against any property owned by protestors who owed the city money. The department told reporters that $234,199 in unpaid fines was prompting this unprecedented move. The liens, they explained, would prevent those property owners who owed anything to the city from collecting money from the sale or transfer of their homes, cars or other assets until they had settled their debts.[88] Other expenditures may also have contributed to the city's hard-line policy. According to the *Pittsburgh Post Gazette,* in 1989 Pittsburgh spent $106,665 on medical leave and lost time due to injuries suffered by police officers while handling abortion protestors and another $76,000 on police overtime.[89] Incarceration costs were similarly astronomical. The *Pittsburgh Press* reports that detaining 130 prisoners for two days in March 1989 cost the county $16,300.[90]

JULY 18–22: ATLANTA, GEORGIA

The Democratic National Convention, an-every-four-year media circus, brought Operation Rescue to Atlanta for a period of sustained mayhem at clinics and hospitals. "It was really unbelievable to see people so willing to get arrested," says Lynne Randall, cofounder of the Atlanta Feminist Women's Health Center (AFWHC) and its codirector until 1993. "Before this, protestors would push the envelope, but they would rarely do things to deliberately get arrested. With OR it changed to a new level. People came to Atlanta to get arrested."[91]

According to Randall, the police tried a variety of tactics to stop the blockades, from erecting barricades, to stationing officers on horseback at clinic entrances. Nothing worked. "I felt like I was watching creatures from another planet," she continues, "when I saw grown adults get on their bellies and crawl dozens of feet under police barricades to blockade doors."[92]

Ann Garzia, executive director of Atlanta Women's Medical Center, remembers arriving at her workplace to find protestors twelve-deep in front of center doors. "The police carried patients over the mostly male protestors to get them in," she says. "They did not arrest OR people at first, but OR antagonized them to get arrested. One day the police blocked the street to keep patients in and blockaders out."[93]

Although Garzia concedes that Feminist got the worst of the protests—four hundred of the 1,235 arrests made that summer were at the AFWHC—because three clinics were located within a one-mile radius, none was exempt. "Atlanta Women's had four 'rescues.' Feminist got it every day. During July and August my staff met daily. We had to be strong for the patients and we did as good a job as possible, but it was a really bad time for all of us," she admits.[94]

While clinics certainly bore the brunt of the difficulties caused by OR, law enforcement was also having a rough time, and police spent untold hours grappling with how best to handle the thousands of antis who had flocked to the city. Frustrated that they were unable to identify those who called themselves Jane, John and Baby Doe, they got a search warrant on July 22 and rifled through the belongings of OR members staying at the Day's Inn. Although police were ostensibly seeking only to identify people who had been arrested, what they discovered confounded them: $50,000 in cash and two fetuses in ice chests.[95]

To the outside world—and even to law enforcement—OR looked strong, well organized and militant. But writer Marian Faux believes that the siege of Atlanta marked the beginning of the end for the organization. Her book, *Crusaders: Voices from the Abortion Front,* states that Randall Terry's followers started to sour on the group when they realized that they had been lied to. "Terry encouraged people to refuse to post bond, claiming that most jails would release them after a few hours because they didn't have room for them," she wrote. "What he didn't always say was that OR would not post bond for its members or necessarily provide them with legal support when they got to trial."[96]

Faux cites a Cajun congregation from South Louisiana that OR had recruited to Atlanta as an example. Terry, she writes, had reassured "them they wouldn't be arrested and promised that if they were, they would get out in a few hours. They were stunned when they were arrested en mass and jailed, and shocked that OR did not spring them. Terry provided no legal support and he got himself out of jail in a few days while the rest of them served a month. Atlanta Police sergeant Carl Pyrdum Jr., head of the Atlanta OR Task Force, said 'We almost had a riot when his followers found out he had stranded them.'"[97]

Follow-up note: A number of people who would go on to make a name for themselves within the most extreme wing of the anti-choice movement met and bonded while in Atlanta's Key Road Detention Facility. Among the future "celebrities" were John Arena, convicted of executing a string of butyric acid attacks in New York state; Rachelle "Shelley" Shannon, convicted for shooting Kansas doctor George Tiller in 1993; the Reverend Norman Weslin, founder of the Lambs of Christ; and James Kopp, indicted in the 1998 shooting death of Dr. Barnett Slepian and in two of the sniper attacks on Canadian physicians.

JULY 30: PITTSBURGH, PENNSYLVANIA

Police Officer Jennie Yauch made the following statement to the *Pittsburgh Press* after she spent several hours hauling 190 noncompliant protestors onto buses for booking.

> I resent protestors chanting such things as "Police kill babies!" The demonstrators have no idea what my personal views on abortion are, and I think I speak for all of my fellow officers when I say that the remark was totally out of line and completely uncalled for. . . . The icing on the cake was the man who left his 14-year-old daughter sitting alone on the sidewalk. When asked what he suggested the police

do with her, his only statement was "take her." While this man was so busy worrying about others' children, he couldn't care what happened to his own.[98]

Many clinics have observed similar behavior on the part of anti-abortion parents. In Florida, babies and toddlers have been paraded in the blazing, tropical sun for hours. In some places police have called child protective service agencies to ascertain if abuse is occurring; in several instances the agency has taken custody of the children.

SEPTEMBER 10: WILMINGTON, DELAWARE

Operation Rescue staged its first "rescue" at the Delaware Women's Health Organization. Clinic doors were blocked for three hours. Although police made more than eighty arrests, the charges against most of the protestors were dropped because the officers were unable to positively identify individual "rescuers" at a subsequent trial.[99] Since photos of protestors had not been taken at the time of arrest, identification of particular demonstrators was impossible, forcing the police to drop the charges.

SEPTEMBER 16: INDIANA

Seventeen-year-old Rebecca Suzanne Bell, a high school senior, died from an illegal abortion. Bell did not want to disappoint her parents by informing them that she was pregnant—a requirement in the state of Indiana for minors seeking abortions—and was also reluctant to go to court for a judicial waiver of the parental notification requirement. Coroner Dennis Nicholas ruled that the teen died of a septic abortion compounded by pneumonia. She is the first known casualty of parental consent/notification laws.[100]

OCTOBER 18: TORONTO, CANADA

The first Operation Rescue blockade in Canada took place at the Toronto Morgentaler clinic. Joseph Scheidler attended. Three days later the American anti-abortion leader spoke at a Campaign Life meeting in Brampton, Ontario.[101]

OCTOBER 29: THIRTY-TWO CITIES

Operation Rescue's first coordinated Day of Rescue led to 2,644 arrests in thirty-two cities across the United States.[102]

CHRISTMAS EVE: DALLAS, TEXAS

The Fairmount Clinic in Dallas, Texas, open since 1973, was set on fire in the late evening. A freestanding building that abuts an alley, the clinic was divided into two sections, administrative and medical. The fire began in the administrative area. A firewall, which owners Dr. Curtis Boyd and Glenna Halvorson-Boyd did not know existed, confined the conflagration to that section of the building. Although the entire clinic suffered water and smoke damage, operating and examination rooms were salvaged; the business offices were completely destroyed.

According to Halvorson-Boyd, at the time of the fire the clinic was scheduled for a two-week break in services; it was expected to reopen in early January. "The fire department was wonderfully supportive," she recalls. "One of the firemen told us about a family whose business was salvaging materials after a fire. I had never heard of such a thing before. We called this family and they said they'd do the job. They worked from Christmas Day through New Year's Day and did all the repairs and cleanup so that we were able to reopen on schedule. It turned out that one of the sons in this family had brought his girlfriend to the clinic for an abortion a few years before. He said that he and she were so well treated by our staff that he convinced his family to work over the holidays. He felt it was the least he could do."[103]

Although the fire was the most devastating event to hit the clinic, Dallas had faced a significant amount of anti-abortion activity since the early 1980s. Like other locales, however, the first few years after *Roe* saw little in the way of anti-choice opposition. In fact, says Halvorson-Boyd, "At first we had strong support from the medical school. They sent residents to us for training. Some of the earliest doctors we trained were residents at the Catholic hospital who were moonlighting with us."[104]

This changed when former California governor Ronald Reagan became president. "Immediately, he issued an executive order that medical schools receiving federal money could no longer train residents in abortion. We also began to see increasing anti-abortion activity at the clinic; the kinds of things that were happening elsewhere began to happen in Dallas. Our parking lot was repeatedly strewn with nails, employees' gas caps were tampered with, and the clinic's locks were filled with glue. Our nursing coordinator was picketed at home by antis carrying signs that accused her husband of homosexuality. At this point, in the early 1980s, the antis became much more invasive and personal in their attacks on us," Halvorson-Boyd says.[105]

An early 1980s invasion—the exact date is no longer available because all of the pertinent records were lost in the 1988 fire—is particularly vivid in

Halvorson-Boyd's mind. She remembers being stunned as abortion foes burst through the door and knocked two completely unprepared staff members to the floor. The protestors then chained themselves to the clinic's exam and surgery tables. Hours later police succeeded in cutting them loose and made arrests. While the penalties meted out for this disruption were minimal, staff quickly learned the necessity of having a security strategy.

Halvorson-Boyd's education took several more turns when, in 1984, she was elected president of the National Abortion Federation (NAF), a position she held through 1986. It was as NAF president that she received her first death threat. Anti-abortion stalwart Joseph Scheidler was at one particular NAF meeting—for years meetings were open to anyone interested in attending, including anti-abortion activists—when outgoing director Uta Landy asked him to leave so that she could say a private good-bye to her colleagues. He refused. "I approached him," says Halvorson-Boyd, "and asked him to walk out with me, which he did. I started to thank him for doing this when he pinned me against the wall and said, 'I'm gonna see the death of you and the likes of you.' I said, 'I doubt it,' and went back inside. A month or so later, at an NAF executive committee meeting, someone asked me what had happened when I'd gone outside with Scheidler. When I told the story people were aghast and said, 'Jeez, Glenna, that was a death threat.'"[106]

Halvorson-Boyd and her husband, Dr. Curtis Boyd, received two other death threats in 1985. Although they contacted local police and other law enforcement agencies, no one was apprehended for sending the handwritten letters and, with one exception in 1991, they have never received another one.

"There were all kinds of creepy things happening in the mid-1980s," adds Halvorson-Boyd, "that let us know that the antis knew more about us and our lives than we thought they should. Our son was in a very serious car accident in 1985. One Saturday, a few weeks after it happened, one of the antis yelled out, as we were walking through the parking lot, 'How's your son? Any more accidents?' They let us know that they knew more about us than we wanted them to."[107]

No one was arrested for the Christmas Eve fire.

1989

AMHERST, BUFFALO AND KENMORE, NEW YORK

Project Rescue Western New York, an Operation Rescue affiliate, began a campaign of sustained blockading, invading and picketing at Erie Medical Center, Buffalo GYN Womanservices and the private offices of physicians who performed abortions. Although there were a few incidents in 1988, between February and December 1989 police were called nineteen times.

A lawsuit filed by the Pro-Choice Network of Western New York, both clinics, and Doctors Paul Davis, Shalom Press and Barnett Slepian charged that "law enforcement efforts by the police departments of Buffalo, Kenmore and Amherst have been ineffective in restoring medical services in a timely manner to patients seeking them at plaintiff providers' facilities." They further argued that they needed an injunction because police had been "unable to prevent blockading activities from occurring and had been unable to prevent closure or delay in the provision of services" at the named locations.[108]

A temporary restraining order/injunction against Project Rescue et al was issued by Judge Richard J. Arcara, a Republican appointed to the bench by Ronald Reagan, on September 26, 1990.[109] According to pro-choice attorney Glenn A. Murray, "Blockading by local Buffalo anti-abortion forces was ended by the injunction and by publicity about the despicable tactics the antis had used. Until the Spring of Life in 1992, local anti-abortion organizations were unable to rally their troops."[110]

Follow-up note: The two-week Spring of Life in April 1992 brought an infusion of out-of-town energy to the Buffalo area. Six hundred fifteen protestors were arrested for violating the injunction and entering a fifteen-foot buffer zone that had been established to separate protestors from patients and building doorways.[111]

Since the injunction was issued, Erie Medical Center has closed its doors, making Buffalo GYN Womanservices the sole clinic in the area. Likewise, Dr. Davis has retired. As a result of Barnett Slepian's murder in the fall of 1998, Dr. Shalom Press is the last remaining private provider in western New York.

NATIONWIDE

For years, National Women's Health Organization clinics had sent their fetal remains to a pathology lab in Northbrook, Illinois, called VitalMed. This arrangement went smoothly until the summer of 1988 when a VitalMed employee, later identified as an associate of Joseph Scheidler, began stealing the fetuses and shipping them to anti-choice activists.

Pat Balagher, a Delaware anti, got a batch in 1989 and subsequently made arrangements with a Catholic cemetery to entomb the "babies." Press savvy, she and her cohorts captured a great deal of media attention for "burying the children." Other activists, including Monica Migliorino Miller in Milwaukee, replicated Balagher's tactic in cities as far-flung as Chapel Hill, North Carolina;

Fargo, North Dakota; Tallahassee, Florida; Ft. Wayne, Indiana; and Chicago, Illinois.

"They obtained the fetal remains illegally. They transported them over state lines illegally. And they buried them illegally," charges former Delaware Women's Health Organization administrator Jennifer Vriens. "But they were never prosecuted. It was terrible. The fetal remains had been identified as coming from the DWHO and former patients were traumatized. We got a lot of calls from women agonizing over whether it was their fetus that the antis were burying."[112]

"The antis were telling the press that they'd found 4,000 fetuses in garbage bags in front of our clinics," adds NWHO president Susan Hill. "In Milwaukee a radio station announced that the antis were going to read the names of the patients who'd aborted out loud at a 'funeral service.' This caused us tremendous problems, confidence problems. It was really brutal. The attorney general in North Dakota called me in and questioned me about whether we were illegally dumping fetuses. The NWHO staff had talked about conspiracy and extortion before, but it was this incident that made us amend the Sherman anti-trust case we had filed against Joseph Scheidler in 1986 to include RICO charges," she says.[113]

Follow-up note: VitalMed refused to press charges against its employee.

Fetuses were also planted in the garbage dumpster of a Boca Raton, Florida, doctor. The "discovery" prompted an exhaustive state investigation; the physician was eventually cleared of improperly disposing the fetal remains.

DALLAS, TEXAS

Ask Lisa Gerard, executive director of Dallas's Fairmount Clinic, about the most horrible anti-abortion experience she's had and a memory quickly surfaces. "We had a patient who was scheduled to come in for the second day of a two-day, second-trimester procedure. She did not speak English. She came to the clinic on the second day and the protestors told her, in Spanish, that the clinic was closed. She believed them and went home."[114]

Meanwhile, inside the clinic staff could not understand why the patient had failed to show up for her appointment. They knew they had carefully explained the procedure to her and made clear how essential it was that she return on the second day. "We got more and more concerned as the day wore on," Gerard says. "This patient had no phone so we decided to send a Spanish-speaking worker to her house. When she got there, she learned what had happened."[115] More than a decade later, Gerard's fury is still audible. "This patient could have died," she blasts. "Laminaria [a fibrous cervical dilating material] can only stay in for so long before it causes what can become a life-threatening infection. We got to her in time and she was okay, but this could have been easily avoided."[116]

PORTLAND, OREGON

Tim Shuck was the director of Lovejoy SurgiCenter when AIDS began to devastate the gay male community he was part of. "In the very early stages of the epidemic I started the Cascades AIDS Project, a social service program for people with AIDS," he says. "I was one of the directors and appeared on a TV program on which it was said that I had the disease. One of Lovejoy's most regular picketers apparently saw it and afterward stood in front of the SurgiCenter yelling, 'Don't go in there. You'll get AIDS.' One day our medical director called me in and said that he'd had a patient who was so scared by what this woman had said that she'd left without having her abortion. When I learned that we'd lost a patient because of this protestor I went over the edge. My friends were dying, I'd been diagnosed, and this lady was being ugly and nasty. I knew I had to do something."[117]

Shuck sued for slander and the intentional infliction of emotional distress and asked the court for $500,000 in compensatory damages. "We brought in witnesses who had heard the screaming to prove that what I was saying this woman had said and done was true," he adds.[118] Shuck won the case and was awarded $150,000. "She paid," he laughs. "The attorney who argued the case got half and I got half, but it wasn't about the money. It was about principle."[119]

WASHINGTON, D.C.

For the first time since making abortion legal in 1973, only four Supreme Court Justices voted to affirm *Roe v. Wade*. In *Webster v. Reproductive Health Services*, the Court upheld a Missouri statute that prohibited the use of public facilities or public personnel for performing abortions. The Court also upheld a requirement that all doctors test to confirm gestational age, weight and lung capacity when they have reason to believe a woman is more than twenty weeks' pregnant.[120]

Follow-up note: States no longer enforce this requirement since clinics have proved that the testing serves no purpose for nonviable fetuses.

JANUARY 25: WILMINGTON, DELAWARE

A second "rescue" took place at the Delaware Women's Health Organization (DWHO). This time the door was blocked with cars and trucks to completely bar people from entering or leaving the facility. Several protestors were locked to the underside of the vehicles.

Police had to cut the locks and tow the cars to get the health center opened. While the clinic was closed for five hours, former DWHO administrator Jennifer Vriens reports that this time the police took videos so that they could later prove that particular people were at the blockade.[121]

FEBRUARY: SAN ANTONIO, TEXAS

When abortion-provision pioneer, the Reverend Myron (Chris) Chrisman, founder of Nova Health Systems, a not-for-profit chain of women's reproductive health clinics, died in February 1989, the last thing anyone expected was anti-abortion protest.

"Demonstrators showed up at the funeral home, signed the guest book and stood milling around the chapel," recalls Chrisman's widow, Marilyn Chrisman Eldridge. "I glanced at them but I was pretty numb and their presence didn't really register. Then we went to the Ft. Sam Houston National Cemetery—Chris was a veteran—for a graveside ceremony and the internment. When we got there we noticed that a video camera had been set up. The antis were standing there, getting ready to film the whole thing. We had to get security from the cemetery to remove them. We eventually got the tape and destroyed it, but the picketing of Chris's funeral was the intentional infliction of emotional distress. I suffered a great deal because of it," she says.[122]

Susan Hill, president of the National Women's Health Organization, was a good friend of Myron Chrisman's—they had both spent five years on the board of NARAL—and was in the limousine with the family when they spotted the picketers. "My twin sister had just been diagnosed with breast cancer so I was sitting in the car and feeling all this sadness and personal loss when we got to the gravesite," Hill recalls. "Suddenly we all noticed that there were two picketers with signs near the site. One guy was standing behind a tree, the other was at the actual burial site. I remember hearing Marilyn and her son and daughter—all at the same time—gasp. It was so horrible. Here we were, dealing with the death of this wonderful man and our right to grieve was being imposed on by political sentiments. There was a lot of motion and movement as everyone tried to protect Marilyn and the family while cemetery security took the men away. The funeral proceeded, but everyone was in knots that Chris couldn't even be laid to rest without this final insult. We related to each other that for all the antis preaching about love, they take every opportunity to inflict pain on people they don't agree with. It was so un-Christian."[123]

FEBRUARY 4: KNOXVILLE, TENNESSEE

When former clinic staffer Deborah Walsh describes the first "rescue" at Knoxville's Volunteer Medical Clinic, it is as if she is narrating a vivid, frame-by-frame documentary that is running in her head. Despite the fact that the protest occurred more than a decade ago, every detail remains within reach as she recounts the day's events.

Walsh had heard a winter 1988 "rescue" described by Belinda Henson, the director of a Birmingham clinic, so when police notified her about an OR blockade scheduled for Saturday, February 4, she thought she knew what to expect. "The police told us there was nothing to worry about. They'd met with OR and knew what would and would not happen," Walsh recalls. "They also told us that the OR people were all good Christians, just like our aunts and uncles. I said, 'No, they're not,' but was totally disregarded. The police told us that a man from Atlanta would keep everything under control. They then told us that OR would be allowed to come onto our property and block our doors, that it would be a symbolic sit-in, like what the civil rights workers did in the 1960s. I asked if we couldn't stop OR at the edge of our property. They said, 'no, it will be a lot more organized if we let them do what they want.'"[124]

Walsh says that although she fully expected a sedate protest, a second conversation with Belinda Henson convinced her that a few people should stay in the building overnight to make sure that clinic doors remained open. Unable to sleep, the three vigilants who did so began checking out the scene at 6:00 A.M. The rest of the staff arrived at 6:30.

"A little before 8:00 we looked out and across the street, coming from the park, was what looked like an army battalion, ten or twelve across, two hundred of them in block formation," says Walsh. "Jerry, my security guard, and I went to the edge of the property to meet them. We yelled, 'You can't trespass. This is private property.' They ignored us and moved toward the door. Police officers were sitting in their cars across the street. Jerry, Willie, an off-duty police officer from a neighboring town, and I ran to the clinic doors. Once OR saw us there, the first row of folks, all of them grown men, sat down. Then the next row sat, as did the others, and all of them started to crawl toward us and push us into the door. The door swung out, so with them pushing us against it, it could not be opened. Fifteen staff members were trapped in the building and OR was elbowing us, punching us, stomping on our feet and pinching us. It was unbelievable. I saw how rough and violent they were. This was not a peaceful sit-in."[125]

"It took an hour to an hour and a half for the police to begin to make arrests," she continues. "They gave OR numerous gentle warnings that they'd be arrested if they didn't leave. They also allowed hundreds of them to go into our parking lot for what they called 'prayer support.' Once the police started to make arrests and put people onto a city bus for booking, their leader asked police to allow them a moment of prayer before each individual arrest. Many of the police bent their heads and prayed with them. Meanwhile, my security guard was bitten on the buttocks. They actually broke the skin through his pants."[126] According to Walsh, it took police more than three hours to arrest the 103 blockaders and trespassers who had failed to disperse.

That evening, when Walsh got home, she discovered bruises up and down the backs of both arms and on her buttocks and legs. "It sounds so innocent now, but we were in a state of shock," she says. "It was the most unbelievable feeling to learn that in this country something like this could happen, that we could be subjected to such brutality. We were physically abused and our business was closed for three and a half hours even though we had done nothing wrong. The news coverage was also horrible. The 'rescue' was portrayed as completely nonviolent. Watching it gave me the most shattered feeling I'd ever had. It was like stepping into a twilight zone where no rules mattered. We had completely cooperated with law enforcement. We had always done what they'd asked us to do."[127]

After watching the TV news coverage, Walsh decided to go to the hospital because she wanted an official record of the injuries she had sustained at the hands of OR's "peaceful entourage." "I told triage personnel that I'd been beaten up by a group of people," Walsh says. "I was afraid to be more specific. I said I was shoved against a brick wall and pinched and bit for hours. They took me to an exam room and as soon as they saw me they said they had to make a police report, that I had to let the police see the bruises. The police officer who came was one of the few who disagreed with the way the city had handled OR. He looked like he was going to cry and said, 'Deb, I'm so sorry. I told them this would happen before it happened.'"[128]

Walsh spent the rest of the weekend trying to regain her equilibrium and on Monday morning called the head of the uniformed police officers, the police public relations office and a few lieutenants and scheduled a meeting for later that afternoon. At the start of the meeting Walsh asked police how they thought things had gone at the "rescue."

"They said they were pleased, that everything was perfect," Walsh recalls. "I said 'no, it wasn't perfect.' I said I knew OR would be back and said I wanted things done differently. I said I wanted a police officer at the door to keep the passageway open and a police tape put around the perimeter of the property so that OR would have to cross a police line to get to the clinic. I also said that when I pointed someone out by name and asked for him or her to be arrested, I wanted them to get a warning and then I wanted them removed. They told me I couldn't have any of these things. I then asked them to help me find the rules for private citizens using stun guns in Tennessee. They said no, that this would cause a big mess for me. I said I understood and would only use the guns within the confines of the law but I particularly wanted my female staff to be armed when OR came back because everyone's family was worried. Everything changed in the room after I said this. They suddenly decided that I could have the first three things I'd asked for. They would do those things."[129]

In addition to meeting with police, Walsh got the names of the 103 people arrested on February 4 and filed a federal lawsuit against them. As a result of the suit, Volunteer Medical obtained a temporary restraining order, later made permanent, which barred the protestors from trespassing or impeding ingress or egress to the building. A few weeks later, on March 18, the injunction was tested by a second OR blockade.

"I was carrying around copies of the court order and had someone following me around with a video camera," says Walsh. "I showed the injunction to each person participating in the action and stated that they were in violation of a federal order. I asked them to leave and told them that if they did not go, it would be a federal offense. To my recollection no one I showed the injunction to left. They shredded them or used them to make rain hats and we got it all on video. When the judge saw the tapes he was livid. So were the police. The captain who in January had told me that OR people were nice Christians was at the front door on March 18 and he physically removed any protestors who got near it. They made arrests quickly this time because they were frustrated. They didn't think the protestors would actually violate the injunction."[130]

The protestors were eventually forced to pay $12,000 in fines to the clinic. "This outcome is extremely rare," says Walsh. "Almost no one ever collects a penny. Things really quieted down in Knoxville after they had to pay up. We had effectively shown these people severe repercussions for trespassing on our property."[131]

MARCH: MILWAUKEE, WISCONSIN

Rembert Weakland, the Archbishop of Milwaukee, long a hotbed of urban anti-abortion activity, held a series of meetings to hear the opinions of Catholic women on abortion. These open forums were the first, and last, of their kind. After the meetings, in which dozens of women from all walks of life spoke, Weakland issued a statement which said, in part, that:

The church's official position has been clear for decades now: Abortion is seen as the taking of human life and, thus, morally wrong. It could also be said that the church would like its moral position to become the legal position in the nation as well. . . . But this unequivocal position does not have the full support of many Catholics, especially of many women, because it seems to be too simplistic an answer to a complicated and emotional question and does not resolve all the concomitant problems surrounding the issue raised in a pluralistic society.[132]

Predictably, petitions were circulated demanding that the archbishop be disciplined, and the Vatican barred the theology faculty of the University of Fribourg in Switzerland from granting Weakland an honorary degree.[133]

SPRING: BOULDER, COLORADO

Dr. Warren Hern of the Boulder Abortion Clinic gets furious when he talks about the callousness of anti-abortion protestors who disregard the circumstances involved in choosing to terminate a pregnancy. One particular case sticks with him. "A couple with a strongly desired pregnancy came from a distant point in another state to have an abortion because the fetus was severely deformed," he recalls. "The woman was diabetic and had forgotten her insulin, so I sent her to the hospital emergency room. Anti-abortion demonstrators followed the couple to the hospital, tried to talk them out of having an abortion, and later tracked the couple to their hotel and harassed them by telephone and knocking on their door. The couple was distraught."[134]

APRIL: CHERRY HILL, NEW JERSEY

Word of Operation Rescue's National Day of Rescue had gotten out and staff at the Cherry Hill Women's Center (CHWC) figured they were a likely hit because police had done little to help them during previous sit-ins or "rescues"; in fact, when OR chose Cherry Hill for its first national blockade in November 1987, the police had passively watched. According to Diane Straus, clinic director from 1986 to 1994, "We just assumed there would be trouble here."[135]

In preparation, Straus instructed staff and volunteer clinic escorts and defenders to arrive at the clinic between 4:30 and 5:00 A.M. Some slept at the facility. "We stood outside, in a single line, mostly women, with our arms linked. I was slightly apart from the line, holding an American flag, which I intended to wave in their faces. When the antis showed up, a few hundred of them, they did not know what to do. It was totally chaotic. Pro-choice people were incensed and told the police that there would only be peace if they removed the protestors who were trespassing. At the same time, I was trying to get patients inside the building. I had parked my car near one of the doors and we told the patients to climb onto the roof and jump off. When they did this, they were near a clinic entrance and could be let in by staff stationed inside. We got twenty-four patients in this way. We were very aggressive."[136]

While this was taking place, the clinic's lawyer was in court seeking an emergency injunction to ban OR from trespassing on CHWC property. After the injunction was granted, Straus read it to the assembled protestors. "I then attempted to enter the building," she recalls, "but I got grabbed and knocked down. I was okay, but I could never identify who pushed me so I could never press charges. Other people, volunteers, staff and patients, were also getting hurt, and for the first time since the protests began the police saw that the people protesting were not as nice, not as peaceful" as they had earlier assumed them to be.[137]

Several months after the blockade, the Cherry Hill police chief, who had previously told clinic staff that he supported OR and other anti-choice organizations, resigned. A new chief was appointed, and, within months, the tenor of law enforcement in Cherry Hill changed dramatically. Although representatives of the pro-choice community had met with the police earlier to press for the speedy arrest of blockaders, only after the new chief was installed did their lobbying find a receptive ear. "I had him talk to Lieutenant Pyrdum in Atlanta, a police officer who would not tolerate clinic disruptions," says Straus. "After this, the police would quickly remove protestors, put them on buses and book them. The secret lies in the police. We had to be in their faces to get them to act, but once word got out about how unpleasant the police were making it for the antis, they moved their disruptions someplace else."[138]

APRIL 9: OCALA, FLORIDA

For the second time in nine days an arsonist hit an Ocala clinic. The first fire caused extensive, but repairable, damage. The destruction from the second blaze was so serious, and the personal trauma so enormous, that the owners—who asked that neither they nor their facility be named in this text—did not rebuild the health center.

At the time of the second fire, most clinic staffers were attending the March for Women's Lives in Washington, D.C. "One of the women who worked at the center went to call her mother in Utah while the rest of us ate lunch," remembers former employee Lena Rabinski (a pseudonym). "Her mother told her that she'd heard on the news that the clinic had been burned. I felt so violated—literally raped. I had worked there for thirteen years. My life was there. It was so awful."

The culprit, says Rabinski, was never caught. "It's very frustrating. For a short period of time the police came in, gung ho. Then it fizzled out when they had no more leads. They didn't investigate very aggressively."[139]

That same night, a clinic in Fort Myers, 150 miles southeast, was fire-bombed. The facility reopened a few months later in a different location; as in the incident at its Ocala counterpart, no one was apprehended.[140]

APRIL 15: MELBOURNE, FLORIDA

Although the Aware Woman Center for Choice had been regularly picketed since moving to Melbourne in 1982 and was frequently victim to phoned-in bomb scares, protests rarely exceeded 150 people and were, for the most part, easily contained. That changed on April 15, 1989, when Operation Rescue organized its first blockade there.

Patricia Baird-Windle: "We had met with the police on March 15 and were told that they'd met with OR and knew what would happen. They also said that 'rescues' in both Tallahassee and Tampa had involved 150 people, so that's what we expected. When we came up to the clinic on April 15 and saw six hundred protestors, about thirty media people and fifty cops, plus my staff and patients, we were baffled. We had no idea what OR had done to organize so many people. The 'rescue' had somehow been arranged in secret, without anyone leaking news of it to us.

"Aware Woman had seven doors, and that morning they blockaded each of them and laid down in our flower beds. Police made 143 arrests in six hours, but it took until 3:30 in the afternoon for us to get inside the clinic; the cops let the antis block the street and the driveway and trample our well-landscaped garden. From that day on, OR was around each and every day. They did occasional 'hit-and-run' blockades where they'd leave before the police arrived, and they once locked themselves together—about eighteen people, two or three in a clot—with kryptonite locks and blocked all of our doors. They also once did an 'ambush blockade,' barricading staff and patients inside the building. Some days they would travel between our clinics in Melbourne, Port St. Lucie and West Palm Beach, blockading all three facilities on the same day."[141]

APRIL 29: NATIONWIDE

Operation Rescue's national Day of Rescue II was considerably smaller than 1988's activities; 1,396 people in fifteen cities were arrested.[142]

MAY: CHERRY HILL, NEW JERSEY

When an anti-abortion group showed up at the Cherry Hill Women's Center in the spring of 1989 for an evening vigil, both staff and police breathed a sigh of relief, assuming that the protest would be peaceful and quiet.

"The police were standing there watching when a group of antis formed a circle around the opening of our sewage drain. They sat down and looked and sounded like they were holding a religious service. Meanwhile, they were quietly pouring concrete into the sewage line," says former health center director Diane Straus. "When we got in the next morning we had to call in a plumber because raw sewage had backed up all over everything. We had to close for several days. By that point in the clinic's history we had elaborate alarms on the building, but they were never activated because the antis did not do anything to the actual structure. What was so maddening was that the police had seen the whole thing and had done nothing."[143]

JUNE: PHOENIX, ARIZONA

Since mid-1987 anti-abortion attorney John J. Jakubczyk and physician Brian Finkel, owner of the Phoenix Women's Center, have gone head-to-head over women's reproductive options. The former president of the Arizona Right to Life Committee, Jakubczyk has defended clinic blockaders and has sued his nemesis for medical malpractice on five occasions.

In the first case, brought in June 1989, "Jane Doe" claimed that the abortion performed by Finkel caused severe "physical and emotional trauma." Six months later the case was dismissed as groundless.[144] By that point Finkel had incurred a $10,000 legal bill and had received word that his malpractice insurance was being canceled. He eventually found a new carrier but has been forced to pay in excess of $29,000 a year for coverage since the lawsuits began.[145]

On November 3, 1990, another Jakubczyk client sued the doctor stating that she contracted pelvic inflammatory disease following an incomplete abortion. On June 7, 1991, Superior Court Judge Alan Kamin dismissed the case and chastised Jakubczyk, arguing that he did not believe that the lawyer "objectively thought the suit was well grounded in fact and warranted by existing laws. . . ." Although an Appeals Court reversed Kamin in 1992, stating that the possibility that Finkel had caused injury was enough to set Jakubczyk into action, not one of the cases against Finkel—or against the other providers whom Jakubczyk has sued—has been successful.[146]

"I take pride in my work," says Finkel, "but there are maloccurrences that happen. I've had them and have always taken care of them. There has never been any malpractice."[147]

Jakubczyk brought his most recent case against Finkel in 1997; once again, the attorney lost.

Meanwhile, the tactic of bringing malpractice lawsuits against providers has become popular throughout the United States and Canada. Although they are rarely found to have merit, such lawsuits are extremely costly, averaging $100,000 to defend; this puts a severe burden on clinics, many of which operate on a slim profit margin.

JULY 1: MARYLAND

The "Interference with Access to a Medical Facility" law went into effect in the state of Maryland. Promulgated at the behest of Planned Parenthood and Doctors for the Right to Choose, the legislation was the first of its kind in the United States. The law states that "a person may not act alone, or in concert with others, with the intent to prevent an individual from entering or exiting a medical facility by physically detaining, obstructing, impeding, or hindering the individual's passage." Earlier bans on blocking clinic doors applied only at the facilities named on court documents; this legislation applied to all health centers in the state and made violations punishable by a $1,000 fine, up to ninety days in jail, or both.[148]

JULY 17: PITTSBURGH, PENNSYLVANIA

The automobile lock-and-block, a technique in which an old, barely running car is used to obstruct clinic doors and serves as an anchor to which anti-abortion protestors lock or chain themselves, was developed by Houston activist Don Treshman, head of Rescue America, in 1987.[149] On June 17 protestors began gathering at the Allegheny Reproductive Health Center at 5:00 A.M. for their first lock-and-block at this site. The group parked in front of the clinic and four men and a seventeen-year-old boy chained, roped and taped themselves to the vehicle's underside.

The *Pittsburgh Press* reports that rescuers had to rely on a power saw to cut through the steel locks and bars, and firefighters had to use a pumper hose and water-soaked towels to protect the demonstrators from flying sparks. Adding to the tension, seventeen-year-old Earl Spencer from Buffalo, New York, taunted authorities with a lit cigarette that he threatened to drop into the gas tank of the car to which he was chained.[150]

Police charged the adults—Kevin Cleary, James Kopp and two others— with reckless endangerment, failure to disperse and conspiracy. They were also charged with contributing to the delinquency of a minor. The disposition of these charges is not known.

A total of forty-four additional people were arrested for simultaneously blocking clinic doors; they refused to give their names to authorities and were taken to the county jail. The day after their arrest, forty-two of the protestors were moved to an unoccupied wing of Mayview State Hospital, a psychiatric facility.[151] Twenty-two of them were released on June 21 after police and guards identified them from photos taken at earlier anti-abortion protests.[152] The remaining twenty identified themselves to prison authorities later in the month. County jail warden Charles Kozakiewicz told the *Pittsburgh Press* that he attributed the arrested protestors' capitulation to the fact that they were treated like other inmates. "It certainly wasn't the relaxed atmosphere" they had previously experienced, he said.[153]

Follow-up note: Years later, the FBI charged James Kopp with the 1998 murder of abortion provider Dr. Barnett Slepian, the 1994 sniper shooting of Dr. Garson Romalis and the 1995 wounding of Dr. Hugh Short, the latter two in Canada. He is currently a fugitive.

AUGUST 21: FT. WAYNE, INDIANA

"The 'rescues' in Ft. Wayne were better organized than anywhere else I saw them," says Susan Hill, National Women's Health Organization president. "There were more camouflage outfits than in other places and the leaders were all young, yuppie-looking white men equipped with walkie-talkies. It looked like a paramilitary thing, like war games. There were three major 'rescues' in Ft. Wayne in 1989 and 1990. Each time the troops, the advance teams, would come in from different directions and all of a sudden seven hundred people would be there, sitting down in front of the clinic. They were very well trained, very well rehearsed.

"In August 1989 I'd flown in to Ft. Wayne from New York. When I got to the hotel my message light was on. My assistant had called. When I reached her, she told me that my father had had a heart attack earlier in the evening and had died," Hill remembers. "It was midnight by this point and I did not know what to do. I called my mother and spoke to her and I called my sister, Nancy, who had cancer and was going through chemo. A few hours later—it was still the middle of the night—I went to the clinic. The administrator was already there. She told me that the security company had called to tell her that they were not sending anyone that day because they thought it would be too dangerous. I didn't tell the administrator about my dad but said that I would cover the front door and she should stay inside. I knew the police weren't going to do much. At 5:00 A.M. the advance people arrived at the clinic, chests out, looking like men in charge. As they pushed me against the door, I kept wondering what my father would want me to do. I decided he'd want me to finish what I'd started and not give in to OR or anyone else.

"This is what it was like for all of us during the 'rescue' years. In the middle of other things in our lives—deaths, illnesses, births and personal crises of all kinds—things that are hard enough to deal with by themselves, we had to face these people and contend with their pranks, disruptions and violence. Meanwhile, we were just trying to make it through the day. People forget that we were dealing with our own lives at the same time that we were dealing with the antis."[154]

AUGUST 29: FT. WAYNE, INDIANA

Activists trailed an abortion doctor for more than a hundred miles, from his Indianapolis home to his Ft. Wayne office. According to the *Post Gazette,* the unnamed physician called police from a Hardee's restaurant and had to wait for state troopers to escort him to his workplace.[155]

SEPTEMBER 8: PITTSBURGH, PENNSYLVANIA

Staff at the Allegheny Reproductive Health Center (ARHC) were elated by the prospect of moving out of the Highland Building. Since early 1988 when a second abortion clinic, the Allegheny Women's Center (AWC), had moved there, things had been unwieldy as anti-choice groups regularly swarmed the building, eager to flex their muscles at two targets at once.

"We had about a year left on our lease when the AWC moved in," says ARHC executive director Claire Keyes, "so we started to look for another space. There weren't many people who wanted to rent to us. It really looked like we would be forced out of business because we didn't have money to buy a building. Then someone told me about a landlord in the East Liberty neighborhood. He liked foot traffic, lots of people coming and going, and agreed to rent to us."[156]

Throughout the time spent searching for space and during the renovation period, AHRC and AWC were blockaded at least once a week by Operation Rescue and local spin-off groups. At first, says Keyes, law enforcement would stand and watch the demonstrations unfold. "The police were conflicted, as if this had to do with how they felt about abortion instead of being about the law being broken. The protestors were often related to the police. For those who were local, everyone knew someone. The police would let them blockade for a while and would eventually ask them to disperse. If they didn't leave after two warnings they started to remove them. But it took forever. Each load was ten or so people, some small number. At times, if there were six or eight hundred protestors, it would take six or seven hours for us to get our doors open. After a couple of Saturdays they started to use city buses to take the protestors for booking. They'd process them and let them go, figuring that would do it. The protestors would return tő the clinic later that same day. It took a while after that for the police to realize that this was costing the city a bundle. It was interesting because they went from being downright sympathetic to the protestors to cursing in disgust at the whole thing."[157]

While this was somewhat vindicating, by 1988 the strain of constant dealings with OR, coupled with overseeing complex renovations at a new space, had a discernibly negative impact on Keyes. "I couldn't sleep. I couldn't eat," she says. "I felt like everyone depended on me. I had to protect the doctors, the patients, the staff, and I didn't know how to do it."[158]

The turning point came in late 1988 after a meeting between Keyes, the chief of police, the local police commander and someone from the mayor's office. "I'd asked for the meeting because it had become clear to me that a coordinated effort had to occur. They needed to talk about this in terms of the protestors breaking the law, even if they were Catholic and didn't support abortion personally. The Pittsburgh Response Team came up with a plan to arrest people and started to impose fines in the hundreds as opposed to $30 or $50."[159]

Keyes found the meeting gratifying and felt that for the first time, she had true access to high-level city officials who were listening to her concerns. "Little by little," she says, "things started moving and I started to feel more in control."[160] That feeling evaporated when Keyes learned that the antis had discovered the clinic's new address and had entered the building to check out the layout. Still, the AHRC moved into the renovated building on August 31. Eight days later Keyes got a call in the middle of the night informing her that someone had noticed flames in the clinic entrance and had called the fire department. Although more than a decade has passed, Keyes still cries at the memory of that moment. "I came into the building at 4:00 o'clock in the morning," she says. "There wasn't anything I could do. I was stunned. There wasn't anyone I could call. The front door was gone. I went upstairs and there was soot everywhere. Luckily, there was a cinder block wall and a steel door in the entrance which saved us. Even though a Molotov cocktail had been thrown, the damage was contained to that one entryway. But there was all this grime, all this black soot. I sat on the front steps thinking that I would guard the building until I could call people, hoping that nobody would come and do anything to harm me. I felt helpless."[161]

While Keyes sat on the building stoop trying to figure out what to do first, the owner of the construction company that had done ARHC's renovations showed up at the site. "He'd heard about the bomb on the news," says Keyes, "and came and asked, 'What do you need me to do?' He told me who to call to do the cleanup. We closed for that day. The construction company took all its men off other jobs to do what needed to be done. We rented big industrial fans to eliminate the smoke smell, which we used for a week or ten days."[162]

Since the fire, holes have been torn in the clinic's roof with pickaxes, locks have been glued, BB shots have been fired into windows and bomb threats have been phoned in. Although the blockades stopped in 1989, a small group of picketers continue to hand gory literature to incoming patients.

The ARHC firebombing was eventually attributed to Marjorie Reed, already in jail for setting fire to the Center for Choice in Toledo, Ohio. She served no additional time for this attack.

FALL: TALLAHASSEE, FLORIDA

Governor Bob Martinez, a Republican, convened a special session of the Florida legislature to make the Sunshine State the first to outlaw abortion.

Patricia Baird-Windle: "All the big names came, Ellie Smeal, Kate Michelman of NARAL, and Ann Lewis of the Democratic National Committee on our side and hundreds of Concerned Women for America on the other. It was a mass hysteria carnival, but it amounted to nothing. Not a single anti-abortion bill passed. Pro-choice people from all over the state came to Tallahassee to lobby, demonstrate and march. Prior to the special session we had forty-seven bed sheets made into large petitions which we had people sign as a show of support for safe, legal abortion. We hung them in front of the governor's mansion. There were thousands of signatures.

"A week or two after the special session, Meredith Trotter Raney, Jr. showed up in Melbourne for the first time to protest at Aware Woman. Before this, all of our protestors had been volunteers. At first I did not understand that Raney and others were being paid. We found that out later, in depositions. What we knew was that the same faces were visible day in and day out and that they had no other apparent support. We heard that they were holding fund-raising events, getting money from involved churches, and constantly sending out money-begging newsletters. Instead of sending missionaries to Africa, some local churches were sending them to Aware Woman."[163]

FALL: TOLEDO, OHIO

Father Norman Weslin, a former Green Beret and one-time operations officer responsible for nuclear missile defenses[164]—and the founder of a militant anti-abortion group called the Lambs of Christ—brought his troops to Toledo, Ohio. "We knew he was coming and we spoke to the police beforehand," says Center for Choice II owner Carol Dunn. "Our police chief insisted he could do nothing until these folks struck. All I wanted was a couple of cops on horses stationed in front of the clinic. On the day the Lambs arrived, between fifty and seventy of them encircled the building and used bicycle locks, put around their necks, to link themselves together. No one could get in or out of the clinic. They descended around 1:00 P.M. The street cops wanted to do something but police management wanted to do nothing. They told us to close down for the rest of the day. They did, finally, make some arrests, but the protestors were quickly released from custody and were back at the clinic within an hour. Meanwhile, patients who had started the abortion process the day before and had laminaria inserted for dilation could not get inside. This could have been life threatening if we had not been able to use Toledo Medical Services, which is five miles away, to treat them."[165]

The Lambs of Christ returned to the clinic October 1990; this time staff and defenders succeeded in physically detaining the eight invaders, holding them until police arrived to make arrests. The center was not shut down and staff resumed operations once the protestors were removed.

SEPTEMBER 30: PITTSBURGH, PENNSYLVANIA

Clinic manager Sandie Matthews was the first staff member to arrive at Women's Health Services (WHS) and remembers opening the door and locking it behind her. As she sat down to eat her breakfast, she heard an odd noise but dismissed it because she knew she was alone. "Suddenly I heard running and looked out," Matthews says, "but I didn't comprehend what was going on. I then jumped up and saw people dressed in neutral-looking clothing standing outside our locked procedure rooms. I later learned that one of the receptionists, who was pregnant, had been thrown against a wall as she opened the door and six people had pushed inside and entered the clinic. They had obviously been here before because they knew where stuff was. And they had these buckets with them. Since I knew the Pittsburgh police were outside I ran and told them that some protestors had come inside. They told me to take it easy, that everything would be okay, and came upstairs with me."[166]

Matthews remembers feelings of abject terror as she reentered the facility, fearing the damage that might have been caused by leaving the abortion foes unattended, albeit briefly. As she looked around she noticed that the protestors were now standing in a straight line with their feet wedged into the buckets they had carried in. "I don't remember them saying a word," she says. "All of a sudden they threw themselves to the floor and tar from the buckets went everywhere, all over the floor and walls, on the cops, on furniture. They were laying in it and the police had to put them in garbage bins on wheels to remove them. We put cardboard down and continued to run the clinic that day; we did not let it stop us."[167]

Although Matthews has worked in the clinic since 1976 and has seen many anti-abortion protests, she says that this incident dramatically altered her views about American jurisprudence. "I was so naive before this happened," she says. "These people were in court, singing, calling us murderers. They swore on the Bible to tell the truth, but they lied and said the police had thrown them to the ground causing the tar to spill."[168] Matthews further explains that she and the clinic director were treated disrespectfully by the court, as if they were the cause, rather than the victims, of the vandalism they had witnessed.

While both staff people continued to decry what they saw as biased court proceedings, they were not the only ones adversely affected by the legal machinations. A memo to the judge written prior to the September 1990 sentencing of the six stated that:

> The full $28,000 cleanup and restoration was not completed until mid-December, 10 weeks after the incident. For over two months, patient services were provided in an ugly, dirty looking setting. . . . The impact on our employees was enormous. During the week following the tarring, some members of the staff who worked in the clinic on September 30th participated in a critical incident stress debriefing. This was followed by a series of weekly meetings which addressed the ongoing anxiety of the staff. These meetings continued until all the repairs were made. . . . The administrator in charge of the clinic on the day of the incident resigned simply because she no longer wanted to work in a place where tarring and court appearances were required of her position.[169]

The culprits in the tarring received sentences ranging from ninety days' probation to a year in jail.

OCTOBER: BLOOMINGTON, ILLINOIS

Methodist minister Walter Carlson, then pastor of a small church in Bloom-
ington, was on the board of a local Planned Parenthood affiliate in 1989, the
year the group marked its tenth anniversary. "I had been asked to speak at the
celebration and had agreed to," Carlson recalls. "I had my infant son in a pack
on my back and all the media were there. That night I was on TV and the next
day I was on the front page of the newspaper. It was my fifteen minutes of
fame."[170]

Unfortunately, Carlson's fame also brought notoriety, and beginning
the day after the event he was besieged with phone calls and letters. "How
could I say these things? Support these things? How could I call myself a
Christian? Some people called me a 'baby killer' and a few said things like,
'How about if I come over and kill your baby?' I got two letters and eight
or ten calls saying this over a one-week period. It scared the hell out of me.
Some people wrote to my bishop complaining about me and three or four
people left my congregation, which had an impact because it was a new
church. Meanwhile, I had not said anything out of keeping with the United
Methodist Church."[171]

In hindsight, Carlson now believes that the antis wanted nothing more than
to scare him into silence. Still, their tactics worked, at least for a while. "My wife
and I spent hours debating what to do. It was a hard decision, either to become
quiet on the issues or to continue to speak out," he says.[172] Carlson ultimately
chose to remain on the Planned Parenthood board but to refrain from making
further public appearances.

His reticence lasted four years. In 1993 Carlson moved to Springfield,
Illinois, where he became instrumental in establishing a clergy committee in
support of that city's Planned Parenthood. "As time has gone on I've
reclaimed some of my righteous indignation over the Christian Right's claims
to moral ground that are not theirs to claim. I speak out now. I don't preach
about this stuff since I don't think that's what a worship service is about. But
I am clear with people that I work with Planned Parenthood. I am one of
about a dozen clergy in Springfield who do problem pregnancy counseling.
It's important to show that the anti-choice folks are not the total religious
voice on reproductive issues. Knowing that prayerful people can be, and are,
pro-choice gives people the fortitude to make extraordinarily difficult choices.
When religious folks take a pro-choice position it takes some power away
from the antis," he adds.[173]

OCTOBER 5: ATLANTA, GEORGIA

Randall Terry began serving two concurrent one-year sentences for violating an injunction against trespassing during the 1988 Democratic Convention. In delivering the sentence, the judge offered Terry a choice: pay a fine or be incarcerated. The OR leader responded by delivering a passionate speech about refusing to pay money to a system that "slaughters" children. Several months later, however, he apparently had a change of heart. On January 31, 1990—after four and a half months behind bars—Terry was released. An unnamed benefactor had evidently paid his fine.[174]

OCTOBER 24: BURLINGTON, VERMONT

Fifty-four anti-abortion protestors invaded the Vermont Women's Health Center and locked themselves together before attempting to "rescue" a woman in an exam room. "There was only one patient in the center at the time and she was there for a colposcopy to test for cervical cancer," says clinic director Rachel Atkins. "They ran into the building screaming that we had blood on our hands and dressed in clothes bought with blood money. The patient they stormed in to 'save' lived an hour away, had borrowed a car and had gotten day care so she could come in. She was furious and would not be 'rescued.' She told them to leave the clinic."[175]

Fifty-one protestors were arrested for trespassing and three were charged with assault for trying to keep police from entering the health center. Nearly all refused to give their names to a District Court judge and were sentenced to three months in jail.[176]

NOVEMBER: NATIONWIDE

Patricia Baird-Windle: "When the Supreme Court issued the *Webster* decision in July 1989, providers thought that it would have a greater impact than it later proved to have. We were scared. Then, at the special legislative session in Tallahassee in the early autumn, we'd seen so much ignorance on the part of lawmakers. At this point two providers from Texas and Utah said, 'We've got to get the abortion leadership in this country together to make plans about how to respond since we are not getting what we need from the Beltway organizations.' Thirty-two providers went to the first meeting of what became known as the November Gang. We represented clinics from all over the country. We spoke about how our agendas were not being met and came up with strategies for dealing with the assaults against us: what to do about the federal courts; how to boost morale; how to better support one another; how to create rituals for grief and improve pre- and post-abortion counseling; how to build better state organizations and networks. That weekend we decided to meet as often as we needed to. We also decided that we'd spend the first day of each weekend attending to our emotional needs and the second strategizing. By the third meeting we found that the logistics were such that if we had more than thirty people it was hard to talk, so we never opened the group up to a more general membership. A few people over the years have called the gang elitist, but it was sized to boost people up and break through some of the isolation we feel. Since 1989 there have been at least twenty-five meetings.

"After the third November Gang meeting, Susan Hill of the National Women's Health Organization called her colleagues, staff and other friends together. This meeting led to the founding of the National Coalition of Abortion Providers (NCAP). It was one of those meant-to-be events. The National Abortion Federation had chosen the medical education model and does a superb job of that and of teaching us to do medical risk management. But there are other things that we need, including specific lobbying that takes into account the routine day-to-day realities at clinics. Ron Fitzsimmons, the man hired to direct NCAP, is an experienced lobbyist. His mandate has been to go to into the field and get a firsthand understanding of the horror of unresponsive police forces, harassment and sabotage. He has seen the selective enforcement of the law and the constant little stuff that is done to us."[177]

NOVEMBER: SAN DIEGO, CALIFORNIA

Bishop Leo Maher of San Diego informed sixty-seven-year-old Lucy Killea, a pro-choice Catholic candidate for the California State Assembly, that she could no longer receive the sacrament of communion—unless she reversed her position on abortion. Killea, considered an underdog until Maher propelled her onto page 1, won the race and credited Maher for her victory.[178]

CHAPTER SIX

From Mayhem to Murder: 1990–1995

George Bush's 1988 White House win may have cheered religious and secular conservatives, but after eight years of Ronald Reagan they were no longer cocky about assuming that a broad-scale social revolution would follow an electoral victory. Indeed, some Christian right-wingers were still smarting over the defeat of their favored candidate, the Reverend Pat Robertson.

In fact, the collapse of the Moral Majority, coupled with Robertson's failed bid for the presidency, left many wondering what to do next. For his part, Robertson took encouragement from Billy McCormack, a Shreveport, Louisiana, preacher who had backed former Ku Klux Klansman David Duke's congressional campaign. At McCormack's suggestion, Robertson formed the Christian Coalition in 1989. He vowed to do things differently than his predecessors and pledged to succeed where others had failed.[1]

"The Christian community got it backwards in the 1980s," said Ralph Reed, the coalition's first executive director. "We tried to change Washington when we should have been focusing on the states. The real battles of concern to Christians are in neighborhoods, school boards, City Councils, and state legislatures."[2]

The coalition tested its mettle in San Diego County's 1990 elections, running ninety candidates for local office. Surprisingly, two-thirds—sixty of the ninety—won races in which virtually no work was done outside the already-organized conservative, religious community. Utilizing a phone bank created by merging the membership lists of one hundred like-minded churches, the candidates called voters and identified themselves as "pro-family" contenders. Then, on the Sunday before Election Day, they blanketed church parking lots with leaflets and voting guides. The effort was so successful that the strategy became known as "the San Diego model."[3]

Three years after its founding, the Christian Coalition had 440 chapters (in every state but Utah) and a national budget of $12 million. And they were not the only conservative Christian group to nettle American politics. Randall Terry's Operation Rescue was still disrupting abortion clinics, and while police and lawmakers throughout the country were getting fed up with them, OR continued to block doors and torment clinic patients and staff—often for weeks or months at a time—during the first years of the decade. In addition, Clarence Thomas, an avowed Christian right-winger, was confirmed as a Supreme Court Justice despite allegations that he had sexually harassed lawyer, now law professor, Anita Hill.

Another group, called Reconstructionists—Christians who hope to reconstruct America in accordance with biblical law—were also becoming a force in national affairs. Based on the theories of Rousas John Rushdoony, a former Presbyterian minister, by the 1990s Reconstructionists were pushing their way into mainstream politics. Their agenda? God's law, as revealed in the Bible, should govern every area of life. Toward that end, local governments, and not the feds, should rule; the death penalty should be imposed for abortion, adultery and unrepentant homosexuality; schools should be run by churches; property taxes should be eliminated; and women and children should be subservient to men.[4]

Lest one think these views too absurd to attract serious notice, representatives of the California Republican Assembly, a Reconstructionist group that bills itself as the "conservative conscience" of the state GOP, have for most of the decade held top spots in the California Republican Party. Likewise, the Allied Business PAC, a political action committee founded by Reconstructionist banker Howard Ahmanson, contributed $5 million to California races in 1993 and 1994. Twenty-eight Allied-backed candidates entered the statehouse in 1992; twenty-four were elected in 1994.[5]

Meanwhile, the popular press ushered in the decade by touting the demise of greed and glitz. Feminists were elated by the 1991 emergence of raucous women-led bands inspired by the Riot Grrrl movement—especially since bland pop seemed to be the order of the day. In mainstream communities Ace of Base, Michael Bolton and Hootie and the Blowfish were making listening easy.

The abortion battlefield reflected society's polarities. While OR and the Lambs of Christ continued to block clinic doors, and the National Right to Life Committee continued to lobby for abortion restrictions, other activists were looking for a more permanent solution to what they saw as the sin of "baby killing." Michael Bray, pastor of the Reformation Lutheran Church in Bowie, Maryland, and a convicted clinic firebomber, was one of many who argued that outright violence was the best means to end legal abortion.

In *A Time to Kill,* a 1994 treatise on "justifiable homicide" against abortion doctors, Bray expressed his viewpoint. "What if the first 10 aborturies built had been set ablaze? What if, after the first abortionist was shot, the pastors of God's churches had sent out news releases saying, 'Amen'? What if Christians individually had simply recognized that a defense was being raised similar to what they would want for their own children?"[6]

Bray's philosophical justification of violence dovetailed with the previously published *Army of God Manual,* a tactical how-to guide that was discovered by law enforcement and the women's health community in 1993. A virtual celebration of arson, chemical attacks, invasions and bombing, the manual offers chilling, practical instructions on bomb making, purchasing and using butyric acid and many forms of general sabotage.

Alongside an array of anti-abortion films and videos, pro-choice activists quickly grasped that these books heralded the arrival of a highly volatile wing of the anti-abortion movement, a movement they feared would physically assault clinic staff. Although the BATF, the FBI and the Department of Justice largely ignored their concerns, by the time the *Army of God Manual* was discovered, one doctor had been killed and several people had been shot.

Murdered? Wounded?

Despite clear warnings that these tactics were in the offing, shock waves rocked the pro-choice community when, on March 10, 1993, Dr. David Gunn was assassinated—shot in the back—as he entered Pensacola Medical Services, a northwest Florida clinic. Within the next twenty months, four others—James Barrett, Dr. John Bayard Britton, Shannon Lowney and Leanne Nichols—would also be killed by anti-abortion fanatics. (Dr. George Wayne Patterson, owner of Pensacola Medical Services, was murdered in August 1994. Although his former colleagues remain skeptical, police blame his death on a bungled robbery and not anti-abortion violence. The pro-choice community continues to point out that Patterson's wallet, cellular phone and Cadillac were untouched by the "robbers.")

More than half a dozen others in the United States and Canada would be wounded and "hit lists" of medical workers slated for death would be compiled by anti-abortion zealots.

Twenty years after *Roe*—in 1993—the country found itself face to face with the worst anti-abortion turmoil it had ever seen. The federal government responded by passing the Freedom of Access to Clinic Entrances (FACE) Act; President Clinton signed it into law in May 1994. FACE allows both the Department of Justice and clinic staff to sue anti-abortion protestors and imposes hefty fines on those convicted of violating its prohibitions.

While most clinics saw FACE as too little, too late, they were nonetheless heartened to see some federal initiative in support of *Roe*. But concern still nagged. Frightened medical workers had to look into their hearts and weigh the risks: as murder became a real possibility, staff had to decide if theirs was a job worth dying for. An amazing number have continued to answer in the affirmative.

1990

NATIONWIDE

Operation Rescue founder Randall Terry's book, *Accessory to Murder: The Enemies, Allies, and Accomplices to the Death of Our Culture,* was published by Wolgemuth and Hyatt Publishers, Inc., of Brentwood, Tennessee. The text lays out Terry's thinking, not just about abortion, but about American democracy, diversity, gender roles, God and secular rule. Some excerpts follow.

> Pornography is legalized—we back up. Prayer and the Bible are made illegal in public schools—we don't fight. Killing children, once a felony, becomes a "fundamental constitutional right"—we stand by and watch the blood flow. Witchcraft and human sacrifice are growing at an alarming rate—we don't believe or simply ignore it. Homosexuals use our money to pollute public museums with filth—we don't fight. My God, what's wrong with us? We don't get angry. We keep backing up. Before long there won't be any place to go.[7]

> The Supreme Court, more than any other legal body, has contributed to the moral cancer and anarchy ravaging our nation. The greatest crimes against humanity committed by these tyrants were *Roe v. Wade* and other subsequent pro-death rulings which legalized child-killing up until the day of birth.[8]

> I don't want conservative judges. I want judges that fear God and believe that what God gave Moses at Mt. Sinai is the bedrock of our society. Most judges have abandoned the Bible as the foundation of law and justice and have little fear of God in their rulings. . . . Like the judge of the importunate widow (Luke 18) they fear neither God nor men.[9]

> We've let the anti-child, career-first, bigger houses rather than bigger families attitude creep into our churches and our families. Christian homes have two

working parents when only one is necessary. We deliberately limit the size of our families, viewing children as intrusions and burdens rather than as the most precious gift on earth short of salvation. We cite the justifications of money, time and work—all the reasons the feminists have. We need to repent of the anti-child attitude in our churches and in our homes and again adopt the Biblical view of children: "Blessed is the man [*sic*] whose quiver is full of them." (Psalm 127:5).[10]

WASHINGTON, D.C.

The Supreme Court ruled that the state of Minnesota *(Hodgson v. Minnesota)* could not require minors to notify two parents before having an abortion unless there were procedures in place enabling them to go to court when it was either impossible, or ill advised, to consult both caregivers. In a second 1990 case, *Ohio v. Akron Center for Reproductive Health,* the Court upheld an Ohio statute that required a minor to notify one parent or obtain a judicial waiver.[11]

WINTER: MELBOURNE, FLORIDA

Patricia Baird-Windle: "In the winter of 1990 Meredith Raney Jr. filed the first of many baseless complaints against Aware Woman. The complaint said that our West Palm Beach clinic was using unlicensed doctors. He has since filed a raft of complaints against all three Aware Woman facilities with the Board of Medical Examiners, the Department of Professional Regulation, the Agency for Health Care Administration and Health and Human Services. He rotates his objections through these agencies, and it takes up to one hundred hours to handle each one. By the sixth or seventh complaint we realized that by filing against us he could find out which doctors were working at which clinics on which days. Once he learned a doctor's identity, either through the filing of meritless complaints or by other invasive and intrusive means, the harassment began in earnest. A 'wanted' poster on Dr. Frank Snydle was given to every nurse at the hospital he worked for. A doctor and his patients were trapped inside a clinic by blockaders. Wives, girlfriends and parents were telephoned and threatened. Imagine it. One tactic isn't all that bad. Two aren't too bad to handle. But fifteen to eighteen a week, every week, is incredibly awful.

"By the time I'd lost the twenty-fourth doctor in seven years, 1989 to 1996, I had hysterics for two days. It averages a hundred hours of staff time to find a replacement physician, and when someone quits the overwork and dread we feel are cosmic. This doctor had only worked for us for four weeks but when the antis threatened her children, who were eight and twelve, she decided the job wasn't worth it. They told her that she needed to be careful, that they knew her kids were in the house alone in the afternoons before she got home from work. Her replacement came from the Midwest, and we had to pay to fly him in and for his lodging and car while he was in Florida. As soon as Dr. Evans (a pseudonym) started, the antis posted his picture on the Internet and created a 'wanted' poster of him which they placed throughout his condo complex in his home state. The first Internet reference insinuated that he was homosexual. They also called his elderly parents and told them that their son was 'a fag abortionist.' First Dr. Evans got really afraid. Then he got stubborn. He is still working for several Florida clinics."[12]

JANUARY 6: KANAWHA CITY, WEST VIRGINIA

Nine out-of-state anti-abortion protestors barged into the Charleston Women's Health Center at 7:00 A.M. and threaded chains through car tires and linked themselves together, chanted quietly and sprinkled "holy" water on each other. They also spoke to the waiting women about their beliefs on abortion.[13] The nine were charged with trespassing and resisting arrest and were held in Kanawha County Jail on $500 bond.

At a bond hearing several days later, Magistrate Ward Harshbarger emphasized that he would not tolerate illegal protest at the clinics. "If you want to remain in Kanawha County and protest, that is your right. Going inside buildings, chaining yourselves together, putting inner tubes over your heads, and disrupting business is not your right. You have cost our county a good bit of money. We are a poor state. . . . You are wasting our money and you are not even from here. This irritates the death out of me."[14] The protestors remained in jail for a week and were released on bond. Although they were later found guilty of trespassing and could have faced a year in jail and a $500 fine, they were required to pay only $50.

FEBRUARY 2: KANAWHA CITY, WEST VIRGINIA

The Charleston Women's Health Center won an injunction limiting the number of picketers at the center to four. The injunction also bars abortion opponents from trespassing on clinic property, threatening or intimidating staff or patients, making false appointments or harassing telephone calls, occupying the building, or blocking parking areas. A ten-foot "safe zone" between protestors and people entering or leaving the center was also imposed. Margi

Hale, the director of the clinic in 1990, said in an affidavit that the injunction was necessary because police refused to make arrests without one.[15]

MARCH: NATIONWIDE

The Reverend Keith Tucci took over as head of Operation Rescue, replacing Randall Terry. The fourth child of Marie Miller, Tucci had been involved in gangs, and was a marginal student and drug and alcohol abuser before his religious conversion in the late 1970s. After completing bible college in 1979, he became assistant pastor at an Assembly of God Church in Trafford, Pennsylvania. In 1987 he purchased an abandoned junior high school in his hometown of Pittsburgh and founded the Pittsburgh Word and Worship Fellowship. Under Tucci's aegis, the church set up crisis pregnancy and prison outreach programs; he also attended his first "rescue"—and was immediately hooked.[16]

"My mother was supposed to abort me," Tucci told the *Minneapolis Star Tribune* to explain his involvement in the anti-abortion movement. Physicians had recommended therapeutic abortion to Miller because of severe medical complications. In addition, several severe beatings by Tucci's father had sent Miller to the hospital, and doctors feared that she would be unsuccessful in carrying the pregnancy to term.[17] Tucci later told reporter Brian Bonner that he was "pro-life" because he "never had a childhood and wanted to give other people that opportunity."[18]

Follow-up note: Tucci masterminded the 1991 Summer of Mercy in Wichita, Kansas, and led protests at the 1992 Republican National Convention in Houston, Texas. Under his leadership, OR-National moved its headquarters to Melbourne, Florida in late 1992; this allowed the group to be at the center of events orchestrated against the three clinics owned by the Windle family. Tucci left OR in 1994 and was replaced by the Reverend Philip "Flip" Benham of Garland, Texas.

APRIL: NATIONWIDE

The Committee for Pro-life Activities of the National Conference of Catholic Bishops hired the prestigious public relations firm of Hill & Knowlton to handle their anti-abortion campaigns. The $5 million, five-year consulting relationship was paid for by the Knights of Columbus. Once the expenditure was publicized, public outcry over both the sum being spent and the fact that the church felt it needed a PR firm to make its message palatable so embarrassed the hierarchy that the arrangement was canceled in 1992. Church leaders attempted to save face by claiming that the ad giant had taught them to handle their anti-abortion efforts themselves.[19]

APRIL 28: PORTLAND, OREGON

All Women's Health Services received a handwritten but unsigned letter postmarked in Las Vegas: "Whores, lesbians, homosexuals, Jews, pornographers, abortionists, NOW members, Planned Parenthood members will burn forever in the fires of Hell. God is man. Man is God. God made woman for man. God made woman to have babies. God made woman unclean. God made woman to serve man. Woman must obey man."[20]

MAY 10: BURLINGTON, VERMONT

Only ten percent of the patients who go to the Vermont Women's Health Center (VWHC) in Burlington want to terminate unwanted pregnancies, but that has not stopped anti-abortion protestors from assailing the facility. Between 1988 and 1991, invasions, blockades and lock-and-blocks occurred with tremendous frequency not just at the VWHC, but throughout the state.

"They picked Vermont because we had a pro-choice, feminist governor, because it is a small state, and because they thought they could cripple the state budget by getting arrested repeatedly," says Rachel Atkins, executive director of the VWHC.[21]

Members of Operation Rescue, the Lambs of Christ, and a local group called Vermont Save a Baby were frequently present at each of the state's clinics. "From the start," says Atkins, "the police were clear that their role was to uphold the law. They brought neither politics nor religion into it."[22] This posture was underscored when, on May 10, 1990, three protestors, one of whom was James Kopp, a man later charged with the 1998 murder of Dr. Barnett Slepian, locked themselves together in front of VWHC. According to Atkins, "the police came, picked them up and carried them across the street to the lawn of the diocesan offices. Twenty hours later they were still sitting there. They never expected to have to get themselves out of the locked device. They expected the police to pry them apart, not leave them chained together. It started to rain on the eleventh so they finally unlocked themselves and left."[23]

MAY 26: KANAWHA CITY, WEST VIRGINIA

For the second time in six months, a small group of anti-abortion protestors invaded a West Virginia abortion facility; this time they used duct tape, leg irons and chains to bind themselves together. Eight police officers and two firefighters equipped with Jaws of Life equipment worked for more than an hour to extricate the demonstrators from Ob-Gyn Associates. The protestors were charged with trespassing and were convicted in November.

Local press denounced the invasion. "Thoreau, Gandhi, and King risked jail in order to expand people's rights—but the abortion protestors are trying to take away the right of women to choose their own future," said a June editorial in the *Charleston Gazette*. "A 14-year-old girl impregnated by her father, a woman impregnated by a rapist, a poor woman unable to feed her too-large brood—all these would be forced into unwanted motherhood if the clinic invaders had their way. The protestors care more about fertilized eggs than about 14-year-old girls and adult women."[24]

MEMORIAL DAY: PITTSBURGH, PENNSYLVANIA

Claire Keyes, executive director of the Allegheny Reproductive Health Center, was at home when she got a call from the clinic's cleaning service informing her that there was a problem at the center that she needed to attend to. "The cleanup guy thought that pipes in the ceiling had broken but that's not what happened," says Keyes. "The call came on the Sunday of a three-day weekend. It had rained Friday night, all day Saturday, Saturday night and Sunday. When he called, it was still raining. Water was pouring in and the clinic was completely flooded. It caused more damage than the [September 1989] fire. It turns out forty-four holes were chopped in the roof with pickaxes. We called in the same company we'd used after the fire and they brought fans in to remove the water. We salvaged what we could. The plasterboard walls got soaked and were ruined. Some equipment was destroyed and some ceiling tiles had to be replaced."[25]

But that was the least of it. Keyes's feelings of vulnerability—she had been through a fire, a lock-and-block, and countless "rescues" over the previous two and a half years—left her feeling bereft, miserable. "I felt awful; I was stunned. I had the same feeling of helplessness I'd had after the firebombing," she says. "I couldn't stop it from happening. I felt so alone."[26]

Keyes eventually rose to the challenge. Within a few weeks both she and the health center were functioning at full capacity. They got the roof patched since they could not afford to replace it, and the landlord put barbed wire around the perimeter of the building top to deter access.

"No one was investigated for doing this," says Keyes. What's more, "these things never occur as single, isolated events. Similar sabotage occurred in other parts of the country at the same time," but law enforcement did little to investigate or determine if a conspiracy existed.[27]

Another pattern also revealed itself. Keyes's insurance carrier paid for needed repairs following the water damage and then canceled the clinic's policy. Like other clinics across the country, Allegheny Reproductive Health Center eventually secured coverage through another insurer, but premiums were significantly higher than they had been before the flood.

JUNE: CORPUS CHRISTI, TEXAS

Rachel Vargas, the director of one of two Corpus Christi, Texas, abortion clinics, was issued a formal decree "separating her from the sacraments of the [Catholic] church, including communion, holy matrimony, and last rites." The decree was signed by Bishop Rene Gracida.[28] Gracida had previously sent Vargas, an eight-year employee of Reproductive Services, Inc., two letters warning her that failure to resign from the clinic would result in her excommunication under Canon 1398 of the Code of Canon Law. The letters called her work "a sin against God and humanity and against the law of the Roman Catholic church" and listed seven offenses that result in automatic excommunication, among them participating in an abortion, attacking the Pope, desecrating the Holy Eucharist and defiant heresy.[29]

By the time Gracida chose to chastise Vargas, his right-wing reputation was already well honed. Within days of his action against Vargas, the *Austin American-Statesman* lambasted him as "notorious within Catholic circles for his conservative and often provocative ways."[30] Furthermore, he was no novice at anti-abortion politics. Gracida had earlier—quietly—excommunicated Dr. Eduardo Acquino, an obstetrician who performed between sixty and seventy-five abortions a month at the New Women's Clinic in Corpus Christi,[31] and had given his support to the vibrant anti-abortion movement then sweeping southern Texas.

The largely Catholic city of Corpus Christi had long been an anti-abortion stronghold. Activists operated on several simultaneous levels. Some attempted to amend the city charter to include a Human Life Amendment, an overt effort to legislate their belief that life begins at the moment of conception into local law. Others, part of a militant group called The Body of Christi, organized "rescues:" twenty-one between November 1989 and August 1990 alone. In addition, law enforcement support for the "rescuers" was blatant, most notably from Nueces County sheriff James T. Hickey. Hickey had attracted the ire of the pro-choice community in early 1990 when he told press that he would not arrest anti-abortion protestors, even if they broke the law, because, "if I were to help by either moving or arresting the rescue workers, then I would be assisting the men [*sic*] who are killing babies."[32] Several months later, in August 1990, Hickey formed Officers for Life, the first such group in the country.

Follow-up note: For all their efforts, anti-abortion activists and the Catholic hierarchy were largely unsuccessful in stopping women from having abortions in Corpus Christi. At the time of Vargas's excommunication, Reproductive Services was performing approximately 2,000 surgeries a year, forty percent of them on women who self-identified as Roman Catholic.

JUNE 17: ST. PETERSBURG, FLORIDA

Susannah Davis (not her real name) still gets panicky when she thinks about the Operation Rescue blockade of the All Women's Health Center in St. Petersburg. "The antis chained themselves to the door, apparently not knowing I was in there. At the time there hadn't been any killings, but I thought to myself, 'These people could justify it. They could kill a person and say it was to save babies for a day.' I'd been inside since 6:00 A.M. I finally got out at 11:00, when the police got a key to the kryptonite locks they were using; they took me out through a back door. It was a very long time to be locked inside," she says.[33]

The clinic was destroyed by arson on August 21, 1995. On November 3, as reconstruction was near completion, a vandal threw a flammable substance onto the building's roof. It did not fully ignite and caused minimal damage. Nonetheless, says Davis, following that blaze, the clinic's owners decided to install a fireproof tile roof to deter potential arsonists and the clinic reopened several months later. Two staff members resigned after the second fire.[34]

JULY 2: CORPUS CHRISTI, TEXAS

Bishop Rene Gracida sent Elva Bustamante, the director of the New Women's Clinic in Corpus Christi, the workplace of Dr. Eduardo Acquino, her first warning letter. The letter, like those sent to Rachel Vargas earlier that year, threatened her with excommunication if she did not leave her job. At the time she received the letter, Bustamante had worked at the clinic for twelve years.

Although Bustamante was fully committed to her work, she took the letter seriously and decided to respond, in writing, and explain her position on both abortion and women's moral agency to the bishop. She posted her response on July 17. "I rely on the Catholic tradition of probabilism which holds, where there is doubt, there is freedom," she wrote. "I believe that each woman who is pregnant must be free to evaluate her own church's teachings on human life, her own view of the issue in light of science and theology, and her own life's circumstances. It is not for me to do this for her, nor is it for me to judge her actions. I genuinely do not believe I am guilty of any sin in the work I do. As brothers and sisters in Christ, we must learn to settle our differences through dialogue, not exclusion."[35]

That dialogue did not happen. On November 8, 1990 Elva Bustamante became the third person in Corpus Christi—and one of only a handful in the nation—to be excommunicated for her pro-choice views.[36]

AUGUST 4: PORTLAND, OREGON

Sarah Walker (pseudonym), a patient at All Women's Medical Services, submitted the following statement in an affidavit about her experience at the health center.

> The lady outside said that I was killing God's child and that the clinic only does abortions for the money and they sell the baby's parts to make cosmetics. She said that last week a girl got hauled out of here in an ambulance and that this is a very dangerous procedure. She also told me that the people here don't care about the patients. I know she is only expressing her opinion, but I feel she was wrong for trying to make me feel worse than I already did about needing an abortion.[37]

SEPTEMBER: MILWAUKEE, WISCONSIN

Matt Trewhella, an avid supporter of citizen militias and former Detroit gang member, founded Missionaries to the Pre-Born. He told supporters that the idea for the group came from the realization that "although Christianity affirms the humanity of the pre-born child and affirms that abortion is murder, not one of the over four hundred Christian missions operating in America has targeted the pre-born child as its people group." Trewhella announced that he intended to right this oversight by establishing Missionaries to the Pre-Born as the first Christian mission in America "dedicated to the ministry of our pre-born neighbor."[38]

To date, the Missionaries have done fund raising to benefit the families of Rachelle "Shelley" Shannon, the Oregon housewife who shot Dr. George Tiller in 1993; John Brockhoeft, a convicted firebomber who torched an Ohio Planned Parenthood in 1985; and Michael Griffin, the man responsible for assassinating Dr. David Gunn in March 1993.

SEPTEMBER 28: NEW YORK STATE

Denis Dillon, District Attorney for Nassau County, called on police unions to adopt a conscience clause that would allow officers to refuse to arrest people blocking access to clinics. He got virtually no support for the proposal. "I don't think a police officer should let religious views enter into his [*sic*] decision to enforce the law," said Suffolk County Police Benevolent Association president Michael Mahoney. "If the law says abortion is legal, we're not judge and jury. We're sworn to enforce the law and that's what we should be doing."[39]

OCTOBER 15: PITTSBURGH, PENNSYLVANIA

When Patty Madden, medical records supervisor at Women's Health Services, returned from lunch, her coworkers were screaming that something awful was happening. As she made her way to the medical records room, she saw that a liquid was pouring through the ceiling. "I was trying to grab files and put them under the desk and was also trying to cover equipment and stuff with plastic," she says. "The smell was atrocious and right away I noticed that my eyes were itching and burning. I washed them out but they kept hurting. I later went to the emergency room. At that point I had no idea what had gotten into my eyes. The hospital flushed them out and released me. For six months after this I had to go to Surgicare to have cysts removed from both eyelids. I never had cysts before, and I haven't had them since, but I got them three times and had to have them removed three times following this incident."[40]

Other staff members suffered serious respiratory problems following their exposure to what they eventually learned was undiluted fish oil. According to clinic director Mary Ellen Tunney, who was not on staff at the time this happened, "the floor above the clinic was vacant and someone got into the space and drilled holes in the ceiling. They then poured fish oil into the holes and turned on fire hoses to flush the oil through. It took staff forever to figure out what the antis had used so that they could find a deodorizer to combat the effects of it. The smell was horrific."[41]

But even with the help of chemical neutralizers, says Madden, the foul odor lingered. "It stayed in medical records the longest because we housed all the files there and the oil was absorbed in the paper. We couldn't throw anything out," she says.[42]

No one was ever caught for this act of vandalism. Worse, the cleanup cost the clinic nearly $12,000, most of which was paid out of pocket. Although insurance covered some of the damage, Women's Health Services' claim for repairs to the fourth floor, which their landlord required as a condition of continued occupancy, was rejected because the space was not clinic property.

DECEMBER 28: NATIONWIDE

The Reverend Keith Tucci sent the following appeal to OR's faithful on letterhead bearing the following exhortation: "If you believe abortion is murder, ACT like it's murder!"

The salutation read "Dear Soldier," and the letter was clearly intended to encourage the weary to keep up the fight:

> We are soldiers, not spectators! We cannot ignore that the battle is raging just because we receive oppression from the pro-death industry, its propaganda mill and the authorities who have sold out to them. . . . The sole reason we are a mobilized army is because of the willingness of people like you to sacrifice in the time of need. Please keep helping. We are presently in need of seed finances to keep going forward. The enemies of God have never understood the value of one committed soldier. Some of you have been on leave. I ask you, in the name of Jesus, to return to camp. Return to the training so that God may use you.[43]

1991

WASHINGTON, D.C.

By a vote of 5 to 4, the Supreme Court upheld federal regulations that prohibited healthcare workers at family planning clinics receiving Title X funds from counseling women about abortion or referring them to options counseling. The so-called gag rule also bars clinic staff from informing patients that abortion is a legal choice.[44]

JANUARY: EL PASO, TEXAS

Almost every weekend between 1989 and 1991, between 150 and two hundred protestors—thirty or forty of them children ages two to fifteen—would show up to block the doors of Reproductive Services. Sabotage, including glued locks and the sprinkling of "holy salt" around the building periphery, was also routine.

"The police were not helpful at first," says Gerri Laster, executive administrator of the clinic. "[A high ranking officer] on the force was anti-choice, and he said he would do anything in his power to close abortion facilities. We organized a campaign against him. Once a month in El Paso there are community meetings. We made sure that the police response to the protestors was on each community's agenda and pointed out that the police could have disbanded the crowds since the protestors never had permits. Instead, they'd watch for hours before doing anything. This was costing taxpayers between $5,000 and $6,000 an episode. This cop eventually retired and since then it's been better."[45]

By January 1991, however, the clinic had developed another tactic to reduce disruptions. "Butch Cappell, our security person at the clinic during business hours, started bringing his trained guard dogs—pit bulls and rottweilers—to the clinic," says Laster. "Bruce would suit up in padded gear on weekends and would go outside and let the dogs attack him to show the protestors what these animals could do. He showed them that the dogs knew to hit the fence if someone were to attach to it. Having the dogs roam around inside the fenced area around the clinic had the desired effect. And it was legal; as long as the dogs were inside our property line, it was perfectly allowable to have them. We now use a German shepherd during the day, and another is here from Friday night until Monday morning."[46]

FEBRUARY 19: PORTLAND, OREGON

Lovejoy SurgiCenter obtained an injunction against Advocates for Life Inc., Operation Rescue and thirty-four individuals including Andrew Burnett, Paul C. DeParrie and Rachelle "Shelley" Shannon. The injunction bars individuals, groups of people, and organizations from:

> obstructing the free and direct passage of any person in or out of the SurgiCenter; threatening, intimidating, coercing or harassing persons entering or leaving the SurgiCenter; demonstrating or distributing literature within the "keep clear" area; shouting, screaming, chanting, yelling or producing noise by any other means, at a volume that substantially interferes with the operation of the SurgiCenter, including the provision of medical services and counseling; trespassing on any private property of the SurgiCenter including the Surgi-Center's parking lot; and damaging property of the SurgiCenter, its employees or its patients.[47]

A jury further awarded the center $8.2 million in punitive damages for property destruction, lost business and the harassment and abuse of staff. "We got a few garnishments of income," says Lovejoy owner Allene Klass. "We were hoping to get them to pay more, but the problem is that they have no money. The bottom line is that the lawsuits were brought to be a deterrent, and they have been. For the first time, people were slapped with huge judgments for their behavior. This means their chances of ever buying a house, a car or getting a credit card are shot. They're gone forever. This is not a judgment that goes away."[48]

SPRING: ASHEVILLE, NORTH CAROLINA

Deborah Walsh, at that time still based in Knoxville, was by 1990 the administrator of a chain of southern clinics owned by the Harris family. She was at the company's Birmingham site when she received a call informing her that twenty-seven people had locked themselves together and invaded the surgery section of the Western Carolina Medical Clinic in Asheville, North Carolina, another Harris health center. Staff and patients—including a woman who had been raped—were unable to get inside the barricaded area.

Upon hearing this news, Walsh called the Asheville SWAT team and was told that police would break down the door and get the protestors out as quickly and safely as possible. But when Walsh called the officer an hour later to check on progress, she was told by Chief Gerald Beaver that plans had changed. "He told me that they didn't want to hurt any of the people locked inside," says Walsh. "I said, 'Why don't you tell them to unlock themselves and get out?' He said that the police were trying to find keys to the locks because the only kind of drill that would do the job was a Dremel drill and it would take until the next day to get these drills from Atlanta. I decided to call Ron Fitzsimmons at the National Coalition of Abortion Providers [NCAP] to see if he had any advice. Ron told me that Asheville got $1 million in Community Development Block Grant [CDBG] money, and failure to enforce trespass laws could result in the government withholding these funds. He said that maybe I could suggest that the police chief speak with the city attorney about this. I got back on the phone with Beaver and the fire chief and said that I'd called D.C. and found out they could lose CDBG money if they didn't act quickly. I also suggested that they didn't want to be the ones to keep people from having low-income housing and parks, the stuff CDBG money pays for. A while later they told me that they had found the drills to undo the locks. But it took from 1:00 P.M., when the protestors came in, until 11:00 P.M. to get them out. Our doctors stayed and all of the patients who were there were seen after 11:00 P.M."[49]

Walsh later learned that the invaders were members of the Lambs of Christ; like all Lambs, they refused to divulge their names and addresses to police and were held in jail for several weeks pending trial. Prior to the court date, says Walsh, clinic workers "kept hearing rumors about them, including stories about their lack of personal hygiene. When I went to the courthouse on the first day of their trial—by this point I'd been in a million courthouses—I noticed several odd things. First, I saw more cops packing more heat than I'd ever seen before in a courtroom. There was a solid wall of uniforms. I also noticed that it was very cold. I then realized that all the windows in the room were open. Everything was blowing and there was a smell, the stench of urine. At one of the breaks I asked Chief Beaver, who was sitting there, about the rumors that the Lambs had been urinating and defecating on themselves. He said it was true, that the Lambs had told their jailers that they were showing their oneness with the unborn."[50]

The twenty-seven protestors were convicted and sentenced to a year in a Raleigh state prison; they served between three and four months.

JUNE 14: FARGO, NORTH DAKOTA

Father Norman Weslin, founder of the Lambs of Christ, was arrested in connection with a clinic disruption on June 14, shortly after announcing that the Lambs had targeted Fargo for a summer-long protest. Weslin told the *Fargo Forum* that "the characteristics of the Lambs are meekness, nonviolence, obedience, but most of all sacrifice. We don't have a game plan. . . . We're led by a little 15-year-old Jewish girl (the Virgin Mary) who calls the shots. . . . This is a colossal war between Jesus Christ and Satan. . . . We become unborn children in order to raise the social consciousness of the people of America. An unborn child has no due process of law and no attorney and it cannot speak for itself. It has no name. It cannot say no to the person who tries to kill it."[51]

By July, sixty-eight Lambs were incarcerated in Cass County Jail, at a cost of $46 per person, per day, not including police overtime charges.[52] They remained in jail for several months.

JUNE 24: ALBUQUERQUE, NEW MEXICO

Curtis Boyd, owner of the Fairmount Clinic in Dallas, Texas, and a physician with a private practice in Albuquerque, New Mexico, received the following handwritten letter: "Hey asshole Boyd—Those babies don't know when they where [sic] dying by your butcher knife. So now you will die by my gun in your head very very soon—and you won't know when, like the babies don't. Get ready your [sic] dead. I am going to burn your offices to the fuck'n ground!" The return address: The Angel, Life Bd., Albuq, NM.[53]

JULY: REDDING, CALIFORNIA

In the midst of a trial in which seven Operation Rescue members were facing charges for trespassing at the Redding Feminist Women's Health Center (FWHC), a four-alarm fire broke out at the clinic. "Everything burned up," says clinic administrator Penny Bertsch. "It looked like arson but the police and fire investigators could not figure out how or why it started. They finally told us that an oscillating fan that we had bought at K-mart, which they knew was off, had blown up and started the fire. We thought this was ridiculous but they sent the fan motor to BATF offices in Washington. A year later a staff person who worked at the clinic got a report from the FBI Crime Lab through the Freedom of Information Act. The report said that the fan was the victim of the fire, not the cause. They never bothered to tell us this and they never really investigated the arson. They did not interview the antis. We wanted to give them their names but they didn't want them, even though we knew that one of the picketers worked in a body shop where he had access to fire accelerants."[54]

The fire caused $100,000 worth of damage and shuttered the clinic for eight months. "We never stopped answering the phones and used a trailer to do pregnancy tests," says Bertsch, "so we were never fully closed down. A van, funded by a foundation, was used to transport women needing abortions to our Chico clinic."[55]

Follow-up note: On June 6, 1992, Richard Thomas Andrews—an activist who had been arrested for blockading a clinic in Yakima, Washington, and who was later convicted of setting fire to eight clinics in four states—torched the Redding FWHC. It was the clinic's third fire since 1989. Damage was extensive, and once more the building required considerable renovation. "The city of Redding clearly did not want us to reopen," says Bertsch. "They made our lives miserable with building code requirements. They said we needed a sprinkler system and we are now the only medical building in all of Redding which has one. No other doctor's office or one-story building has been required to install such a system. Then, when they came to do the final inspection before we started up again, they told us they needed to see the wiring so we had to rip the wall back out."[56]

The clinic reopened in February 1993. Less than a year later, on October 4, Andrews struck again. "An hour and a half before he got to us he blew up the Planned Parenthood in Chico," Bertsch says. "The Chico police immediately called the Redding police and said they were concerned that our clinic would be the next target. The Redding police did nothing. There used to be a house of prostitution right behind the clinic, and the guy who ran it saw Andrews set the fire. He called 911 and when the cops came, he screamed, 'That's him. Get him' as Andrews was driving away. But the police did not stop Andrews. Instead, they questioned the man from the house of prostitution."[57]

The fourth fire was particularly devastating for clinic staff. "You start seeing these things as a regular part of your day," says Bertsch. "You get so you know exactly what to do, how to handle the press, get a contractor, call the feds, and get a clinic relicensed. I resigned after I acknowledged that I was treating these things as routine. I returned two years later. I love the health center, the women I work with, and the work itself. But I needed to leave so I could return with a good perspective."[58]

Richard Thomas Andrews is currently serving a seven-year sentence. In 1989 he told the *Sacramento Bee* newspaper that he participated in the anti-abortion movement as an "act of repentance" for a series of personal tragedies that included a divorce, the suicide of a son, the estrangement of a daughter, and the diagnosis of another child with cystic fibrosis.[59]

JULY 13: SANTA FE, NEW MEXICO

Operation Rescue and Holy Faith Rescue descended on the Santa Fe, New Mexico, office of Dr. Curtis Boyd (closed in 1992), bringing approximately one hundred demonstrators to the site. This was OR's first and only "rescue" at this location. "This was a big demo for Santa Fe," says clinic staffer Glenna Halvorson-Boyd, "and twenty arrests for trespassing were made."[60]

On September 4th, Santa Fe Municipal Judge Tom Fiorina dismissed the charges against fourteen of the defendants and appointed a local Roman Catholic nun to serve as their "probation officer"; the duration of her service was not specified.[61]

JULY 15: WICHITA, KANSAS

Operation Rescue stormed into Wichita for a seven-week blitz against the three clinics open there. By the time the "Summer of Mercy" was over, police had arrested 1,734 people for 2,657 acts of trespassing, resisting arrest and violating injunctions against blockading.[62]

According to the Reverend George Gardner, pastor of College Hill United Methodist Church and the founder of Religious Leaders for Choice, "The word on the street was that Randall Terry and Operation Rescue had an open invitation from then-Mayor Bob Knight to come to Wichita. Whether that's true or not I don't know. As far as I could tell, Knight did nothing to curtail their activities. We'd had race riots in Wichita in 1968 and

1969 and things were turbulent then. But we'd never had anything like this. The city was being held hostage."[63]

Although the clinics had for months been following reports about Operation Rescue's planned one-week appearance, they were caught off guard by the number of protestors that OR had mobilized. "Before OR arrived the police told us that whether the clinic was officially open or officially closed we'd be closed because they could not guarantee us access to our patients," says Dr. George Tiller, owner of Women's Health Care Services (WHCS). "I did not want to close but we struck a deal with the police. We would close for the week if they would guarantee us access to the clinic beginning the Sunday night of the week before OR was supposed to come. We had nine late-abortion patients fly in, gave them a code word and told them to wait in front of their hotel with a photo ID and their money. We said we'd pick them up between 6:30 and 7:00 P.M. The police told us to be radio silent so we could not be picked up on a scanner. We drove a circuitous route to the clinic on back streets, agreeing to arrive at the clinic at 7:30. Five police cars were out front when we drove in and the gates were open. We did the abortions on these nine women on Sunday, Monday and Tuesday. Everyone was discharged on Wednesday and we closed for the following week. Then, on Saturday or Sunday of that first week, Randall Terry announced that because of the tremendous outpouring of support he'd received, OR would stay in Wichita for the rest of the summer."[64]

In subsequent weeks staff and patients never knew if they would—or would not—be able to get inside their facilities on a particular morning; some days they arrived to find 2,000 protestors standing, sitting or praying in front of their doors. "For weeks some staff stayed in the clinic three or four nights a week," says Cathy Reavis, patient coordinator at Women's Health Care Services. "Remember, all of the patients and their escorts were staying here, inside the clinic. Once we brought them in, we kept them because we were afraid we would not be able to get them back inside if they stayed in a hotel. Everyone was pulling together. It was us against them."[65]

Yet as determined as staff were—and as desperate as patients were to have their abortions—everyone was frustrated by the inadequate response of lawmakers and police. "You can start with the Bush administration and work your way down to the Wichita mayor," says former WHCS public relations specialist Peggy Bowman. "People who had the power chose actions that facilitated and encouraged OR right down the line."[66]

Finally, on the ninth day of demonstrations, police made 210 arrests; by the end of that week 825 had been charged with breaking the law. Then, in late July, Federal Judge Patrick Kelly issued an order banning protestors from blocking clinic entrances and harassing Dr. Tiller and his family at their home. Violation of the order, he said, would result in a $25,000-a-day fine for the first offense and $50,000-a-day fines for successive breaches. Randall Terry thumbed his nose at the ban.[67]

On July 27, one hundred United States Marshals were brought in to enforce Kelly's order. Still, support for OR continued to build. Kansas Governor Joan Finney spoke at an OR rally, and a Cessna Stadium event drew 30,000 to hear such well-known crusaders as the Reverend Pat Robertson.[68] "The antis were picking up ten grand a night and someone was paying to put them up at the Holiday Inn. Judge Kelly was getting heavily criticized and I started getting calls asking me if anyone was going to stand up to Terry and OR," says the Reverend George Gardner. "At the time I had two associate pastors working with me, and we started to call all the ministers and rabbis in town. It was August, many were away, but we got seventeen people together and created Religious Leaders for Choice. We called a press conference and read a statement. Our mission was to support Judge Kelly and show that you could be religious and affirm a woman's right to make reproductive choices, including abortion. We were the first religious voice in support of the clinics in Wichita."[69]

The protests finally ended around Labor Day, when people had to return home for the start of school; by that time, $553,000 had been expended on police overtime and court costs. Although several OR leaders, including Randall Terry and Keith Tucci, served short jail sentences, the *Wichita Eagle* reports that the first 288 people arrested were fined just $25 each. While penalties increased as the protests continued, the newspaper states that despite Judge Kelly's threatened $25,000 and $50,000 fines, penalties for repeat offenders averaged less than $100.[70]

Follow-up note: Following a mid-September "rescue" and an early October clinic invasion, the Wichita City Council passed an ordinance imposing a mandatory $250 minimum fine on individuals who had been previously convicted of blocking access to a legal business. The fine for a first conviction was left to the judge's discretion.[71]

"Abortion tore this community in half in 1991," says the Reverend Gardner, "and we have not come back from it. The rise in gangs can be traced to that summer because law enforcement was tied up with riots at the clinics."[72] Still, while Gardner believes that the issue remains one-quarter inch under the surface, he thinks that mainline religious groups can make an appreciable difference in promoting tolerance between contending political positions.

"Each religion—Hindu, Jewish, Christian, Buddhist—defines the experience of finding a spiritual dimension differently," says Gardner. "The first thing we need to do is admit that our understanding of that spiritual dimension is relative, not absolute, made up of doctrines, creeds and liturgical practices that reinforce a religion's relative point of view. We have to speak to our followers, teach them that nobody knows the absolute truth, that no one should use religion as a justification for absolute right and wrong, good and bad."[73]

SEPTEMBER 6: BELLEVUE, NEBRASKA

When Dr. LeRoy Carhart opened the Abortion and Contraception Clinic of Nebraska in the Omaha suburb of Bellevue on May 1, 1992, he did it as an act of public defiance. Carhart had been doing abortions since 1972 and had been a "circuit rider," serving clinics in Indiana, Ohio, Pennsylvania, Nebraska, New Jersey and Wisconsin for more than fifteen years. Nonetheless, it was only after his horse farm was destroyed by arson on September 6, 1991, that he bought his own clinic and hunkered down, in one community, for the long haul.

Prior to the fire, Carhart had experienced what has come to be viewed as routine anti-abortion harassment. He was met regularly at the Omaha airport by small groups of people who screamed their denunciations of him, labeling him a murderer, a baby killer, a devil. In addition, all of the clinics that employed him experienced frequent picketing and were targets of petty vandalism including glued locks, broken windows, and graffiti on doors and outer walls. But as awful as these things were, they pale in comparison to the destruction of Carhart's sixty-two-and-a-half acre farm.

"The fire happened on a Friday afternoon. My daughter Janine had been working at the clinic with me, counseling and assisting with procedures. That day was her twenty-first birthday and we'd planned a big party for that night. It was going to take place in the barn. Janine had left the clinic about noon to go buy food and other party supplies. I got a call from the sheriff's office at about 2:30, informing me that there was a fire at the farm. I took off immediately to find my daughter and wife. The three of us got home about 2:45 or 3:00, and by that time everything had been leveled, the trailer we lived in, the barn, our trucks. Everything was gone. We had the clothes we were wearing and the three vehicles we were driving. That was it. We lost seventeen horses that afternoon. We had a forty-three-stall barn with twenty-one horses; only four survived, blistered and bruised," says Carhart, his voice ruefully controlled as he struggles, nearly a decade later, to remain composed as he recounts what he, his wife and daughter confronted that afternoon.[74]

"We'd lived there since 1979 and ran horse shows once a month. My daughter was one of the top riders in the Midwest at that time, and she had trained most of the horses we lost. Some were ready to be sold as racehorses and others were our pets. My wife, daughter and I lived in a trailer on the land. We had plans to eventually build a home to replace the decrepit, 1,700-square-foot house that was already there," he continues, "but we had not yet started construction."[75]

The day after the blaze, September 7, the Women's Medical Center in Omaha, one of the clinics that employed Carhart, received an unsigned letter with no return address. The typed missive justified the conflagration as retribution for the doctor's "crimes against humanity." Although the letter was long ago lost or misplaced, Carhart still bristles when he speaks about the response of state fire marshals to the arson and the vindictive document that followed it. "The marshals told us that even though this was obviously arson—it was clear that the fire had been started from multiple origins—Nebraska has a two percent conviction rate for this crime. He actually said, 'we don't expect to catch anyone,' and they didn't."[76] The marshals did, however, bring front-loading trucks to the farm to remove the dead horses from the property.

For the Carharts, rebuilding their lives has been both traumatic and slow. "At first we stayed with friends. Then we had to get an apartment and buy everything from scratch," Carhart remembers. "I haven't ever healed. None of us has. But as a result of the fire I stopped doing abortions three days a week and started doing them seven days a week. I basically said, 'If the anti-abortion movement's goal is to intimidate people to stop providing services and I stop, they win. But if I become more aggressive, we win.' I went into medicine to help people. I'm a general surgeon by trade, and there is no patient in this field who is unrewarding. There is no down side to this work. I don't know what else I could do that would be as gratifying."[77]

The Carhart family stayed away from the farm for six years. "We continued to make payments on the land," the doctor says, "but we simply could not face going back. We finally felt ready, in late 1999, to start over, and we're presently trying to borrow money so we can build a house and return to live there."[78]

Follow-up note: Once the Carhart family came to terms with the fact that the fire had rendered their dwelling uninhabitable, they had to find a suitable rental property; their new address was apparently leaked to anti-abortion activists. "The first Saturday we were in the new place the antis entered the apartment through the balcony when we were out," Carhart says. "Our neighbors saw them breaking in and called the police."[79]

While the protestors were gone by the time Carhart and his wife returned, telltale indicators of their visit remained visible. A placard warning the community that "a baby killer lives here" was posted, and hand-lettered signs urging the doctor to repent were strewn throughout the apartment and hung on walls.

In addition, on the Saturday following the fire, a nurse at Women's Medical Center in Omaha received a phone call at 2:00 A.M. warning her to check her garage. Although she initially thought the call was a prank, when she went outside she found the garage engulfed in flames. Anti-abortion literature was strewn near the building. Damage was minimal and no one was apprehended.[80]

SEPTEMBER 28: BUFFALO, NEW YORK

The Reverend Paul Chaim Schenck and the Reverend Darren Drzymala lay down in the street in front of a car driven by Dr. Barnett Slepian to prevent him from entering the parking lot of Buffalo GYN Womanservices. As Slepian exited the vehicle, Schenck screeched that the physician was a "murderer" and a "pig."

Judge Richard J. Arcara fined Schenck $20,000 and Drzymala $10,000 after viewing a videotape of the incident.[81] Schenck balked at the rebuke and told the judge that his financial situation made it impossible for him to pay such a substantial fee. The fact that his wife was expecting their seventh child was also repeatedly mentioned.[82]

"Some money was collected from Paul Schenck," says attorney Glenn A. Murray. "Deductions were taken through his church, New Covenant Baptist, in 1994. We got a few hundred dollars a paycheck until Schenck moved out of town in August 1994, but we did not have the resources to chase him to another state once he left" to work for the Reverend Pat Robertson's American Center for Law and Justice.[83] An additional problem, Murray continues, is that many antis avoid having property or other assets in their names. Worse, "when it comes to income from the church it is difficult to obtain disclosure about amounts. State reporting requirements for religious institutions are less stringent than they are for nonreligious institutions."[84]

OCTOBER: WICHITA, KANSAS

Nails were found scattered throughout the driveway of Women's Health Care Services and a fishy-smelling substance was spread on the ground outside the clinic. Picketers told patients that the odor came from burning babies. They were also told that if they went inside the facility "their insides would be slashed" and they would "bleed to death and never have children."[85]

OCTOBER: MASSACHUSETTS

The Planned Parenthood League of Massachusetts won an injunction against Operation Rescue. In granting the order, Judge Peter Lauriat stated, "The right to persuade another not to have an abortion is not the right to prevent her from doing so. A woman choosing an abortion should not have to assault a citadel of human blockaders by climbing over or crawling through those individuals in order to exercise her constitutionally protected rights."[86]

The injunction was issued in response to numerous blockades that began during the 1988 presidential campaign. "They were horrible experiences," says former PPLM president Nicki Nichols Gamble. "I remember getting to the clinic at 6:00 A.M. and literally racing to the door. We had huge blockades during Thanksgiving 1988 and on New Year's Eve 1989, but smaller groups would gather virtually every Saturday in one or another church. The police did surveillance to see which clinics they were going to hit. There would be a lot of communication in the mornings," and caravans of cars filled with pro-choice people would roam around Brookline in order to defend whichever clinics OR selected for a blockade or protest. "We never knew where the antis would land," says Nichols Gamble.[87]

As tense as it was not knowing when or where OR would be on a particular weekend, the response of Brookline-area law enforcement was extremely good. According to Nichols Gamble, as soon as OR started protesting in Brookline, the City Council and head of the selectmen called a meeting between the town's four clinics and the police department to make sure that the health facilities got the coverage and protection they needed. "The Boston police and the state police put hundreds of officers out front when OR threatened to close the clinics. No Planned Parenthood in Massachusetts was ever shut down by OR. We were delayed a few times but never closed," says Nichols Gamble.[88] "At one point over Thanksgiving weekend, 1988, we told our patients to go to a church and we met them there. The state Highway Patrol then marched the patients into the clinic. They'd been called because the city police could not handle the number of protestors."[89]

The injunction was upheld in April 1994 by the state's highest court.

OCTOBER: CAMBRIDGE, MINNESOTA

Dr. Susan Wicklund had been an abortion provider since October 1989— regularly traveling between Minnesota, North Dakota and Wisconsin—when the anti-abortion movement decided to turn up the heat in an effort to dissuade her from her work. "It started building that summer when they leafleted Cambridge with handbills that said, 'Your neighbor is a baby killer.' They passed these out to the 3,000 people in town and at my daughter's school," Wicklund says. "They also distributed 'wanted' posters with my name and address. One Sunday morning they put them on every car in the parking lots of all the churches in town."[90]

As bad as things were in Cambridge, they were worse, says Wicklund, at the clinics that employed her. "I remember having to have tunnel vision. I had to be totally focused. I was on a plane every day or every other day and I participated in almost nothing else, family-wise or socially. It was like being on a battleground all the time. The most peaceful hours of my life, ironically, were when I was inside with patients. I was so absorbed with each individual that it made the antis go away for a while."[91]

Still, it was on October 1, 1991, that the protest against her reached an apex. That day, Wicklund had planned to sleep in since she did not need to be anywhere until midmorning. "I generally left the house at 5:15 A.M. and they obviously knew my routine. At about 4:30 A.M. about two dozen people arrived and began waiting in our driveway. They surrounded the house, which is on five wooded acres, about two hundred yards from the end of a road. They came up to the driveway and put up twenty-foot cloth banners that had been spray-painted with the words, 'no more dead babies' and 'stop killing babies.' They also left a wicker bassinet filled with fake money and a doll sprayed with red paint on my doorstep. I'd been sleeping when they arrived and thought I was dreaming when I heard someone chanting, 'Susan, stop killing babies,'" she says.[92]

Once Wicklund figured out what was happening, she called the police. A squad car arrived and moved the protestors off her property and into the street. The police also gave Sonja Mitchell, Wicklund's fourteen-year-old daughter, a ride to her high school and escorted Wicklund out of the house so that she could catch a flight to her job for that day.

"I remember using my Spanish book to cover my face," Mitchell recalls, "so they wouldn't get me on videotape as I was leaving. At that point I didn't know that home pickets were standard. I had seen my mother getting more and more stressed, needing security at the airport, but I had no concept that they could bother us at home."[93]

For thirty consecutive days, until Halloween, the Wicklund residence was the site of picket lines and demonstrations. On at least one occasion their driveway was blocked with cement-filled barrels, and one morning they awoke to discover that someone had broken in while they were asleep and placed anti-abortion literature throughout the house. That same month someone poured sugar into their gas tanks and slashed the tires of their cars.

Coincidentally, Wicklund and her family were in the throes of moving to another part of Cambridge when the protests began. "We'd already bought another house about four miles away but needed to sell this place before we moved," says Wicklund. "We did not have 'for sale' signs up because we did not want the antis to know our plans. Apparently they found out anyway. One woman, a Lamb of Christ, went to the real estate people and posed as a buyer. That's how they got in. That's how they learned where the entrances were, where the bedrooms were, everything. I saw this woman inside the house one day, then a few days later I saw her picketing in Fargo. She had distinctive red hair so she was very visible."[94]

The protests ended serendipitously on October 31, when a thirty-six-inch snowfall made it impossible for the protestors to get near the house. "Our neighbors got together and used a snowmobile to clear the snow away from our entrances and exits. They then helped us move all our stuff to the new place. It took the antis quite a while to find us once we moved," Wicklund recalls. "When they did, a Baptist minister in our new neighborhood brought a group of eleven or twelve men to the corner where the antis had gathered. I don't know what was said but the protestors never came back and that was the end of our home pickets."[95]

Follow-up note: At the same time that her home was being subjected to daily picket lines, sabotage and anti-abortion street theater, Wicklund's daughter, Sonja Mitchell, was also being harassed. "I remember late in October the antis leafleted my school with a flyer about my mother that said, 'This woman kills babies.' I didn't know about it and was at lunch. One of my friends had been to gym, and she told me that the class had spent the whole period outside picking the leaflets up," says Mitchell. "She showed the paper to me and I remember getting very upset. Then on another day a number of young protestors came into the school library to look through the yearbook for my picture. It was stupid since I was in ninth grade and was not in the yearbook yet, but these people knew my name and tried anyway. They were escorted out of the building but were not prosecuted for trespassing."[96]

Despite the stress of having her school visited and leafleted, Mitchell says she is grateful for the "amazing support" she received from her teachers, friends and school administrators. "Everyone was completely supportive and understanding," she says. "They all tried to give me whatever help I needed."[97]

Nonetheless, the protests took their toll. "After you have protestors at your house you alter your way of living," she admits. "There was a woman who used to drive down our street very slowly with binoculars. She was a bird watcher but we were sure she was an anti. My stepdad eventually stopped and talked to her and confirmed that she was there to see birds. It's ridiculous, but you assume all people are antis after a while. Another time I was home alone and a man knocked on our door to ask directions. I was terrified. It was more than the standard 'don't let a stranger into the house' rule. I locked the doors and was too scared to help him."[98]

NOVEMBER 5: FARGO, NORTH DAKOTA

The Fargo Women's Health Organization (FWHO) went to court seeking a temporary restraining order against the Lambs of Christ, Focus on Fargo, Help and Caring Ministries and a host of individual protestors.

The clinic's legal brief chronicles an array of protest activities in addition to standard picket lines: the attempted epoxy gluing of demonstrators to the clinic building on July 9; the stalking of clinic staff, including Dr. Susan Wicklund, in August, September and October; the continual interference with cars entering or leaving the parking lot; the following and taunting of a staff member's nine-year-old daughter as she walked to school; periodic phoned-in bomb threats; and the storming and occupation of the facility.[99]

The temporary restraining order was granted on November 14; the order is now permanent.

Although clinic staff had documented dozens of incidents of trespassing and harassment, it was the testimony of a nineteen-year-old former patient that pushed the court to grant the injunction, says National Women's Health Organization president Susan Hill. "This particular woman was young, innocent and apolitical," she says. "She told the judge what it had been like to climb through protestors when she'd come to the clinic a year and a half before. She testified about being screamed at and having recurring nightmares of mean faces yelling at her. She went on to tell the court that she'd even left town for a few months because she was so scared of seeing the protestors again. She cried when she told her story, and you could hear spectators sobbing in the courtroom. She said she didn't want anyone else to go through what she'd gone through. She was there to tell her story, not about the politics of abortion, but about being attacked, and she was incredibly compelling."[100]

NOVEMBER 8: NATIONWIDE

The Yellow Page Publisher's Association issued revised guidelines for anti-abortion organizations wishing to advertise their services. The new strictures followed congressional hearings on phony clinics, held earlier that fall, and were meant to dispel confusion over the crisis pregnancy centers that were proliferating across the country. The guidelines mandated that anti-abortion groups be listed under "Abortion Alternatives" and said that ads should clearly state that these organizations do not provide abortions or abortion referrals.[101]

DECEMBER 28: SPRINGFIELD, MISSOURI

A man in a ski mask walked into the Central Health Center for Women and asked to see a doctor. When he was told that the physician had already gone for the day, the man pulled out a sawed-off shotgun and fired it. He seriously wounded the clinic receptionist and the owner of the building. The gunman was not apprehended, and the clinic closed its doors in early 1992.[102] The pair were the first victims of an abortion-related shooting.

1992

UNKNOWN PLACE OF ORIGIN

The name "Army of God" (AOG) entered the American lexicon in 1982, when a group claiming to be the Army kidnapped Dr. Hector Zevallos and his wife, Rosalee Jean, owners of the Hope Clinic in Granite City, Illinois. At the time, the three perpetrators of this crime were seen as bizarre aberrations, and law enforcement was (and remains) uncertain about whether there was an official group bearing the AOG moniker or if it was a name adopted by a few violent individuals. During the early 1980s, the groups' logo was seen several more times. In 1984, when a Norfolk clinic was firebombed, the letters AOG were found scrawled on a wall; that same year someone claiming to be the AOG sent a threatening letter to Supreme Court Justice Harry Blackmun, berating him for his role in writing the *Roe v. Wade* decision. The acronym was also found near a Sarasota, Florida clinic.[103]

But it was in 1993 that the AOG mentality—whether generated by an organized group or by a loosely affiliated network of like-minded souls—fully established itself in public consciousness. In August the arrest of Oregon activist Rachelle Shannon for the shooting of Wichita abortion provider Dr. George Tiller led to revelations about a guidebook, believed to be a year old, called the *Army of God Manual*. The manual was found hidden in the backyard of Shannon's residence.

What law enforcement found when they read the manual proved that pro-choice warnings of a violent turn among the anti-abortion movement's most fanatical wing had been correct. Indeed, the manual proved that at least some abortion foes were ready to take matters into their own hands and launch a one-sided war.

Unlike Joseph Scheidler's *Closed: 99 Ways to Stop Abortion* and Kevin Sherlock's *Abortion Buster's Manual,* both published in 1985, the *Army of God Manual* boasts no authors. The over 100-page text also separates itself from its written predecessors by encouraging a range of illegal activities, including the direct sabotage of clinics and the outright execution of abortion personnel. Furthermore, its methods were clearly employed long before the manual was discovered by either law enforcement or pro-choice communities.

The Army of God's most benign recommendations are these:

> The pro-life activist can use a simple glue, such as Super Glue, to save babies' lives. By simply walking by the doors of an abortuary and squirting glue in the locks, you have effectively stopped the opening of the killing center, at least until the abortion mill personnel have left the mill, gone to a phone, called a locksmith etc. to gain access to their own chamber of horrors.[104]

> The most beautiful kryptonite park-ins to date are where rescuers lock their ankles to the axle or feather springs of a junked car which they have towed to the doorway of the mill. Attach a human being as closely as possible to the place where the fire department must cut to remove the rescuer—so that the fire department will hesitate to risk injury to the rescuers in a clearly non-emergency situation.[105]

> Don't forget park-ins: Any car can be driven onto the lot. Wheels should be turned in such a way that a tow-truck cannot pull the car directly out without making the car crash into another.[106]

> Flat tires can also save babies when bestowed upon the abortionist at his [*sic*] place of residence. One 50 lb. box of one-inch long roofing nails or tacks with large heads is enough to adequately cover the parking lots and residential areas of all the killers and staff in an average city.[107]

> Do you know how pesky roof leaks are? A hole can find its way into a roof and you will not know it until it rains several months later. Remember that you will need either a portable electric drill or a hand-drill like the old-fashioned coffee grinder type that telephone men used to have. The latter is quieter and less expensive.[108]

The manual then moves from tactics that are extremely irritating to ones that are more directly disruptive and harmful to patients and staff.

Project Noah: Use the abortionist's garden hose or import one, place it through the mail slot, turn it on, and let gravity do the rest.[109]

Any college chemistry student will recall with distaste his or her acquaintance with the uncontrolled substance called butyric acid. The least-risk method of obtaining butyric acid, otherwise known as liquid rescue or LR, is for each termite [the AOG's name for a saboteur] to obtain his or her own. Chemical suppliers listed in the Yellow Pages can be interviewed without revealing your identity. But use caution: If you get more than a gallon or two at once, or fail to establish some kind of story about how you are a teaching assistant at Podunk U, vandalism will cross the mind of your vendor, even though that thought will rarely, if ever, stop the sale. . . . A large veterinary-type syringe and needle, which can be purchased at any feed store, can be used to great advantage. Someone using the killing center's rest room can make a small hole in the wall with an ice pick, which will never be noticed, and inject LR between the walls in a number of places. After a few days . . . phewwww. The syringe and needle can be used to inject LR into the ceiling. The syringe can also be used to inject LR through the front door where double doors come together. The weather stripping around windows and doors will also admit a needle, and a later small squirt into an abortionist's high-dollar car can act as frosting on the cake.[110]

Nearly everyone has heard of teenaged tragedies where kids playing around bulldozers at a construction site got one hot wired (easy to do), and started it rolling, only to jump off in fear when they realized that they couldn't stop it just before it plowed into a building. Tragic, simply tragic.[111]

The Fourth of July or New Year's Eve are great times for gunshots. It has been suggested that hollow-point bullets might make glass shatter. A trusty shotgun can also serve the purpose.[112]

Final judgment by phone means simply a good ol' fashioned bomb threat. The main thing to remember is never, ever, make a bomb threat from anywhere other than a generic phone, i.e. a pay phone. And don't use the same pay phone twice. Go to different phones just to be safe. Mask your voice right from the start. One of the simplest ways is to purchase a voice digitizer, but a Radio Shack rapmaster is a cheap alternative.[113]

Scenario: You are given three months to live. You commit to torching two killing chambers every other day in different cities for 11 weeks. That's 77 destroyed death camps! This is a once in a lifetime tactic. Not everyone will be so blessed with this opportunity.[114]

The manual's appendices offer step-by-step advice for making one's own C-4 plastic bombs and using chemicals such as ammonium nitrate and nitromethane. Other sections detail the creation of detonators for explosives and cover what the AOG calls "beta celibacy: The final solution for life." Here activists are urged to remain single and pursue a life of one-dimensional activism.

> Celibacy has rarely been discussed in Protestant circles. Catholics don't talk about the subject like they once did. All Christian folks know that God sometimes calls individuals to a life of single-mindedness, the possibility of a life of single-minded covert activism. Practically speaking, a covert activist with no ties could save thousands of children and their mothers in a lifetime. Once an activist is married, and especially after having children, the constraints of parenthood are profound. Compassion for one's own brood will curtail the level of covert activity, and a lot of other activity as well. Most termites are going to be busy making the next generation of warriors. But for those few exceptions—carry on proudly with unbridled and righteous fury.[115]

Most chilling is the manual's epilogue, added in November 1992, after the first edition was already in the hands of extremists. They write:

> The use of force is woefully inadequate against mass murder, unless that force is directed against the perpetrator of the crime. Imagine an investigator discovering a killer. He knows where the crimes are committed. He knows the building contains all the instruments of torture that this criminal will be using. So the investigator goes out in the middle of the night and destroys the murder weapons, and even the structure where the killer did his crimes. So the psychopathic mass murderer packs up, moves down the street, reinvests in more instruments of torture, and continues killing. Our Most Dread Sovereign Lord God requires that whoever sheds man's blood, by man shall his blood be shed. We are forced to take arms against you. You shall not be tortured at our hands. Vengeance belongs to God only. However, execution is rarely gentle.[116]

By the time this epilogue was appended, three people—a clinic receptionist and building owner in Springfield, Missouri, and Houston doctor Douglas Karpan—had been wounded by people purporting to be pro-life. Karpan, an employee of the Women's Medical Center, was shot in an parking garage on his way to the bank. He survived the attack but his assailant was never apprehended.[117]

DENTON, TEXAS

Marketing consultant Mark Crutcher formed Life Dynamics Inc. (LDI), an organization whose principle purpose is the filing of malpractice lawsuits against abortion providers. LDI believes that is important to sue health workers "not just to protect women, but to force the abortionists out of business by driving up their insurance rates."[118] Crutcher claims to have pulled together a network of more than seven hundred attorneys, as well as psychologists and other expert witnesses across the fifty states, for women wishing to sue for reproductive malfeasance.

But lest litigation not provide a quick or sure enough result, LDI has a wide array of other tactics up its sleeve. One of its earliest programs was "The 800 Club." Described in a brochure distributed to anti-choice groups throughout the United States and Canada in 1992, the club gave "members" the toll-free 800 numbers of more than two hundred abortion providers. "Obviously, some pro-life activists may choose to repeatedly call these numbers for the purpose of harassing these abortionists or creating what might be called an 'electronic rescue' of the abortion mill," the brochure told readers. "At the end of the month businesses that have an 800 number receive an activity report, which allows them to identify anyone who repeatedly called them during the previous month. This would obviously not apply to calls made from pay phones." A year later, in an April 1993 *Life Dynamics Update,* the group crowed that, "The 800 Club is a pro-life tactic that seems to be gaining popularity across the country. . . . When pro-lifers call in large numbers, others cannot call and set up abortion appointments."[119]

WASHINGTON, D.C.

The Supreme Court issued its decision in *Planned Parenthood of Southeastern Pennsylvania v. Casey.* The 7 to 2 decision found that a Pennsylvania law intended to impede access to abortion was largely legal. The Justices said that it was permissible for physicians to give anti-abortion information to patients, including pictures of fetuses at various stages of development, in an effort to discourage them from ending unplanned pregnancies. A mandatory twenty-four-hour waiting period following the lecture was also ruled to be legal, as was a requirement that young women get the consent of one parent (or the court if parental consent would be an undue burden) before having an abortion. The only thing the Justices nixed was a provision requiring married women to get their husband's consent before terminating a pregnancy.[120]

"Casey has significantly overruled *Roe v. Wade* even as it reaffirmed the right to abortion," wrote attorney Rhonda Copelon in *Reflections After* Casey: *Women Look at the Status of Reproductive Rights in America.* "In allowing states to protect potential human life so long as the burden is 'not undue' throughout pregnancy, the Court undid the key structural protection of *Roe.*"[121]

JANUARY 16: MELBOURNE, FLORIDA

A patient at the Aware Woman Center for Choice received the following letter from the Women's Legal Action Coalition, an anti-abortion group founded by Meredith Raney. Her address was obtained from Florida motor vehicle records following Raney's acquisition of her license plate number.

It has come to our attention that you may be one of the 20,000 women who have had an abortion at the Aware Woman Clinic in Melbourne, Florida. We know that it may be difficult and painful for you to even think about this period of your life. Please be assured that we mean you no harm or embarrassment. We are a group of concerned citizens organized specifically to help women having problems after an abortion. We know that many of these 20,000 women have been damaged either physically or emotionally or both by abortion at the Aware Woman Center.

The following symptoms may indicate abortion related damage: Heavy or continued bleeding; severe cramping; elevated temperature; intense head-aches; depression or suicidal tendencies; hallucinations, nightmares, etc.; inability to get pregnant again; or inability to carry a baby to term, miscarriage or premature birth. . . . If you are having any of the problems listed above, please write us and describe your experience. You don't have to identify yourself but please let us know your story and how we can help you. We have trained counselors who can help you overcome emotional problems. We have doctors who can help you with any physical problems related to abortion. We have lawyers who can help you assert your right to compensation for any injuries you may have suffered, whether physical or mental. All of our services are provided at no cost to you.[122]

The patient recognized the letter as anti-abortion propaganda and immediately reported its receipt to the Aware Woman Center for Choice.

In a sworn deposition given in 1998, Raney admitted that there was no organization called the Women's Legal Action Coalition. He also admitted that he had no credentials as an investigator, despite the fact that he signed all outgoing letters, "Chief Investigator, WLAC." Both were fictions that he alone had created.

WINTER: A PENSACOLA, FLORIDA, SUBURB

"One Sunday in either January or February 1992 my child, who was then nine, called me and said there were people in front of our house yelling," says Sandy Sheldon, administrator of Pensacola Medical Services. "A regular protestor at a clinic I worked for in Mary Esther, Florida, and a few others were out front holding signs saying 'a baby killer lives here.' I called the police and they restricted where they could be. Then, every Sunday for five or six months, the group came back to the house. At around the same time that the home protests started, one of the protestors started following me around. I'd look up in the grocery store, the bank, the post office—he'd be there. I was in the bank one day and he came in and took photos of me which were put on a 'wanted' poster. He or someone from his group stuffed these in the mailboxes of all my neighbors. Everyone in my community was supportive of me but none of them wanted to file a complaint with the post office. I finally went to a lawyer. He listened to my story and said that what I was describing was not just harassment, it was stalking. We went to the state attorney's office and the state attorney agreed that I was being stalked. The attorney took the case and in the spring of 1993 the man was found guilty. I got an injunction ordering him to stay 1,000 feet away from me and the clinic. He violated the injunction twice and was taken to jail and held for several days. I have not seen or heard from him since."[123]

Follow-up note: Sheldon tells the story calmly, quickly reeling off the stalker's actions against her. The veneer begins to crack, however, when she addresses her daughter's safety. "I would go with her to the bus stop and I watched her get on and off the bus," she says. "For several years I was afraid to have birthday parties for her because I feared the pickets might show up. I was also scared to let her friends sleep over."[124] Sheldon and her daughter spent a year and a half in counseling following the man's conviction.

APRIL 21–MAY 2: BUFFALO, NEW YORK

"Randall Terry came to Buffalo in September of 1991 and said he'd lay siege to the clinics on the following Saturday. He said he would not let an injunction stop him," says Elena Schweitzer (not her real name), a historian and active member of Buffalo United for Choice (BUC). "He was pronouncing a

showdown. The next Saturday nothing happened. We were out at the clinics at
5:00 A.M. OR retaliated by saying they'd be back in the spring of 1992."[125]

Buffalo's anti-choice Mayor, Jimmy Griffin, in power from 1977 until
1993, announced that he would roll out the red carpet for all who came to
protest. "If they can close down one abortion mill, then I think they'll have done
their job," he bellowed.[126]

Pro-choice activists knew that with leaders like this, clinic defense would
invariably fall to them. "We began to organize Buffalo United for Choice in
January," Schweitzer continues. "BUC was to do defense and the Pro-Choice
Network of Western New York was to do escorting. In January and February
there was chaos in BUC. No one could figure out what to do and meetings went
on for hours, discussing theory. It was all talk and no show. There were also
tensions within the group and between BUC and the Network. The Network
wanted to do the safe stuff, like writing their legislators. Old hostilities erupted.
Some people were angry that ACT-Up was in the coalition. Others hated the
International Socialist Organization. It created real stress because it meant we
were at odds with one another. One day in March [BUC member] Cathy
McGuire announced that she was prepared to do clinic defense training and
invited people to come. She moved people into real action. She had studied a
lot and knew how to keep clinics open using nonviolent strategies; she knew
how to build a line of defense and do surveillance."[127]

Within weeks of McGuire's announcement the training began. "BUC had
a mailing list of 2,000 and we taught between five- and six hundred people to
do defense," says McGuire. "It was amazing. Some people took vacation to be
at the clinics every day OR was in town."[128] The Feminist Majority Foundation
also contributed to the training, supplying technical know-how and materials,
such as walkie-talkies, as well as experience gleaned from previous "rescues."

While OR brought approximately five hundred protestors to Buffalo for
the "Spring of Life," pro-choice activists gathered about 1,500 counter
demonstrators over the two weeks OR stayed in town. Chanting "you're not
in Kansas any more," they dubbed the event the Spring of Lies and appeared
wherever OR appeared. They also did whatever they could to keep patients,
doctors and clinic staff safe.

"Their first hit was on a Wednesday," says Schweitzer. "I remember calling
Steve Calos, the minister of Sweet Home United Methodist Church. He and I
talked about what was going on and he offered us the church as a staging area
for patients going to Dr. Shalom Press's office since it was close by. I told Dr.
Press's staff to tell patients to arrive at the church, that they would be escorted
to the clinic from there. Apparently the antis made phony appointments so our

plans were found out. That Friday the church was surrounded. The congregation also started to get bomb threats and death threats, about thirty in all. Steve was fabulous throughout. Clergy were coming out of the woodwork to help counsel, and ministers and rabbis from all over the area came to escort women to Press's office. Some even brought food. Saturday, however, was a big mess. It was rainy and cold and a few clinic defenders were arrested in a melee with the antis. Then, early on Sunday morning, I got a call from Laura Calos, Steve's wife. She said she'd heard that Keith Tucci, the head of OR at that time, was coming to the church later that morning. I had planned to go to the service anyway, and when I got there the place was mobbed with antis who were picketing and shouting. I got inside and Pat Mahoney and other OR leaders were already there. Keith Tucci was seated and had church ushers flanking him."[129]

Schweitzer remembers several unusual things happening during the course of the day's worship. For one, the antis could be heard speaking to one another throughout the ritual. For another, in the middle of the service, the Reverend Calos sat on the steps leading up to the altar and invited all the children in the room to join him. "He asked the kids if they were scared of the protestors," Schweitzer says. "They said no. Steve said, 'Well, I am.' He also said he was unclear about why the protestors were so angry at him, that all he'd done was open a door and offer women sanctuary. He then walked up to Tucci and said, 'You're a man and I'm a man. We both love Jesus so I'm not sure what the problem is here.' Tucci did not respond. Steve went on to talk about peace, about resolving conflict. At the end of the service he asked Tucci to come up and read the benediction with him. Tucci got up and read the rescue passage. Then he went out quietly. Tucci was treated with such loving compassion by a man who was supposed to be his enemy. That Monday, the next day, OR announced that they were going to retreat and do a fast. They fasted Monday and Tuesday. On Friday we again used the church for patients and the harassment started up once more. We took patients to Press's office from the church and ministers in collars drove them to the clinic."[130]

Although local OR leaders tried to close the clinics and private offices of abortion providers, their efforts failed. "Getting up at 5:00 A.M. was the worst part of it," says Susan Ward, counseling supervisor at Buffalo GYN Womanservices. "I'd escort patients in. We'd meet at a different location every day and take the patients down a narrow corridor that had been set up as an entryway. People would push and shove us. It was awful to have to step over people to get inside, but the Spring of Life was not as bad as an earlier invasion of our waiting room had been. The invasion of our space got to me far more than the protestors outside did."[131]

Follow-up note: The last Spring of Life blockade occurred on June 5. But residual fallout from the protests continued to be felt long after the demonstrators had packed their bags and returned home. The Niagara Frontier Transportation Authority, for example, billed the cities of Buffalo and Amherst $7,283 for buses used to haul the 615 protestors who were arrested from demonstration sites; local police and Sheriff's Department fees for overtime and other services came to nearly $500,000.

While Mayor Griffin spent the weeks OR was in Buffalo decrying the arrests and criticizing Judge Arcara's enforcement of an injunction against trespassing and blockading, most people in the city were fed up with the disruption and sick of the costs they, as taxpayers, were being forced to bear. Throughout, Griffin refused to budge. Reflecting on Buffalo's declining population, he told reporters that the 90,000 abortions in Buffalo and Erie Country—and not the stagnant local economy—were responsible for the area's population loss.[132] Griffin was defeated in 1993, after four terms.

A Spring of Life reunion in April 1999 brought approximately two hundred abortion foes to Buffalo for Operation Save America. The group targeted abortion providers as well as purveyors of books OR considers child pornography. They picketed Barnes & Noble for selling "indecent" materials and brought their message to local high schools. Throughout the seven days OR was in Buffalo, police provided the one remaining clinic, Buffalo GYN Womenservices, with twenty-four-hour-a-day protection. An injunction barred protestors from going within sixty feet of the health center's entrance, and police made it clear that they would enforce it at the first sign of infraction. In addition, pro-choice Mayor Anthony Masiello told demonstrators that his administration would not tolerate blockades or illegal protests.

Although outreach materials were sent to 60,000 people, most saw the small turnout as indicative of OR's shrunken appeal. No one was arrested during the week-long protest.

Shortly after their 1999 Buffalo reunion, however, OR announced that it had changed its name. Effective immediately, the group would be known as Operation Save America.

SPRING: CHARLOTTE, NORTH CAROLINA

By her tenth anniversary in the abortion field, Deborah Walsh, an administrator at a string of clinics throughout the South, was exhausted, suffering from severe headaches and insomnia. "I began to realize I was going to die from the extreme vigilance," she says, "the every-day, twenty-four-hour-a-day, seven-day-a-week physical, mental and emotional hell you go through when you do this work. The fear for your loved ones gets to you after a while."[133]

Yet giving up the stance of what she calls "the winning warrior" was not easy. Her first step was deciding to stop arresting blockaders for trespassing. "They hated not being arrested," Walsh says. "That is part of why they quit coming. They want the notoriety. If there are no arrests there is no media coverage of their blockades."[134]

But in addition to shifting her strategy in dealing with OR and other "rescuers," Walsh also decided to put energy into herself, to start paying attention to her own physical and spiritual needs. "The decision was to focus on the positive," she continues, "not in a way that shut the door on my messes, but to put energy on positive growth and stop trying to fix anyone else. I realized that it is not my job to stop someone from standing outside the clinic with a sign. If you realize you can't control it, it makes it easier."[135]

Staff at the clinics she administered also decided to begin telling patients to expect confrontations with anti-abortion protestors when they came for appointments. "We told them that they should roll up their windows and lock their doors when they came into the parking lot, that one staff person from the clinic would be in the lot to help them get inside. We chose to explain it in a very matter of fact way: 'If you want to talk to the antis you can, but you don't have to.' We set it up so it was no longer as much fun for the antis to come to the clinic. It was no longer exciting once we stopped screaming and calling the police," Walsh concludes.[136]

Walsh also went from sneering at the antis to periodically speaking to them. One particular incident stands out. Walsh was at Family Reproductive Health, a clinic she owns in Charlotte, North Carolina, and her sole place of employment since the mid-1990s, when she overheard a protestor telling a patient that clinic staff routinely lied when they denied that the procedure terminated a life. Like Charlotte Taft at the Routh Street Clinic, Walsh decided to use the opportunity to educate the protestor about what actually goes on inside a clinic.

"I went up to her and showed her the color pictures of fetal development and fetal remains as well as the pictures from the ultrasounds that we show every single patient," says Walsh. "I showed her the consent form we use which lists all the risks of the procedure including the fact that you can die. I said, 'My clinic does all these things, so tell the truth.' I challenged her on her honesty. I then said, 'Look into my eyes and go home and pray on it. See if Jesus tells you I'm lying. See what Jesus tells you.'"[137] Except for one lone demonstrator, the antis have not come back to the clinic since this encounter.

JULY 14: NEW YORK CITY

Harley Belew, Joe Foreman and the Reverend Robert Schenck were arrested after they lured presidential candidate Bill Clinton from his bulletproof limousine—they had begged him for an autograph—and thrust a fetus wrapped in a towel at him. The three were charged with unlawful possession of fetal remains and health code violations.[138]

AUGUST: MINNESOTA

When Jeri Rasmussen, director of the Midwest Health Center for Women, got to her fortieth high school reunion, she was shocked to see an anti-abortion picket line out front. "I am proud of what I do but it was difficult for other people," she states. "Some of my former classmates wanted to beat the protestors up; other people's first response was to engage them verbally. The protestors finally left, but they were there for long enough to upset the reunion for everyone."[139]

AUGUST 12: FT. WAYNE, INDIANA

Dr. Ulrich George Klopfer, physician at the Ft. Wayne Women's Health Organization, had to be driven to his workplace by police after pro-life protestors stole his car keys from the parking lot of the motel where he was staying. Klopfer told authorities that a young woman had gotten on the ground in front of his vehicle and blocked his path as he prepared to leave the motel. When Klopfer got out of the vehicle to tell her to move, a man reached in and grabbed the keys from the ignition.[140] The incident delayed Klopfer's arrival at the health center by thirty minutes.

AUGUST 6–20: HOUSTON, TEXAS

A few weeks before the Republican National Convention, scheduled for August 17 to 20, the leaders of Operation Rescue and Rescue America held a press conference at which they announced their plans to shut Houston clinics. A Planned Parenthood videographer captured the event on tape.

After viewing the film, local health centers knew that they had to act preemptively. A request for a temporary restraining order charged the antis with tortious interference to shut a legitimate business and adversely impact revenues. Judge Eileen O'Neill granted the temporary restraining order on August 6; the order mandated that protestors stay at least one hundred feet from clinic entrances and prohibited the use of loudspeakers.

"As the GOP Convention was starting, several hundred protestors arrived at Planned Parenthood, but it was impossible for them to blockade the clinic's doors without charging a police line," says Judy Reiner, former senior vice president of Planned Parenthood of Houston and Southeast Texas.[141] "The police kept them on the other side of the street. Although there were frequent shouting matches between the two sides, there were no physical confrontations. TV reporters were all over the place, and during one of the first days of the convention Pat Mahoney tore up the temporary restraining order right in front of the cameras. We went back to court and showed the judge a videotape of Mahoney doing this and he was found in contempt."[142]

Over the course of the convention, eight OR, Lambs of Christ and Rescue America leaders were arrested and jailed for flouting the injunction. Sentences ranged from one to three weeks.

"The Houston providers later sued the eight for negatively impacting our services and sought a permanent injunction to keep them away from us," says Reiner.[143] A very high-profile, high-press, costly and lengthy trial on the clinics' claims of tortious interference took place in 1994. "I testified about my personal knowledge of the ways the antis had violated the injunction both before, during and after the convention," says Reiner. "Plus, by the time of the trial, Dr. Gunn was dead, many of our doctors had received death threats, and doctors were regularly having protestors show up at their homes. We were able to impact the jury with the drama about what it is like to be threatened and have your family threatened."[144]

In the first phase of the trial, the clinics asked the jury to award them actual damages for vandalized property. "Planned Parenthood staff told the court about numerous incidents, including having to pull up tiles and replace floorboards and wall panels after a butyric acid attack; other clinics spoke about similar disruptions. After all the clinics testified, we got a permanent injunction and all the damages we'd asked for," says a still-elated Reiner.[145]

In the second phase, the jury had to decide if the clinics' pain and suffering merited punitive damages; they decided in the affirmative and returned a $1.1 million verdict against Operation Rescue. "By that point, Rescue America had reincorporated, but we were able to show that Operation Rescue National, which was now based in Dallas, was the same as Operation Rescue, and we got an order forcing them to either pay the judgment or let us seize their assets. On the day of the Oklahoma City bombing, Planned Parenthood staff went to Dallas with the constable and watched as OR's stuff was put in a county warehouse. It was later auctioned off," Reiner says.[146]

"It was always my belief that if we stuck with this we could have collected a lot more of the money they owed us," Reiner concludes. "But Planned Parenthood was not interested in pursuing these judgments. The litigation unit in the national office in New York is not well staffed, and I could not get local support to keep going after them. After a while I gave up. But if the Planned Parenthood Federation of America and the chief executive office here had been more intent on collecting the money, we could have done it. I believe that not following through on this was a huge error. Look, OR's leaders claim to be impoverished but they fly all over the world. How do Flip Benham and Keith Tucci travel everywhere—to Europe, Belize, Guyana, Russia and the Ukraine—if they have no money? Where does the money come from? A good asset-tracing firm can figure this out."[147]

Follow-up note: The antis remained in Houston for nearly two weeks and demonstrated at GOP platform hearings and at the conference itself. "The police knew that Houston was going to be on display and they didn't want another Wichita or Atlanta," says Susan Nenney, vice president of communications at Planned Parenthood of Houston and Southeast Texas.[148] "They were great. They assigned liaison officers to the clinics, and we started meeting to plan a response five months before the antis were scheduled to show up. We also started meeting with other providers and used May, June and July to train volunteers to be clinic escorts and defenders."[149]

Thanks to assistance from the Feminist Majority Foundation and other experienced activists, Houston's pro-choice community became well coordinated and ready to take on OR and other foes. "We had walkie-talkies and always got to the clinics before the antis," says Nenney. "We kept the doors open. We also used humor. The Lambs of Christ were in Houston during the convention, and one of our favorite chants was: 'Lamb chops for breakfast. Lamb chops for lunch. Cross that line and munch, munch, munch.' We'd gather our volunteers each day at 5:00 A.M. It was hotter than blazes—Houston in August—but we developed an effective system to get our patients into the health center. We set up an ice house and had spritzers which we used to spray the crowd and distributed ice water continuously."[150]

While clinic workers and pro-choice activists were battling to keep OR from closing the city's reproductive health centers, pro-choice Republicans inside the convention were battling an increasingly right-wing, anti-woman agenda. "The campaign team had planned carefully," wrote a disgusted Tanya Melich. "Abortion was only one issue on the agenda; the Bush campaign gave the Religious Right carte blanche to fashion planks on education, the arts, environment, morality, health care, the family, and even land use."[151]

SEPTEMBER: MELBOURNE, FLORIDA

Patricia Baird-Windle and her husband, Ted, were on vacation when they received a call warning them that Operation Rescue was bringing an event they called "The Impact Team," the Institute of Mobilized Prophetic Activated Christian Training, to Melbourne in January 1993. Several days later, fearing a repeat of Wichita, they returned to Florida to plan their response.

Baird-Windle: "Although the Impact Team was advertised as running from January 10 until April 10, 1993, many OR leaders—Flip Benham, Joe Slovenic, Pat Mahoney, Richard Blinn, Randall Terry, Keith Tucci, about thirty national figures—began arriving in Melbourne in late November and early December 1992. One guy, Chet Gallagher, came in September 1992. He had previously been a police officer in Las Vegas, Nevada, but had been thrown off the force in 1989 for refusing to arrest anti-abortion protestors. Most of OR's leaders stayed in town until 1995, and as soon as they showed up the number of disturbances at central Florida clinics skyrocketed."[152]

FALL: BREVARD AND PALM BEACH COUNTIES, FLORIDA

"Wanted . . . Wanted . . . Wanted . . . Wanted . . . Wanted . . . Wanted" read the banner headline on a poster distributed throughout central Florida. The text ran as follows:

> The following physicians are wanted for crimes against humanity. Specifically they kill unborn children for a fee. Unbelievable as it may seem, this is a legal profession under chapter 390 of the Florida statutes. There are rules under this statute that regulate the practice of this profession.
>
> A $1,000 reward is offered for information leading to the arrest of these so-called physicians or revocation of their licences [*sic*]. The following names of physicians, their addresses and phone numbers are being provided for information or educational purposes only and not to encourage harrassment [*sic*], of any type. This list of physicians is by no means complete; we will continue to update you of all abortionist [*sic*] in the state of Florida. Although we are short of funds we already have mailed 10,000 of this letters [*sic*] to homes, businesses, hospitals and schools in Palm Beach County alone.

Twenty-five doctors were enumerated on the crudely typed poster. Many had never performed abortions.[153]

FALL: NATIONWIDE

Operation Rescue distributed 140,000 pamphlets urging followers to vote against Bill Clinton. "Christians beware," the missive warned, "to vote for Bill Clinton is to sin against God." The brochure bore the endorsement of the Reverend Lou Sheldon, chair of the California-based Traditional Values Coalition. Sheldon argued that Clinton's campaign was an "attack on Christianity itself."[154]

FALL: PORT ST. LUCIE, FLORIDA

Patricia Baird-Windle had opened another Aware Woman Center for Choice in Port St. Lucie in 1988. (The clinic closed in 1994 after severe anti-abortion pressure on their landlord caused the center to lose its lease.) In the fall of 1992, the twelve-year-old son of the clinic's office manager died, and Baird-Windle was concerned that anti-abortionists would either disrupt the funeral—as they had when the Reverend Myron Chrisman died in 1989—or harass the family at the funeral home. The police agreed to be visible at both locations and, on several occasions, were forced to turn protestors away.

Baird-Windle: "When the boy's mother returned to work, she began receiving terrible sympathy cards saying things like, 'if you hadn't worked for a baby killer, your son would not have died.' She lasted about two weeks before resigning."[155]

OCTOBER: DALLAS, TEXAS

Anti-abortion activists launched Operation John the Baptist, a nationwide campaign intended to intimidate doctors into stopping the provision of abortions, in Dallas. The campaign was orchestrated by a coalition involving Operation Rescue, the Dallas Pro-Life Action Network (Dallas PLAN) and Missionaries to the Pre-Born. Thomas Cyr, president of Dallas PLAN, kicked off the operation by unveiling a statement he had written for approximately twenty Dallas-area doctors to sign. The statement read, in part, "I, [name], swear that I will never participate directly or indirectly in abortion, whether legal or not. . . . I will cease all contracting with women's clinics listed in the yellow pages [*sic*] as providers for abortions; I will not enter the premises of any of the same clinics for any reason whatsoever." Its cynical closing line asked doctors to "warrant that I am entering into this agreement of my own free will and not under any coercion whatsoever."

In October Dr. Norman Tompkins, in practice for twenty-six years and on the faculty of the University of Texas Southwest Medical School, was approached in the driveway of his home by a group of people including Cyr. They identified themselves as Christians and told Tompkins that they were morally opposed to abortion. According to a lawsuit brought against the anti-abortion activists in 1993, Cyr told Tompkins that "he had organized a protest against Clay Alexander, another local physician, until Dr. Alexander finally agreed to stop performing abortions." Daniel Scott, an anti who witnessed this conversation, testified that Cyr threatened to make Dr. Tompkins's practice "go away" if he did not sign the pledge. Dr. Tompkins refused the ultimatum and the interaction ended.[156]

But the protests and confrontations did not. For the next nine months, demonstrators carrying signs calling Dr. Tompkins a "tool of Satan" picketed the Tompkins home every Saturday morning and Sunday afternoon. They were there every weekday morning when the doctor and his wife left for work and every evening when they returned. Dallas PLAN also organized demonstrations at the Boy Scouts of America, where Carolyn Tompkins was employed, and at the Highland Methodist Church, where the couple worshipped. Hundreds of letters and postcards were delivered to their home urging Tompkins to "stop the slaughter."[157]

According to the lawsuit, the Tompkinses also received "numerous phone calls at all hours of the day and night. Several anonymous callers made death threats. . . . Dallas PLAN organized a surveillance of plaintiff's residence. Several defendants parked their cars in a cul-de-sac that runs behind their house and kept a near constant watch of plaintiffs inside their home. Plaintiff's neighbor, Linda Pennington, testified that the defendants often had binoculars and a camera with them while they sat in the car."[158]

The intrusions went so far as to include following the Tompkinses to a party. One of the protestors, Oldrich Tomanek, disturbed the couple's 1992 Thanksgiving dinner by rattling their front gate. On another occasion they returned home to find their front lawn covered with dozens of small white crosses simulating a graveyard. The lawsuit further charges that "on the evening of November 12, 1992 Tomanek rushed at Mrs. Tompkins as she opened the garage door to take out the garbage. Tomanek got very close to her and continued to yell as she put the garage door down. On another occasion, Tomanek ran up to Mrs. Tompkins while she tried to get the mail. He shouted 'Stop the killing now. Aren't you afraid, Mrs. Tompkins, that I'm going to shoot you?'"[159]

As a result of the shrill tenor of Operation John the Baptist, the Tompkinses hired twenty-four-hour-a-day bodyguards. Dr. Tompkins began wearing a bulletproof vest when he was out in public and installed a bomb detection device in his car. Still, the pressure became so intense, and their emotional distress so acute, that the Tompkinses moved from Dallas in April 1994.

Follow-up note: The Tompkinses eventually took legal action to stop the campaign against them. They sued eleven individuals, including Philip (Flip) Benham of Operation Rescue, and Dallas PLAN members Richard Blinn, Thomas Cyr and Oldrich Tomanek. The initial charges, filed in state court, accused the defendants of the intentional infliction of emotional distress, tortious interference, invasion of privacy, civil conspiracy and related torts.

In July 1993 the court issued a preliminary injunction restricting demonstrators to one twenty-minute protest per day and ordered them to stay at least three hundred feet from the Tompkins' home. The injunction also barred them from picketing on Sundays at either their home or church and ordered them to cease intruding "by the use of voices, sound amplification equipment, musical instruments, or other noises."[160] The case moved to federal court after the Tompkinses amended their pleading, and arguments were heard by a jury from October 11 to 17, 1995. The jury found in favor of the Tompkinses and awarded them $2,248,000 for the infliction of emotional distress and $2,800,000 for invasion of privacy. Ten defendants were further ordered to pay a total of $3,450,000 in exemplary damages, for a total of $8,498,000.[161]

The Fifth Circuit Court of Appeals affirmed the decision in the spring of 2000. Pro-choice attorney Linda Turley is currently conducting postjudgment discovery to ascertain if the antis have any assets that can be acquired.

OCTOBER 13: MOBILE, ALABAMA

Patricia Mitchell, owner of the Center for Choice in Mobile, was in Texas visiting her daughter and meeting her first grandchild when her clinic was attacked with butyric acid. She remembers receiving a frantic call from staffers who opened the center that morning to find a foul smell permeating the entranceway and making it difficult to enter the building. She also remembers them telling her that paint was visibly blistering on the walls and that plants in the waiting room—thriving the night before—were now dead. At the time staff had no idea what had hit them.

Mitchell's first move was to call the National Coalition of Abortion Providers (NCAP). After describing the nauseating odor to NCAP director Ron Fitzsimmons, NCAP suggested that she contact Renee Chelian, a Michigan provider who had experience with butyric acid and had developed considerable expertise in handling the noxious chemical.

"Renee asked if it smelled like vomit times a thousand. I said yes, and she tentatively identified it. I then called the state forensics lab and said that I thought we'd been hit with butyric acid and needed confirmation. The police, meanwhile, had been called but they said it smelled bad and were not about to go inside. Finally, my attorney pressured the police enough that they went in and gave us a case number. The forensics people could then take a sample and identify the chemical," Mitchell says.[162]

According to the Occupational Health and Safety Agency (OSHA), butyric acid can cause eye, mucous membrane, and skin irritations as well as respiratory distress. Although it can be neutralized with repeated applications of baking soda, water, bleach, or citrus cleansers, the smell lingers and, particularly in humid climates, remains faintly detectable years after an attack. The National Abortion Federation (NAF) estimates that cleanup for the ninety-nine recorded butyric acid attacks that occurred between 1992 and July 1998 has cost clinics more than $1 million.[163]

No arrests were made for the acid attack, and the Center for Choice reopened the following day. Unfortunately, the attack was only one of a slew of disruptions that had begun to plague the clinic. "In early 1992," says Mitchell, "the protests that we'd always had started to get increasingly ugly. There was a Catholic priest named Father Ed Markley who had a church in Foley, fifty-two miles from Mobile. He began leading the demonstrations. He and his followers would scream at patients, calling them 'murdering whores,' 'murdering bitches.' Markley would bring people to the clinic six days a week."[164]

Staff became increasingly edgy after learning that Markley, a Benedictine, had been convicted in 1984 of using a sledgehammer to destroy thousands of dollars' worth of medical equipment at the Birmingham Women's Medical Center and had been arrested for splattering red paint on the front door of a Huntsville, Alabama, clinic. Markley spent a year in jail for the Birmingham destruction and was released in July 1987.[165]

"By 1993 we were constantly in court with Markley and others for all kinds of things, blocking the driveway, trespassing and sabotage like glued locks," says Mitchell. "One time we came in to find feces smeared all over our front door. The police told us it was human feces so this came from a very sick mind."[166]

Despite evidence of countless acts of vandalism and sabotage, Mitchell was profoundly disappointed that the courts rarely did more than slap the hands of the protestors; as a result patients and staff were continually harangued and abused by Markley and his supporters.

In fact, things escalated. In August 1993, within days of the murder of abortion provider Dr. Wayne Patterson, a second priest, Father David Trosch, began to picket the clinic. A colleague of Markley's, Trosch had founded Life Enterprises Unlimited, a "crisis pregnancy" center that arranged the adoption of unwanted newborns, in 1983. A Chicago native, he had been a California businessman before his 1982 ordination.[167] "I have always been outspoken about abortion," says Mitchell, "and when Trosch started showing up at the clinic he would say things like, 'Pat Mitchell should be dead. She needs to be killed.'"[168]

But Mitchell was not the only adversary Trosch wanted to eliminate. The same month that he started picketing the Center for Choice, he appeared at the offices of the *Mobile Register* and the *Pensacola News Journal* with a cartoon that rationalized the murder of providers. Trosch attempted to convince the papers to run the cartoon as a paid advertisement; both refused. Nonetheless, ten days later the *Birmingham Register* ran a lengthy feature on the renegade priest that quoted him saying, "If 100 doctors need to die to save over one million babies a year, I see it as a fair trade."[169]

Immediately after the media exposed Trosch's position on abortion, Archbishop Oscar H. Lipscomb, his superior, issued a public statement denouncing the priest's activism. "The Catholic Church cannot espouse the teaching that abortionists are to be killed in defense of human life," he wrote. "It is a basic principle that a good end does not justify the use of an evil means."[170]

For more than a year following Lipscomb's rebuke and the *Mobile Register*'s article on the priest, debate over justifiable homicide raged, both within the church and within secular communities. Letters to the editor continued for months as people on both sides of the issue were galvanized. Throughout, Trosch's rhetoric remained high-pitched and hateful. In a June 20, 1994, letter to Joseph Cardinal Ratzinger of the Congregation for the Doctrine of the Faith he wrote: "Imminent danger is the reason why the use of force, either in self-defense of an innocent person or persons, is justifiable even though such force is deadly force. . . . The deaths of the innocent should not be allowed when there is an immediate solution, i.e. the death of the killers, the murderers, the practicing abortionists. . . . Justifiable homicide should be seen as the correct moral solution to the imminent deaths of innocent persons."[171]

A month later Trosch further upped the ante in a letter addressed "Dear Congressman." The July 16, 1994, missive warned that, "In time, the killing in protection of the innocent will begin to spill over into the killing of the police and military who attempt to protect them [abortion providers]. . . . It will begin to affect those who direct them to protect abortion providers. This will include city councilmen [*sic*], mayors, governors, representatives, senators, the president and his staff, judges and others seen in any way as fostering the protection of mass murderers."[172]

Follow-up note: Trosch was eventually relieved of his duties as pastor of St. John the Baptist Catholic Church in Magnolia Springs, Alabama. He was, however, never defrocked and remains a priest. Trosch was last seen at the Center for Choice in 1995. His Web site continues to include horrible rants against abortion providers. According to Mitchell, Markley still periodically protests at the clinic although his rhetoric is far less vitriolic than it used to be.

"FACE [the Freedom of Access to Clinic Entrances Act, signed into law in May 1994] is in effect," concludes Mitchell. "And after the Atlanta clinic bombing in 1997, local police started to patrol the clinic and respond to our calls more quickly. We also have an unofficial contact on the police force. This officer has admitted that he remembers women who died from illegal abortions. He believes that folks who don't like abortion should stay away. After Atlanta we spoke fairly frequently. And as horrible as the 1998 Birmingham clinic bombing was, the fact that the bomber killed a policeman made it better for us. The police take anti-abortion violence a lot more seriously now."[173]

OCTOBER 25: DALLAS, TEXAS

The Reverend Bruce Buchanan, associate pastor for program at Dallas's First Presbyterian Church, had a funny feeling in the pit of his stomach as he was preparing the order of service on Sunday, October 25. "As I was getting ready, I thought to myself, 'What would I do if Operation Rescue disrupted?' I then put the thought out of my mind, but for some reason, I noted a hymn number as I was getting things ready and jotted the number down on my sermon."[174]

Buchanan's feeling was preceded by a host of warnings that OR was mounting an increasingly aggressive campaign against the church. Like the concurrent torment being waged against Dr. Norman and Carolyn Tompkins, since 1989 Dallas PLAN, OR and individuals including Philip (Flip) Benham, Thomas Cyr and Oldrich Tomanek had assailed the church for allowing a coalition of groups—including the Boys & Girls Clubs, the Dallas Urban League, the Girl Scout Council, the YWCA and Planned Parenthood of Dallas—to hold what they called the "Teen Savvy" conference in their auditorium. Although a brochure billed the event as "developing leadership skills for adolescents to enhance a youth's self esteem," the anti-abortionists saw Planned Parenthood's participation as sanctioning youthful immorality.

On November 3, 1990, at the second annual conference, OR picketed First Presbyterian with huge signs depicting mangled body parts. A year later OR demonstrated outside the church on the Sunday before the conference. Then, on November 9, 1991, the antis again showed up, this time blocking the doors of the buses that brought teens from throughout the region to the site. The next day, Sunday, congregants had to go through an OR picket line to get into the sanctuary.

The following year, November 1992, the third annual Teen Savvy conference was again scheduled to take place at the church. A week before, at Sunday services, Buchanan recalls looking up and seeing a group of unfamiliar people in the sanctuary. "I noticed a group of men with big, floppy Bibles. They looked like televangelists. I greeted them. We had frequent Sunday visitors at the church so even though they looked a bit suspicious I proceeded. As I started to preach two men stood up and started to scream that I was a murderer. There were about one hundred people at the service. We have a police officer who works for us off-duty. I called the usher and told her to get the police officer, and I then announced that the congregation should turn to the hymn I'd noted on my sermon earlier that morning. The organist played, and we sang, 'A Mighty Fortress Is Our God' until the officer escorted the protestors out. Then, as soon as I started the service again, two more men stood up and started shouting. I motioned to the congregation and they did the same thing again: They sang the hymn. In the course of the service we evicted seven people. It hit the news that night and it backfired for OR. Flip Benham was denounced."[175]

The 1992 Teen Savvy conference, while picketed, went off without a hitch. This undoubtedly annoyed OR, and by 1993, the group had a new plan to dissuade the church from sponsoring the confab again. For two weeks prior to the convention, OR members picketed and screamed outside First Presbyterian during Sunday worship services; in the afternoon they brought their protest, complete with bullhorns and gory posters, to Buchanan's residence. "One of my kids was four and the other was nine," says Buchanan, "and they were terrified."[176]

"Operation Rescue complains that Planned Parenthood usurps the parental role in providing sex education and contraceptive information to children," adds Carol Adams, Buchanan's wife. "But when they thrust bloody fetal images in the faces of our children at church, and then brought those same images to the sidewalk in front of our house, they usurped our parental role. In retrospect, the time was past due for us to explain to our nine-year-old about the abortion controversy. But is there ever an appropriate time to teach a four-year-old about such things? For me, the saddest thing in all this happened about two months after the last home picket. I was baking bread at Christmas time and speaking to my four-year-old about the Christmas Eve service. He got very serious and asked, 'Will Operation Rescue be there?' What a world when a four-year-old has to be worried about Operation Rescue."[177]

But the Buchanan-Adams boy was not alone in his concern. Church staff worried about future disruptions and feared that the congregation would lose members over the conflict. On October 25, 1993, the day after OR demonstrated against the fourth Teen Savvy conference, Rita Odom, director of children's ministries, sent a letter to church members. "First Presbyterian Church voted to allow Teen Savvy to use our building for a one-day event with programs for leadership development, decision making and developing self esteem. Because Teen Savvy is sponsored in part by Planned Parenthood, this protest group (called Operation Rescue) has targeted us for their protests. Until this is over, there will be extra security inside and outside the building and members of our congregation will be concentrated around the entrances of the church."[178]

Bruce Buchanan, writing in the *National Christian Reporter,* added a more political edge to the issue. "In other eras people reinforced ignorance by burning books so as to prevent people from reading and learning. Today our Christian compassion, our common sense, and our freedom to worship are at stake, threatened with fear and intimidation. Future generations will certainly face their tests and likewise be called to examine and practice their faith; may what we do today guide them as they face their tests."[179]

On November 6, 1993, the District Court of Dallas issued a temporary restraining order protecting the Reverend Buchanan and the First Presbyterian Church. The defendants were "immediately restrained" from harassing and invading the Buchanan family's privacy at home and disrupting First Presbyterian Church's Sunday worship services.[180]

Neither the 1994 nor subsequent Teen Savvy conferences were held at the First Presbyterian Church of Dallas. The church, however, lost no members and remains a thriving, socially committed parish.

NOVEMBER: BOZEMAN, MONTANA

Dr. Susan Wicklund was at the Fargo Women's Health Organization for her weekly shift, getting the operating room ready for the day and listening to the shrill screams of protestors outside the facility. "The phone was ringing," she recalls, "so I picked it up. It turned out to be a doctor from Bozeman, Montana. He'd heard about the pressure I'd been under and was calling to offer me his support. He also told me that he was seventy-two and wanted to retire, but had been unable to sell his clinic. By that point I was working in five places and needed a break. I also had a strong desire to start my own clinic. A week after the call I went out to Bozeman to look at the place. I opened the Mountain Country Women's Center on February 2, 1993."[181]

Within a month of moving to Bozeman and opening the clinic, Wicklund's newly rented apartment was broken into by someone who left anti-abortion literature in her bedroom. "They took nothing so it was not a robbery," she says. "I left that apartment right after this happened and moved into a room on a ranch owned by people who were very pro-choice. They agreed to help insure my personal safety and security."[182]

Security at the clinic, however, was another matter. During its five-year existence, the clinic was repeatedly hit with both butyric acid and a hunting chemical that replicated the smell of skunk. Vandalism was nearly constant, and in March 1997 a protestor named John Jankowski was caught setting a fire on the clinic's roof. In addition, a spate of threatening letters from abortion foe Michael Ross added to Wicklund's uneasiness. "I was scared all the time. I hid out when I was not working. The clinic had extensive security but I never ate out or went to the movies until Ross went to jail," she says.[183]

Why does she continue? "It's the patients," she says. "People who have not been inside a clinic don't understand this, but to help a woman get through an unwanted pregnancy is incredibly rewarding."[184]

Although Wicklund has no intention of giving up her work, she admits that the threat of violence scares her. "I watch my back," she says. "I carry a loaded gun and have a trained guard dog that I take everywhere I go, including to work. My security is part of my thinking day in and day out. When I drive to work, I stop at different rest stops and I vary my routine. It's become part of who I am and what I do."[185]

Wicklund closed the Mountain Country Women's Center on January 1, 1998, and donated all of the medical equipment to nonprofit health centers. Although the clinic was both financially successful and well received, Wicklund left shortly after her mother was diagnosed with a life-threatening illness and she decided to move to Wisconsin to help with her care. She continues to work at clinics in Fargo and St. Paul.

John Jankowski is in federal prison for attempted arson at the Women's Center. Michael Ross, convicted of felony intimidation for letters sent to Wicklund and others, was sentenced to ten years in Montana State Prison on December 20, 1993. He was released in the spring of 1999.

DECEMBER 31: CHARLESTON, SOUTH CAROLINA

Lorraine Maguire, executive director of the Charleston Women's Medical Clinic, remembers that New Year's Eve call as every parent's worst nightmare. She and her husband were at home, hoping to spend a quiet evening together.

Their only child, a teenage daughter named Shelley, was with friends. "Around ten o'clock I got a call that Shelley had been in an accident and was in the hospital. They said she was in bad shape. I was scared to death but I got enough wits about me to call the number where she was supposed to be. She was there, right where she said she would be, and she was fine. There had not been an accident. The next day that the clinic was open, January 2, our most vocal protestor, Cathy Rider, was out there screaming. When I went outside she smiled at me and said, 'So, Lorraine, did Shelley have a nice New Year's Eve?'"[186]

At the time of the call, Maguire and Rider had been locked in battle for nearly two years. They became acquainted after Rider—a seasoned anti-abortion activist with a long arrest record for blockading clinics around the country—moved to Charleston and arrived at Maguire's clinic.

Rider was the first sustained anti-abortion protestor at the health center; between 1980, when Maguire began working there, and 1991, when Rider appeared, things at the Charleston Women's Medical Clinic were quiet and staff served their patients without having to contend with the anti-abortion activity that plagued so many of their colleagues. "Rider simply came into the clinic one day in February 1991, took a brochure, and told our receptionist that she was going to picket," Maguire recalls.[187] With that pronouncement, and accompanied by one or two others, including the adolescent daughter she was home-schooling, Rider set out to make life hell for everyone connected with the clinic.

From the first, says Maguire, Rider bombarded patients with antagonistic taunts. "She tailors her comments to individual clients. For example, when a Black couple comes out of a car, she goes up to them and says, 'So, you've joined the KKK today in annihilating your race.' She goes up to guys on the breezeway and says, 'So, your manhood lasted as long as your erection.' If she sees a mother and daughter she screams, 'So, Grandma, if you had been a better mother your daughter wouldn't have been out whoring and she wouldn't be here today.' If a father brings a girl in, she screams, 'It must be incest.'"[188]

Maguire does not believe that Rider's jibes have kept many people from terminating their unwanted pregnancies. Nonetheless, she concedes that her adversary has badly upset countless patients and their escorts. Many enter the clinic in tears or are so angry they want to assault Rider for her behavior. In either case, clinic counselors must work what amounts to a double shift; they must calm the agitated before beginning the counseling that their patients are seeking.

But as awful as Rider's abuse of patients has been, it is the staff who have born the brunt of her harangues and confrontations. And although no one working at the clinic has been exempted, it is the Maguires—Lorraine, her husband, Mike, and daughter, Shelley—who have received the worst of

Rider's virulent fixation. When Shelley was still in high school, Rider would bellow, "Don't you know, your mother has killed all your brothers and sisters. Aren't you afraid she'll do away with you?" any time she saw her. "She still screams this whenever she sees me," says Shelley, now a nurse at a Charleston hospital.[189]

Indeed, Lorraine feels as if she and her entire family have been under Rider's constant gaze since 1991. "She researched me. She knew my father had been a marine and she knew I didn't have a good relationship with him. She knew I'd had an abortion as a teenager. When she sees my husband at the clinic on Saturdays she points to her pictures of aborted fetuses and she'll say, 'Mike, this is your son. If you'd been more manly then and talked her out of her abortion, he'd be here with you today.' Other days she has approached me and said things like, 'That sure is a nice oak table in your kitchen,' or, 'That sure is a nice swimming pool in your backyard.' She's talked about my dog. She has obviously looked in our windows. After she made these comments we started to close our blinds, and we now keep them closed all the time. We have to live in a dungeon to keep her out. We even installed a house alarm."[190]

Maguire reports that Rider has also threatened her. "She once told me that I needed to get protection from the marshals, that she had a gun bigger than the one my security guard had and that I needed to start wearing a bulletproof vest. She made the last statement ten days after David Gunn was murdered in March 1993," she says.[191] One particular Saturday Maguire saw Rider conversing with a man who had unsuccessfully attempted to persuade his girlfriend not to abort. When Maguire went outside, "Rider pointed at me and told this man that I was the one who was going to kill his baby. She told him that I had a daughter and said, 'Why don't you go to her house and kill her child?' She then screamed out my address and phone number and wrote it down for him while I was standing there."[192]

Rider's intrusion into the Maguires' life reached a pinnacle in May 1992, when the Charleston police chief called Lorraine and told her about a call he had received. "Rider had asked him if she needed a permit to protest at the Citadel where Middleton High School's graduation was being held. That was the year Shelley was graduating," says Maguire. "The police chief said that he feared that when Shelley's name was called, Rider would do some sort of protest."[193]

The chief met with the school officials and forged a plan to close all but the front entrance to the Citadel. People were posted at every door with a picture of Rider. The band and the choir were instructed to start playing and singing as loudly as they could if they were told to do so. "When Shelley's name was called to get her diploma, the police moved from all the closed entrances to see where Cathy was and they were ready if she started to cause any trouble. There was even a paddy wagon outside," Maguire recalls. "The police were good because a disruption would have affected so many people; 340 were graduating."[194]

In the end, Rider did nothing, but fear that she might cast a pall on what should have been a night of celebration. (Six months later, Shelley got married and the family experienced similar feelings of anxiety. Fearing that the nuptials would be protested, they opted against running a marriage announcement in local newspapers and kept the event as quiet as possible.)

While the police went to great lengths to ensure a disruption-free graduation, Maguire has not seen the same law enforcement tenacity at the clinic. In fact, she says that until June 1999, when Rider signed a court order agreeing to temper her activities, police response had been extremely lax. "The police seemed afraid of her, and it was like beating your head against a wall to file complaints," she says. "The city has rules governing picketing that prohibit the use of signs on sticks. They never enforced these rules in the small front yard at the clinic. They let Cathy set up a beach umbrella and lawn chairs on the right-of-way fronting the clinic. She called it a parade float and had two cribs that she puts huge, five-foot pictures of aborted fetuses on. They let her hang a clothesline up on a tree out front and she flew baby clothes with a sign that said, 'I'm your son or daughter. Please don't kill me today.' Her posters blocked peoples' view as they exited the driveway so when you looked right or left you couldn't see the road. I needed to have someone, my own security person who I hired, out there to direct traffic."[195]

In late 1992, however, the police were forced to take action when Rider sprayed Mace at a clinic employee; Rider was convicted of assault in January 1993 but received a slap on the wrist, in essence warning her not to do it again.[196] Then, in March 1993, Maguire finally succeeded in having Rider arrested for harassment and stalking. Ninth Circuit Court Judge Luke N. Brown Jr. sentenced Rider to one year in jail and fined her $1,000 but suspended both parts of the sentence in lieu of five years' probation. Brown told the court that he would have sent Rider to jail had Assistant Solicitor Amie Clifford not recommended probation.[197] The judge also ordered Rider to stay five hundred feet away from the clinic, all clinic employees, and members of the Maguire family during the probationary period.

Follow-up note: Rider's anti-abortion road show returned to the clinic immediately after an appeal of her stalking conviction was filed. Five years later, in June 1999, litigation to curtail her activities finally resulted in a stipulation barring Rider from violating the Freedom of Access to Clinic Entrances (FACE)

Act and intimidating or interfering with staff. At that time Rider told the court that she was "burned out" and would permanently refrain from illegal protest at the Charleston Women's Medical Clinic.

1993

DALLAS, TEXAS

When Operation Rescue announced that Dallas would be the site of year-long protests, staff at the Routh Street Women's Clinic met to discuss how best to respond. They decided to drape a fifteen-foot banner with the words, "At the Routh Street Women's Clinic we do sacred work that honors women and the cycle of life and death. When you come here, bring only love" from their balcony. They also put the message on T-shirts.[198]

"What it did," says former clinic director Charlotte Taft, "is create a different atmosphere from what we'd previously had. We had a different energy. The protestors came, saw the banner, and had no idea how to respond. They weren't the opposite of us any more."[199]

DENTON, TEXAS

In an effort to dissuade medical students from providing abortions, Life Dynamics Inc. mailed 30,000 aspiring doctors a "comic" book entitled *The Bottom Feeder*. Among the "jokes":

Q: What do you call an abortionist with an IQ of 50?
A: Gifted.

Q: What would you do if you found yourself in a room with Hitler, Mussolini and an abortionist, and you had a gun with only two bullets?
A: Shoot the abortionist twice.[200]

As a result of the mailing, a number of aspiring doctors formed Medical Students for Choice. Since its formation in 1993, the nationwide group has grown to include more than 4,000 members. Its agenda includes: building an information network for pro-choice students and residents; reforming medical curricula and training to include abortion and reproductive health; increasing educational and training opportunities for residents and students; and advocacy of reproductive choice.

JANUARY: MELBOURNE, FLORIDA

"As pro-life forces grow, we are facing a serious need for fresh and better trained leadership. For this purpose, Operation Rescue National (ORN) is announcing the first IMPACT (Institute of Mobilized Prophetic Activated Christian Training) Team to be held in Florida, January 1993," the Reverend Keith Tucci, then-ORN head, wrote to people affiliated with the group.

> The Team will be sent to a Midwestern city in the Summer of 1993. . . . The IMPACT Team concept is the most aggressive plan ORN has ever undertaken. Pro-life leaders from around the country will take 100 people in two groups of 50, to train them to be part of a whole new generation of leaders—people who not only understand the battle, but are equipped to win it. They must be willing to commit for 12 weeks to get the training needed to be a prophetic leader. The goal is to turn the Summer of Purpose into a lifetime—a lifetime for the thousands of children that are scheduled to die each day in our nation and a lifetime of purpose for the Christians and the sleeping church.[201]

A subsequent IMPACT brochure went even further, urging "Christians with a serious attitude problem" to sign on for the training: "We are looking for Christians who are serious about making a difference, serious about seeing their lives count, Christians with an attitude of righteousness, an attitude of victory and an attitude of team work, who want to be a problem to the kingdom of darkness and liberal pro-death agenda."[202]

JANUARY: NATIONWIDE

The National Committee for a Human Life Amendment delivered more than five million postcards to churches across the country for distribution to parishioners. The cards urged members of Congress to vote against the Freedom of Choice Act.[203]

JANUARY: DENTON, TEXAS

Life Dynamics Inc. covertly mailed "Project Choice: The Abortion Provider— A Self-Analysis" to 961 clinics across the United States. The multipage survey, with handsome graphics printed on fancy, colored paper, was ostensibly issued by a group of Texas students who told the clinics that they were attempting to do something about the constant harassment of doctors. According to Canadian pro-choice activist/researcher Will Offley:

> The story was that they had applied to a foundation for a grant and the foundation was making them conduct a survey to prove there was harassment and to assure that the students were worthy of funding. The survey was conducted professionally. Four days after the packets—complete with self-addressed, stamped envelopes—were received, a follow-up call was made to the recipient. Eventually, a follow-up postcard was mailed urging completion. By early February Life Dynamics judged that they had received all the surveys they would get and began tabulating the results.[204]

LDI claims that a total of 285 surveys were returned, a 29.66 percent response rate. LDI used the survey's purported findings to bolster the morale of the antis within its orbit; a *Life Dynamics Update* gleefully reported that 36.71 percent of respondents said that anti-choice activity had caused them to consider not providing abortions; 29.79 percent reported that harassment and violence had forced them to curtail some personal activities; 54.1 percent said that anti-abortion violence had negatively impacted their families; and 26.8 percent admitted that their competence level decreased during periods of sustained anti-abortion protest.[205]

Adding insult to injury, an October 20, 1993, *Clinic Support Update* issued by the National Abortion Federation told clinics that the return envelope enclosed in the LDI packet had been treated with ultraviolet-sensitive ink.

> The materials informed the reader that all survey information would be confidential and, since they were not asked to include their names on any part of the survey, responses could not be traced back to the individual provider. They lied. Bill Price, former president of the defunct Texans United for Life, told a Dallas-area reporter that he had been on the founding board of Life Dynamics but had resigned after director Mark Crutcher revealed the secret one-two punch of the survey. The envelopes were all coded with invisible ink, indicating which provider received the envelope. Thus, if Dr. Doe sent back the survey in the conveniently provided envelope, all of Dr. Doe's confidential responses were immediately identified as his and recorded as such.[206]

JANUARY 1: DULUTH, MINNESOTA

When the Women's Health Center (WHC) received word that its lease would not be extended when it expired on January 1, 1994, clinic director Tina Welsh knew that the center had to make some changes in the way that it functioned. Since this was the second time in four years that their lease was not being renewed, Welsh realized that she and her coworkers had to figure out a way to combat the violence and harassment that made others see them as undesirable tenants.[207]

The clinic opened in October 1981, on the same day that former President Ronald Reagan was shot. "The antis had collected 7,000 signatures against us in the weeks before we opened and had announced that they were going to stop us," says Welsh. "That first day we made arrangements with the YWCA to have patients go there instead of coming to the WHC directly. We had drivers pick them up and bring them to the center through the drive-in garage. But because Reagan was shot and the whole country was in shock, the antis' plans fizzled and we got through the day without incident."[208]

Shortly afterward, however, the antis started calling Welsh's home and threatening her children. "I had foster kids living with me when I opened the center. All of them were teens—two were seventeen, one was eighteen and one was sixteen—and all of them had been either sexually or physically abused," says Welsh. "We got about fifty calls in the first several weeks from people who would say things like, 'Your mother believes in killing babies. How will she feel if you're dead in the morning?' The kids were really frightened and really pissed. One morning we got up and found a dead rabbit with its stomach cut open on our porch. We reported the calls and the rabbit incident but the authorities did nothing. It was also awful at the clinic. A local priest and a picketer who has since died, used to come up to our floor— our offices were on both sides of the hallway—and would make it impossible for people to get from one side to the other. They tormented us until we finally got a restraining order against them in 1993."[209]

Between 1981 and 1993, when the restraining order took effect, things continued to escalate: WHC was the first clinic in the United States to be hit with butyric acid; their doctors were routinely followed and tormented en route to and from the airport, and on several occasions someone tampered with their plumbing so that raw sewage shot out when they flushed their toilets. In addition, a particularly hard-line Catholic bishop, Roger Schweitz, lobbied the state legislature to limit women's reproductive and sexual options.

By the time Welsh received the eviction notice from her landlord, she had grown used to keeping an eye on both the antis and the Minnesota legislature. But unlike other clinics that had reacted to the nonrenewal of a lease by purchasing a building, Welsh had bigger ideas. She knew that she did not want the WHC to be freestanding because she was convinced that there was safety in numbers. As wheels turned and conversations germinated, Welsh decided that the clinic's best bet would be to join an array of groups in a Women's Building.

"I started by going to the community," Welsh recalls. "I wrote a letter to all twenty-two of the women's groups in town and said that we needed to have a meeting. Either the clinic got some help or I was out of there. We needed money. WHC had filed for an injunction and the case went all the way to the Minnesota Supreme Court, costing us $37,000. Along with two other clinics we had sued the state to get Medicaid funding restored. We had to pay for an off-duty policeman, $25 an hour with a four-hour minimum, and now we had to pay to move. I told these groups as well as a few individual feminists—movers and shakers of northern Minnesota—that I was interested in buying a building with other organizations. We would be the third Women's Building in the United States and the first one to house an abortion clinic. Rosie Rocco of PAVSA, the Program to Aid Victims of Sexual Assault, and Karen Diver, the YWCA director, were interested although the Y later became a limited partner. We formed a committee made up of women who knew where the money in town was and looked at twenty-seven buildings to see if any were suitable."[210]

Welsh also consulted with a group that had conducted successful capital campaigns and was given a referral to a woman-owned development company that focused exclusively on nonprofits. While grant proposals were written, the committee planned fund-raising events with well-known feminists. "We wanted to have an event with Gloria Steinem, Dr. Jane Hodgson, and attorney Janet Benshoof of the Center for Reproductive Law and Policy and were looking for a place to hold it. A friend suggested that I call Joan Drury, a local woman with a big house and some money. Two days later," says Welsh, "Joan called and said, 'We have a mutual friend who told me you'd never call me, so I'm calling you.' She said we could use her house for the fund raiser and set up a meeting to talk about the building. We went to dinner, then returned to her place. I told her the idea, said we'd already raised $100,000 but needed another $800,000 at six percent interest. She said she'd give us $400,000 at eight percent. Since interest was fourteen percent at the time, this was a good deal and we suddenly had enough money to proceed."[211]

The group bought a building for $330,000 but continued to pursue grant money because they estimated that the renovation of the warehouse they had purchased—and the security system they would need to install—would cost approximately $2 million, more than twice their initial projection. For five years the Building Committee met to plan activities, review progress and discuss strategies for raising additional revenue.

WHC moved into the three-story, 21,000-square-foot Duluth Building for Women in January 1994, when their lease expired. Other tenants, including Joan Drury's publishing company, Spinsters Ink; a rape crisis center; the League of Women Voters; a branch of the American Association of University Women; the Aurora Lesbian Center; and Norcroft, a writer's space and retreat, have since joined them.

Not surprisingly, the road to this point was far from smooth. According to Welsh, the local Catholic diocese, students from St. Scholastica College and several priests picketed the building during construction and attempted to intimidate contractors into severing their agreements with the women. "One contractor, the guy who was drilling for the elevator, was told that we had no money and would never pay him. He came to us and said we had to pay him up front. I said no, that I'd pay him as to contract. He did the job, but since he is the only driller in a three-state area, if we had lost him we would have been in real trouble," Welsh admits.[212]

Catholic clergy also denounced the building from the pulpit and printed flyers listing the names and addresses of all the foundations the building had appealed to. The Bush Foundation, a huge Twin City fund, told Welsh that their trustees received as many as thirty-two calls an hour demanding that they deny the building funding. The pressure caused the foundation to defer discussing the group's eligibility until the public outcry died down.[213]

In addition to contacting philanthropic groups, in December 1993 the Catholic diocese withdrew its $40,000 contribution to the Duluth United Way. Enraged that the group provided funding to PAVSA and the YWCA, organizations they now deemed conspirators in a pro-choice plot against family values, Bishop Schweitz also resigned from the United Way board.[214]

Welsh says that the bishop's action generated tremendous criticism from all sectors of Duluth's population. "The Protestant and Jewish mainstream got very angry at the Catholic diocese," she says, "and they decided to bless the building. We got rabbis, Native American shamans, and Protestant clergy to come to a packed ceremony on October 11, 1994."[215]

Since opening its new offices, WHC has performed approximately 1,200 abortions a year on women from northern Minnesota, Michigan and Wisconsin. While protest continues, Welsh calls the police department "very fair" and says that she is cheered that "they interpret the law impartially."[216] She is also encouraged by a recent decision to situate Technology Village near the Women's Building. A high-tech project run in cooperation with the University of Minnesota, the village will be the center of the computer world in the Duluth area. "We are the only building in a two-block area that will not be demolished," says Welsh. "The city has eminent domain and wants to negotiate with us for our parking lot. We need the lot, but we can negotiate because it will make us much safer to be adjacent to Technology Village."[217]

Things at the WHC have calmed significantly over the last several years, says Welsh. "I think the bishop and the College of St. Scholastica had to take a good look at their own trustees, some of whom gave us money for the building. They received a lot of criticism for their efforts to close us down. I think they are finally figuring out that they have better things to do with their money than fight a clinic."[218]

JANUARY 10: MELBOURNE, FLORIDA

As soon as the Impact Team arrived in Melbourne, anti-abortion activity— always vigorous—became a 24/7 occupation. *Time* Magazine called the team the "nation's first formally trained class of abortion protestors."[219] The twenty-two students who attended the four-month program—twelve women and ten men ranging in age from sixteen to sixty-seven—came from all over the United States. One student came from Canada. According to *Time* reporter Paul Gray, classes were comprehensive. A private detective lectured on how to obtain information about people associated with clinics, and sessions taught partici-pants how to trace home addresses from automobile license plates and use Social Security numbers to ascertain information about a provider's financial status. Schemes for infiltrating waiting areas and operating rooms, doing "sidewalk counseling" and using all types of technology were also described.[220]

Patricia Baird-Windle: "As soon as the team assembled, one of our doctor's, Monthree Ruangsamboon's, private office was attacked. Someone threw a baby bootie filled with cement through a vent in his roof, which cost him $3,200 to repair and closed him down for several days. His office was later hit with butyric acid and his home was blockaded. On another occasion, after invading Dr. Monthree's waiting room and refusing to leave, Chet Gallagher, an ex–Las Vegas cop, spent more than thirty days in the Seminole County jail for trespassing. Another of our doctors had acid thrown onto the roof of his antique Mercedes. The wife of still another physician, a guy who filled in for us as needed and who wanted to have his identity protected, received a videotape of her husband entering and leaving our clinic. That was the last day he worked for us. Shortly thereafter, Dr. Frank Snydle, an out-of-town physician employed by Aware Woman, was greeted by a gaggle of protestors when he got to his Melbourne hotel.[221]

"But doctors were not the only victims. We'd put a ten-foot fence around the clinic and the antis poked dozens of holes in it, trying to see who came and left, and which physician was working on a particular day. They also got a ladder, which they would stand on and scream from. One protestor, named Jessica, a red-headed teenager from North Dakota, used to stand on a tall, A-frame ladder and shriek 'Mommy, Mommy, I had blue eyes. Why did you kill me?' Eric Johns and Mark Gabriel would scream from over the fence, from the top of a large panel truck. I was followed around as I shopped in Wal-Mart, and our police captain told me that he had also been followed. The message was: You can't get away from us. From January 10 on, Impact Team members were all over town, turning up everywhere. It was an eighteen- to twenty-two-hour-a-day event, every day for more than sixteen weeks. My staff, family and I lost all sense of autonomy as a result of it.[222]

"The Impact Team was orchestrating a zillion-ring circus, with a continually shifting range of tactics. Although the schedule varied, Team leaders usually taught 'classes' in the mornings and brought hundreds of protestors to Aware Woman—and periodically to clinics in Orlando, Port St. Lucie and West Palm Beach—in the afternoons. Streets around the clinic were routinely blocked and there were constant traffic tie-ups. In addition, picketers descended on my condominium every day at 7:00 A.M. and would stay until 9:00; other clinic staff were also disturbed at home. They had a load of other dirty tricks up their sleeves. People from forty-nine of the fifty states began calling the clinic's 800 number with hang-up or open-line calls. This barrage, clearly orchestrated, would see the phones literally ring hundreds of times an hour. Frustrated staff would answer only to hear silence or have people curse or threaten them. Only the most intrepid of clients and friends could get through.

"When the phone bill came for February, the computers had registered a total of 7,500 calls in one four-week period. They came from every state except Hawaii. It took us a few more weeks to get our 800 line disconnected. By the time we did, 2,900 more calls had come in. Imagine the frustration and anger staff felt, having to answer the phone over and over, never knowing whether it was a patient in need or someone who would scream at them for 'murdering babies.' I estimate that more than 200 women who needed birth control, medical care or abortions were forced to go elsewhere during this short time because they could not reach Aware Woman to schedule an appointment. Many other clinics were zapped by this tactic during the 1993–95 period. Many felt they had no choice but to disconnect their 800 numbers. Some of us have tried to have our 800 lines reconnected, but a variety of new harassing phone tactics have been used against us.[223]

"Although the Feminist Majority Foundation (FMF) sent Kathy Spillar and other organizers to Melbourne to beef up local pro-clinic activism, nothing seemed adequate in the face of so much anti activity. In late February Kathy Spillar called Ellie Smeal, the FMF head, and said that it was worse in Melbourne than she'd ever seen it before and said that things were out of control. These early March days—and our press conference to alert media to the problems we were facing—are covered in the Introduction of this book. I returned to Melbourne in time for a big event called by Randall Terry for the seventh of March.[224]

"It was at this event that Terry played to the crowd and issued his threat to me: 'You kill babies. You'll have no place to hide. We're going to run you to ground. It will be fun.' I cannot tell you what that felt like. From that day on, I believed my life was in danger. This interaction was covered by more than fifty media, some international, and several from the networks. The blatant threats Terry made to close my clinics were glossed over in the coverage. No one got it. Except us. That afternoon Kathy Patrick, a Texas lawyer who had previously crafted an injunction against illegal trespassing and blockading during the 1992 Republican Convention in Houston, began to hammer out a lawsuit to protect us from OR, the Impact Team and individual activists."[225]

FEBRUARY: CORPUS CHRISTI, TEXAS

Arson destroyed Reproductive Services, the clinic whose director, Rachel Vargas, had been excommunicated by the Catholic church in June 1990. "It was just too expensive to rebuild," remembers Marilyn Chrisman Eldridge of Nova Health Systems, the nonprofit management company that ran the clinic. "Our insurance would have covered some of it, one-third to one-half, but we didn't have enough money to finance the rest of the reconstruction."[226]

Reproductive Services had been one of six Texas and Oklahoma clinics in the Nova chain. "We operate on such a slim financial margin that it would have been a drag on our other facilities to rebuild since the clinic had been burned to the ground. It was an awful decision but we reluctantly decided not to rebuild since it would have cost several hundred thousand dollars," Chrisman Eldridge concludes.[227]

No one was arrested for setting the fire. Adjacent offices in the strip mall that housed Reproductive Services were also damaged, but these businesses were able to make the repairs necessary to resume operations.

FEBRUARY: MELBOURNE, FLORIDA

Janet Williams (a pseudonym), a part-time lab assistant at the Aware Women Center for Choice, had been screamed at by anti-abortion protestors since she began working at the clinic in 1985. During the Impact Team, however, she was physically intimidated by them. "They would block your car as you tried to enter the parking lot," she says. "The worst was a guy we called 'Speed Bump.' As I drove in, he threw himself down on the ground in front of me. It seemed like thousands of antis then surrounded my car and began to rock it back and forth. I had visions of them taking out clubs and beating me. I was also scared that the car would roll over since they were rocking it really hard. I was almost panicking, but the clinic escorts were there and I think they dragged 'Speed Bump' out of the way. One of the escorts spoke to me, calmly telling me to keep moving. I did, driving very slowly until I got into the parking lot. I finally got inside the building and went to work since it was a busy surgery day."[228]

Follow-up note: Car rocking is an oft-repeated tactic. In most cases, the antis try to provoke the car's driver into a physical confrontation. If they can get the driver to leave the vehicle, they videotape the exchange, hoping to catch him or her in an act of battery or threatening behavior.

According to Patricia Baird-Windle, perpetrators have gone so far as to pretend to be hit and in some cases have actually let themselves be gently bumped by a passing car. In Youngstown, Ohio, and other cities, she saw the tactic documented on the evening news.

FEBRUARY: CENTRAL FLORIDA

Dr. Monthree Ruangsamboon, a gynecologist employed by the Aware Woman Center for Choice, woke up to find his home surrounded by Impact Team protestors. "Monthree is a small, nonreactive person," says Patricia Baird-Windle. "When he loses his temper he shakes. He was really mad that morning but was determined not to let the antis stop him from doing what he had to do. Monthree had an eight-year-old son who needed to get to school, and he decided that there was enough room for him to pull his car out of the garage. He then drove across his lawn and across his neighbor's lawn to get out. When he got to his office it, too, was blockaded."[229]

Ruangsamboon resigned from the clinic a month later, immediately following the murder of Dr. David Gunn in Pensacola. He is currently practicing medicine in Thailand, his home country.

FEBRUARY 19: MELBOURNE, FLORIDA

Lisa Merritt Sanford, staff administrator at the Aware Woman Center for Choice since August 1991, knew that anti-abortion harassment had hit a new low when, during the Impact Team, her then-thirteen-year-old son was lured in. Joey (a pseudonym) told Sanford that he had met a teenage girl several weeks before and was delighted when she called him up and invited him to go to Burger King. "Since he hadn't given her his number, when she called he asked her how she'd gotten it. She said, 'Oh, I can always get a cute guy's number.' He was flattered and decided to go out with her and a woman he thought was her mother," says Sanford. "When they got inside the restaurant the two put a Bible on the table. They told him that he and I would burn in eternal hell because of what I did for a living. Joey thought he was ten feet tall and bulletproof, so he tried to be brave and argued with them, telling them that he believed in a higher power, not God. They then said they knew about the Narcotics Anonymous meetings I went to and the karate classes he took. At that point he got scared and left."[230]

"I was livid," she continues, "and when I got home Joey and I had a heart-to-heart about what I do and about how he had to be careful and not get into a car with people he didn't know. He was so scared that he was pretty much willing to listen. The next day I woke up and looked outside my window and there were picketers outside my apartment. Joey started crying and begged me not to go outside. I went out anyway and saw their signs labeling me a baby killer. I got in their faces and told them to leave. They refused. They were leaning on my neighbor's car and he came outside and told them to get off it. They asked him if he knew I was a murderer. He said he knew I was God's daughter, a woman who cared for her terminally ill mother and a good mother to her son. My boyfriend called the police and the picketers were forced to move out to the sidewalk in front of the complex. This was a Saturday. I told Joey not to go out, to have friends over, which he did while I went to work. When I got to work there were hundreds of protestors there, outside the clinic."[231]

Follow-up note: When Sanford met with detectives to discuss the Burger King incident, she was told that since Joey willingly got into the car, there was nothing they could do. "I said that I thought that was awful and was told that if I was so scared as a mom I should quit my job. They don't understand what I've gotten from this work. Before I came to the clinic, I hadn't thought much about feminism. I came to Aware Woman and learned so much about what women deserve, about courage and strength. I no longer accept what is unacceptable."[232]

MARCH: NATIONWIDE

Convicted clinic firebomber John Brockhoeft released the first issue of *The Brockhoeft Report*. Since Brockhoeft was incarcerated at the time the magazine was launched, he had Oregon activist Shelley Shannon mail it for him. Among the report's musings: "It is a well-known fact that some people who deliberately and knowingly worship Satan take jobs in abortion chambers. How could a real Satanist resist an opportunity to participate in human sacrifice with immunity from prosecution? In some Satanic covens a young woman must submit to the initiation of getting pregnant and aborting the baby." The report was mailed to approximately two hundred people.[233]

MARCH 1: MELBOURNE, FLORIDA

Naomi Oliver (a pseudonym) received the following letter from Meredith Raney, "Chief Investigator" of the Women's Legal Action Coalition, five weeks after having an abortion at the Aware Woman Center for Choice.

> Your vehicle was seen at the Aware Woman Clinic in Melbourne, Florida on December 23, 1992, a day when abortions were performed. We are a group of concerned citizens organized specifically to help women having problems after an abortion. If you or your loved one are hurting after an abortion, please let us help. Many women have been damaged either physically or emotionally or both by abortion at the Aware Woman Clinic. We have doctors in Melbourne who can help with these problems. The Aware Woman Clinic's doctors come from at least 60 miles away. Their doctors are only there on abortion days, usually Wednesday and Saturday. The people there on other days are not doctors, they are nurse practitioners or physician's assistants. If you are hurting, see a doctor not a nurse or practitioner.[234]

Like other letter recipients, Oliver was annoyed that Raney had traced motor vehicle records to obtain her address. She was not swayed by the letter; in fact, she reported Raney's intrusion to clinic staff and expressed her willingness to testify against him if legal action was initiated.

In a sworn deposition in 1998, Raney admitted not only that the Women's Legal Action Coalition did not exist as an organization, but also that he had no license to work as an investigator.

MARCH 3: WASHINGTON, D.C.

Sixty-three members of Congress signed onto a letter to the Honorable William Sessions, director of the FBI:

Dear Mr. Sessions,

In 1992 over 40 women's health centers were targets of noxious butyric acid attacks. . . . In many cases the fumes from the chemical have forced police and staff to be hospitalized. Some establishments have been forced to close for several days. Clinics have incurred thousands of dollars of damage as they have had to replace carpets, walls and equipment. Based on the number of nationwide attacks that have occurred and the clear threat to public health and safety that they present, we believe that the FBI should begin an investigation of these attacks.[235]

MARCH 10: PENSACOLA, FLORIDA

Jeanne Singletary, assistant to the clinic administrator at Pensacola Medical Services (PMS), knew something was wrong the second she arrived at her office. Although she had worked at the clinic for two years, she had never before seen picketers at the facility. In fact, the closest she had ever come to anti-abortion protestors was driving past The Ladies Center or viewing photos of disruptions on television or in newspapers.

"I usually got to work at the crack of dawn and our doctor, David Gunn, usually got here between 8:30 and 9:00," she says. "That day I walked among the protestors and watched them. What made me wonder was that they were all dressed up, in church clothes, so I knew something was up. Donny Gratton, John Burt and young women from Burt's group home were marching out front. There were about fifteen of them. The staff thought we should try to stop Dr. Gunn from coming in. We wanted to let him know that protestors were here. We beeped him but he did not answer the page. He probably thought, 'I'm on my way. We'll talk when I get in.'"[236]

Shortly thereafter, Singletary remembers hearing an explosive noise. Another staffer went upstairs to look out a window and when she screamed, Singletary says she instinctively knew what had occurred. "David was lying near the rear entrance out back. We got blood pressure cuffs out and worked on him. I went crazy. I was screaming and screaming," she says. "Meanwhile, the protestors out front didn't even come to the back of the building to see what had happened. They knew. I started screaming at Burt and Gratton: 'You killed him. What kind of people are you?' The cops were out front and patients were in the building. The police got us all in one room and made us close the curtains and windows. The six of us working that day were questioned one at a time, all day long. Calls were forwarded to a clinic in Mary Esther [Florida] that was owned by the same doctor who owned PMS. We reopened two days later."[237]

Although David Gunn was rushed to the hospital, the forty-seven-year-old doctor from Eufaula, Alabama, was pronounced dead later that day, the first fatality in the one-sided war against abortion.

"When we found out that he had been shot, we tried to reach his family," says Linda Taggart, administrator of Community Healthcare Center of Pensacola, Inc., the second Pensacola clinic that employed Gunn. "CNN broadcast it before we notified them. By the time they called the hospital he had died. That was no way for the family to hear."[238]

"We had begged David to get a car phone," she continues. "It might have saved his life; at least it might have stopped the antis that day."[239] Tears stream down her face as she describes the impact of losing both a friend and colleague, and she repeatedly points to the many photographs of Gunn decorating her office. "David worked with us from 1986 or '87. As soon as he came it was as if family had arrived," she says. "He was funny, flirtatious, interesting. Every Friday when we were through he'd come into my office and we'd discuss all the problems in the world. He was very political. He wanted to help women maintain pregnancies when they wanted to be pregnant or help them when they did not. He would ask every patient on the table if she was registered to vote. If she was not he gave her a lecture. David was five foot five and about 125 pounds. He'd had polio as a child and had been tormented because of this affliction and because he had to wear a brace on his leg. Maybe it made him more sensitive. He was one of the best physicians I have ever known. He could do anything. He was our only doctor, and we closed for about two weeks after he died, until we could find another. For the first three or four weeks after we reopened we had temporary doctors step in."[240]

The Ladies Center (the Center was renamed the Community Healthcare Center of Pensacola, Inc., in the late 1990s) had begun to use volunteer escorts to assist patients several months before Gunn was killed. Taggart believes this influenced Michael Frederick Griffin, the man who pulled the trigger killing Gunn, since PMS did not use attendants.

Griffin—a former nuclear power plant supervisor who had spent six years in the navy—had a rocky personal history. The son of a Pensacola dentist, he and his wife, Patricia, had lived in Bremerton, Washington, before moving back to Pensacola in April 1987. The couple separated in March 1991, after nearly a decade of marriage. Michael filed for divorce on August 14, 1991; his petition asked for joint custody of their children. Patricia filed a counter petition demanding sole custody. Her response claimed that Michael "suffers from great fits of violence" and stated that he had been abusive to both her and the children.[241] While the Griffins reconciled in March 1992, the pastor of Charity

Chapel, a church they attended in the months before the killing, told the *Pensacola News Journal* that, "I am afraid people will think he did this because he was impassioned about the pro-life movement. But he had other problems. He was obviously a very angry person."[242]

Likewise, the Reverend John Kilpatrick, pastor of the Brownsville Assembly of God, a church the Griffins had belonged to in 1987, told the press that "Griffin was real hard on his family . . . abusing all of them, slapping them around. Mike was rigid in his views."[243]

Griffin's rage may also have been fueled by John Burt. At Griffin's trial Burt testified that Patricia and Michael had volunteered at Our Father's House prior to the slaying. He further testified that he had shown them two anti-abortion videos and encouraged them to attend anti-abortion events.

Follow-up note: Griffin's trial began on February 21, 1994. He was convicted of first-degree premeditated murder by a twelve-person jury on March 5. Escambia Circuit Court Judge John Parnham gave him a mandatory sentence of life in prison with no chance of parole for twenty-five years.[244]

Michael and Patricia Griffin are now divorced.

MARCH 10: MELBOURNE, FLORIDA

Shortly after noon on March 10, clinic consultant Ruth Arick came running into Aware Woman to report that a Pensacola doctor had been shot and killed. Because Melbourne had been in the news since the January arrival of the Impact Team, swarms of media immediately converged on the city for an up-close look at a clinic under siege.

"The *St. Paul Pioneer Dispatch,* a Mobile, Alabama, paper, the BBC and dozens of reporters from all over the world arrived," says Patricia Baird-Windle. "The *Montel Williams* show called me, and while our lawyers were attempting to polish the legal papers asking for an injunction, and staff and I grieved for David, I flew to New York. During this period I was doing between twenty and sixty interviews a day and was having horrific nightmares. One of the ones that kept repeating had me trying to hide from the antis. In the dream I kept breathing noisily, and I would wake up terrified that the only way to avoid detection was to literally stop breathing, to die. I would be shaken up for hours afterwards."[245]

Other clinic workers, including Susan Hill of the National Women's Health Organization and Merle Hoffman of Choices Women's Medical Center in New York City, also appeared on national TV talk shows in the days following Gunn's murder. Likewise, Paul Hill, a Pensacola extremist who would commit two abortion-related murders in 1994, appeared on programs including the *Phil Donahue Show* and *Nightline*. It was the clinic staffers' first exposure to him and his debut as a national anti-abortion spokesman.

MARCH 11: GRANITE CITY, ILLINOIS

Tim Dreste, second in command of the Missouri Militia, showed up at the Hope Clinic for Women the day after David Gunn's assassination carrying a home-made sign that named the clinic's medical director and asked: "Dr. [name], Do you feel under the Gunn?"[246]

MARCH 11: WICHITA, KANSAS

The same day that Dreste scared Illinois clinic workers, a Wichita gynecologist woke up to find all four tires on his car slashed. A picture of a dismembered fetus was stuck to the vehicle's windshield. The unnamed doctor resigned from his job at a family planning clinic within weeks of the vandalism.[247]

MARCH 13: SHOREVIEW, MINNESOTA

Since 1991, following the acquisition of a permanent injunction limiting protest at the Midwest Health Center for Women in Minneapolis, anti-abortion groups have put their energy into disturbing Jeri Rasmussen, the clinic's director, at her suburban home. Picket lines, "wanted" posters, derogatory leaflets and petty vandalism have become everyday events.

Immediately after the murder of David Gunn, Rasmussen found roofing nails in her driveway; her vigilance foiled their impact, and she cleared them away before they damaged her tires. The next night, however, Rasmussen was startled awake by a disturbing phone call at 3:00 A.M. "Quit killing babies, Jeri," the caller told her. "Around 6:30 or 7:00 A.M. I went downstairs," Rasmussen recalls. "It was a Sunday, a wonderful late-winter, early-spring snowy day, brilliantly bright. But I felt like something was strange when I went into my dining room. The sun was streaming in and I finally realized that my whole table was covered with broken glass. I then found a rock with a note wrapped around it saying, 'don't kill babies.' The police came out and took pictures but made no arrests. There is no police department in Shoreview. The County Sheriff provides service to the suburbs. The officers were nice to me, but I believe they had someone above them putting the kibosh on doing anything more. I paid out of pocket to replace the window in my dining room, and clean up and fix a chair that had been gouged by glass."[248]

MARCH 23: WASHINGTON, D.C.

Senator Edward M. Kennedy [D-MA] introduced the Freedom of Access to Clinic Entrances (FACE) Act in the United States Senate. In his opening remarks Kennedy reminded his colleagues that, "Over 100 clinics have been torched or bombed in the past 15 years. Over 300 have been invaded and over 400 have been vandalized. Already this year, clinics have sustained more than $1.3 million in damages from arson alone." He then stressed that only federally enacted laws can stop the rising toll of nationwide extremist acts and the resulting damage to property and to the well-being of clinic patients and staff.[249]

A *Congressional Research Service* report sided with Kennedy and argued in favor of FACE, concluding that prosecution by local law enforcement agencies had proven inadequate in protecting clinics from destruction and sabotage.

> Small towns faced with large organized blockade activities have had to divert significant amounts of money to fund additional police protection, arrest processing procedures, and incarceration costs for demonstrators. Even still, some towns have been unable to effectively deal with the number of protestors, and medical clinics have become temporarily inaccessible. . . . A further concern is that local officials may be reluctant to take action against demonstrators. In some cases, prosecutors have refused to prosecute blockade cases, law enforcement officials have refused to arrest protestors, and judges have refused to convict. In other cases, law enforcement officials have been passive, or even active participants along with the demonstrators in their blockade.[250]

FACE was signed into law by President Bill Clinton on May 26, 1994, and prohibits the use of force or the threat of force or physical obstruction to "injure, intimidate, or interfere with providers of reproductive health services or their patients." FACE also makes it a federal crime to damage or destroy the property of a reproductive health center.[251]

There are two types of FACE actions, civil and criminal. Criminal actions can be brought only by the Department of Justice; the law stipulates that convictions for nonviolent obstruction of a clinic can result in fines of up to $10,000 and six months in jail for a first offense and up to $25,000 and eighteen months in jail for each subsequent violation. Other breaches can lead to $100,000 in fines and a year in jail for the initial offense and $250,000 and three years in jail for later infractions. Civil FACE cases can be brought by a state attorney general, clinic staff, doctors or patients, and the courts can grant injunctions or actual or punitive damages as relief.[252]

FACE has been upheld by every Federal Circuit Court of Appeals in the United States.

MARCH 26–28: MELBOURNE, FLORIDA

The Aware Woman Center for Choice appeared in state circuit court to request an injunction against illegal anti-abortion activities. During the three-day hearing, Judge McGregor's home phone line was jammed and both his residence and courtroom were picketed.

McGregor issued the injunction on April 7 and mandated a thirty-six-foot buffer zone around clinic entrances and driveways. He also barred the antis from making excessive noise or using sound amplification equipment.

The antis appealed the ruling to the Fifth District Court; the court refused to hear their argument and bumped the case to the Florida Supreme Court.[253]

SPRING: MILWAUKEE, WISCONSIN

The National Abortion Federation (NAF) reported increased tensions in Milwaukee due to a daily talk-radio program giving voice to Missionaries to the Pre-Born and other hatemongers. NAF's *Clinic Support Update* quotes a program in which Joe Foreman, a Missionaries leader, compared abortion providers to man-eating tigers. "When a tiger in India starts attacking and killing and eating human beings, you have to go and take it out," he told listeners. "Well, what you have in the case of an abortionist is somebody who is in the midst of a very complex medical field, and they've just gotten a taste of human blood, that's all."[254]

According to NAF, Missionaries founder Matt Trewhella took Foreman's statements even further when he urged his audience to buy weapons. "The reason we should have guns is because we are Christians," he said. "The reason we should have guns is because of our government."[255]

Complaints to the Federal Communications Commission (FCC) proved fruitless; the FCC told NAF that the comments were not in violation of FCC regulations.

MARCH 29: MISSOULA, MONTANA

"It was kind of out of nowhere," says Anita Kuennen, executive director of the Blue Mountain Clinic in Missoula, Montana, about the firebombing that rocked the city's oldest abortion clinic that early-spring night. "We did not expect such violence. We'd had some 'rescues' (in 1989 and again in 1991) and had received a few personal threats and some hate mail from a man named Michael Ross. We'd also had pretty consistent protests outside, but we had escorts to help our patients get in and we generally felt that we functioned pretty well."[256]

The fire was ignited by Richard Thomas Andrews, a longtime abortion foe from Wenatchee, Washington. Andrews was convicted in the winter of 1997 of setting eight clinic fires (including two at the FWHC in Redding, California) in four western states—California, Montana, Oregon and Washington—during a three-year period.

The Blue Mountain fire was started when a gas can was thrown through a window and ignited. "The clinic was in a row of buildings," Kuennen says. "It was not a quality structure and it burned very quickly. We had been there a long time and the clinic was completely destroyed. We were able to save a lot of files, but that was all we could salvage. We had to oxygenate them, a lengthy process that allows you to separate the pages to remove the smoke scent and damage."[257]

Despite the overwhelming destruction, Kuennen says that staff never considered closing shop. Instead, they operated out of a donated space for nineteen months until a new facility, complete with bullet-resistant windows, firewalls and an enclosed parking lot, became ready for occupancy in October 1995.

Raising the money to create this new, highly secure space was, however, extremely difficult and required a multitiered fund-raising strategy: from applying for corporate, philanthropic and matching grants, to holding special events, to selling bonds. Gloria Steinem traveled to Missoula to help the clinic raise money, as did other nationally prominent leaders. All told, nearly $1 million was gathered.[258] Community support, says Kuennen, was immediately evident. The day after the firebombing, pro-choice activists held an impromptu speak-out so that people could express their outrage about the violence. Surprisingly, she says, many local anti-abortionists appeared contrite. "Most of them no longer seemed as comfortable standing outside yelling at patients. In a community this small, people don't want to have that association with violence, or even with the potential for violence. Most are now more legislatively focused, more active on the political level with electoral stuff."[259]

Unfortunately, while most of Missoula's anti-abortion activists were cooling their heels in seeming embarrassment, an encouraged Michael Ross was increasing his harassment of clinic staff in other parts of the state. A letter to Dr. Susan Wicklund, the Bozeman clinic owner whose Minnesota home had been the site of a month-long protest in 1991, underscored the continuing threat facing everyone who worked in reproductive health: "Isn't it awful that a clinic was torched in Missoula?" he wrote just days after the fire. "Tsk. Tsk. Could it happen in Bozeman?"[260]

"The bombing was really devastating," Kuennen admits. "We were in shock but we also got a sense of secret gratification from what happened. We got to be the phoenix. We not only affirmed our place in the community but we prospered as a result of our misfortune. We were able to rise above it. Of course, we're not glad it happened, but we were able to come out of it stronger, with a much nicer building for patients and staff to work out of."[261]

Indeed. As a result of a successful capital campaign, The Blue Mountain Clinic has expanded its services and now reaches a greater number of Missoula's 70,000-plus people. A "full family practice," it offers health education, acupuncture, pediatric care, prenatal exams, routine gynecological services, vasectomies, mental health counseling and massage, as well as approximately five hundred abortions a year. Several years ago, the service shift caused staff to remove the word "women's" from their name to reflect their more comprehensive offerings.[262]

Richard Thomas Andrews is currently serving a seven-year sentence for his arson spree. Ross was sentenced to ten years in state prison for felony intimidation; he was released in 1999.

APRIL: ORLANDO, FLORIDA

The Women's Health Center, one of four clinics in the greater Orlando area, had been using private security guards for more than a decade when Dr. David Gunn was killed in Pensacola. Tammy Sobieski, the clinic's owner, says that within a month of the murder she approached the Country Sheriff about hiring off-duty police officers to perform security functions, a safety measure employed by health centers across the country. "The previous sheriff had been good to us, but once this man took office I was no longer sure if we would get any support," says Sobieski. "I knew that he belonged to a church whose students had picketed the Orlando Women's Health Organization, but when Gunn was shot I decided to call his office and make my request. When I got called back, the person said that the new sheriff had instituted a ban on cops working at clinics, even if off-duty. I went back and forth with them on this for a year. After Dr. Tiller got shot in August, several providers including Patricia Baird-Windle, Kathy Spillar of the Feminist Majority Foundation and I met with the governor and complained that the sheriff would not let off-duty cops work at clinics, but the governor was not at all helpful. Then, in July 1994, Dr. Britton and James Barrett got shot. When the newspapers called me for a comment, I again complained about the policy prohibiting cops from working to protect us. I also said that if anything happened to us I was going to sue. A few days later I got a call from the person who handles off-duty officers. I was told that the ban had been lifted." The center now employs off-duty officers, at a cost of $18 an hour, whenever it needs additional protection.[263]

APRIL 8: MELBOURNE, FLORIDA

According to Aware Woman Center for Choice co-owner, Ted Windle, the day news of the clinic's injunction against the antis hit the newspapers, Operation Rescue, the Impact Team and Operation Goliath, a local "rescue" group, held a press conference. "Keith Tucci announced that some antis had bought the house directly across the street from the clinic and would now keep a twenty-four-hour-a-day, seven-day-a-week presence at Aware Woman," he says.[264]

Although the title originally rested with a woman unknown to the clinic, within the first year ownership passed to anti-abortion activist Jay Rogers, editor of *The Forerunner,* an arch-conservative Christian newsletter and website. "Rogers lived in the house and they used it to store stuff and as a gathering place," Windle continues. "They also apparently installed long-range microphones so they could hear our conversations. One time a reporter told Patricia, in confidence, that she was leaving the newspaper for another job. They had this conversation while sitting in the garden. The reporter later went across the street to interview the antis and the first thing they said was, 'So, how are you going to like your new job?'"[265]

The house has also served as a staging ground for a host of tactics against the health center. In the spring of 1994, for example, Windle went to the clinic over a long weekend to find that fast-growing grass seed had been sprinkled on the lawn, spelling "the killing place." Shortly thereafter Windle was told that Rogers and friends had registered the name, "The Killing Place," with the county as a certified business. "The next thing we knew they erected a mailbox with 'The Killing Place' painted on it. The box was attached to a thick, telephone pole–sized stake to keep it from being knocked over," he says. "This mailbox has been up ever since."[266] In addition, patient license plate information has been copied by "scribes" from the house's front stoop.

Follow-up note: Jay Rogers moved out of the building in the summer of 1998; another activist has taken occupancy and has converted the space into a crisis pregnancy and spiritual center.

APRIL 10: MELBOURNE, FLORIDA

The Melbourne police had made no arrests during the Impact Team's assault on the Aware Woman Center for Choice until the clinic received an injunction limiting the antis' activities.

Patricia Baird-Windle: "Police would only charge protestors if they trespassed, and the antis, for the most part, stayed on legal territory although they did block the driveway when law enforcers were present. Then, on the Saturday before Easter, April 10, the supposed last day of the Impact Team, they did a fairly massive blockade and violated the injunction. The police took their time, but they eventually made more than seventy arrests. Every Saturday after that, for years, the antis would return to violate the injunction."[267]

APRIL 12: SATELLITE BEACH, FLORIDA

The Reverend Susan Beem-Berry penned the following letter to National Public Radio in response to a program she felt understated the danger of anti-abortion harassment.

I am an Episcopal clergy woman. The Melbourne newspaper, *Florida Today* (part of the Gannett chain that publishes *USA Today*), published an article that I wrote articulating a pro-choice Christian perspective. After my article was published I received numerous threatening and annoying phone calls. I received signed and unsigned letters chastising me for breaking ranks with the "Christian family" on this issue. Anti-choice people visited my church one Sunday morning looking for me. The bishop of this Episcopal diocese has received a deluge of mail protesting that I would dare present an alternative Christian perspective on abortion.

My experience, however, is nothing compared to the brutal harassment of Dr. Frank Snydle, a doctor who recently resigned from working with our local clinic. He told a BBC reporter that the OR people in Melbourne are the meanest and most vociferous group of pro-life demonstrators that he has ever encountered. On one occasion they phoned the doctor's 82-year-old mother in the middle of the night and told her that Dr. Snydle had been killed. Another time they called the doctor's house and told him that his 18-year-old son had been in a serious car accident and was in the hospital ER. The doctor, of course, rushed to the ER only to find that it was a cruel hoax. This does not even begin to take into account the hundreds of death threats, the picketing of his home, the phone calls in the middle of the night, the "wanted" posters, and the times that OR followed Dr. Snydle all over the state.[268]

APRIL 18: MELBOURNE, FLORIDA

A week after the Impact Team officially left Melbourne, local clinic defenders and patient escorts decided that the time was right for a celebratory they-never-shut-the-clinic-down picnic. Held in a public park by the beach, the activists used the occasion to kick back, relax and swap stories. "It was Holocaust Memorial Sunday so I had to leave early to get to a service," says clinic defender, the Reverend Susan Beem-Berry, "but my husband, John, who had also been active in clinic defense, stayed. The group was laughing, telling jokes and generally carrying on. When I got home there was a message on my answering machine. Playing it, I heard John's laugh, and I heard someone else telling a joke. John's laughter was clear. It was obvious that the antis had recorded our party; not only had they done surveillance, but they wanted me to know they had done surveillance. This had to have been recorded from at least fifty yards away since we hadn't seen any recording equipment anywhere near the picnic site. I called the police and the sheriff came and took the tape. He also agreed to drive around our house more often to keep an eye on things. The sheriff was good; he would not take shit from these people. But the police in Melbourne see Patricia as the problem—their attitude is that she should just close the clinic—and they did not do much of anything to help her or Aware Woman."[269]

MAY 19: KANSAS CITY, MISSOURI

Shots were fired into the playroom of a house owned by Dr. Robert Crist. No one was injured in the middle-of-the-night incident. At the time of the shooting, Crist was employed at a clinic in Springfield, Missouri, and had recently taken a job at Planned Parenthood of Kansas City.

On May 10 a toll free anti-abortion hotline told callers that Crist had been seen at Planned Parenthood and speculated that he had become a regular physician there. The message added that "we have been assured that he will be monitored and appropriate action will be taken." Nine days later someone fired into his home.[270]

SUMMER: SHOREVIEW, MINNESOTA

Jeri Rasmussen, director of the Midwest Health Center for Women in Minneapolis, was in a local grocery store picking up a few items for a relative who had broken her foot when she noticed a male store patron smiling at her. "It was around 10:30 at night. I was going around with my cart and I thought the guy was just being friendly. He was in every aisle I went in," she says. "Finally, in the entertainment aisle, he came up to me and said, 'Jeri, Jesus loves you. Stop killing babies, Jeri.' Nothing else happened but it was pretty unnerving."[271]

Follow-up note: This tactic is called "St. John the Baptisting" and is widely reported by clinic workers and their families. Ted Windle was accosted in the grocery store and at the post office. Reid Windle, Ted and Patricia's oldest son, was confronted in the supermarket.

JUNE: ANAHEIM, CALIFORNIA

The Reverend Steven Mather, pastor of the First Presbyterian church and president of Planned Parenthood of Orange and San Bernardino Counties, came home to find his community blanketed with an unsigned "Neighborhood Alert." A large photo of Mather graced the leaflet, and his home and workplace addresses were prominently displayed.

The flyer's message was direct:

It has come to our attention that Rev. Steven J. Mather, an ordained Presbyterian minister, has disgraced the body of Christ by aligning himself publicly and unequivocally, with Planned Parenthood of America, the nation's largest abortion provider and number one murderer of innocent unborn children in America. As a resident of this community and neighbor of Rev. Mather, you have a right to know that his active support of such a monstrous organization, while claiming to represent God in his community and congregation, makes him a danger to unborn children throughout southern California. . . . Please join us in denouncing the activities of Rev. Mather by confronting him directly, by calling the church to voice your outrage, or by writing a letter to him at his home or work address (listed above).

"While not directly threatening," Mather wrote in 1999, "the leaflet certainly was a bit intimidating. But in the end it only made most of my neighbors upset at the sentiments of those distributing them."[272]

At the time that the one-page sheet was distributed, the Planned Parenthood that Mather worked with did not provide abortion services; the affiliate began providing them in 1998.

JULY: SEVEN CITIES

Operation Rescue's Cities of Refuge campaign—ten simultaneous demonstrations slated for Central Florida, Cleveland, Dallas/Fort Worth, Jackson (Mississippi), Minneapolis, Philadelphia and San Jose—were lightly attended. Not wanting a repeat of what happened in Wichita, pro-choice forces mobilized and law enforcers acted swiftly to curtail illegal activities. Prior to OR's arrival in Minnesota, for example, Attorney General Hubert H. Humphrey III sent the group a letter warning that "physical interference with the right to obtain an abortion cannot and will not be tolerated in this state."[273]

JULY: PENSACOLA, FLORIDA

Anti-abortion activist Paul Hill, founder of a group called Defensive Action, issued a statement declaring his organization's support for violence as a tactic to end abortion. The statement read: "We declare the justice of taking all Godly action necessary to defend innocent human life including the use of force. We proclaim that whatever force is legitimate to defend the life of a born child is legitimate to defend the life of an unborn child. We assert that if Michael Griffin did, in fact, kill David Gunn, his use of lethal force was justifiable providing it was carried out for the purpose of defending the lives of unborn children."[274]

Although Hill told the *Pensacola News Journal* that Defensive Action had only five members, the statement was signed by such "pro-life" luminaries as Michael Bray, Andrew Burnett, Paul DeParrie, Paul Hill, Roy McMillan, Matt Trewhella and Father David Trosch.

JULY 16: LANCASTER, PENNSYLVANIA

Someone lit a wick in a bottle filled with gasoline and threw it at the front door of a Planned Parenthood clinic. The bottle did not explode and caused only minor damage. Nine weeks later, on September 29, firebombers finished the job, destroying the clinic's examination rooms, a business office and equipment. The facility performed medical exams, including screening for cervical cancer, AIDS and other sexually transmitted diseases. It did not provide abortions.[275]

AUGUST 19: WICHITA, KANSAS

Dr. George Tiller, one of the country's premier providers of second- and third-trimester abortions, had just completed an application to the World Population

Council to request that Women's Health Care Services be allowed to participate in a study of RU-486, a chemical abortifacient. "It was 7:00 P.M. on a Thursday night. I had just finished the paperwork and was all pumped up," he recalls. "As I drove out I noticed five, six, seven antis and remember thinking, 'Gee, the spooks are here late tonight.' Then someone approached my car. She had something in her hand and I thought she was going to give me a leaflet. It turned out she was holding a gun. As she got closer I gave her the finger and turned the car to the right. If I hadn't given her the finger I might have gotten the bullet in the chest. Instead, I was hit in both arms."[276]

Tiller knew that he had been shot. Nonetheless, he tried to chase his assailant as she attempted to flee from the clinic's parking lot. "She was on foot," he says, "and I wanted to stop her. I was looking at her through the window she'd shot out. But after a few minutes I realized that I was pretty woozy so I went back to the clinic. I recall saying I'd drive myself to the hospital but there was a police officer standing there and he told me to lie down and wait for the ambulance so I did. It seemed like suddenly everybody and their brother was around. I had no idea why these people were there. My time perception was way off."[277]

A clinic nurse, who had also been working late, saw the woman who fired at Tiller and had the presence of mind to write down the license tag number and physical description of the car she was driving. The shooter turned out to be Oregon activist Rachelle "Shelley" Shannon, the woman who had mailed the first issue of *The Brockhoeft Report* as a favor for incarcerated pal John Brockhoeft and in whose yard the *Army of God Manual* was found. She was apprehended when she returned a car she had rented days earlier to an Oklahoma airport.

Peggy Bowman was the public relations specialist at the clinic from 1988 to 1998 and was at a fund raiser for the Pro-Choice Action League (PCAL) the night Tiller was wounded. "It was terrifying," she says. "I went to the clinic immediately after being called and learned that Dr. Tiller had already been taken to surgery, so I went to the hospital and waited for news. When he got out of surgery to remove the bullets I spoke to him. I then spent until 2:00 A.M. handling calls from all over the world. I mean literally, nonstop. At 6:00 A.M. it started again and did not let up. It was absolutely incredible. The irony of the whole thing was that in addition to the enormous trauma of the event, we were having another PCAL fund raiser that night, August 20, and had planned a surprise roast of Dr. Tiller. I assumed it would be called off. But he insisted that the party not be canceled."[278] The fund raiser went off as scheduled and was a huge success. Bowman says that despite everyone's frayed nerves, "it allowed our closest friends and supporters to come together at a moment of incredible crisis and it was really, really wonderful."[279]

Patient coordinator Cathy Reavis also remembers her reaction to news of Tiller's shooting. She had just gotten home from work when she was called by the nurse who had witnessed Shannon fire her semiautomatic handgun at the doctor. "My first thought was that the patients who were in for multiple-day procedures would freak out if they heard about this on the news. I knew I had to return to the clinic and get patients' phone numbers so I could tell them that Dr. Tiller was okay, not in serious condition. I told them that things would be fine, not to worry, that doctors from all over the country were calling to offer their help and that we'd take good care of them. Fifteen or sixteen patients were scheduled for that Friday."[280]

Although Reavis says that on the surface things at the clinic returned to normal fairly quickly—Tiller showed up for work the day after being shot—the threat of violence became an insidious undercurrent in the center's day-to-day functioning. "Everyone reacted to the stress in one way or another," she says. "I found myself being short with patients. I wanted them to understand that we were doing this for them. I wanted them to be grateful for the risks we face. We got together with a mental health counselor about a week after the shooting because we were all so angry. That helped. But it takes a long time and there is always the suggestion of something else happening. You never know what you'll find when you turn into the parking lot."[281]

Follow-up note: Shelley Shannon was found guilty of one count of felony aggravated assault and was sentenced to eleven years in prison in April 1994.[282] At her trial, the unrepentant activist, who was also linked to arson attacks in Eugene and Portland, Oregon, and to butyric acid attacks in Reno, Nevada, and Chico, California, rambled to the court that, "I believe there are occasions when a person becomes so evil and perhaps to stop the crimes they're causing or to stop them from murdering all kinds of other people, such as in the case of Hitler, or maybe others, that it may take something like their death to stop what they're doing."[283]

Dr. Tiller has slight nerve damage in both hands but continues to work at the clinic full time. In 1993 he was awarded the Faith and Freedom Award from the Religious Coalition for Reproductive Choice, and in 1994 he received the Christopher Tietze Humanitarian Award from the National Abortion Federation.

AUGUST 21: MOBILE, ALABAMA

The owner of Pensacola Medical Services (PMS), Dr. George Wayne Patterson, was shot to death outside an adult movie theater.[284] Patterson had begun working at PMS after the murder of Dr. David Gunn five months earlier; he was one of two physicians working there at the time of his demise.[285]

Although the case was never solved and was officially designated a robbery, Jeanne Singletary, assistant to the clinic administrator at PMS, says that she does not believe police reports that classified the killing as the result of a bungled theft. "He had a car phone, a wallet and a new car. Nothing was taken," she says.[286] Instead, both she and clinic administrator Sandy Sheldon believe that the murder was abortion related. They refer to a "wanted" poster, which described Patterson and his car, issued in April 1993, to add weight to their claim. Nonetheless, the contention that Patterson was killed because he was a provider has never been proved; to this day, clinic staff are frustrated by the reluctance of law enforcement to affix blame for the murder on anti-abortionists.

Despite misgivings, staff have dealt with their grief by picking up the pieces and, where possible, finding medical replacements for the slain physician. "There was nobody to do anything after Dr. Patterson was killed," says Sheldon. "It was unreal. We had to close a clinic he owned in Mary Esther, Florida, about an hour's drive from Pensacola, and three he owned in Mobile, Alabama, because we had no one to provide medical care. Overnight, Mobile went from having four clinics to having one."[287] Dr. Patterson's son currently owns PMS, and doctors were found to replace him at that site.

"If I let myself get incensed I'll be consumed by the injustice and not be good for anything," Sheldon concludes. "At this point there is nothing I can do, so I have had to let the anger go. Keeping PMS open is the best memorial we can give doctors Gunn and Patterson."[288]

AUGUST 28: MOBILE, ALABAMA

Nine days after Dr. George Tiller was wounded by Shelley Shannon in Wichita, Kansas, and one week after Dr. George Wayne Patterson was found murdered in Mobile, someone fired into the Center for Choice. No one was injured.

"The owner of the building happened to go by and saw that someone had shot through our front doors," says clinic owner Patricia Mitchell. "Whoever did it used a large-caliber armor-piercing bullet. It went into a wall, but it could have gone through a bulletproof vest."[289]

The shooting left Mitchell feeling more vulnerable than ever. "Before Wayne [Patterson] was killed we thought that David Gunn's murder was an isolated incident. Now there was no fooling ourselves."[290] Days after the building was shot at, Mitchell added a full-time armed security guard to the clinic's payroll.

SEPTEMBER 1: SOUTH FLORIDA

"We were at the end of our ten-year lease," says Carlyne Smith (a pseudonym). "The building we were in had been sold and the new landlord wanted us out. We found a new place and thought we were all set to go. We'd painted, put up wallpaper, everything. On moving day we loaded the truck and drove over but when we got to the new offices we found ourselves locked out. We later learned that the landlord had received several phoned-in death threats and the building had been leafleted by antis. The landlord obviously panicked. We went to court with a pro-bono lawyer, but we got a lousy judge who let the owner break the lease. So there we were, in the parking lot with all our stuff packed in a truck, and no office to go to."[291]

For two months the clinic (which asked not to be named for fear of attracting increased anti-abortion activity) stored most of its equipment in a warehouse while staff searched for new quarters. Throughout, it maintained a small, triage health service. Calls were forwarded to the clinic director's home, and staff members conducted what they call a "MASH operation" out of a local doctor's office. What kept them going, they say, was the outpouring of community support they received. Within weeks of losing their office, $15,638 was raised, much of it in $10 and $20 increments. The Virginia-based Feminist Majority Foundation sent organizers to assist with fundraising and provided the center with a $20,000 low-interest loan. Even the Realtor who ultimately found a new site for the beleaguered clinic donated her commission. By November 1993 they had relocated to an office that Smith says is "newer, bigger and better" than any of their previous ones.[292]

Nevertheless, anti-abortion activity remains a chronic problem at the facility. Recurrent bomb threats still require them to evacuate for hours at a time, and patient harassment is a daily event.

FALL: MELBOURNE, FLORIDA

Nurse administrator Roni Windle, formerly on staff at the Aware Woman Center for Choice, says that she felt sick when she opened her mailbox and found a photograph of a fetus with a picture of her twelve-year-old daughter's head superimposed on it. "I watched Lilia (a pseudonym) like a hawk for weeks and weeks," Windle says. "The police were called and told me they considered it a death threat. They took it as evidence but never arrested anyone for it."[293]

OCTOBER: BELLEVUE, NEBRASKA

Abortion providers know, deep in their souls, that the truism is correct: They who laugh, last.

Dr. LeRoy Carhart still chuckles when he speaks about the one and only arrest of anti-abortionists for illegally entering the Abortion and Contraception Clinic of Nebraska. At the time of the arrest, the clinic was located in an office building about one hundred yards from a doughnut shop. A medical assistant was outside, taking a break and smoking a cigarette, when she saw four anti-abortion activists run into the building through a back entrance clinic staff later learned had been propped open with a rubber eraser. The staff member, suspecting that a clinic invasion was under way, ran into the shop to call the police only to find five officers already there, eating and drinking, looking like a scene from a TV sitcom.

The police caught the intruders and arrested them; seasoned activists with histories that included prior arrests, the four received sentences ranging from thirty to 120 days in jail.[294]

OCTOBER 1: BUFFALO, NEW YORK

Six western New York abortion foes were fined a total of $110,967.42 by Judge Richard J. Arcara. William Ostrowski, an anti-abortion attorney in Buffalo, told the press that the punishment was putting a dent in the activities of the "pro-life" movement. "The offenses people are being charged with have been magnified from being at the level of a parking ticket to being some kind of federal crime," he said.[295]

Despite Ostrowski's statement, the six did not take their reprimand very seriously. According to pro-choice attorney Glenn A. Murray, no money was ever collected from those charged.[296]

OCTOBER 3: FT. WAYNE, INDIANA

Two hundred fifty abortion foes showed up at the Catholic cemetery on Lake Avenue for a service in memory of "children murdered by abortion." They unfurled American flags, piled fifty roses on a white casket the size of a bread box, and prayed for the 1,126 fetuses they estimated had been aborted at the Ft. Wayne Women's Health Organization between September 1, 1992, and August 31, 1993. According to the *Journal Gazette*, the number was calculated by protestors who had spent the year picketing outside the clinic.[297]

DECEMBER 3: ANAHEIM, CALIFORNIA

A former clerk at the Anaheim Police Department was sentenced to three years probation and two hundred hours of community service for giving the addresses of four abortion clinic staffers to anti-abortion demonstrators. Three of the four, including the director of Doctor's Family Planning Clinic in Tustin, California, were targeted for home picketing following the staffer's disclosure.

The former police worker admitted that she had obtained the data from confidential motor vehicle records.[298]

1994

NATIONWIDE

Despite repeated complaints that abortion opponents had limitless access to motor vehicle information—which providers say they used to harass clinic patients and staff—it was only after actor Rebecca Schaeffer was brutally murdered in the doorway of her Los Angeles apartment by a man who got her address through the Department of Motor Vehicles (DMV), that the federal government began to take heed.

The Federal Drivers' Privacy Protection Act of 1994 makes it a crime for a state DMV to knowingly disclose or make available personal information obtained in connection with a motor vehicle record. The law allows damages of up to $2,500 per offense plus punitive damages for "willful or reckless disregard of the law."[299]

Follow-up note: The United States Supreme Court upheld the Federal Drivers' Privacy Protection Act by a unanimous vote in 1999.

JANUARY: PORT ST. LUCIE, FLORIDA

Patricia Baird-Windle: "The Aware Woman Center in Port St. Lucie opened in 1988 in a twelve-unit professional building owned by two doctors. The building housed an optometrist, an optician, two dentists, a day care center, some lawyers and a Sears' sales office.

"Starting in 1993 the antis—who had previously blockaded several times and picketed the clinic on surgery days—went on a campaign that involved taking down the license number of every car entering the building's parking lot. They then sent out letters warning people that because there was an abortion clinic located at the site, their safety could not be guaranteed. Every parent of a child enrolled in the day care center got a letter saying that their kid was in danger. Shortly thereafter the landlords told us that they would not renew our lease when it expired in January 1994. By this point we were so worn out by the Impact Team and the constant chaos that we couldn't think clearly. We simply gave in and closed. This meant that the community we'd served for six years was without a provider."[300]

JANUARY 21: MELBOURNE, FLORIDA

Patricia Baird-Windle: "I was sick in bed when I got a call from a news reporter informing me that the United States Supreme Court had agreed to hear *Madsen v. Women's Health Center,* the case involving our injunction against the Impact Team and OR. Aware Woman had been working with a cobble of lawyers including Susan England, Talbot 'Sandy' D'Alemberte, Steven Gey and Kathy Patrick. Oral argument was scheduled for April 28. Two days after I got this call, I was in New York, appearing on *Good Morning America* to discuss whether an anti-abortion conspiracy existed."[301]

In early February a meeting of progressive and women's organizations was convened by the Feminist Majority Foundation (FMF), and groups were asked to submit amici, or friend of the court, briefs in support of the injunction. Several unions, as well as the American College of Obstetricians and Gynecologists, the American Civil Liberties Union, Planned Parenthood, Center for Reproductive Law and Policy, NOW, NARAL, NOW Legal Defense and Education Fund, American Medical Association and People for the American Way attended the day-long planning and strategy session.

Baird-Windle: "Most of the people at this meeting were initially uncomfortable with our injunction, fearing that we were violating the First Amendment rights of the protestors. We had to educate them about the antis, showing them proof that these venal extremists had crossed the line into abusive, medically dangerous behaviors. We showed them that the oft-repeated anti mantra, 'We're only exercising our right to free speech,' is a lie. The people at the meeting simply did not know how bad it was at clinics; after we explained things, most came around to support us and the women who use our services."[302]

FEBRUARY: WASHINGTON, D.C.

The FBI announced that it would, for the first time, begin investigating death threats received by doctors and other abortion clinic staff in the states of Florida, Indiana, Kansas and Wisconsin. The Bureau also said that agents would begin gathering evidence from local law enforcement officials about protests that had turned violent. According to the *Wall Street Journal,* during the Reagan-Bush era the FBI resisted community efforts to get it to investigate abortion-related violence. FBI officials denied jurisdiction and argued that local authorities should address the problem. The article concludes that while some local and state police departments responded, most were unwilling or ill-equipped to mount major investigations.[303]

MARCH: HOUSTON, TEXAS

The funeral of abortion provider Dr. John Coleman, who died of congestive heart failure on March 5, was picketed by Rescue America leader Don Treshman and his followers. According to the National Abortion Federation, Treshman told at least one church elder that he was "like a religious leader in 1940s' Germany, attempting to pull Hitler's remains out of the ashes for a funeral."[304]

MARCH 10: WASHINGTON, D.C.

President Bill Clinton sent the following letter to the National Coalition of Abortion Providers (NCAP) to mark the one-year anniversary of Dr. David Gunn's death. "In a nation committed to upholding the rule of law, we cannot allow violent outlaws to restrict the rights of women. I am pleased that you are continuing your work to stop the violence. By heightening public awareness of this tragic problem, you play a vital role in helping to ensure that all women have access to the safe, quality health services they need."[305] He said nothing, however, about the federal government's role in this endeavor.

MARCH 20: LOS ANGELES, CALIFORNIA

Dr. Paul Hackmeyer, a gynecologist who performs abortions, was shot and wounded in the driveway of his home. Police classified the shooting as a robbery although nothing was taken. No arrests were made.[306]

SPRING: BELLEVUE, NEBRASKA

The Abortion and Contraception Clinic of Nebraska, located in Bellevue and owned by Dr. LeRoy Carhart, has conventional-looking locks on its front and back doors, but these locks are only for show. Staff enter and exit the building by activating electronic, keyless locks. Twice during the spring of 1994, says Carhart, anti-abortionists glued the keyholes only to discover that their acts of intended sabotage had no impact on clinic functioning. "We didn't even notice it for quite a while," he laughs. "I guess they got frustrated because the week after the second gluing they brought five-gallon buckets of hog manure and piled it up against the clinic door. It stunk really badly but the police said we could just spray it away with water. The sewer drain was right there and the smell does not linger, so once it was washed away it was gone."[307]

Although Carhart makes light of the incident, large-scale manure spills have been linked to both human illness and environmental destruction. According to writer Kristin Kolb, manure spills killed approximately 700,000 fish in Iowa, Missouri and Minnesota in 1996. In addition, in Virginia, Maryland and North Carolina, excrement from huge pig and chicken farms has been linked to outbreaks of *Pfiesteria*, estuary-based organisms that produce toxins believed to cause abnormal brain function, burning skin and respiratory distress.[308]

Follow-up note: No arrests have ever been made for either the gluing or manure dumping at Carhart's Abortion and Contraception Clinic.

Health centers report that replacing and installing multiple locks often costs upward of $1,000.

SPRING: MASSACHUSETTS

After the shooting death of Dr. David Gunn in Pensacola, Florida, Attorney General Janet Reno offered to provide extra security to clinics that needed it. Need was determined by an evaluation conducted by the government.

Nicki Nichols Gamble, president of the Planned Parenthood League of Massachusetts until June 1999, told the *Boston Herald* that Boston had been deemed ineligible for added assistance because the city was not considered as dangerous as other locations.[309]

Clinics in eleven cities were ultimately given marshals' protection: Des Moines, Iowa; Falls Church, Virginia; Fargo, North Dakota; Ft. Wayne, Indiana; Gulfport, Mississippi; Jackson, Mississippi; Melbourne, Florida; Milwaukee, Wisconsin; Pensacola, Florida; Washington, D.C.; and Wichita, Kansas.[310]

APRIL 29: WASHINGTON, D.C.

Although the United States Supreme Court had been scheduled to hear arguments in *Madsen v. Women's Health Center* on April 28, the death of former president Richard Nixon pushed the case forward by one day. "We had been involved for months in the process of preparing the case," says Ted Windle, co-owner of the Aware Woman Center for Choice in Melbourne. "We'd held press conferences and moot courts and had tried to train our lawyers in what it was like to be under attack. I remember telling lawyer Sandy D'Alemberte to imagine himself as a young teenager. I took him through the scenario: You're scared to death, trying to keep this pregnancy from your parents. You've rounded up the money for an abortion, but you still don't know what will happen. You've listened to people who've told you what to expect but you don't want to be at the clinic and you don't want to see all those people out front. It's noisy. There are news trucks with towers and video cameras, people are screaming and crowding the streets, and someone is banging on the windows of your car. All you want to do is run. If you manage to make it through the crowd, you still have to calm down and get through surgery. I repeated this over and over, trying to make him understand, to have a picture of what it was like."[311]

"On the day of the oral arguments at the Court," Windle continues, "it was obvious that [Justice Antonin] Scalia was not sympathetic to us. He treated us as if, you get into the oven, you've got to expect some heat. The other justices paid attention for the most part and asked questions to see if the lawyers knew what they were talking about."[312]

After the hearing and a post-court press conference, Windle and his wife returned home.

Patricia Baird-Windle: "I admit I was simply unable to function. I was whipped by it all and scared that we were going to get a bad ruling. For twenty-three days I sat by the phone and accomplished nothing except talking to the media. Years later I realized that my responses were those of a woman who had been emotionally battered."[313]

JUNE: LINCOLNWOOD, ILLINOIS

A national meeting of eighty pro-life bigwigs in this Chicago suburb led to a split over the use of violence as a tactic "to save the unborn." Former roofer Andrew Burnett, the executive director of Advocates for Life Ministries and a leader of the faction that refused to denounce violence, responded by forming the American Coalition of Life Activists (ACLA). ACLA was formally launched in August 1994.[314]

Some of ACLA's founding members had already achieved notoriety as signers of Paul Hill's justifiable homicide declaration: Andrew Burnett, David Crane, Paul DeParrie, Michael Dodds, Roy McMillan, Cathy Ramey and Dawn Stover among them. "Violence isn't always wrong," Burnett told the press. "It isn't always wrong to kill. Violence doesn't necessarily beget violence. Sometimes it solves violence."[315]

ACLA's constitution states that "ACLA is an association of pro-life organizations dedicated to First Amendment activities that glorifies [*sic*] God by obeying His word which commands that we expose to public scrutiny, opprobrium and shame all facets of the abortion/euthanasia family by making public God's judgment against both those who participate in it as well as the church, society and civil government that tolerate it, along with God's offer of hope and healing if they should repent and flee it."[316]

JUNE 6: MILWAUKEE, WISCONSIN

Less than two weeks after President Clinton signed FACE into law, six protestors were charged with blocking the entrance to Affiliated Medical Services and delaying the clinic from opening for three hours. They were the first anti-choice activists prosecuted under FACE legislation.[317]

Three of the six received six months in jail, the maximum allowable for first-time, nonviolent offenders. They were also ordered to reimburse the city for the cost of arresting them, a fee of more than $10,000.[318]

JUNE 10: PENSACOLA, FLORIDA

Shortly after David Gunn was shot to death, Linda Taggart, administrator of the Community Healthcare Center of Pensacola, Inc., noticed a new demonstrator at her clinic. "The first time I saw him, it was not a procedure day and he was just standing there. He looked really spooky," she says. "I went inside and called the police and said that some man was standing near the clinic and making me uncomfortable. Two cars with four policemen came over, and one of the officers came inside and told me the man's name. It was the first time I'd heard of Paul Hill."[319]

It was not the last. Over time, Hill, the founder of Defensive Action and a well-known proponent of "justifiable homicide" to end abortion, escalated his activities at the clinic, moving from standing and staring to screaming at incoming patients.

"After President Clinton signed the FACE law, Paul Hill was incensed," says Taggart. "On June 10, I was doing an ultrasound and he was shrieking so loud it sounded like he was inside the building. I looked out and Paul was standing right next to a window. The police said they could arrest him under a city noise ordinance but I wanted to arrest him under FACE. I called BATF and they told me to call the FBI. I did and they said they'd send an agent. The local police were holding Hill in the parking lot but no one knew what to do. The

FBI agent got to the clinic in about forty minutes. I was working. I came downstairs a while later and talked to him. He told me he was at the clinic to make a report, and said that it was up to city police to arrest Hill. I was very angry and called the Department of Justice. They transferred me to Kevin Forder in the Civil Rights Division. I told Forder what had happened. He said, 'We know about Paul Hill and we know about your clinic. But this is not the time to make an arrest. We don't want to test the law in Florida.' I asked him what I should do. He said, 'Have him arrested under city ordinances.'

"I was still very agitated but by this point Hill was gone," says Taggart. "The next week, on June 17, Hill was back out there shrieking and I told police to arrest him under the noise ordinance. They did, but he was only gone for about an hour. After this he didn't scream as loud. He'd approach patients as they came in and yell at them, but it wasn't as bad so we went along, as if this was okay."[320]

JUNE 30: WASHINGTON, D.C.

The Chief Justice of the Supreme Court, William Rehnquist, delivered the opinion in *Madsen v. Women's Health Center, Inc.*—a case brought by the Aware Woman Center for Choice—upholding the right of a clinic to have a thirty-six-foot buffer zone around entrances and driveways. According to the decision: "The 36-foot buffer zone protecting the entrances to the clinic and the parking lot is a means of protecting unfettered ingress to and egress from the clinic, and ensuring that petitioners do not block traffic. . . . We hold that the limited noise restrictions imposed by the state court order burden no more speech than necessary to ensure the health and well being of the patients at the clinic. The First Amendment does not demand that patients at a medical facility undertake Herculean efforts to escape the cacophony of political protest."[321] The justices added that the freedom of association guaranteed by the First Amendment "does not extend to joining with others for the purpose of depriving third parties of their lawful rights."[322]

Patricia Baird-Windle: "I had spent the day of the decision at the clinic dealing with the press. Most of the media had peeled off to do their stories by midafternoon and I'd come home around 4:30. A group of us—Ted, me, some staff and key volunteers—were going out to dinner to celebrate, but I wanted to sit for a while before showering and changing my clothes. Ted and I were relaxing with one of our volunteers when we heard a war whoop. Our oldest son, Reid, came in and said, 'Mama, don't you know the antis are out there?' He also said that Melbourne Beach police were parked out front. I looked out and saw that demonstrators had surrounded the house, all 380 feet around the corner property. I was afraid. The antis had lost the case and I had no idea what that meant to them. I went to one of the cops and asked what he was going to do. He said he planned to watch and maybe take some pictures. He then said he'd heard that an anti from Tampa, a guy who had signed Paul Hill's Justifiable Homicide petition, had bought an AK-47. He told me to go back into the house since a sniper could be hiding in the overgrown lot across the street. I went inside and picked up a camera and went out the garage door intending to hide behind some bushes and take pictures. As I was hurrying out, I fell in the garage. Right away I knew I was injured and panicked. I was somehow able to crawl to the car so my husband could take me to the hospital. By the time I lifted myself into the car, dusk had fallen and the antis had left. But I was still terrified that they would follow us to the hospital."[323]

X rays revealed that Baird-Windle had broken both feet; she was forced to wear heavy casts until mid-August.

JULY 7–9: LITTLE ROCK, ARKANSAS

The city of Little Rock spent $100,000 in police overtime during Operation Rescue's Summer of Justice. Twenty-six people were arrested for trespassing during the three-day protest.[324]

"We saw patients the whole time OR was here," says Carolyn Izard, director of Little Rock Family Planning Services, one of four abortion providers in the city. "I ran an ad in the newspaper before they came saying that we would see patients on Saturday even though we are not normally open on weekends. I wanted people to know that we would accommodate the need for service during this period. I wanted to put out that we would be here no matter what."[325]

The clinic further thumbed its nose at OR by hanging a huge banner from its entryway: "Jesus, Protect Us From Your Followers." A similar banner was flown in front of the home of the clinic's physician. In addition, the Feminist Majority Foundation sent staff to train local activists in clinic defense, and Izard reports a groundswell of community support.[326]

JULY 29: PENSACOLA, FLORIDA

In the spring of 1994, clinic escort Hallie Joyce did not want to believe that anti-abortion protestor Paul Hill could be an assassin. "One morning when I showed up to escort at The Ladies Center, Paul was there and I found myself watching him. There was also a policeman there. The cop saw me watching Paul and he said, 'You're not thinking of escorting alone, are you?' I said, 'Well, actually, I was.' He said, 'No. You should wait for your buddy to show up because that man is dangerous.'"[327]

Although Joyce took the warning to heart, she was nonetheless shocked when, several months later, Hill shot Dr. John Bayard Britton, the sixty-nine-year-old physician who had replaced Dr. Gunn, and his escort, seventy-four-year-old retired Air Force Lieutenant Colonel James Barrett, to death on July 29. Hill also wounded June Barrett, a sixty-eight-year-old former public health nurse and Jim's wife of four years. The Barretts had retired to Pensacola in 1991 and had become escorts following Gunn's murder.

"It was a little before 7:00 A.M.," says Keri Taggart, assistant administrator of the clinic and Linda's daughter. "Paul Hill was here when I came inside. One of the staff was near the TV and we were talking when we heard this 'pow.' Then we heard it again and I said, 'That was a gun shot.' Our first action was to lock the door. I then pushed the door to my mother's office in and called 911. I told the operator my name and where I was calling from and said that someone was outside shooting. Next I tried to call my mom because I knew she was on her way. I had seen Doc Britton and Jim pull up, but at that time we still didn't realize that anyone had been hurt. I remember a firefighter coming inside and I kept asking, 'Is Doc okay? Is Doc okay?' I think I was hyperventilating. I finally looked out the window and saw the blood running down the driveway. I saw Doc and Jim lying there and I knew."[328]

Keri was five and a half months pregnant at the time, and the paramedics who arrived on the scene were concerned that she was going to go into premature labor. As a precaution they took her to the hospital. "I was hooked up to machines and kept thinking, 'This has to be a bad dream.' I was very scared," she continues. "For the first couple of weeks after the shootings I could not sleep at night. I could only sleep with the lights on or in the daytime. I needed to be around a lot of people for a couple of months and stayed out of work for about a week. As the days went by, it got better. Since I was pregnant I knew I had to keep myself okay."[329]

Keri eventually delivered a healthy baby girl, but her joy was marred by the absence of Britton and Barrett. "I used to pick Doc up from the airport a lot of the time and we were really close," she says. "And Jim and I would talk and talk and talk. Jim and Doc were like my two dads."[330]

Britton had begun working at the health center several months after David Gunn was murdered. "I had gotten his name and called his office and left my name and number," says administrator Linda Taggart. "He called back and sounded skeptical, but he said he didn't want to see us closed down and would come in and help us until we found someone permanent. He was a character, a big, tall, lanky, Lincolnesque man. He had to duck his head to get up and down the stairs. He had this truck that was constantly breaking down and he didn't have a car phone. I just knew he was going to get stranded on the interstate one day. We finally convinced him to fly to Pensacola since it was a six-hour drive from his home in Fernandina Beach on good days and an eight- or nine-hour drive in bad weather. He would work ten- or twelve-hour days and did a full exam on every woman, listening to her heart, her lungs. He was also very up-front and would wear a name tag. I didn't want him to wear it because I did not want him to be identified, but he would not listen."[331]

On the day of the murders, Linda Taggart was running late and remembers noticing an unusual backup of traffic as she neared the health center. She finally pulled into a shopping center parking lot and walked to the clinic. "I saw Jim on the ground but it did not register and I was trying to get them to let me into the building. While I was waiting I could have sworn I saw Doc open the door and look out. I still didn't know what had happened. I'd never seen a vision before, and I haven't seen one since, but I swear I saw Doc Britton at the door. Maybe it was his last appearance. As I rounded the corner I saw that the police had Paul Hill on the ground. I was not shocked that he had done something violent, but as I learned what had happened I was just blown away. I went home and could not stop crying. On top of everything, the press descended. I remember the doorbell ringing at my house. I don't know why I answered it, but I did, and it was a CNN reporter. I said, 'Don't even think about it. If you want to talk to me you have to do it at the office.' They had no respect for my privacy and grief. Meanwhile, I could not believe that Doc was dead. I thought I'd never go into the clinic building again."[332]

Despite being in an acute state of mourning, Taggart knew that she could not leave the job, that the months ahead would require her leadership and vision. "Right after the shootings I set up psychologists for us to see but slowly people started to leave the job. Two women took other positions and then came back, but I had to hire practically a whole new staff. We have two doctors now and keep their anonymity. We just call them Doc. But it took until about 1998 for the staff to feel cohesive again."[333]

Follow-up note: The day the clinic resumed operations, federal marshals were on the premises. Taggart says that she was so angry when she saw them that she called Kevin Forder, the man at the Department of Justice whose help she had begged for weeks earlier. "I said, 'Is now the time to make an arrest?' He said, 'Hill has been arrested and the marshals are at your clinic.' I still believe that these deaths could have been prevented had the Department of Justice acted sooner," Taggart says.[334]

Paul Jennings Hill was indicted on August 12, 1994, on two counts of first-degree murder, one count of attempted murder and one count of shooting into an occupied vehicle. He was also charged with violating the FACE act and using a firearm to commit a felony.[335]

Before his trial, details about Hill began to emerge and revealed a deeply troubled, unstable man. His public problems began in 1971, when he was seventeen. At that time, his father signed a warrant against him, charging him with assault. Oscar Hill told police that both he and Hill's mother wanted Paul to get treatment for a drug problem.[336] Apparently he cleaned up, and in 1984, after completing a master's in divinity program at the Reformed Theological Seminary in Jackson, Mississippi, he was ordained as a minister in the Presbyterian Church in America. From 1984 to 1989 he ministered two churches in South Carolina. In March 1989, however, he transferred his credentials to the Orthodox Presbyterian Church; several years later, in 1992, he was removed from the ministry at his own request. He and his wife then moved to Pensacola and started an automobile detailing business.

To this day, Hill has expressed no remorse for the murders. In fact, he told *Florida Today* reporter Cindy West that, "I felt so strongly that this was the right thing for me to do, that there was no question for me not to do it. It would have been a sin for me not to do it. I honestly could not have looked at myself in the mirror if I hadn't. Now I can."[337]

Hill represented himself at trial and presented no evidence and cross-examined no witnesses. He was found guilty of violating FACE and of using a firearm in a violent crime. On December 6, 1994, United States District Court Judge Roger Vinson—the same judge who presided over the Christmas 1984 trial of clinic bombers Matthew Goldsby, James and Kathren Simmons and Kaye Wiggins—sentenced Hill to die for killing Britton and Barrett.[338] He is currently on death row and has refused to participate in the appeals process mandated by law. Instead, Hill has repeatedly insisted that he wishes to be executed.

June Barrett returned to her home state of Maryland within a year of her husband's death.

Following the murders, an eight-foot buffer zone was established to protect Pensacola clinics.

JULY 29: MELBOURNE, FLORIDA

Patricia Baird-Windle: "The day Dr. Britton and James Barrett were shot, I was sitting in my wheelchair with plaster casts on my broken feet, when I heard bang/bang on the door. I asked who it was and a man called out 'United States

Marshals Service.' I asked the man to step back and hold out his badge so I could see it. I peeked out the living room window to see who he was and then I let him in. He said the government was going to give Aware Woman marshals' protection because of the killings. For the first four months we had round-the-clock coverage. Then it tapered off to sun up to sun down coverage on surgery days. The marshals stayed in Melbourne for eleven months, and it was interesting to see their arc of belief shift. There were marshals who started off thinking the antis were good, devoted Christians. By the end of two months both of them knew better. On two separate days, one of the marshals had pulled his gun on the antis when they refused to follow his orders against trespassing and blocking entrances."[339]

AUGUST: BUFFALO, NEW YORK

Barnett Slepian, a physician at Buffalo GYN Womanservices, wrote the following letter to the editor of the *Buffalo News:*

> The members of the local "non-violent" pro-life community may continue to picket my home wearing large "Slepian Kills Children" buttons, display the six-foot banner with the same quotation at the entrance of my neighborhood, proudly display their "Abortion Kills Children" bumper stickers, scream that I am a murderer and a killer when I enter the clinics at which they "peacefully" exercise their First Amendment right of freedom of speech. They may also do the same at a restaurant, at a mall, in a store, or, as they have done recently, while I was watching my children play. . . . But please don't feign surprise, dismay, or certainly not innocence when a more volatile and less-restrained member of the group decides to react to their inflammatory rhetoric by shooting an abortion provider.[340]

AUGUST: MELBOURNE, FLORIDA

Patricia Baird-Windle: "I had just gotten the casts off my feet and was headed to the movies when my husband told me about an incident that had occurred that afternoon. Ted said that a reporter had come to the clinic and told him that two people had overheard a death threat against me. The pair worked with a guy who was a major anti, and they told the reporter they often heard this guy's tirades against me and my family. On this particular day they heard him say, 'I'm gonna have to kill her. Nothing else is working.' The two went to the newspaper even though they were afraid of the man and said they feared losing their jobs. The reporter heard the story, saw how scared these people were of their coworker and asked them to repeat the story to her managing editor. Neither journalist knew what to make of the information. We somehow sat through the movie and when we got out I decided to go to the clinic and speak to a marshal on duty about the threat. I said that I thought it should at least be investigated. The marshal looked at me and said he could do nothing about it. I was so scared I left on the next plane and stayed in an out-of-town hotel for a week."[341]

Follow-up note: "I spoke to the marshal again in April of 1999," says Baird-Windle, "and in the course of our conversation he told me he agreed with 'the other side.' I was outraged and called his supervisor in Washington, D.C. The person I talked to assured me that they would speak to him and put a disciplinary letter in his file, but I doubt that he was actually reprimanded for his impolitic statement."[342]

In fact, he has since been promoted.

AUGUST 10: BRAINERD, MINNESOTA

The offices of Planned Parenthood of Minnesota, Inc., were burned to the ground in a fire the BATF confirmed was arson. The facility did not perform abortions. Four other businesses located in the shopping mall that housed the clinic were also damaged.[343]

FALL: RHODE ISLAND

When Citizens Bank of Rhode Island named Dr. Pablo Rodriguez to its board of directors, the bank was immediately contacted by the Respect Life Office of the Diocese of Providence. The diocese demanded that the nomination be rescinded because of Rodriguez's work with Planned Parenthood of Rhode Island. They also launched a campaign to get Catholics to withdraw their money from the bank. According to Citizens Bank, "only a handful" of account holders obeyed the order. The bank also held firm, writing the diocese that, "Dr. Pablo Rodriguez is a recognized leader in the Hispanic community with an extraordinary record of community service. We do not and will not ask our customers, employees or our directors for their views on any one issue—particularly one as personal as abortion."[344]

SEPTEMBER: NATIONWIDE

Convicted firebomber Michael Bray, editor of *Capitol Area Christian News* and pastor of the Reformation Lutheran Church in Bowie, Maryland, published his first book, *A Time to Kill.* An effort to rationalize "justifiable homicide" against abortion providers, the book is an intellectual exploration of scriptural doctrine in support of violent resistance. Unlike the shrill rhetoric of *The Army of God Manual* or *Closed: 99 Ways to Stop Abortion, A Time to Kill* is reasoned, heavily footnoted and rooted in theology. It is not a how-to guide, but rather a denunciation of Christian pacifism. "Justifiable homicide" supporter Andrew Burnett, the founder of the American Coalition of Life Activists, was the book's publisher.

"Force is not equivalent to violence," Bray writes. "Still less is it to be equated with evil. It is amoral; it can be used for good or for evil. The Christian policeman does not live by an absolute code of peaceful and non-violent behavior. Neither does the Christian soldier or executioner. And just as it is ethical to use force for good, it is on the other hand immoral to refrain from using force on some occasions."[345]

Examples follow. "Force, even lethal force, is not only commanded by God and performed by Him on innumerable occasions in the older Scriptures, it is also prescribed in the Law for citizen participation. When a man sacrificed his own children to a false God, the whole community was obliged to participate in an execution by stoning (cf. Lev. 20:2–4). Use of force is not only commanded as a judicial act, but granted to the individual in cases of self-defense or the defense of others."[346]

And abortion? "The legality of abortion is disputed by those who argue (Constitutionally, a la the Tenth Amendment) that the Supreme Court is not supreme over matters where states retain jurisdiction (among which rights are all those not specifically ceded to the federal government). The legality of abortion, finally, is denied by that great throng of Christian American citizens who contend specifically on the grounds of Biblical law and historic Christian theology that abortion constitutes nothing less than the murder of an innocent child."[347]

The solution Bray advocates is armed struggle, a second American revolution. "The people of God are never enjoined to unconditional submission. When tyrants ruled, God sent deliverers to the people. The Scriptures are full of examples of righteous disobedience and revolution," he writes.[348]

Appendix A, "Entertaining Questions," concretizes Bray's arguments and further explicates his thinking.

Q: Are you advocating the murder of doctors?
A: No. We are not embarrassed about stopping short of advocating the slaying of government-approved childkillers. . . . We simply declare that the slaying of (even) government-sanctioned childkillers is justified. We do not know the best strategy to resist the evil of abortion. But we cannot condemn that forceful,

even lethal, action which is applied for the purpose of saving innocent children.[349]

Q. The Sixth Commandment says "Thou shalt not kill." How can you defend killing?
A. Scripture does not condemn all killing. It legislates capital punishment (Deut. 19:12; Gen. 9:6) and provides guidelines for warfare (Deut. 20-21) and self-defense (Ex. 22:2). Killing is so common, the Hebrews had numerous words to express the act of taking the life of a person. Those who use lethal force to stop a murderer are not themselves committing murder. They kill, or terminate, or slay, or neutralize; they do not murder.[350]

Q. How can an individual take the law into his [sic] own hands and punish another person? That is God's right, not ours.
A. The individual, in defending himself [sic] or another innocent person, is authorized by God to exercise lethal, defensive force (Ex. 22:2). A distinction must be made between the use of defensive force and retributive force which is reserved for God and those to whom He delegates it (Rom. 13; Deut. 19:12).[351]

Q. If you defend the shooting of abortionists, why not the guilty mothers as well? And what about the abortuary owners and other employees?
A. Those involved with the propagation of abortion rights and all the processes leading up to the commission of the same are distinguished from the one who does the deed. Government has the duty to prosecute conspirators and accomplices. Christian citizens have the duty to defend their neighbors from imminent death. It is true that the mother acts as an accomplice to the murder of her child when she submits to the abortionist's knife. However, efforts to stop her with lethal force would result in the death of both mother and child. Furthermore, the mother is distinguished from the abortionists as one who may change her mind and leave the abortuary at any time. In contrast, the abortionist has unequivocal intentions to kill innocent children. He [sic] is a murderer by profession.[352]

SEPTEMBER 24: FT. WAYNE, INDIANA

"FACE-less," an editorial in the *Journal Gazette*, revealed deep problems with local enforcement of the FACE act. The editorial quoted the congressional testimony of Police Sergeant Bill Walsh, assigned to patrol the Ft. Wayne

Women's Health Organization, who said that he lacked "the authority to enforce the Act. . . . The U.S. Marshals who have the power don't use it." Walsh also told Congress that "when he arrests protestors for trespassing, U.S. Attorneys won't prosecute."[353]

SEPTEMBER 30: WASHINGTON, D.C.

The Feminist Majority Foundation sent the following letter to members, seconding the Ft. Wayne *Journal Gazette* and alerting them to problems with the government's enforcement of the FACE bill:

> With the exception of the charges against Paul Hill and the clinic blockaders in Milwaukee in June, the Department of Justice has moved at a snail's pace in enforcement. Too many incidents of terrorism, violence and obstruction at the clinics since FACE was passed have not been prosecuted. To date, no charges have been brought against extremists for threats and intimidation against doctors. In Jackson, Mississippi, Dr. Joseph Booker reported to the FBI that he was threatened the day of the Pensacola murders in a face-to-face encounter by a leading anti-abortion extremist and signer of Hill's Justifiable Homicide petition. Although Booker continues to receive federal Marshals' protection, the alleged threat has not been prosecuted. . . . In Des Moines, Iowa two staff members were physically blocked as they were attempting to leave the clinic by a known anti-abortion extremist. The U.S. Attorney has declined to press charges, mistakenly claiming that only physicians and nurses are covered under the FACE law. Other clinic administrators and doctors around the country have received death threats and have been stalked. Even in Ohio, where an anti-abortion extremist was arrested by local police for stalking a physician from the clinic to his home and attempting to force the physician's car off the road, no federal charges have been filed.[354]

OCTOBER 1: PENSACOLA, FLORIDA

Three members of the Ku Klux Klan picketed in front of The Ladies Center to protest federal intervention in "daily life." The protestors were particularly annoyed that federal marshals had been stationed at the clinic since the July 29 shooting of Dr. John Bayard Britton and escort James Barrett. A month and a half earlier, KKK members held a similar protest at the Aware Woman Center for Choice in Melbourne, Florida, one of twenty-four clinics under marshals' protection.[355]

OCTOBER 6: FARGO, NORTH DAKOTA

The following is excerpted from a memo sent to the Department of Justice by Jane Bovard, a former administrator of the Fargo Women's Health Organization.

> I feel frustration and growing anger about the way the Marshal Service is handling the directive to do whatever it is they are supposed to be doing at our facility. . . . Several times I have told the head of the U.S. Marshal Service for North Dakota, that what I really need is for them to transport the doctor since he is followed regularly to his plane and motel by several protestors. Never has he been even escorted anywhere with another car following the one he is in, let alone transported to and from his destination. Dr. Miks initially told the Marshals he was leaving for the airport and said, "You know, the protestors are going to follow me there," which they did. The Marshals just shrugged their shoulders and continued to sit in their cars in our parking lot.[356]

NOVEMBER: NATIONWIDE

For the first time in forty years, Republicans took control of both the U.S. House and Senate. According to researcher Sara Diamond, "On Election Day about 30 percent of those who voted were Evangelical Christians and among these, about 69 percent voted Republican. Though right-wing Christians represented only an estimated nine to 10 percent of the population, their disproportionate electoral participation made them a force to be reckoned with."[357]

NOVEMBER 1: RENO, NEVADA

When Dr. Damon Stutes moved the West End Women's Medical Group, northern Nevada's only abortion clinic, to a new site at the end of 1994, he facetiously dubbed the health center Fort Abortion. "From 1974 to 1994 we were in a 2,000-square foot freestanding building on an eighth of an acre, right on a public street. The sidewalk was two feet from the building entrance," he says.[358] Butyric acid attacks, hate mail, fires, broken windows, crank calls, blockades, bomb threats, damage to the building's wooden deck and the gluing of the clinic's doors occurred on a regular basis. Indeed, Stutes counted fifty-six instances of violence and harassment in the two years prior to the move.[359]

Not so at the new location. "This is a $1 million building," boasts Stutes. "I spent $40,000 for a security system that includes pan-and-tilt cameras that see all around the building as well as inside. They can zoom in and get face shots. The walls are bulletproof concrete. We have a steel roof and steel-reinforced ceilings, five exits with remote, magnetic locks on the doors, secondary circuits in case power lines are cut, speakers to create a sound curtain so if there are protestors we can't hear them, an enclosed parking garage for staff, and doors that are wide enough to bring an ambulance gurney through in case of emergency. The guys who do security systems at the casinos were my security consultants, and the architect who designed the building specializes in hospitals, medical centers, and prisons. Can I be killed? You bet. But I've reduced the risk."[360]

Stutes began performing abortions in Reno in 1987, when he bought the clinic from a physician who was retiring. He credits his desire to work in reproductive healthcare to a tragedy he learned of while attending a Michigan junior high school in 1963. A twelve-year-old classmate, he says, abruptly stopped coming to school. When he inquired about her, he was told that she had died from an illegal abortion. "I thought it was terrible that she had died. But everyone else I talked to blamed her. She shouldn't have had sex. It seemed so ridiculous to me. Whether or not you agree with abortion, killing women who have them is unacceptable," he says.[361]

The outspoken Stutes is an imposing man, six foot ten inches tall, with a shaved head and piercing blue eyes. Wearing multicolored Hawaiian shirts instead of medical scrubs, he sings while he works and laughs frequently, brashly and loudly. Nonetheless, he is extremely serious about the work he does and his right to do it. "My day-to-day life is more rewarding than I ever thought it could be," he admits. "You can't fake the genuine, sincere appreciation of the 5,000 women a year who come here for all kinds of gynecological problems including unwanted pregnancies. But I don't want to be in constant fear to do my job. I now have a license to carry a weapon and there is a gun within a few feet of me at all times. I will shoot and use deadly force if I have to. Am I a control freak? Maybe. But I like taking care of women and feel that I have stamped out certain diseases like a bull in a china shop. I love that I get to demonstrate my morality as part of the job. At the same time, I know that I have done my best to keep myself, my staff, and my patients secure and safe."[362]

NOVEMBER 7: WASHINGTON, D.C.

Ninety clinic owners and staffers, all members of the National Coalition of Abortion Providers (NCAP), met with the Department of Justice (DOJ) to press their concerns about government inattention to anti-abortion terrorism.

Patricia Baird-Windle: "Ron Fitzsimmons of NCAP wanted providers to come to D.C. and lobby. Someone suggested that as long as we were going to be in town we should meet with DOJ. James Reynolds, the chief of domestic terrorism, was at the meeting with three DOJ attorneys. Reynolds had an I'm-the-chief-and-I-own-the-room poise, and he opened the meeting by saying that he shared our concerns and was investigating what laws could be used to help us. He also said that he supported FACE.

"I concede that the group was ill-prepared for the meeting, having no detailed agenda to present. Nonetheless, I also believe that Reynolds missed a wonderful opportunity to hear, firsthand, about the range of tactics being employed by anti-abortionists across the country. As soon as providers started to express their anger about violations of restraint of trade laws, conspiracy and interference with interstate commerce, Reynolds started to do the bureaucratic conga. Renee Chelian, a provider from Michigan, stood up and said, 'Don't you understand that we are afraid?' Nebraska doctor, Lee Carhart, said, 'My house went up in smoke.' I said, 'What you have in this room are the people who have been the most victimized providers in the United States.' I suggested that he debrief each of us. He said, 'Okay, give me your phone number. I'll have you debriefed.' This is not what I was suggesting; I wanted him to debrief all of us, not just me.

"The day after the meeting, Dr. Garson Romalis was shot by a sniper while in his Vancouver, Canada, home. I called Reynolds, got through, and asked if he remembered me. He said, 'Oh yes, you're that aggressive woman.' I said that whether or not I was aggressive didn't matter, that he should have taken advantage of our expertise while we were there. He did not and the meeting was a one-shot deal. We never went back to DOJ as a group, and, as I anticipated, no agents ever called me, as Reynolds had promised."[363]

NOVEMBER 8: VANCOUVER, CANADA

Dr. Garson Romalis, an employee of the Women's Health Centre and the Elizabeth Bagshaw Clinic, was shot in both legs by a sniper hiding behind his house. Romalis had been eating breakfast in his kitchen when he was hit by bullets fired from a high-powered rifle. The impact shattered his femur and severed his femoral artery; the doctor bled profusely before he was able to phone for emergency help.[364]

The shooting occurred three days before Remembrance Day, a Canadian holiday that honors those killed during World War I—a time appropriated by anti-abortion groups in the early 1990s—and five days after Paul Hill's conviction for the murders of Dr. John Bayard Britton and James Barrett in Florida.[365]

Canadian law authorities suspect that James Charles Kopp, a full time anti-abortion zealot, is the shooter. He is being sought by both Canadian and American law enforcers but is currently a fugitive. The total reward posted by the two countries for his capture and conviction exceeds $1 million.

NOVEMBER 9: ALLENWOOD, PENNSYLVANIA

Randall Terry began serving a five-month sentence in federal prison for ignoring an injunction against disrupting the 1992 Democratic National Convention and presenting then-candidate Bill Clinton with an aborted fetus.[366]

WINTER: MELBOURNE, FLORIDA

Patricia Baird-Windle: "I was so thoroughly disgusted that the tactics being used against providers were not being adequately discussed that I decided to organize a national conference, called Connections, for February 5–9, 1995, in Orlando. As I envisioned it, the conference would be a time for targeted clinic principals, major defenders, and those we call trackers, people who monitor the antis and document their activities, to address the tactics used to harass and intimidate us, as well as a time to strategize about fighting back. I recognized the overwhelming need for the people who were keeping watch on things across the country—the clinic defenders, the right-wing watchers and targeted providers themselves—to share information. Although fifty-five people attended the meeting, including several from key media outlets, I came to believe that the antis were remote call-forwarding our faxes. I suspect that some of the materials I sent to clinics across the country were diverted due to this and other telephone tactics because people I knew I had faxed invitations to said that they'd never received the information. Plus, Keith Tucci had a press conference in late January where he read from the conference brochure. Although there was no direct proof, we assume that was how he got it. It felt like death by a thousand tiny cuts, the constant, extreme, personal violation of my autonomy."[367]

Nonetheless, those in attendance hail the confab as a milestone. "Researchers and providers tend to work quietly, in isolation," says Anne Bower, former editor of *The Body Politic,* a defunct magazine that covered reproductive health issues. "What the conference did was give us—providers as well as the premier researchers in the United States and Canada—our first real opportunity to be in the same place as one another. We were able to do an information exchange.

We had photos of particular antis and asked, Who is this or that person? Where was he last seen? Hundreds of photos were exchanged. We were also able to talk about our differences. Some people believed in confrontational tactics. Others didn't. But all of the major organizations were represented, and we were able to talk about our politics and ideas and know people as human beings. It opened a lot of avenues for information sharing that have carried over to this day."[368]

MID-DECEMBER: BOSTON, MASSACHUSETTS

A doctor employed by Planned Parenthood in Brookline got a telephone call at his home at 2:30 P.M. on December 10 warning him that, "you, your family and your house" are going to be "blown away." On December 12, a second call came in. This time the physician's spouse was asked, "How do you feel about being the wife of a murderer?" Tracers were installed on December 13, but somehow missed the caller's third communication on the fourteenth.[369]

Attorney General Janet Reno was contacted after the second call and was urged to provide protection to the doctor. She did not do so.[370]

Two weeks later the doctor, who had been an abortion provider for more than twenty years, was given twenty-four-hour protection from the United States Marshals Service following the fatal shootings of two Brookline abortion clinic workers: twenty-five-year-old Planned Parenthood receptionist Shannon Lowney and thirty-eight-year-old Preterm employee Leanne Nichols.[371]

DECEMBER 30: BROOKLINE, MASSACHUSETTS

The last Friday in 1994 began like most others at the Planned Parenthood League of Massachusetts' Brookline office. Sixty women were scheduled for appointments, more than half of them for contraceptive counseling, pregnancy tests, or pap smears. Alice Verhoeven, the director of the clinic, was in her office. "I was on the phone and heard what sounded like electrical sparking. It was an odd sound. We had been having electrical problems so I put the phone down and went to check on what had happened. When I got to the front of the office, I saw staff rushing around. I smelled gunpowder and saw Shannon [Lowney, the receptionist] on the floor. One of the nurses and our doctor were running to tend her. I backed up and called 911."[372]

Seconds later Verhoeven heard someone scream that people in the waiting room had also been shot. A nurse went to investigate and Verhoeven followed her. "When I realized people in the waiting area were hurt, I called 911 back and said, 'Bring more ambulances. A lot more people are shot.' For some reason

I went outside to direct the vehicles. Two nurses were tending the injured people and our doctor was cradling Shannon. She died in his arms. There was nothing he could do to save her. EMS came in. An EMT hovered over Shannon for a few minutes, then he got up to help someone else. I said, 'No, she's the most seriously injured. Please don't leave her.' He was very, very calm and gently told me, 'No ma'am, she's expired.'"[373]

Within what seemed like minutes, says Verhoeven, the clinic was crawling with local and state police, the FBI and the media. The crime scene was cordoned off with yellow police tape and the damage was assessed. Shannon Lowney, a twenty-five-year-old Boston College graduate and aspiring social worker who had worked at the clinic for nine months, was dead. Three others—Anjana (Anu) Agrawal, a thirty-year-old part-time medical assistant, and thirty-two-year-old Antonio Hernandez and twenty-two-year-old Brian Murray, who had accompanied friends to the clinic—were wounded. The clinic itself was a shambles.[374]

The Brookline shootings marked the first time that nonphysicians were killed by anti-abortion violence. "Before 1994 it was not on our radar screen that someone could walk in and murder receptionists," said Nicki Nichols Gamble, former president of the Planned Parenthood League of Massachusetts. "We knew physicians were targets, but after December 30 we found out that they weren't the only targets."[375]

As the story unfolded, Verhoeven and Nichols Gamble learned that a man, later identified as John Salvi III, had come into the clinic and asked if it was Planned Parenthood. When he was told that it was, he leveled his rifle and shot Lowney in the neck. He then fired several more times and fled the scene. Salvi apparently drove two miles down the street and at approximately 10:30 A.M. entered Preterm Health Services, another Brookline clinic. There he shot thirty-eight-year-old receptionist Leanne Nichols to death while shouting, 'This is what you get. You should pray the rosary.' He then shot and wounded twenty-nine-year-old office worker Jane Sauer and forty-five-year-old security guard Richard J. Seron.[376]

Despite being hurt, Seron fired back at Salvi from the Preterm entranceway; although he did not hit the gunman, he scared him, and in his haste to leave the clinic Salvi dropped a black gym bag he had been carrying. The bag contained receipts for the gun and the ammunition he had purchased, as well as a .22 caliber Colt handgun, bullets and a detachable magazine that held more than five rounds.[377]

While the police began searching for Salvi, clinic staff had a multitude of things to do. Nicki Nichols Gamble had taken the thirtieth off as a vacation day and had been called at home as soon as the shooting stopped. "I walked in within thirty minutes of Salvi, and police and media were everywhere. Shannon was dead on the floor. She had to stay there for a number of hours before they could move her because the spot was the scene of a crime and they had to take photos. Most of the staff moved to another part of the building to wait for the police to question them, but some of us had to move back and forth," to confer with press people or police investigators. This meant walking by the body again and again.[378]

Verhoeven recalls, "The incident was very quickly on the news, and I told everyone to call their families and tell them they were okay. Then, within an hour or two, David, Shannon's fiancé, called and I had to tell him that Shannon was dead. He started to scream at me. Someone, luckily, had the good sense to call Beth Israel Hospital to get a crisis team in and Nicki called a psychiatrist she knew."[379] The staff met with trauma specialists that day and again on the thirty-first, to begin sorting through what had happened and deal with the violence they had witnessed. Support groups, sponsored by Brookline Mental Health, met weekly and then monthly for nearly a year; additional one- or two-session meetings were offered for the children and partners of staff. Individual help was also provided for those suffering from acute anxiety or sleep disorders.

Meanwhile, the clinic remained a designated crime scene for four days. During this time, responsibilities were divided. Verhoeven handled internal issues, including staff needs and cleanup, while Nichols Gamble and Susan Weber, vice president for operations at PPLM's administrative offices, handled press and organized a memorial.

"The next few days are a blur," Verhoeven says. "I was very concerned with how to deal with staff, how to rebuild. Before we could reopen we had to pull bullets out of the walls in the waiting room and repair the sections of wall that were torn apart when we removed the bullets."[380] Staff also had to clean blood off the floor, walls and furniture.

PPLM resumed client services on January 4; Preterm reopened in mid-month. "Some staff were able to pick up the pieces immediately. During those first weeks, one of our nurses and our nurse practitioner came in every day to manage patients. They handled it all. The doctor who had received death threats two weeks earlier, the one who had tended to Shannon, was wonderful. But another doctor, who was not here the day of the shooting, resigned. We also lost a few other staff. A woman with a newborn baby felt she could not continue and our lab tech quit, but for the most part people came back. Some took time off before returning; others came at once. But I have to tell you, the outpouring of concrete support, particularly from former staff, was incredible. One RN who used to work with us took vacation time from her current job to help us for a few weeks."[381]

"The climate in Boston," Nichols Gamble says, "is effusively supportive of choice. We were embraced by the community. Dozens of people came by to help, to do trauma work, to do security, to rebuild stuff and to bring food. We got tons of cards, letters and flowers." In addition, $500,000 was raised to help PPLM beef up security, $100,000 of it from one anonymous donor."[382]

Nichols Gamble continues: "I felt at the time that my life would never be the same." In fact, a few days after the shootings she received a phoned-in death threat warning that "we're gonna kill you." The call resulted in around-the-clock protection, at both her home and office, from Massachusetts state troopers. This lasted for about two weeks. "Finally I decided that I couldn't live with it anymore," she says. "One of the lessons I learned is that you can't make yourself one hundred percent secure and still live a life. You ultimately have to decide if you're going to do this work or not. But it's harder, much harder, if you have young children. At the time it wasn't clear to me that I had what it takes to get through this."[383]

But get through it she—and PPLM's Brookline affiliate—did. Within three months of the shootings, negotiations were under way to join Preterm and Planned Parenthood. The merger was completed in January 1996, and Planned Parenthood/Preterm moved into a 40,000-square-foot, state-of-the-art building in September 1997. PPLM raised $7 million for the new Boston site.[384]

Follow-up note: Anu Agrawal still has one bullet lodged between her heart and spine; likewise, Brian Murray has a bullet in his rib cage. Medical experts say that both projectiles are too close to vital organs to be removed.[385]

DECEMBER 30: MICHIGAN

Renee Chelian, owner of Northland Family Planning, a three-clinic chain in the Detroit area, was getting ready for work when she received a call informing her that two receptionists had been shot to death in Brookline, Massachusetts. Her first reaction was to call her clinics, her doctors and her husband. While the morning's conversations are now lost to her, Chelian remembers that she began to cry as she conveyed the scant information she had been given. "My daughter Lara, who was fourteen, was in the room with me. She was also crying and said, 'Please don't go into work today, Mom.' I said I needed to go and meet with the staff, that I had a responsibility to thirty employees. By this point she was crying really hard and grabbed onto my leg and said, 'But what if they kill you? What will I do without a mother?' It was the hardest thing I've ever done, leaving her that day. I literally had to peel her off me. She was so scared. We had always talked about security, but this time it was different."[386]

Chelian, her husband and two daughters had long understood that clinic workers were potential targets of anti-abortion violence. Still, the Brookline shootings brought the message home with powerful veracity. Although the Northland clinics had been picketed since opening day, and the Chelian home had been picketed in 1988, the December shootings forced Lara to confront her worst fear: that her parents would be killed or maimed because of their pro-choice activity.

Prior to this, she had always been easily reassured. A city ordinance, passed in the late 1980s, restricts residential picketing. In addition, injunctions keep most protestors from trespassing at Detroit-area clinics. Now, with the shootings of Lowney and Nichols, Lara understood that the landscape of anti-abortion protest had changed and she feared that the violence would hit her personally.

Growing up, she had seen her younger sister, Jennifer (a pseudonym), develop a plethora of fears following the picketing of their residence; both she and her mother attribute Jennifer's extreme concern about safety to her early exposure to anti-abortion violence. "For more than a year after the protestors came to our house for the second time, Jennifer, who was then three, was petrified," Chelian recalls. "When my husband and I would tuck her into bed she'd scream, 'Make sure I'm safe. Hug me. Kiss me.' She'd say these things over and over, for hours every night. And she would not play in the yard or in the driveway because she thought she'd be harmed."[387]

Chelian and her husband were so concerned that they eventually consulted a psychologist about how best to handle their child's terror. "He told us that children don't always say what they mean. He felt that she could not say that she was afraid for us and would instead say, 'Check on me. Make sure I'm safe.' He told us that she wanted to see us to make sure we were okay. We started to turn on the house and car alarms and tried to reassure her as much as we could. But she still wanted her bedroom windows bricked in. She would say, 'I don't want those people to get in.' Until she was twelve she did not open her bedroom blinds. We would open them, she'd close them. She kept them closed, with the windows locked, at all times," she says.[388]

Since the home pickets Chelian and her husband—with whom she runs Northland—have attempted to shield their children from day-to-day protests at their clinics. Yet she concedes that they have not always succeeded in keeping their home and work lives separate. For thirty consecutive months in the late 1980s and early 1990s, for example, "rescues" required the pair to leave home at 3:30 A.M. With the children in the care of a baby-sitter, they went to their clinics to troubleshoot and orchestrate law enforcement, patients and staff. "We'd be gone by the crack of dawn and return late in the day completely exhausted," says Chelian. "We tried to keep the media out of the house as much as possible so the kids would not see TV coverage of the 'rescues,' but they always seemed to know what was happening."[389]

For their part, Lara and Jennifer have processed their parents' professional lives differently. Beginning in the summer of 1996, when she was sixteen, Lara took a job at one of the clinics, assisting in the recovery room, cleaning up, doing paperwork and filing. "During the fall of 1997, on a Saturday, Lara was again working with us and someone she knew from her school came in for an abortion," says Chelian. "Lara went up to her and told her she was safe at the clinic, that she worked there and knew that everything was confidential. She went into the procedure room with this girl, cried with her and held her hand during surgery. After it was over she told me that she now understood what a difference this care makes. She had seen it help someone she knew. Everything came together that day, everything I'd told her for the past ten years clicked."[390]

Follow-up note: Jennifer Chelian is still in high school and, as of this writing, has expressed no interest in working in the field of reproductive health. Lara is now a full-time college student and active supporter of Students for Choice.

DECEMBER 31: NORFOLK, VIRGINIA

The day after shooting two Brookline, Massachusetts, clinic workers to death and wounding five others, John Salvi III was captured in Norfolk, Virginia. He had driven more than five hundred miles, passing approximately 180 abortion clinics, before stopping in Norfolk.[391] At the time of his arrest, he had $1,277.94 in cash in his wallet.[392]

According to Suzette Caton of Norfolk's Hillcrest Clinic, "We had heard about what had happened the day before in Massachusetts and were very concerned but we had no clue that we might also be victims. Saturdays at the clinic are extremely busy. I'd worked in the morning and had just left. As I was driving home one of the counselors called me on my car phone and said I had to return. I knew it had to be important. By the time I got to the clinic the police had captured Salvi and had started to tape off the area. One of our security officers was outside and I asked her what was going on. She said that she'd gone outside to check the parking lot after our regular protestors left and a man approached her and asked her where Burger King was. She said there wasn't one nearby and had just started to walk back inside when the man started firing.

Fortunately, Salvi's gun jammed and he ran to his vehicle. Coincidentally, there had been an arson at an ATM machine located outside our building. The arson investigator happened to be there at this particular moment and he called the police. They caught Salvi a block from here. Within an hour they confirmed that the man was the same guy who had killed two people in Massachusetts. Salvi had fired twenty or thirty shots at Hillcrest. He broke all the windows in the lobby, but that was the only damage that was done." While staff were badly shaken, a workshop on violence and personal safety, held the following Monday, helped calm frayed nerves; Caton reports no staff losses as a result of the incident.[393]

CHAPTER SEVEN

Rx for Safety:
1995 to the Present

Since 1993 seven people—eight if you include Wayne Patterson, a physician killed in what police have deemed a bungled robbery—have been murdered because they worked in U.S. abortion clinics. Dozens more have been injured: shot, stabbed or blown-apart by flying shrapnel. Compounding this, abortion-related arsons doubled between 1996 and 1997; bombings tripled.[1]

Many antis attribute escalating violence to FACE, petulantly asserting that because of limits on permissible demonstrations, anti-choice activists have no recourse but to destroy women's health centers and the people they employ. Coupled with scores of Web pages bearing inflammatory rhetoric about baby killers, genocide and mass extinction, true believers eager to end the "abortion holocaust" have no shortage of people and propaganda egging them on. Debates about the boundaries of free speech notwithstanding, at present no strictures have been placed on their calls to arms.

Yet change is in the air, and limits on allowable public conduct that goes beyond constitutionally protected speech, first articulated in the Supreme Court case of *Madsen v. Women's Health Center,* may be in the offing. But that is not the only change that is evident; in fact, movement observers have noted discernible shifts in the way anti-choice zealots now claim violence. Assassins Michael Griffin and Paul Hill, the men responsible for slaying clinic escort James Barrett and Doctors John Bayard Britton and David Gunn, actually waited for police to take them away after pulling their respective triggers. Eager martyrs, they proved compliant once the killings were over. Similarly, although John Salvi III fled after shooting Shannon Lowney and Leanne Nichols, he marked his trail so clearly that he was easily apprehended. Not so James Kopp and Eric Robert Rudolph. Demonstrating no urge to claim their victories, the pair have eluded law enforcement since the 1998 murder of Dr. Barnett Slepian and the bombing of the New Woman All Women clinic in Birmingham, Alabama. Hit-and-run terrorists, they continue to frighten the pro-choice community with the threat that they might, at any time, strike again.

Indeed, the entire right-wing bears watching as it, too, continues to strike at anything it considers obscene, anti-family or blasphemous. No longer obsessed with the National Endowment for the Arts, rightist groups have begun to eyeball state and city funding of cultural programs, a strategy in keeping with their focus on grass-roots, community politics. According to People for the American Way, a Washington, D.C.–based group that monitors the Christian and secular right, 137 challenges to artistic expression in forty-one states and the District of Columbia were launched in 1995 alone.[2] In one incident, a Christian Coalition chapter in Clearwater, Florida, organized to keep a city-funded theater from presenting Tony Kushner's award-winning *Angels in America* because of its gay content. Although the play was performed, the City Commission passed a resolution warning the theater to be "sensitive to and aware of community standards in booking performances."[3]

In another instance, the Texas-based Christian Pro-Life Foundation and a local Christian Coalition chapter lobbied the San Antonio City Council in 1998, pressuring it to eliminate $62,000 in funding to the Esperanza Peace and Justice Center. The reason? Esperanza had sponsored a lesbian and gay film festival in 1997.[4]

Although opposition to homosexuality and abortion are unifying threads for many Christian conservatives, their agenda is far broader, something that was clearly demonstrated in a bizarre challenge to Christian hegemony in San Jose, California. Local activists there sued the city over a $500,000 statue of the Aztec and Maya god Quetzalcoatl that had been erected in a neighborhood park. The plaintiffs argued that the sculpture "violated their religious freedom by honoring a non-Christian deity."[5] In late 1996 the Ninth Circuit Court of Appeals ruled against the Christians and declared that the statue was a secular tribute to Latino culture.[6]

Theater, sculpture, painting, performance art and words both spoken and written: all have been scrutinized by the eagle eye of a Christian right that includes anti-abortion groups. Unlike the National Right to Life Committee, which confines itself to fighting abortion and assisted suicide, groups like the

American Life League and Operation Save America (formerly Operation Rescue) have broadened their scope to include the fight against "godlessness" in numerous arenas. Their agenda now includes advocacy of school vouchers, prayer in the schools, the teaching of creationism and the posting of the Ten Commandments in public buildings. Conversely, they oppose pornography, sex education, human cloning, assisted suicide/euthanasia and lesbian, gay, bisexual and transgender rights.

And they have made some headway. Almost all of the state Republican platforms passed in 1996 include endorsement of school prayer and five call for the teaching of creationism in public schools. Other platforms support the posting of the Ten Commandments in classrooms. Incredibly, Alaska, Iowa, Oklahoma and Texas have issued planks declaring homosexual conduct illegal, and Grand Old Party stalwarts in Iowa and South Carolina have approved a program that would bar gay men and lesbians from teaching in public schools.[7]

Nonetheless, the trajectory of right-wing growth has been uneven, and disagreements and organizational problems are obvious. Donations to the Christian Coalition have plummeted since Ralph Reed's 1997 departure as organizational head, and in 1999 the organization gave up its tax-exempt status after years of fighting with the Internal Revenue Service. In addition, despite a hard-fought campaign to impeach Bill Clinton for sexual misconduct, the right's attempt to impose a Calvinist morality on everyone but itself has failed. New Right mastermind Paul Weyrich conceded this in a May 1999 appearance on *60 Minutes.* "If there was a moral majority we would have ousted Clinton," he said. "Christians have lost the culture war. We failed. Christians should withdraw, drop out" of American politics. Similarly, *Blinded by the Might,* a 1999 book by former Moral Majority leaders Cal Thomas and Dr. Ed Dobson, argues that political change is impossible without moral change. "If the so-called religious right focuses mainly on politics to deliver us, we will never get that right because politics and government cannot reach into the soul. That is something God reserves for Himself," they write in the book's introduction.[8]

While Pat Robertson, Randall Terry and others remain steadfast in their belief that religion and politics are flip sides of the same coin, their detractors are forcing them to confront the fact that despite some community-level victories, pluralism and tolerance remain American ideals. Hence there are two opposing right-wing poles, with the majority of Americans quietly living their lives—having both affairs and abortions—nestled snugly in the middle. The future? In terms of popular culture, journalist Barry Yeoman envisions a big chill on controversial productions. "As local governments feel the pressure not to subsidize provocative art," he writes, "some impresarios will decide that survival is more important than social commentary. . . . How many directors will decide, in the name of placating a city council, not to bring in the next (Terrence) McNally or (Tony) Kushner? The most damaging effect of the new funding paradigm might be the absence of those works we'll never know we've missed."[9]

As to abortion, anti-choice activists will continue to do what works, whether that is lobbying to winnow away access, bombing clinics or shooting workers. While the FBI has placed both James Kopp and Eric Rudolph on the Ten Most Wanted List and has expended considerable resources on their capture, many pro-choice activists believe that more can be done, not just to find them, but to curtail illegal opposition to abortion and reproductive healthcare. As longtime New York City clinic defender Susan E. Davis says, "If it had been banks being bombed, set on fire, shot at or hit with butyric acid, they would have found the culprits years ago."[10]

1995

JANUARY: BOSTON, MASSACHUSETTS

Within days of the shootings in Brookline, Boston's Bernard Cardinal Law called for a moratorium on clinic protests. "It's my judgment that it would be good to refrain from such manifestations at this time," he said. "We need to restore a sense of calm."[11] His words were ignored. Picketers resumed their protests at Planned Parenthood the day the clinic reopened.

JANUARY: MILWAUKEE, WISCONSIN

Dr. James Schwartz (a pseudonym) had been performing abortions for twenty years when he got a phone call from a colleague in Milwaukee asking him to fill in for a doctor who had become unable to work. He readily agreed. What he found shocked him. "Up until that point," he says, "I had experienced minimal personal harassment from the antis. The protestors had come to my house a few times, but it was not an ongoing thing. My work in Milwaukee involved much more personal harassment, continual, every-single-day harassment, than I'd ever seen before."[12]

The Pennsylvania resident agreed to work in Milwaukee two days a week; his plan was to spend the rest of each week providing abortion and gynecological care at the southern New Jersey clinic he had purchased in 1994. "The Milwaukee clinic had been closed for four months because the owner had some personal problems. The protestors did not expect it to reopen. The first few times

I went there, in December 1994, it was fine. The local antis didn't know who I was, and it took them a while to realize that we had opened again. By January, by the third or fourth time I went, they had figured it out. The antis met me at the airport. A guy came up to me and took my picture. He told me it was for a promotion, that I was the one hundredth person to sit in that chair or something. I didn't buy it and assumed the photo was for one of those 'wanted' posters. A week or so later, again at the airport, another man walked up to me as I was boarding and said, 'Aren't you the man who kills babies at the clinic?' I tried to ignore him, but it was obvious that the antis knew who I was. This then became the standard thing. Different people, always men, met me at the Milwaukee airport each time I came into town and each time I left. And there were always protestors screaming at the clinic. They'd use my name to yell at me as I came and went. For a while they also called my hotel room at 3:00 A.M. whenever I was in town to tell me to stop killing babies. I finally asked the hotel to stop putting middle-of-the-night calls through to me, which solved that problem."[13]

But Schwartz's other problems—the harassment he experienced while traveling and while at work—were not so easily quelled. In fact, they became worse when Milwaukee activists contacted like-minded people in Pennsylvania, where Schwartz lived, and in New Jersey, where he owned a clinic, and began to coordinate their activities. "One day when I tried to leave my house, I saw a car sitting in the cul-de-sac blocking my entrance. I had to call the police. They made the owner move the car so I could drive past him. The driver then followed me to the Philadelphia airport. When he got to the waiting area he made a loud announcement to everyone on my flight that they 'were flying with a doctor who works in an abortion mill and kills babies.' A few people offered me their support and a few told him to shut up," but the incident was still unsettling.[14]

Schwartz worked at the Milwaukee clinic until the summer of 1996, when the facility closed. "I was always adamant about getting the clinic open, getting myself in and getting patients in. I would sometimes try disguises to fool the protestors, hoping they wouldn't know it was me. I'd put on different hats and sunglasses. I'd ask different people to drive me to and from the airport in unfamiliar cars, but I would not give in; I never let them stop me from doing my job. Of course doctors are intimidated and frightened. But the antis also make us very determined, very stubborn. We get really angry. Maybe doctors who do one or two abortions a week or a month will stop because of pressure from the antis. Maybe doctors considering becoming providers will go into something else. I never chastise people who don't want to do abortions, but those of us who provide them believe in what we do and we will keep doing them," Schwartz says.[15]

Schwartz currently works full time at his southern New Jersey clinic. Protest there is sporadic and usually peaceful. "The police and the township learned in the late 1980s, when there were frequent blockades, that they could save themselves a lot of time, money and effort if they had a presence at the clinics," Schwartz says. "The police have become aggressive and their support has been essential. I am absolutely convinced that having a police presence at the clinic has helped thwart illegal anti-abortion activity there."[16]

JANUARY 2: BOSTON, MASSACHUSETTS

A memorial service for Shannon Lowney and Leanne Nichols, clinic workers murdered by John Salvi III on December 30, was held at the Arlington Street Church. More than 2,000 mourners attended. Actor Kathleen Turner read a passage from Edna St. Vincent Millay's *Dirge Without Music:* "I am not resigned to the shutting away of loving hearts in the hard ground. . . . Down, down, down into the darkness of the grave / Gently they go, the beautiful, the tender, the kind; / Quietly they go, the intelligent, the witty, the brave. / I know. But I do not approve. And I am not resigned."[17]

JANUARY 3: SOUTH CAROLINA

The South Carolina legislature passed an amendment to a state law regulating all medical facilities that perform five or more first-trimester and/or any second-trimester abortions per month. The regulations were slated to go into effect on June 28.

Under the aegis of setting "quality standards" for the licensing of abortion clinics, the new rules set guidelines for everything from the required frequency of fire drills, to the required width of hallways and thickness of doors. They also barred clinics from performing abortions on women with diabetes, AIDS, hepatitis or high blood pressure.

In response, the Greenville Women's Clinic, the Charleston Women's Medical Clinic and a doctor who performs in-office procedures sued the state to stop the regulations from taking effect. Their challenge argued that the regulations were unfairly burdensome to abortion providers. Other ambulatory surgical facilities, they charged, did not face the same stringent requirements, nor did they face the same fines for noncompliance. With help from the Center for Reproductive Law and Policy, a New York City–based think tank and public interest litigator, the plaintiffs spent four years in court, repeatedly asserting that the rules discriminated against providers.[18]

Their persistence paid off and the regulations were ruled invalid on February 9, 1999. "Simply put," said Judge William B. Trexler, "they [the state] have gone too far—imposing costly requirements that are at best medically unnecessary and at worst contrary to accepted medical practice. . . . The regulation is permeated with provisions which are either not sufficiently supported by the state's interest in maternal health or not designed to further that goal."[19]

The providers, while pleased by the verdict, were not surprised. More than fifteen years before South Carolina's attempt to control outpatient abortion services, *City of Akron v. Akron Center for Reproductive Health* found that a state bears the burden of demonstrating that any regulations it seeks to impose are "justified by important state health objectives. . . . Specifically, the preservation and protection of maternal health." Almost ten years after the 1983 Akron decision, in 1992, *Planned Parenthood v. Casey* found that "a statute which, while furthering the interest in potential life or some other valid state interest, has the effect of placing a substantial obstacle in the path of a woman's choice cannot be considered a permissible means of serving its legitimate ends. Unnecessary health regulations that have the effect of presenting an obstacle to a woman seeking an abortion impose an undue burden on that right." At least three other challenges to the kind of burdensome state regulations sought by South Carolina have been similarly successful.[20]

JANUARY 5: BOSTON, MASSACHUSETTS

After a delay of several days, John Salvi was extradited from a prison in Virginia to one in Massachusetts. Over the next few weeks, details emerged about the twenty-three-year-old man. The only child of French Canadian parents, he was raised in Ipswich, Massachusetts, and moved to Naples, Florida, when he was thirteen. Like Michael Griffin and Paul Hill, Salvi had long shown signs of mental imbalance. According to the *Boston Herald,* Salvi was fired from his first job after high school for exposing himself to a woman while on a rooftop.[21] He left Florida in 1992 and settled in Portsmouth, New Hampshire, where he immersed himself in the study of anti-abortion literature and hairdressing. He had attended several "rescues" at Planned Parenthood in Brookline and was videotaped at March 12 and May 14, 1994, events there.[22]

Investigators also discovered that Salvi had been fired from his job as an apprentice beautician on December 23, a week before his Brookline shooting spree. Richard Griffin, owner of The Eccentric Hair Salon in Hampton Beach, described Salvi as "a very odd character," and said that he had been fired following an altercation with a customer. He further told reporters that Salvi's truck had sported a large, gory picture of a mangled fetus until his coworkers complained about having to look at it.[23] Doreen Potter, the salon manager, added: "When you talked to him, he either stared you down or walked away."[24]

By all accounts Salvi was deeply religious. A frequent churchgoer, he confided to a neighbor that he was drawn to the abortion issue "because he wanted other kids to have a better chance than he had."[25]

A search of Salvi's apartment after he was arrested revealed a large cache of materials including tracts entitled "Bomb the Abortion Clinics?" and "Abortion: Will There Be a Civil War?"[26] Also found were the phone number and address of Donald Spitz, head of Pro-Life Virginia and an outspoken advocate of murder and violence against abortion providers.[27] Spitz's work, conducted from an office in Chesapeake, Virginia, had been profiled in the November 1994 issue of *Life Advocate,* the pro-violence magazine of the now-defunct American Coalition of Life Activists (ACLA). Pro-choice watchdogs believe that Salvi's awareness of Spitz may have prompted him to go to Virginia after fleeing New England. Nonetheless, Spitz was never charged in the murders.

JANUARY 6: DEDHAM, MASSACHUSETTS

The day after being extradited from Virginia, John Salvi pled not guilty to two counts of murder and five counts of assault with intent to murder. He also submitted a rambling six-page letter to the judge asking to be put to death if found guilty. The letter further stated that if he was exonerated, he intended to become a Catholic priest.[28]

JANUARY 9: LONG ISLAND, NEW YORK

Four Long Island clinics found signs on the outside walls near their entrances when they opened for the day: "Danger. This is a war zone. People are being killed here. Like Boston you risk injury or death if you are caught near these premises."[29]

Several days later, one of the clinics, Long Island Gynecological Associates, was told by its landlord that it had to stop performing abortions because "doing so endangered the building's other tenants."[30] In February, when the clinic had not ceased terminating unwanted pregnancies, the building owner began eviction proceedings. A strong editorial in the *New York Times* put the eviction into perspective: "Long Island Gynecological Associates is not the one putting other tenants in presumed jeopardy. It is the domestic terrorists who made the bomb threats, demonstrated outside the clinic and posted the threatening placards. . . . By moving to evict Long Island Gynecological Associates, the clinic's landlord is not just caving in to criminals. It is also giving a green light to those who would harass abortion rights out of existence."[31]

JANUARY 21: PORTLAND, OREGON

Anti-abortionist David Crane introduced the "Deadly Dozen" poster at a press conference held during a meeting of the American Coalition of Life Activists (ACLA). The poster bore a large banner headline—GUILTY OF CRIMES AGAINST HUMANITY—and offered a $5,000 reward for "information leading to the arrest, conviction and revocation of license to practice medicine" of twelve "abortionists," including Doctors Robert Crist, Warren Hern, Elizabeth Newhall, James Newhall and Karen Sweigert. The posters listed the physicians' names, addresses and telephone numbers. During the press conference, Crane likened the ACLA campaign to the Nuremberg Trials of 1945 and 1946 during which alleged war criminals were interrogated about their participation in the Nazi Holocaust.[32]

"The FBI called to warn me about the list within a few hours of its release," says Dr. Elizabeth Newhall. "They offered me a guard at my home, which I declined. I did not want an FBI agent living in my house. At first I dealt with the threat by bravado: 'You're not going to do this to me.' But they scared me enough to buy and wear a bulletproof vest, wear wigs and other disguises to drive to work and install a silent alarm in my home. This whole thing politicized my kids and even though they did not act afraid, I knew they were. We talked about it a lot."[33]

On top of the upheaval caused by the poster, Newhall and her children were also going through a difficult personal transition. She had recently separated from her husband, Dr. Jim Newhall, and was plodding through a divorce and joint custody agreement. "This was an awful time for us," Newhall admits. "It was a lot for our kids to go through but they were champions."[34]

Part of coping, she says, involved figuring out how best to counter the list; in addition to installing alarms and wearing disguises, both she and her former spouse decided to sign on to a lawsuit, *Planned Parenthood of the Columbia/Willamette v. The American Coalition of Life Activists*. The suit charged ACLA, Advocates for Life Ministries and fourteen abortion foes with violating the Freedom of Access to Clinic Entrances (FACE) Act of 1994, the Racketeer Influenced and Corrupt Organizations (RICO) Act and the Oregon Racketeer Influenced and Corrupt Organizations (ORICO) Act. Plaintiffs charged that ACLA et al had instigated a "campaign of terror and intimidation" and argued that the Deadly Dozen poster, "when viewed in the context of violence against abortion providers," constituted a "true threat" for which they should be punished. Defendants, in turn, maintained that the poster was a form of free speech protected by the First Amendment.

A jury sided with the plaintiffs and awarded them $107 million in February 1999. "Whether any of the money awarded will ever find its way to Planned Parenthood or its co-plaintiffs is uncertain at best," wrote *New York Times* reporter Sam Howe Verhovek. "In three other major cases against militant abortion opponents, in Portland and in Houston and Chicago, juries have ordered smaller damage amounts, but many of the defendants have either refused to pay or asserted that they have transferred all their assets to others and thus have no way to pay."[35] More significant than the financial award, however, was the finding that the Deadly Dozen poster, along with a Web page called the Nuremberg Files that was first posted on the World Wide Web in January 1997, posed a "blatant and illegal communication of true threats to kill, assault or do bodily harm to each of the plaintiffs." It was further found that both the list and the files were specifically intended "to interfere with or intimidate the plaintiffs from engaging in legal medical practices and procedures;" the court concluded that neither the list nor the Web page were protected by the First Amendment.[36]

JANUARY 21: PORTLAND, OREGON

"The Deadly Dozen list was released on a Saturday," says Dr. James Newhall, an abortion provider at the Downtown Women's Center in Portland and the ex-husband of Dr. Elizabeth Newhall. "I got a page that afternoon from the FBI. I was shocked when a man called and identified himself from the Domestic Terrorism Task Force. At first I was incredulous when he told me I was on the list. He suggested I get a concealed weapons permit and a bulletproof vest. I considered getting a handgun but I have two boys. They were eight and thirteen in 1995, and I didn't want a handgun at home. But I did buy the vest and I will wear it until everyone agrees that abortion is necessary. The clinic workers in Brookline were shot with a .22. A vest would stop a .22 and is some protection against handguns; it is not protection against rifles, which are higher velocity. At the time the list came out, there was a flurry of publicity and I got letters from all over the state, as many as one hundred from people I never met. All but one were supportive. I was a hero to these people. A lot of the people writing sent money, and the vest was paid for by their contributions. I have no quarrel with people who think abortion violates God's law. It's when they act on God's behalf that I have a problem with them. I am a stubborn person. The more people tell me I can't do something, the more I say, 'Fuck you, I shall.' They harden my resolve. Yes, they could shoot me, but I really don't think that will happen. Of course, David Gunn didn't think it would happen either. This is a holy war, a jihad. We look down our noses at the Muslims, but this is the same thing."[37]

LATE JANUARY: JACKSON, MISSISSIPPI

Since 1973, when a then-twenty-three-year-old Susan Hill first got involved in the provision of abortion services, her dream has been to open as many clinics as possible in underserved areas. Shortly after Dr. Gunn was killed in 1993, she and her colleagues began to consider opening a facility in Jackson, Mississippi. Their first move was to consult with local NOW and ACLU people.

"Once we connected with them and got their encouragement, we started to look for a building," she says. "We found one next to the office of Dr. Helen Barnes, an obstetrician/gynecologist. She had done the first legal abortion in Mississippi in 1973 and was the first Black woman in the state to become a gynecologist. She became our guardian angel, our godmother. She was semi-retired when we opened but said she would work with us."[38]

On December 30, 1994, the day of John Salvi's rampage in Brookline, Hill was interviewing prospective staff at what was to become the Jackson Women's Health Organization. "Our existence became a media dream, because despite the murders, a new clinic was opening in, of all places, Mississippi," Hill laughs. "Shortly after the shootings, the Department of Justice issued marshals to us because we'd gotten death threats. Police vans were posted around the building. On the night we had scheduled our staff orientation there were cameras everywhere."[39]

While Hill hoped the thirteen medical technicians, nurses and counselors she had hired would attend the training, she worried that the political violence surrounding abortion would scare off at least some of her new employees. Her fears were unfounded; all the women showed up, passing through a line of police, federal marshals and media to get inside. "I started the meeting by asking each person why she'd returned for the job," recalls Hill. "One woman, a twenty-three-year-old with a twenty-one-month-old baby, said she and her husband had talked and prayed all night long. They had decided that she needed to do what was right because what the antis were doing was so wrong. Another woman, a licensed practical nurse from Pocahantas, Mississippi, said she'd called her mama and asked her if God would judge her harshly for working in an abortion clinic. She told us her mama said no, God wouldn't judge her, but He would judge the people who bombed clinics. One by one we went around the table. Dr. Barnes told us about delivering babies and said we'd all come too far as women to let these anti-abortion bastards stop us. A *Nightline* producer in the room with us likened the meeting to a revival, with everyone pouring out their hearts. I got to see feminism twenty-five years later. Only maybe two of the women there that night had ever voted, but they still knew they had to come in and do something. They weren't political when they got here but they are now. They've seen politics affect their lives, their jobs."[40]

Shortly after opening, the Department of Justice charged protestor Roy McMillan with violating FACE and obtained a federal injunction against him. The injunction orders McMillan to stay one hundred feet from the clinic; Susan Hill reports that the mandate is well enforced. "McMillan is the most personally frightening of the protestors," she says. "He's a lurker, a drive-by-twenty-times-a-day, follow-you-in-the-shopping-center kind of guy. He likes to get very close to you, in your face, and yell. When we came to town he didn't do much at first but jump in and out of things. Then he made threatening remarks to staff. A few months after the Salvi murders in Brookline he made a motion with his fingers and said, 'I could just shoot you like a birdie in a tree' to several workers. We got additional legal relief off that comment because the judge agreed that it was threatening."[41]

JANUARY 27: DEDHAM, MASSACHUSETTS

Anne Marie and John Salvi II, in Massachusetts for their son John's trial, issued a heartbreaking public plea to other parents of disturbed children: "Don't let your love for your child blind you to problems that exist. We want to urge all parents who notice unusual or strange behavior on behalf of their children to seek out professional help."[42]

FEBRUARY 23: MELBOURNE, FLORIDA

Meredith Raney, "Chief Investigator" of the fictitious Women's Legal Action Coalition (WLAC), sent the following letter to Chelsea Pierce (a pseudonym) in an attempt to scare her into suing the Aware Woman Center for Choice. Raney had illegally obtained Pierce's address by tracing motor vehicle records.

> We understand that you or someone you know received services at Aware Woman Center for Choice in Melbourne on February 11, 1995. . . . We apologize for having to write you, but because of suspicious activity involving deliberate concealment of certain persons entering Aware Woman com-

pounded by us seeing no known doctors there on the day of your visit, we
have reason to believe that Aware Woman may be using unlicensed doctors
to perform their services. It would be a great help to our investigators if you
would send us a copy of your discharge papers that shows the name of the
"doctor" who performed the surgery [*sic*]. If you send us a copy of your
paperwork we will send you a copy of our investigation report when it is
complete if you include your name and address. . . . Patients have been seen
leaving Aware Woman in obvious distress. If you were one of these patients,
please contact us. We want to help you. We have doctors to help you get
better. We have lawyers who can file malpractice lawsuits on your behalf if
you have been hurt. All of this is at no cost to you. You may not be having
problems now, but please keep this letter in case you start having problems
in the next weeks or even months.[43]

According to records subpoenaed by Aware Woman in a court case, at least
twenty-five antis maintained full surveillance of the clinic for ten years, using
long-range video cameras, binoculars, long-range microphones and other high-
tech equipment. These devices enabled them to copy license plate information,
track the women and send them letters.

MARCH: PENSACOLA, FLORIDA

The Southern Poverty Law Center (SPLC) filed suit against John Burt for the
wrongful death of Dr. David Gunn. The suit alleged that Burt had provided
Michael Griffin with literature calling for the execution of abortion doctors and
had shown him a life-size effigy of Gunn that depicted the physician with
bloodstained hands and a rope around his neck.[44]

The case was settled in July 1996 when the Gunn family was given
possession of a tiny plot of land, owned by Burt, located next door to the
Community Healthcare Center of Pensacola, Inc. (formerly called The Ladies
Center). Burt had previously erected scaffolding above the eight-foot fence and
had used the platform to scream at women entering the center.[45]

MARCH: FLORIDA

An incarcerated Michael Griffin, convicted of murdering Dr. David Gunn, told
reporters that, "I used to believe in justifiable homicide. I don't anymore. My
change of mind has come from reading the Bible and praying. I've had two years
to think about it."[46]

MARCH 16: MELBOURNE, FLORIDA

"We apologize for having to write you but we suspect that Aware Woman may be using a doctor with a questionable reputation," said the letter from Meredith Raney's letterhead-only WLAC to patient Renata O'Connell (a pseudonym). "They take him in and out of the clinic under a blanket in the back seat of a car. Obviously they are trying to hide something. We need for you to send us a copy of your discharge papers that shows the name of the doctor who performed your surgery so that we can investigate his reputation. Please help us identify this questionable doctor."[47]

Follow-up note: Following the deaths of Dr. John Bayard Britton and James Barrett, abortion providers *were* running scared of anti-abortion extremists. Like most clinics across the country, Aware Woman tried to hide the identity of its medical workers, providing wigs and other disguises for them to wear. They also used a series of decoy cars to convey doctors to and from the airport and hotels, and regularly shielded them under blankets to protect them and their anonymity.

SPRING: VIENNA, VIRGINIA

Randall Terry was awarded the third annual Andrew Jackson "Championship of Liberty Award" from the ultra-right-wing U.S. Taxpayer's Party (since renamed the Constitution Party). In his acceptance speech Terry told the audience that:

> The greatest crisis we face is not child killing. It's not the Sodomites, it's not land tax, it's not the intrusion of the federal government into our lives, into our families, as they crush our liberties. The greatest crisis we face is a crisis of leadership. We are facing a crisis of righteous, courageous, physically oriented, male leadership. Male leadership! God established patriarchy when He established the world. If we're going to have true reformation in America, it is because men once again, if I may use a worn out expression, have righteous testosterone flowing through their veins.[48]

During the course of the speech, Terry also told the crowd that, "The Declaration of Independence is an intrinsically Christian document. The four references to God there can only be the Christian God."[49]

APRIL: PORTLAND, OREGON

When the American Coalition of Life Activists (ACLA) kicked off the Stigmatize, Harangue, Agitate, Mortify and Expose (SHAME) Campaign, one of their first targets was Jude Hanzo, executive director of All Women's Health Services from 1986 to 1996.

"On April 14 I found a copy of *Life Advocate Magazine* on my doorstep," Hanzo says. "I knew they knew where I lived. I told the cops that they were going to picket me but they said that since I didn't perform abortions I would not be hit. Somebody once told me, 'You go after the executive director, you go after the heart of the organization.' The antis knew this."[50]

The day after finding the magazine on her stoop, Hanzo received a postcard depicting a fetus on a cross and bearing the message, "Father, forgive them, for they know not what they do." The card was signed "a neighbor." A week later, on April 22, nine ACLA protestors led by Paul DeParrie marched in front of Hanzo's home with placards stating, "Hanzo lives comfortably in her home because she makes good money as an abortionist who kills children. Let her know that you think she should not kill children for a living."[51]

Shortly thereafter, the clinic's medical director received a leaflet that said, "These abortionists have been exposed." The one-page sheet listed the names, addresses and phone numbers of five abortion providers, including Hanzo. Within the next few months ACLA returned to Hanzo's residence several more times and in January 1996 conducted a "Jericho Walk," a loud demonstration that moved through Hanzo's neighborhood, denouncing her and her work.[52]

"It became increasingly difficult for me to continue this work once I was personally targeted," she says. "I could never get away from abortion. I'd get home and a neighbor would want to talk about it. I couldn't blame her, but I could never get away from the issue. The feeling of vulnerability was horrendous. Was I really in danger? Or was I overreacting? When you put a bulletproof vest on—which I'd been doing—you admit that there is danger. My partner also had to deal with the issue all of the time. We moved—and I resigned as executive director—about a year after the home picketing started."[53]

While Hanzo feels that the police were minimally responsive, she says that her neighbors were wonderful. "They sent me letters, came over and invited me to meet with the Neighborhood Association to see what we, as a community, could do. I never met with them because I resigned from the clinic and we left the city. It felt like a good time for me to leave All Women's Health Services. I wanted to move on. I'd done abortion work for more than twenty years, but I still have mixed feelings. The antis won because I left, although I am now the president of the board of the Chico Feminist Women's Health Center and am still connected to a lot of people in the pro-choice community via letter, phone and e-mail."[54]

Follow-up note: Hanzo sued DeParrie for stalking and won an injunction barring him from demonstrating at her home. DeParrie appealed and the Oregon Appellate Court sided with him, concluding that the protests were an expression of legitimate free speech. The Oregon Supreme Court declined to review the appellate decision.[55]

MAY: WASHINGTON, D.C.

Representative Charles Canady [R-FL] introduced a ban on dilation and evacuation (D & E or D & X)—so-called partial birth—abortions. Although the House and Senate passed the Partial Birth Abortion Ban Act in late 1995, President Clinton vetoed it, charging that the ban would threaten the health of women by denying them access to a safe surgical procedure. Opponents countered that the technique was infanticide.

According to researchers at the Alan Guttmacher Institute, D & Es account for between 0.03 and 0.05 percent of the 1.4 million abortions performed annually.[56] And they are necessary, even life-saving. A fact sheet composed by the New York state chapter of the National Abortion and Reproductive Rights Action League reports that D & E abortions are often performed to remove a dead fetus from the pregnant woman. "Fetuses with severe abnormalities—often detected late in pregnancy—have a huge chance of dying in utero, before labor begins, posing a severe health threat to the woman. When a fetus dies, the tissue begins to break down and toxifies the woman's circulation. This increases the likelihood of needing blood products, emergency hysterectomy or can lead to death."[57]

Follow-up note: Since 1995, twenty-eight states have passed legislation banning D & E abortions. Most of the prohibitions have been struck down in court as overly vague.[58]

MAY 1: DALLAS, TEXAS

Writer Carol Adams, wife of pro-choice activist the Reverend Bruce Buchanan, associate pastor of the First Presbyterian Church of Dallas, bid $3,325 to purchase seventy-eight items of Operation Rescue property being auctioned off to satisfy a Planned Parenthood lawsuit against the group. In 1994 Planned Parenthood won a $1.3 million judgment against OR and two anti-choice activists. All were held liable for conspiring to interfere with clinic activities during the 1992 Republican National Convention in Houston. In order to make at least partial restitution, OR was forced to sell its office equipment—six computers, printers, loudspeakers and sound equipment.[59]

"The speaker system had been used to terrorize my children and my church," says Adams. "I know what my family experienced was infinitesimal compared to what clinics experience. But that auction felt wonderful, like a rare opportunity to one-up them. Now their property was my property. It would never undo what they had done, but it was still sweet."[60] Adams told the press that she planned to donate the office equipment to several not-for-profit organizations.[61]

MAY 18: MELBOURNE, FLORIDA

Meredith Raney had begun writing patients of the Aware Woman Center for Choice in 1991 but had been so unsuccessful in his attempts to get them to file complaints against the clinic that he continually escalated his rhetoric.

"Aware Woman is concealing the identity of the doctor that they used on the day of your visit," he wrote patient Sharon MacGregor (a pseudonym).

> They take him in and out of the clinic under a blanket in the back seat of a car. Obviously they are trying to hide something. It is unimaginable that any reputable doctor who spent many years and much money going to medical school would lower himself to being carried in and out of work under a blanket in the back seat of a car. . . . We are concerned enough about the reputation of this doctor that we are offering $300 cash to the first person to give us her original discharge papers [no copies] showing the name of a doctor other than Dr. Whitney who we already know. Remember, only the first person to contact us will get the $300.[62]

Due to repeated complaints filed with the Florida Agency for Health Care Administration by Raney, inspectors visited the clinic three times in twelve months to ascertain whether the medical staff was properly credentialed. On all occasions, everything was found to be in order and personnel were found to be in compliance with state licensing requirements. Unfortunately, the pattern of filing utterly ridiculous complaints with city, state and federal agencies absorbed an enormous amount of staff time and forced workers to expend energy on something that benefited no one.

JUNE 22: FT. PIERCE, FLORIDA

West Palm Beach resident Dr. Lino B. Rodriguez received the following warning from Meredith Raney's WLAC: "Part of our charter is to expose anyone who participates in the abortion industry. We understand that you perform abortions at A Woman's World Medical Center in Ft. Pierce. This is your right under the present laws of this country. It is also our right to peacefully picket. This letter is to notify you that we will be picketing at your office and other appropriate places to inform the public as to what we understand you do at A Woman's World."[63]

AUGUST: DEDHAM, MASSACHUSETTS

Despite attempts by John Salvi III's attorney, J. W. Carney Jr., to have his client declared criminally insane, Judge Barbara Dortch-Okara found Salvi competent to stand trial. Had Salvi been found guilty by reason of insanity, he would have been sent to a state psychiatric hospital until medical experts felt that he no longer posed a danger to himself or society.

District Attorney John Kivlan successfully argued that Salvi's actions were premeditated and meticulous, making him legally sane and responsible for his actions.[64] Salvi agreed, testifying that he was mentally fit and eager to stand trial.

AUGUST 3–5, 1995: GRANITE CITY, ILLINOIS

Early in the summer of 1995 staff at the Hope Clinic for Women got word that the American Coalition of Life Activists (ACLA), the group responsible for the Deadly Dozen list, would be holding their annual convention in St. Louis, Missouri, ten minutes from the Granite City health center. "Our medical director made the decision to leave town with his family since he had a 'wanted poster' on him, and we supported his decision," says administrator Sally Burgess. "We have four doctors on staff, and one of our other physicians said that if we provided him with an escort he could come in on Saturday. We hired a fairly expensive escort and security service—they needed a $1,000 retainer plus hourly expenses—and they picked the doctor up in a van from a remote location. He wore a helmet and vest when he was traveling to and from the clinic."[65]

According to Burgess, ACLA arrived at the clinic on Thursday, Friday and Saturday at 5:15 A.M. "Thursday and Friday were relatively quiet," she says, "since we were not seeing patients on these days, but Saturday was a zoo. All the media were here with cameras and recorders and ACLA had close to a hundred people. You wouldn't have believed the circus atmosphere. On top of ACLA and the media, the police, the state patrols and pro-choice forces were all here. What was so odd was that the patients acted like they expected this. I think they'd been so inundated with pictures of clinics under siege by Operation Rescue that this is what they thought you got when you came to a clinic. All of the patients were treated that day because the police were wonderful. They'd been here when OR showed up in 1989, and they let them know that blockades would not be tolerated in this community."[66]

SEPTEMBER: ATLANTA, GEORGIA

When Ann Rose, former public relations and marketing director at Atlanta's Midtown Hospital, started Abortion Clinics On-Line in September 1995, she wanted to provide an Internet forum for clinics across the country to publicize their services and give potential patients a virtual tour of facilities in their area.

More than 160 clinics currently participate in Abortion Clinics On-Line, and Rose says that for the most part, electronic harassment has been minimal. Nonetheless, in 1997 and 1998 she had several chilling experiences. In the first, Rose was besieged with what she calls "e-mail bombs," 1,000 copies of a message saying "Go to Hell, you filthy murderer." In the second instance, someone signed her into the Auburn University Football Chat Group; until she was able to unsubscribe, the nonfootball enthusiast received up to two hundred pieces of correspondence a day. In both cases Rose was able to trace the mail and turn in the perpetrators. "Unfortunately, all the listserves can do is cancel their accounts for harassing behavior," she says.[67]

OCTOBER 25: MELBOURNE, FLORIDA

Meredith Raney, now in his fourth year of sending guilt-tripping letters to patients of the Aware Woman Center for Choice to induce them to sue the clinic, was becoming more and more desperate. A new form letter, on Women's Legal Action Coalition letterhead, bore a photo of Dr. Randall Whitney in the upper right hand corner.

> Your vehicle being at Aware Woman Center for Choice in Melbourne on October 14, 1995 indicates that you or someone you know used their services. We want to alert you to the fact that Aware Woman is hiding the identity of the doctor they used on the day of your visit. They may not even have told you his correct name,

said a letter to Cassie Robertson (a pseudonym). The letter continues:

> Dr. Randall Whitney, pictured above, is a known doctor who works at Aware Woman one or two days a week. We did not see Dr. Whitney there on the day of your surgery. Aware Woman may have used someone to operate on you and

told you it was Dr. Whitney. Please check your paperwork. If Dr. Whitney's name is on your paperwork or medication, but the picture above is not of the man who operated on you, you need to contact us at once. Fraud may have been committed and the man who operated on you may not be a licensed doctor. We have helped three women file complaints recently. All of these women are being represented by our lawyers. Our lawyers will also represent you if fraud has been committed against you or if you have been damaged by the man who operated on you.[68]

Raney eventually found someone who was willing to sue the clinic for alleged malfeasance in July 1999. Both he and the woman lost the federal lawsuit, which they appealed.

NOVEMBER: NATIONWIDE

A year after a sniper shot abortion provider Garson Romalis in his Vancouver home, the Reverend Michael Bray penned "Tale of Two Armies—and Their Manuals" for his column in *Life Advocate Magazine*. His attention first turned to the *Army of God Manual,* a text, he writes, that "provides all kinds of jokes and inspiration for folks who really want to stop abortion." While he further described the manual as "witty and charming," he suggests that serious saboteurs utilize materials put out by the United States armed forces. "Our military has much better literature on violence than one reads in those dirty tricks books," he writes.

I am short on shelf space so I traded my copy of the *Army of God Manual* for the army's *Sniper Training and Employment.* And it is uplifting! There are some exciting concepts such as that stated under "Mission: The importance of the sniper cannot be measured simply by the number of casualties he inflicts upon the enemy. Realization of the sniper's presence instills fear in the enemy troop elements and influences its decisions and actions. . . ." The very presence of sniper-minded people serves to instill fear into those who take it upon themselves to slaughter babies. The fact that three percent of the population believes that lethal action against abortionists is justifiable (according to a CNN poll taken in August of 1994) probably "instills fear" enough to influence the potential targets to make life-preserving decisions. . . . The fear of the sniper can influence the abortionist to consider the end of his life and the judgment to come. Such fear can lead the abortionist to cease killing babies and repent unto salvation! The *U.S. Army Manual* further states: "The sniper must be capable of calmly and deliberately killing targets that may not pose an immediate threat to him. It is much easier to kill in self-defense or in defense of others than it is to kill without apparent provocation. The sniper must not be susceptible to emotions such as anxiety or remorse."[69]

NOVEMBER 11: ANCASTER, ONTARIO, CANADA

Dr. Hugh Short was left permanently disabled by a sniper attack, the second shooting in Canada. The gynecologist was watching television in his home when a bullet smashed through a window and shattered his right elbow. According to *Pro-Choice News,* a publication of the Canadian Abortion Rights Action League, Short provided the majority of abortions at Hamilton Henderson Hospital, a facility that had previously been subjected to heavy picketing and harassment by anti-choice activists.[70]

Short was sixty-two at the time of the shooting and never returned to the practice of medicine. The perpetrator, believed to be James Charles Kopp, remains at large.[71]

DECEMBER: MISSOULA, MONTANA

Deb Frandsen, executive director of Planned Parenthood of Missoula, Montana, received a letter from incarcerated anti-abortion zealot Michael Ross. "How many children have you killed at Planned Parenthood today? My friends in Missoula want to hold funeral services for these dear children," he wrote.

Staff at Missoula's Blue Mountain Clinic also got a letter from Ross: "We are watching Sally Mullen [the clinic's executive director at that time]. We have a file on her and a snapshot. Flyers are being posted identifying her as a blood-flecked piece of dog feces."[72]

1996

NATIONWIDE

Randall Terry, Flip Benham of Operation Rescue National, Judie Brown of the American Life League, Joseph Scheidler of the Pro-Life Action Network and the New York State Right to Life Committee announced their endorsement of Howard Phillips, presidential candidate of the U.S. Taxpayer's [now Constitution] Party. "As president I would approve U.S. Attorneys who would prosecute abortion mills and abortionists," he promised. "I would name to the federal bench judges who publicly acknowledge the legal personhood of the unborn child."[73]

And that's not all. In addition to advocating the reversal of *Roe v. Wade*, Phillips also pledged to withdraw U.S. participation from the United Nations and NATO; end federal funding for the National Endowment for the Arts; curtail federal support for AIDS education and "special legal protections and privileges for practitioners of buggery"; and close the Department of Education.

Phillips, head of the Office of Economic Opportunity under President Richard Nixon, also expressed his support for governing America by precept of biblical law:

> Each of the states at the time of our founding had explicitly Christian legal systems rooted in the British Common Law and traceable to Holy Scripture. Neither Congress nor any other component of the federal government had any right to interfere with those Christian law systems. Today America is in trouble because we have departed from the original premise, the original design, the original contract. . . . No human law should put us at odds with God's instruction. The intentional killing of an innocent human being is always illegal to God, whatever may be the opinion of appointed judges or elected politicians.[74]

JANUARY: LANDOVER, MARYLAND

Michael Bray, author of the 1994 book *A Time to Kill*—and a convicted firebomber whose ten targets included the Hillcrest Clinic in Norfolk, Virginia, and the National Abortion Federation in Washington, D.C.—sponsored the first White Rose Banquet to honor anti-abortion zealots who have been incarcerated, as well as those whose acts have gone undetected by law enforcement. The event has since become an annual fund raiser for the most violent sector of the "pro-life" movement.

The fourth annual banquet, in 1999, was held in a Holiday Inn just outside Washington, D.C., and attracted seventy people, including butyric acid proponent John Arena; convicted firebombers John Brockhoeft and Joshua Graff; and the Reverend Donald Spitz of Pro-Life Virginia. Twelve items were auctioned off to raise money for Bray's cause: a camouflage hat, scarf and baby booties knitted by an imprisoned Shelley Shannon, an anonymously donated sweatshirt advertising "Explosives and Professional Services," and sketches of Mother Teresa drawn by convicted firebomber James Mitchell.[75] Mitchell had been arrested in February 1997 for setting fire to the Commonwealth Clinic in Falls Church, Virginia. He is currently serving a ten-year sentence.

According to Amanda Ripley, a journalist who attended the 1999 "festivi-ties," a recently penned letter from Paul Hill, passed out to those assembled, was greeted enthusiastically. The letter reminded the crowd of Hill's continued pride: "When I finished shooting, I laid the shotgun at my feet and walked away with my hands held out at my sides, awaiting arrest. When they later led me to the squad car, a small crowd had assembled. I spontaneously raised my voice, 'One thing's for sure, no innocent people will be killed in that clinic today.'"[76] Letters from other jailed comrades further imbued the crowd with the spirit of armed struggle.

But it was Jayne Bray, a mother of ten and the wife of the Reverend Michael Bray, who got the troops revved up for battle. "I think changing abortion laws will mean as much as changing slavery. I think we'll end up in a civil war," she told them.[77]

JANUARY 25: WASHINGTON, D.C.

Attorney General Janet Reno announced that a grand jury convened after the 1994 murders of Dr. John Bayard Britton and James Barrett had found no evidence of a national anti-abortion conspiracy. The grand jury had conducted eighteen months of research and had questioned more than fifty witnesses, only one of them an abortion provider.[78] Among the anti-abortionists questioned: Michael Bray, John Burt, David Crane, Matt Trewhella and Father David Trosch.[79]

FEBRUARY 5: DEDHAM, MASSACHUSETTS

The trial of John Salvi III for the murders of Leanne Nichols and Shannon Lowney and the wounding of five others began. Anti-abortion activists picketed the court with signs reading, "Salvi Saved Lives" and "Execute Murderers, Abortionists and Accessories."[80]

MARCH: LINCOLN, NEBRASKA

A month after the formation of the Nebraska chapter of Call to Action, a national organization formed in 1979 to push for liberalization of the American Catholic church on issues of sexuality and ordination, Lincoln, Nebraska, Bishop Fabian Bruskewitz told Call members that they had to resign from the group. Stating that Call to Action was "inimical to the Catholic faith, subversive of church order and destructive of church discipline,"[81] Bruskewitz gave the three hundred members until April 15 to resign. Failure to comply, he told them, would first result in interdict, a ban on receiving the sacraments, and then in outright excommunication.

Call to Action was not the only group on the bishop's hit list. A total of twelve organizations were targeted, including Planned Parenthood, Catholics for a Free Choice, five Masonic lodges and several conservative Catholic societies that support the exclusive use of Latin to celebrate mass.

Reaction to Bruskewitz's order was swift. Monsignor Timothy J. Thorburn, the diocesan chancellor of Lincoln, fanned the flames by declaring that "the name Catholics for a Free Choice is as offensive to Catholics as the intrinsic contradiction Jews for the Holocaust would be to Jewish people."[82] Meanwhile, Call to Action members, including a former priest and nun active in the group, announced that they would defy the order, stating that it violated basic principles of justice.[83]

Frances Kissling, president of Catholics for a Free Choice, issued a news release three days after Bruskewitz's pronouncement stating that:

> The Bishop provides not one specific fact about the views of any of the groups—that is, he offers no information to enable individuals to define in what way their membership in these groups is incompatible with membership in the church. He cites no specific canon of church law that they allegedly violate, nor does he cite the canons that are the basis of his action. Even within the minimal due process provisions of canon law and the feudal nature of a bishop's arbitrary power, such disregard for people's rights shows a profound lack of respect for the dignity of these Catholics.[84]

MARCH 16: MELBOURNE, FLORIDA

A medical resident sent a letter to Christians for Life announcing his resignation from the Aware Woman Center for Choice effective April 1, 1996. The resignation followed the picketing of both the resident's home and the medical center where he worked in the obstetrics and gynecology department. Although he told a hospital colleague that he was leaving the clinic because of fear for his safety, his letter to Christians for Life affirmed his commitment to reproductive choice. "Understand that I am proud of being able to provide reproductive services to women of all ages and that my activities were known amongst my colleagues, friends and family," the resident wrote.[85]

Patricia Baird-Windle: "Flip Benham of Operation Rescue went to the hospital where this man worked and rallied the anti troops. He also threatened to challenge the hospital's accreditation because they allowed residents to moonlight at abortion facilities. The hospital responded by barring residents from working at clinics. This posed a huge potential problem since eight of Florida's fifty-four clinics relied on residents. Our tactic, as providers, was to threaten back. We argued that because Florida is a right-to-work state, they were in trouble on two grounds. Eve Gartner, then at the Center for Reproductive Law and Policy, successfully argued that the ban deprived residents of their right to work. Secondly, they were being deprived of their right to training. We won, but by this point the resident was so scared he resigned and had to be replaced."[86]

MARCH 18: DEDHAM, MASSACHUSETTS

John Salvi III was convicted of murdering Leanne Nichols and Shannon Lowney and wounding five others in a December 1994 attack on two Brookline, Massachusetts, clinics. He was sentenced to two life terms without parole, plus one hundred years.[87]

APRIL 28: MELBOURNE, FLORIDA

Patricia Baird-Windle: "The *Madsen* decision giving the clinic a protected buffer zone went into effect on April 8, 1993. The police enforced it pretty consistently while it traversed its way to the United States Supreme Court. The High Court heard the case on April 29, 1994, and upheld the buffer zone on June 30. Until April 28, 1996, the police stationed a car at the clinic on surgery days and did regular drive-bys on nonsurgery days and at night. Once I was also given a police escort. Aware Woman got this type of protection for one year and ten months after our Supreme Court victory. The Melbourne Police Department stopped providing police assistance after two different judges—one of whom was up for reelection that year—ruled that clinic protestors were not acting in concert with Operation Rescue when they trespassed on our property and thus were not in violation of the injunction. The way the injunction was written, only OR, and groups allied with them, could violate it. The judge blithely stated that OR was little more than a slogan on a bumper sticker. That was the day I started really going downhill. A bedrock of mine had always been a flag-waving pride in being American. I assumed the system would work for me. It didn't. I just wanted to be left alone to do my work and I wasn't left alone. The loss, frustration and rage I felt was indescribable. I am healing, but wouldn't you assume that going all the way to the United States Supreme Court would solve the problem?"[88]

MAY: LINCOLN, NEBRASKA

Bishop Fabian Bruskewitz announced that he would not formally record the names of those Catholics who had been excommunicated for their membership in groups he found objectionable to the church and confessed that he had no way of knowing if people were heeding his ban on receiving the sacraments. Although he never admitted that his denunciation of Call to Action, Planned Parenthood, Catholics for a Free Choice and nine other groups went too far, he told reporters that compliance with his March order "will be left to the person's conscience."[89]

MAY 28: ORLANDO, FLORIDA

Patricia Baird-Windle: "Janet Reno had been saying that clinics around the country who thought they had FACE violations needed to meet with the United States Attorneys in their area to discuss their situations. So I made an appointment with Rick Jancha of the Orlando U.S. Attorney's Office; from the first he was extremely rude. He started off by telling me that we didn't need a meeting. I responded by saying that we had protestors who were violating the intimidation portions of FACE. He finally agreed to meet, but said he would see me and me alone. I told him that I was going to bring my husband, Ted, and my lawyer, Susan England, with me because both had been clinic defenders and had been to the Supreme Court on *Madsen* and were integral parts of what we needed to discuss. On the day of the meeting we went in prepared, with an agenda and sixty-pages of evidence in notebooks I had made up with the names, dates and places mapped out. I also had copies of the letters Raney had been sending to patients.

"Jancha came to the meeting with FBI Agent Edward Bodigheimer, a phalanx of other men in suits and a man from the United States Marshal's office who had never been to the clinic. Jancha did not include the marshals who had been assigned to Aware Woman from August 1994 until July 1995. Nonetheless, I was hopeful. Jancha had at least two militia cases on his plate at the time, so I thought he would at least be alert to the terrorism component of the anti-abortion movement. He opened the meeting by asking me what I wanted. I told him that I wanted him to bring federal RICO charges against the antis. He said he could not do this and began yelling at me. I was flummoxed but I asked him to be polite and hear us out, stressing that he needed to listen if we were going to have any kind of relationship. He responded by telling me to disabuse myself of the notion that there was going to be a relationship between Aware Woman and the United States Attorney's Office. The whole thing lasted about forty-five minutes. Right before we left I decided to pass out the materials I had prepared.

When I looked over I saw that Bodigheimer was asleep. We got up. There was no point in being abused this way.

"A year later, in August 1997, Pamela Chen of the Civil Rights Division of the Department of Justice came to Melbourne and interviewed me and my staff. She was very respectful and thorough but ultimately said that there was nothing DOJ could do; our experiences were not egregious enough to litigate."[90]

MAY 31: NATIONWIDE

Georgetown University law professor Father Robert Drinan—a liberal, democratic congressman from 1971 to 1981, when he was forced to leave elected office by the Holy See—once more angered church authorities by writing an editorial in support of President Clinton's veto of a ban on "partial birth" abortions. The editorial ran in the *National Catholic Reporter* on May 31 and in the *New York Times* on June 4.

"Even if one assumes that some of the 17,000 women who each year request an abortion after 20 weeks of childbearing are seeking a termination of their pregnancy for personal reasons rather than a compelling medical reason, it does not make sense, for the first time in history, to enter into such a complicated arena of specialized professional and ethical issues," he wrote.[91]

Seven days after the piece was published, the Georgetown Ignatian Society wrote Drinan challenging his use of the word "Catholic" to describe himself.[92] The society also petitioned James Cardinal Hickey, asking him to remove Drinan's priestly faculties in the D.C. Archdiocese unless he publicly retracted his statements.[93] John Cardinal O'Connor and Bishops James McHugh and Thomas V. Daily echoed the society's demands.

"The arm-twisting should be pretty evident," says Frances Kissling, president of Catholics for a Free Choice.[94] And it was effective. On May 12, 1997, Drinan wrote a second op ed piece for the *Times:* "I see abortion—particularly partial birth abortion—as a grave evil and can understand why church leaders are urging lawmakers to ban it. I do not want anything to impede that effort. On the contrary, I join in that effort and stand ready to promote laws and public policies that aim to protect vulnerable human life from conception until natural death. I support the Catholic Bishops in their efforts to exercise moral leadership in the fight against abortion."[95]

JUNE: MISSOULA, MONTANA

Jailed anti-abortion fanatic Michael Ross, sentenced to ten years for felony intimidation in 1993—a man whose offenses include mailing Dr. Susan

Wicklund sixty-two pieces of hate mail over a three-month period and sending threatening letters to Hillary Rodham Clinton—sent Sally Mullen, former executive director of the Blue Mountain Clinic in Missoula, the following from his jail cell: "Why do you murder little boys and girls created in the image of a holy God? You must realize, deep in your heart, that some day, perhaps very soon, this mighty God will hold you to account for killing these wee children." A subsequent letter called Mullen "a yellow, baby-killing whore."[96]

JULY 12: SPOKANE VALLEY, WASHINGTON

A Planned Parenthood satellite clinic in the Spokane Valley, eighteen miles from the central office in the city of Spokane, was bombed by a militia group based in Sandpoint, Idaho. Called the Phineas Priesthood, the white supremacist organization based its ideology on Numbers 22, an Old Testament story about a mixed race pair killed for violating a prohibition against such couplings. Like the contemporary Phineas Priesthood, the biblical murderers said they were obeying the law of God and had taken it upon themselves to be the law's enforcers.

The men who participated in the Priesthood's attacks on the clinic—Charles Barbee, Robert Berry, Verne Jay Merrell and Brian Ratigan—were adherents of the Christian Identity Movement, a religious/political network steeped in anti-Semitism, misogyny and racism. "They participated in largely symbolic actions," says Bill Morlin, a reporter for the *Spokesman-Review* who has covered right-wing movements since the early 1980s. "A common thread to Christian Identity and militia groups is the need for visible targets. Abortion clinics are just one possibility. Some groups are compelled to print counterfeit money, firebomb an adult bookstore or spray graffiti on a synagogue. They think they're soldiers of God and feel biblically driven. They feel they'll get higher stature in the kingdom of heaven by doing these earthly deeds."[97]

The Phineas Priesthood got its first public recognition on April 1, 1996, when the group bombed the offices of the *Spokesman-Review*. That same day, while investigators were nosing around the newspaper's offices, the Priesthood robbed a U.S. Bank. "My theory," says Morlin, "is that after we printed pictures of militia members in the paper they were pissed. Then Morris Dees, the head of the Southern Poverty Law Center and their archenemy, used our photos on the cover of his book. The book came out in March 1996 and they were angry at us for selling Dees the pictures. I think they bombed us as a diversion for the robbery, but they also knew that they'd get coverage in the paper for their exploits if they got us."[98]

On July 12 the foursome repeated their bombing and robbery scheme, this time choosing the Planned Parenthood satellite office as their target. "It was during the day," says John Nugent, CEO of Planned Parenthood of Spokane and Whitman Counties. "Fortunately, we were closed for a staff training so no one was hurt but the clinic was completely gutted. After they bombed us they went to a different branch of the same bank and robbed it. For a while the police, FBI and BATF treated us as if we were a diversion for the robbery. Since it was a newspaper in April, law enforcement felt like the perpetrators were just looking for a distraction and we were it."[99]

A few weeks after the bombing, however, Nugent received a typed letter with the name Phinehas [sic] as the return notation. "So sorry to have missed you July 12th, and you missed the note about Psalm 139," the letter said. "Will do better next time. HalleluYah! (Praise ye Yah)." "This convinced BATF that we were their intentional target," says Nugent. "During the cleanup they had found a matchbook cover that had a handwritten note on it about Psalm 139. No one thought much about it until the letter arrived, but it had been saved. When we got the letter they started to make connections."[100]

The firebombers were captured in October after Christopher Davidson, a military surplus dealer, heard the men bragging about their exploits and turned them in for a monetary reward. Fear of militia retribution forced Davidson to enter the federal witness protection program once he identified the perpetrators to law enforcement.

Barbee, a former $50,000 a year AT&T supervisor who had worked in Florida, Georgia and Idaho, was sentenced to two life terms, as were codefendants Robert Berry and Verne Jay Merrell. Ratigan received fifty-five years and is in a federal prison near Seattle, Washington.[101]

The more than $100,000 stolen from U.S. Bank was never recovered.

Planned Parenthood's Spokane Valley office—which does not perform abortions—was closed for a year after the bombing. Repairs cost $500,000, and while insurance covered much of the reconstruction, the policy was canceled shortly after the claim was settled.[102]

AUGUST 6: WASHINGTON, D.C.

Deval Patrick, then an assistant attorney general in the Civil Rights Division of the Department of Justice, wrote to Patricia Baird-Windle in response to numerous complaints from her about DOJ inaction.

> Let me reassure you of this administration's commitment to combat violence against health care providers and to protect reproductive rights. Any time that we receive allegations of actions that might constitute a violation of the

Freedom of Access to Clinic Entrances Act the incident is thoroughly investigated and, if warranted, vigorously prosecuted. While primary responsibility for responding to security and law enforcement concerns rests with local law enforcement officials, I assure you that DOJ has and will continue to be vigilant in seeking to deter and punish acts of intimidation and violence.[103]

Patricia Baird-Windle responded: "When 90 clinic owners and administrators from around the country met with James Reynolds (DOJ's Chief of Domestic Terrorism) and his staff in November of 1994, Mr. Reynolds could barely contain his disdain of us while giving us the royal run-around. . . . The technique Reynolds used was a classic effort of a lawyer to try to convince nonlawyers that there are no laws to help us. At the meeting I suggested to Reynolds that he should make an effort to debrief all those present to discover, firsthand, the scope of the similar and identical tactics used against us. The room was full of people who have been seriously victimized for years. Reynolds refused to ask any questions, manifesting no curiosity whatsoever, even after a heartfelt plea from one of our group. Mr. Patrick, if you don't look, you won't find."[104]

OCTOBER 31: MINNEAPOLIS, MINNESOTA

Staff at the Midwest Health Center for Women take Halloween seriously, dressing in outlandish costumes for their own, and their patients', amusement. That day the receptionist was sitting at her desk in a bathrobe, her hair in curlers; clinic director Jeri Rasmussen was dressed as a witch. "Starting early in the morning we got twenty or thirty calls from a man who said he had a high-powered rifle and could pick us off one at a time," says Rasmussen. "The police came, listened in and heard the guy making the threats. But they refused to put a tap on the phone. They didn't take him seriously at all," treating him as nothing more than a Halloween prankster.[105]

The next day staff learned that the man had been apprehended after making similar calls to a federal building in Wisconsin. "Until a police officer was killed at a Birmingham clinic [in January 1998], the police here did not investigate the things that happened at abortion clinics very seriously. The only reason they got the guy who called us was because he threatened a federal building," Rasmussen concludes.[106]

NOVEMBER: LOUISIANA

Less than a week before the 1996 presidential elections, retired New Orleans (Catholic) bishop Phillip Hannan urged Louisiana's Catholics not to vote for

President Clinton or Democrat Mary Landrieu, a candidate for state senate, because of their support of legal abortion. Despite his directive, both candidates won their races.[107]

NOVEMBER 29: MASSACHUSETTS

John Salvi III, the man responsible for the Brookline murders, committed suicide by suffocating himself with a plastic bag. Investigators found detailed suicide plans in his prison cell. He was twenty-five.[108]

DECEMBER: NEW ORLEANS, LOUISIANA

Dr. Calvin Jackson was stabbed fifteen times, losing fourteen pints of blood, outside the Orleans Women's Clinic. The assailant was captured by police later that day when he barged into a Baton Rouge clinic, fifty miles from New Orleans, shortly before their physician was scheduled to arrive.[109] The man served no jail time for the stabbing; his current whereabouts are unknown.

DECEMBER: MILWAUKEE, WISCONSIN

When Diane Pogrant took the job as administrator of the Summit Women's Health Organization, local anti-abortionists wasted no time in trying to persuade her to quit. "There was glue in the clinic's locks on day one," she says. "Within the first week someone put a screw in one of my tires, which caused a slow leak, and someone put a kryptonite lock through the front doors of the clinic so the staff had to wait in a coffeeshop for the police to arrive and let us in."[110]

A few months later three of her four tires were slashed, her home was picketed and her neighborhood was leafleted by people accusing her of living in a house purchased with blood money. But Pogrant appears unaffected by the protestors. "I've learned to ignore them," she says. "They're looking for a reaction but I won't give them one. Some of the clinic's escorts have snappy comebacks and that's their style. It's not my style so I don't try to engage them."[111]

DECEMBER: WEST PALM BEACH, FLORIDA

A can of pork and beans, with a screw poking through its lid and electrical tape wrapped around its rim, was found between two cars in the parking lot of the Aware Woman Medical Center. The suspicious object forced the evacuation of the building in which the clinic was housed. No one was arrested for the caper.[112]

DECEMBER 26: CHARLESTON, SOUTH CAROLINA

"HO HO HOW HORRIBLE, EH?" read the bright pink leaflet that was distributed in the neighborhood where the executive director of the Charleston Women's Medical Clinic and her family lived at that time.

> But this is what your neighbors, Lorraine and Michael Maguire of [the house address] have spent another year doing to more than 2,500 helpless unborn babies. Have you ever wondered how the good citizens of Nazi Germany could have remained silent? Have you ever wondered how they could justify their silence and apathy to the pain and suffering of others? You and most of the people in this city have, for the sake of your ease and comfort, remained silent while 40 million babies have been killed since the 1973 *Roe v. Wade* decision declared war on the unborn. . . . The irony here is that these baby killers, along with most of you, are celebrating Christmas. You all are celebrating the BIRTH of the BABY Jesus when just yesterday, they spent part of the day killing about 15 unborn babies. Our question is, "When would it have been okay to have aborted the fetus Jesus??? When was He not fully G-d yet fully human???" After all, Mary was a 16 year old unwed mother. A crime punishable by stoning in her day. And know that your neighbor would have done it. She would have asked no questions, took [*sic*] Mary's money and killed the Savior of the world.[113]

The anonymous screed was distributed to hundreds of households; the Maguires received dozens of supportive phone calls and notes from neighbors disgusted by the holiday invasion of privacy.

1997

JANUARY: INTERNATIONAL

The Nuremberg Files, a Web site maintained by Georgia anti-abortion activist and computer consultant Neal Horsley, appeared on the Internet for the first time. On top of the first page of the site were the words "VISUALIZE Abortionists on Trial." This was followed by:

> The American Coalition of Life Activists (ACLA) is cooperating in collecting dossiers on abortionists in anticipation that one day we may be able to hold them on trial for crimes against humanity. . . . One of the great tragedies of the Nuremberg Trials after WWII was that complete information and documented

evidence had not been collected so many war criminals went free or were only found guilty of minor crimes. We do not want the same thing to happen when the day comes to charge abortionists with their crimes. We anticipate the day when these people will be charged in PERFECTLY LEGAL COURTS once the tide of the nation's opinion turns against child killing (as it surely will).[114]

More than two hundred individuals—some of them with little or no connection to clinics or pro-choice organizations—were then named and divided into categories: "Abortionists: the baby butchers; Clinic Owners and Workers: their weapons providers and bearers; Judges: their shysters; Politicians: their mouthpieces; Law Enforcement: their bloodhounds; Third Trimester Butchers; and Miscellaneous Spouses and Other Blood Flunkies."

In February 1999 a jury found the Nuremberg Files, along with the Deadly Dozen poster unveiled in 1995, to be "true threats" not protected by the First Amendment. The Web site was subsequently shut down; several months later, in the spring of 1999, a Dutch list server agreed to post the page from Amsterdam. It has since bounced between Internet service providers.

Follow-up note: Horsley does not confine his political activism to abortion; he also maintains the Web page of the Creator's Rights Party, where he sells a variety of items. For a mere $3 one can purchase: Legalized Abortion is War, Queers Suck, Abortionists Kill Babies for $, Jail Faggots, and Unconditional Love is Impossible bumper stickers.

JANUARY: LINCOLN, NEBRASKA

"We are not identified as a pro-choice church," insists the Reverend Carl Horton, associate pastor of Westminster Presbyterian Church in Lincoln, Nebraska. "We have members who are 'pro-life' and members who are pro-choice. Our goal has always been to maintain the unity of our congregation. We have never gone out on a platform which is pro-choice, although ordaining an abortion doctor as an elder speaks for itself."[115]

That elder is Dr. Winston Crabb, a longtime provider of gynecological services at reproductive health clinics in Omaha and Lincoln. When word of Crabb's ordination got out in late 1996, anti-choice reaction was immediate. The first Sunday after Advent, Larry Donlan, head of Rescue the Heartland, showed up at the church with a group of protestors. According to former Westminster pastor Don Smith, from that day on the 1,400-person congregation was subjected to aggressive picketing and loud comments frightening to the children of parishioners. Smith calls it "verbal violence."[116]

"They stand on all four sides, surrounding the church, with four by six-foot signs of late-term aborted fetuses," says Smith. "They hold them up to cars entering the parking lot and especially aim them at the backseat where children are sitting. They also yell at the kids, things like, 'Aren't you glad Dr. Crabb didn't abort you?' and 'Do you know that there is a man in your congregation who cuts up babies inside their mothers and pulls the pieces out with his hands?'"[117]

On several occasions, adds Horton, members of Rescue the Heartland entered the church after services were over and confronted Crabb during coffee hour. "At that point we wrote a letter to the police to tell them that these people were trespassing and that they had to put down their signs if they wanted to worship with us. From that point, they confined themselves to harassing people on the way in. They usually stay on the sidewalk, not trespassing on our property, but we consider the whole property to be sacred. We think it's wrong that they follow people, lunge at people with their signs as if to say, 'You must look at this picture because it's the truth.'"[118]

In addition to contacting police, the church launched several simultaneous initiatives to deal with the personal impact the protests were having on individual congregants. For one, they called a series of meetings for church staff and parents to discuss the situation. Together they developed recommendations, none of which was ideal, for dealing with the trauma they and their children were experiencing: play penny-pick-up on the floor of the car, or sing songs, to distract very young children when pulling into the parking lot, and put sweaters or jackets over children's faces to protect them from bloody imagery before coming inside. They also discussed how best to talk to older children about reproduction, including abortion.

In addition, Westminster Presbyterian pressured the City Council to take action to restrict the picketing Rescue the Heartland and groups like them could legally engage in. An appellate court ruled against the church, finding the proposed ordinance unconstitutional, and picketers continue to menace parishioners each Sunday. Although Rescue the Heartland has inexplicably ceased its activity, Policemen for Life and other organizations still demonstrate outside sanctuary doors.

Follow-up note: Associate Pastor Carl Horton admits that between twenty-five and thirty families have resigned from the church since the picketing began. "We've had an exodus of people who don't want to cross a picket line to get into church or put their children through the stress and harassment," he says. "Some people who left saw Dr. Crabb as the problem and felt that he should resign or be removed. Had the picketers not arrived, I don't believe we would have had a problem making him an elder. This outside group has done this to us. It's been very hard on Dr. Crabb. He's been very tight-lipped, but it's been an enormous burden on him because he knows, at root, that his vocation has caused harm to this congregation. But God has called us to this place for a reason. We are not so privileged that we can avoid social agenda items as a congregation."[119]

Although Winston Crabb's term of service as an elder ended in January 2000, this has had no appreciable impact on the protestors.

JANUARY 1: TULSA, OKLAHOMA

A Molotov cocktail was thrown through a window of Reproductive Services of Tulsa, Oklahoma. The firebomb did minimal damage to the clinic's break room, destroying several windows and ceiling tiles. A three-month-old carpet in the room had to be replaced.[120]

JANUARY 16: SANDY SPRINGS, GEORGIA

Northside Family Planning, a clinic just north of Atlanta, was bombed at 9:30 A.M. The health center had been bombed thirteen years earlier when a Molotov cocktail was thrown through a window; that attack remains unsolved. The 1997 blast badly damaged the operating, counseling and waiting areas; according to the *Atlanta Constitution,* the bomb's volley was so intense that it rattled windows two and a half miles away.[121]

Federal agents, rescue workers and media rushing to the scene were shocked when, at 10:30 A.M., a second bomb, hidden nearby, detonated. "The second explosion was clearly designed to maim or hurt those who were coming to assist," Sandy Springs Mayor Bill Campbell told the *Miami Herald.*[122] Six people, including an FBI agent and TV cameraman, were injured by flying shrapnel.

The clinic reopened several weeks later at a different location. The still-at-large Eric Robert Rudolph was charged with the bombing in the summer of 1998.

Clinic staff across the country note that since this bombing, both the FBI and media have taken clinic violence much more seriously.

JANUARY 16: TULSA, OKLAHOMA

Sixteen days after a Molotov cocktail was thrown through a window of Reproductive Services in Tulsa, Oklahoma, several grenades filled with shrapnel ripped through the clinic. "The FBI, BATF, city police and bomb squad began heavily monitoring the building after the January 1 firebombing," says Sherri

Finik, the clinic's executive administrator. "But because some FBI guy went to the bathroom at the wrong time, no one saw the perpetrator approach the building. The FBI had a lot of egg on its face and the monitoring was again increased" after this incident.[123]

The grenades damaged the same room that had been affected by the earlier bombing.

FEBRUARY 6: TULSA, OKLAHOMA

For the third time in five weeks, Tulsa, Oklahoma's Reproductive Services was attacked. "The perpetrator broke a window, came into the building with a 9 mm handgun, and went into a room, shot up an FBI monitor, shot a procedure table and some medical equipment, and fired some random shots. Then he left," says administrator Sherri Finik. "We had cameras up everywhere and this time we got a picture of him. That picture ran in the newspaper and he was turned in."[124]

The assailant turned out to be a young man, one month shy of his sixteenth birthday. He had ridden his bicycle from Bixby, Oklahoma, about twenty miles south of the clinic. "I was never told the full details of the case because he was a minor," says Finik. Nonetheless she has learned that the boy was charged with three federal felony offenses: possession of a firearm by a juvenile, damaging a building with an explosive device and using a firearm in the commission of a violent crime. The teen was released from custody when he turned eighteen.[125]

The young man's parents were also involved, pleading guilty in October 1997 to federal charges of possessing an unregistered destructive device—a grenade—and unlawful transfer of a 9 mm semiautomatic pistol to a child.[126]

For his part, in October 1997 the perpetrator sent Reproductive Services a check for $3,000, the first installment of a $19,000 restitution order issued by the court. No other monies have been received at the time of this writing. Total damage to the clinic for the three attacks was $38,000. "There is still significant damage to the building that we've never been able to repair," says Finik. "There are holes in our refrigerator, sink and cabinets that we've decided we can live with."[127]

In a conundrum common to abortion clinics, Reproductive Services had to decide whether to file for compensation from their insurance carrier for the damage caused by the shooting. Since policy claims increase premiums and often lead to outright cancellations of coverage, clinics have to weigh whether it is in their interest to risk the loss or increased cost of property insurance or to absorb the cost of repairs out of pocket. In this case, the health center opted for the latter.

FEBRUARY 19: BUFFALO, NEW YORK

Schenck v. Pro-Choice Network, a lawsuit challenging an injunction issued by Judge Richard J. Arcara, pitted pro-choice doctors, clinicians and activists against Pat Robertson's American Center for Law and Justice. The Supreme Court generally sided with pro-choice arguments and upheld the fifteen-foot buffer zone that keeps protestors away from clinic entrances and driveways. Nonetheless, the Justices also threw a bone at anti-choicers by overturning a fifteen-foot "floating buffer zone" around patients entering or leaving reproductive health offices. Clinic escorts say that this has no impact on either the provision of care or patient safety since the concept of a floating area was always too ill-defined to be of practical use.[128]

MARCH 19: NEW YORK

Syracuse, New York, talk-radio host Richard Bucci, a born-again Christian affiliated with the Lambs of Christ, was ordered by United States District Court Judge Kimba Wood to close the Web site he had opened under the domain name plannedparenthood.com. The court found that the site bore a deceptive banner reading "Welcome to Planned Parenthood" before offering visitors a look at articles by such anti-abortion heavyweights as Lambs' founder Father Norman Weslin.

In an affidavit submitted to the court, Weslin said that he considered the Web site "a highly effective instrument by the Roman Catholic church in exposing Planned Parenthood's efforts which seek to impose the culture of death upon the culture of life and to inform not only the Roman Catholic faithful but also those who are opposed to Planned Parenthood. . . ."[129]

Judge Wood disagreed and enjoined Bucci from using either the Planned Parenthood domain name or identifying his site as belonging to the reproductive health organization.[130]

MAY 22: PORTLAND, OREGON

Lovejoy SurgiCenter is licensed as an outpatient ambulatory care provider and offers routine gynecological care, vasectomies, tubal ligations, radial keratotomies to correct nearsightedness, foot care and some plastic surgery. But because it is also Oregon's oldest and largest abortion provider, anti-choicers have zeroed in and have long blockaded, vandalized and picketed outside its doors. The owner's primary residence and beach house have been demonstration sites, and hate mail and crank calls routinely divert staff from the patient care they were hired to provide. Indeed, Portland's antis have been so obstreperous that a jury punished them by awarding the health center $8.2 million in compensatory damages in February 1991.

Over 1997's Memorial Day weekend, however, everyone connected to the center was dumbfounded when a fire broke out at 2:52 A.M. Although firefighters arrived within minutes, the blaze caused more than $500,000 in damages. According to the *Oregonian* newspaper, on the night of the fire police found a fifty-five-gallon drum with a hose running into the Surgi-Center. They also noticed a blue 1981 Chevrolet Citation parked in the lot behind the building.[131] No one has been apprehended despite the posting of a $100,000 reward by the Planned Parenthood Federation of America and the National Abortion Federation.

"The fire burned a lot of our supplies," says center director Carye Ortman. "All told, we lost $175,000 in clinic contents including a $70,000 ultrasound machine. All our computers had to be cleaned of smoke and there was $270,000 worth of structural damage to the building that had to be repaired. Cleanup costs alone came to more than $65,000. On top of this, after the fire we needed round-the-clock police protection because our alarm system had been destroyed. For four weeks we had twenty-four-hour-a-day off-duty police officers sitting in our lobby. We had to have someone here but it cost us $7,600 a week."[132]

The SurgiCenter also lost what staff had called the "war room," an area packed with archival materials, patient and personnel files, and mementos of their transformation since opening as an ambulatory rehabilitation hospital in 1969. Ortman finds this to be the most traumatic aspect of the fire since the destroyed materials were largely irreplaceable. "We had a patient in 1995 who had been raped," says Ortman. "Her court case was just coming up at the time of the arson and all the records were now gone. Another woman who had worked at the SurgiCenter until 1996 was trying to buy a house and the bank needed her employment records. Without the files, it took me twelve or thirteen hours to re-create her employment history. Plus, all our videotapes, all our evidence about what the antis had done and said was gone, all the affidavits and the depositions from our court cases, our pictures and albums, all our press clippings—our whole documented history was destroyed."[133]

As if this were not enough, staff also had to contend with numerous bureaucracies in order to rebuild. The freestanding cinder-block building that housed Lovejoy had been erected in 1952; upgraded building codes now required the SurgiCenter to comply with numerous new requirements, many of which were not covered by insurance. "I spent a year after the fire as a clinic director and insurance adjuster," quips Ortman. "Getting insurance for an abortion clinic is never an easy feat and after a $500,000 fire it's even harder. Our carrier is on the East Coast, in Virginia, so we had to use an independent adjuster. This meant we had two middlemen instead of one and faced more red tape and delays than usual."[134]

Despite a mountain of paperwork and hours of negotiations, the Surgi-Center reopened three days after the fire. Large metal sculptures, plants and colorful abstract paintings now decorate the waiting areas and lounges, providing the illusion of safety.

JUNE: MILWAUKEE, WISCONSIN

Staff at the Summit Women's Health Organization had been looking forward to their annual "employee appreciation" dinner for months. Clinic administrator Diane Pogrant had made reservations at one of the nicest restaurants in town, a swanky place with darkened-glass windows. "The best we can figure, someone who worked at the restaurant must have seen the reservation and informed the antis that we were coming. They came to the restaurant and right outside the window near our table, did this street theater thing where they pretended to be killing babies," says Pogrant. "There was nothing we could do. We'd all been anticipating a nice, relaxed, social evening. Instead it was a very stressful night."[135]

JUNE 4: MELBOURNE, FLORIDA

Patricia Baird-Windle wrote the following plea to DOJ staffers Mellie Nelson and Pamela Chen about the reprehensible tactics used by abortion foes in Melbourne to identify doctors working at the Aware Woman Center for Choice.

> Using long-lens still cameras and video cameras to photograph the doctors as they enter or leave the building, the resulting pictures are then compared against those license photos on file at the Bureau of Professional Regulation and/or the physician's licensing board to arrive at identification. When we realized that this method was being used, we started bringing the doctors into the clinic in disguise, hiding under blankets in our cars, erecting entrance and egress blinds to shield them from identification, using decoy cars and decoy sham doctors. The antis then began developing counter measures such as climbing up to the twenty-five foot level of one of the trees to try to get photos from above or around the shielding device. No one should have to enter or leave their workplace under such conditions.[136]

JUNE 26: PORTLAND, OREGON

Don Treshman of Rescue America led a session of imprecatory prayer at Planned Parenthood of the Columbia/Willamette. "It was very creepy," says executive director Lois Bachus. "Treshman asked for our financial ruin, not illness or death like they used in other places, but he was still asking God to smote providers with misfortune so we'll get out of what he considers a 'shameful business.'"[137] Imprecatory prayer services have been held throughout the United States and Canada for the express purpose of asking God to punish providers and force them to repent for their "sins."

SUMMER: INDIANAPOLIS, INDIANA

Since 1993, federal law has allowed Medicaid coverage for the abortions of recipients who fall into three categories: those with documented evidence that their pregnancy resulted from rape, incest victims and those for whom carrying a pregnancy to term would be life endangering.

"A few years ago, in the summer of 1997, we got a call from a woman who had been raped," says clinic counselor Katrina Douglas (a pseudonym). "She was on welfare and had a Medicaid card but neither the hospital nor the Medicaid office knew how to get payment for her abortion. We had to do tons of advocacy to get them to pay. Indiana's Medicaid office acted like they'd never heard such a request before, like it was a completely new issue, when we called."[138]

The would-be patient had reported the rape to police and had a copy of the paperwork. Still, says Douglas, the run-around lasted three weeks. "This woman had no phone and the hospital she went to had no 800 number. She would call me on the clinic's 800 line and I'd call the hospital and then call her back at a pay phone where she was waiting. She was really tough, this woman, and had already been through a lot, but if she had not persevered she would never have gotten the coverage."[139]

Follow-up note: From 1981 to 1993 the Hyde Amendment, sponsored by Representative Henry Hyde [R-IL], prohibited federal Medicaid funds from being used for abortion unless it was needed to save the woman's life. In 1993 the amendment was expanded to include pregnancies resulting from rape or incest. At the present time, only fourteen states provide Medicaid coverage for the abortions of all benefit-eligible women who need one, regardless of reason.[140]

JULY: MILWAUKEE, WISCONSIN

Monica Migliorino Miller, director of Citizens for a Pro-Life Society and an outspoken anti-abortion protestor with a long record of civil disobedience activities, was arrested for child neglect after leaving her two-year-old son locked in a car. According to *NCAP News,* "the child was sopping wet, his hair dripping sweat," when he was removed from the vehicle.[141] The charges against Miller were eventually reduced to a disorderly conduct misdemeanor to which Miller pleaded no contest. She was sentenced to one day in jail, the time spent in custody after she was arrested.

JULY 22: TUSCALOOSA, ALABAMA

The fire at the four-year-old West Alabama Women's Center happened on the night Hurricane Danny came through Tuscaloosa. Clinic owner Gloria Gray remembers the evening vividly. "I got a call at 1:00 A.M. from the security company telling me that the alarm had gone off. I told them to call the police and to call me back if there was a problem. Then I went back to sleep, thinking the storm had set off the alarm. A few minutes later I got another call saying the police had seen smoke and had called the fire department and that I needed to come to the clinic right away. I got there and the fire chief told me that whoever started this fire knew how the building was constructed because everything hit the surgery side. Even though the business side was not hit directly, because the temperature inside the building was 2,000 degrees, we lost everything with the exception of some furniture in our doctor's office," Gray says. "Even stainless steel instruments, which I thought were indestructible, were gone. The clinic had to be totally gutted at a cost of $450,000."[142]

The clinic reopened three months later thanks to a construction team that worked nights and weekends on top of standard hours. "The amount of support we got was incredible," says Dr. Louis Payne, the clinic's physician and a part owner of the facility. "People who don't give us support from day to day came forward to help us. The builder gave us a temporary office so that our phones could continue to operate, and the construction people worked fast despite roadblocks set up by the state health department."[143]

Those roadblocks forced clinic staff to jump through a plethora of hoops before they were allowed to rebuild. Despite the fact that Payne and Gray wanted the clinic to exactly replicate the one destroyed by the fire, they were told that they needed to hire an architect to develop new plans for the site. These plans had to be presented for Health Department approval. "It took two weeks for us to get the permits," says Payne, "because they made us amend the plans. We had to put in a janitor's closet even though we don't have a janitor and we had to install automatic closure devices on it. They made us make our hallway one inch wider. The electricians had to add something and there were other ridiculous things to deal with before we could proceed."[144]

In addition to state requirements, the clinic had enormous difficulties with their insurance carrier. Although the company paid their arson claim, their policy was canceled shortly thereafter. "We kept hitting our heads against a wall," says Gray. "Most companies we approached turned us down. One company said they'd insure us but required a police officer on duty twenty-four-hours a day, seven-days-a-week, which we could never afford to do. We eventually found an insurer but we were now high risk. Our premiums went from $2,000 to $5,000 a year and the company required us to put in outside and hidden cameras."[145]

"BATF and the local police were good," Gray continues. "They responded to our needs. The FBI made an appearance but the agent didn't even introduce himself to us. As far as we could tell, the FBI did nothing."[146] No one has been apprehended for the fire. Law enforcers told Gray and Payne that they believe the arsonist chose this particular evening because the severe weather made fingerprints untraceable.

JULY 29: WASHINGTON, D.C.

Donald Treshman of Rescue America led a protest at the funeral of Supreme Court Justice William Brennan. Treshman said that he was there to denounce the Justice's support for the *Roe v. Wade* decision.[147]

AUGUST: CHARLESTON, SOUTH CAROLINA

When Dr. Richard Mulligan (a pseudonym) arrived at the Charleston Women's Medical Clinic for his two-day shift, he told his coworkers that he was not feeling well. "He traveled in every week from Knoxville," says clinic director Lorraine Maguire, "and that Friday when he came in and said he was sick we did blood work on him. It was normal. He assumed he just needed to go to his hotel and sleep. The next day when he came in his face was gray and he was vomiting so I took him to the hospital. The protestors saw me leave with him. It turned out he was having a heart attack. Before he even got to his intensive care unit bed, the hospital had gotten five calls: 'Tell Richard that God is paying him back for all those lives he's taken.' The antis had phoned all the hospitals in the area to see if Dr. Mulligan had been admitted. The hospital he was in had to take his name off the computer roster of admitted patients. They finally established a policy where if you called to check on his status you had to give a code word. Only his wife and I had the code. But we still removed the phone from his room to protect him from harassment, just in case. The nurses were totally appalled that people would go to that length to hurt someone."[148]

This type of "protest" has been recorded in numerous locations. Patients with abortion complications and hospitalized clinic workers have been harassed while recovering from their ailments.

SEPTEMBER 25: LITTLE ROCK, ARKANSAS

It was supposed to be a day of celebration and racial healing. President Bill Clinton was in town for a ceremony to add Central High School to the National Register of Historic Places, and all eyes were on Little Rock. Apparently eager for a moment in the spotlight, an anti-abortion activist elbowed his way into the news by crafting a sure-fire attention getter. The man rented two large, bright yellow Ryder trucks and parked them in the entryway of two of the city's clinics. "There is a little message with a Ryder truck," says Carolyn Izard, director of Little Rock Family Planning Services. "Since that was the truck used in the April 1995 Oklahoma City bombing of a federal office building, law enforcement took no chances and evacuated all of the businesses in the area, including a cardiologist's office and a day care center, for four hours."[149]

The perpetrator was arraigned by a grand jury in August 1998 and the following November was convicted of threatening violence. In January 1999 he was sentenced to three years' probation with one year of house arrest.[150]

SEPTEMBER 25: WASHINGTON, D.C.

"America's Health Held Hostage: How Politics is Paralyzing Medical Advances," a congressional briefing sponsored by the National Abortion and Reproductive Rights Action League (NARAL), brought doctors, lawyers and ethicists together to urge federal funding for human embryo research. Although President Clinton had lifted a fifteen-year ban on fetal tissue research in January 1993, those testifying asked lawmakers to lift the prohibition on studies involving human embryos. Pandering to anti-abortion pressure not to do so, they charged, was unacceptable. NARAL supporters cheered Dr. Allan Rosenfield, dean of the Columbia School of Public Health, when he reminded the audience that if the "political climate that exists today existed 35 years ago, oral contraceptives would never have been brought to market."[151]

R. Alta Charo, a law professor at the University of Wisconsin, testified that, "Private sector research on human embryos has already led to breakthroughs in in vitro fertilization and pre-implantation diagnosis. Additional research is needed to improve these techniques and to understand better the process of conception so that treatments of infertility can be found."[152] Charo also testified that human embryos hold promise for providing skin grafts and regenerating skin for burn victims and could prove helpful in helping scientists understand cancer.

Dr. Eugene Redmond, professor of neurosurgery at Yale University Medical School, touted the promise of fetal cells even further, stating that embryonic tissue may advance the treatment of people with AIDS, leukemia, sickle cell anemia, Parkinson's disease, diabetes, retinitis pigmentosa and spinal cord injuries.[153]

Follow-up note: A panel appointed by President Clinton to study the advisability of lifting the ban on embryo research issued a report in May 1999 in support of doing so.

OCTOBER 1: MELBOURNE, FLORIDA

Meredith T. Raney filed a seven-page lawsuit with the Middle District Federal Court in Florida, alleging that his rights were violated by three arrests at the Aware Woman Center for Choice (AWCC).

According to a brief submitted by attorney Christopher F. Sapp:

> Plaintiff Meredith T. Raney Jr. was unlawfully interfered with, threatened and physically prevented from providing reproductive health services by the Melbourne City police, who as agents of and taking direction from the defendants, threatened plaintiff with physical removal from the facility and then physically took plaintiff away from the facility. In doing so, defendants violated the civil rights of plaintiff Meredith T. Raney and caused him suffering, financial loss and the need to incur attorney's fees and the various costs in bringing this action.[154]

Aware Woman lawyer Roy Lucas responded:

> The FACE law expressly protects medical clinics and professional offices, and their buildings, from the kind of obstruction and harassment engaged in by Mr. Raney. . . . It makes no sense to suggest that a medical clinic in Melbourne, Florida could control or employ the police of a city whose mayor denounces Roe v. Wade every January 22. The city hires, trains, outfits, mobilizes and pays the police, not AWCC. The video made by Mr. Raney of his arrests plainly shows city vehicles on city property warning and then arresting him for violating a state court injunction that has been upheld by the United States Supreme Court, Madsen v. Women's Health Center.[155]

NOVEMBER: INDIANA

Indiana's "informed consent" law went into effect, mandating an eighteen-hour interval between scheduling an appointment for an abortion and having the actual procedure. Indiana is currently one of fourteen states to impose a waiting period on women wanting to abort unwanted pregnancies. Although waiting periods vary from state to state (most are twenty-four hour), Indiana's requires that all prospective abortion patients converse with a clinic doctor, nurse practitioner or nurse midwife about the abortion procedure, its risks and potential side effects, fetal gestation, and adoption and other reproductive options before the termination is performed. This counseling, unique to abortion surgery, can be delivered in person or by telephone.[156]

According to counselor Katrina Douglas (a pseudonym), on staff at Indianapolis's Clinic for Women, under the guise of advocating comprehensive informed consent the Indiana legislature has enacted an enormous roadblock to women's reproductive health. "Our patients are terribly inconvenienced by this," says Douglas. "Most can't come into the clinic twice, once for the counseling and again for the abortion. A lot of our patients live outside of the city and have to travel in. Some come from as far as four hours away. Many women feel that they spent a lot of time deciding to have an abortion and are ready to have it by the time they call for an appointment. They don't want to wait by the phone for a call back before they can end the pregnancy. We also have a number of patients without phones, and we need to schedule a time for them to call us back so that they can speak to an authorized person. For other women the requirement touches on privacy issues. They don't want to be called at home by someone who identifies as working at the clinic. They may not want their partner, their parents or other relatives, or even a roommate, to know what they're going through. In the worst cases some of our patients are afraid that having a stranger call the house will lead to violence against them."[157]

NOVEMBER 11: WINNIPEG, CANADA

Dr. Jack Fainman, a Winnipeg obstetrician for more than forty years, was shot by a sniper hiding outside his home. The bullet hit him in the right shoulder, leaving him wounded but in stable condition. Fainman was the third Canadian physician to be hit by a sniper in four years.[158]

MID-DECEMBER: MILWAUKEE, WISCONSIN

"Right before Christmas, I came outside after work and found that someone had filled gold Christmas tree ornaments with red paint and thrown them at my car, the guard's car and the doctor's car," says Diane Pogrant, administrator of the Summit Women's Health Organization. "Pieces of glass ornament were lodged in the paint and there was gold glass all over the ground. The ornament they threw at my car splashed paint onto the side of it. The other two cars were hit squarely on the back windshield and trunk. A Christmas ornament can hold a lot of paint. I got an estimate of $1,000 to have it removed, so it's still there."[159] The other staffers did not have this option since the paint destroyed visibility out of their back windows; both had to replace their rear windshields before the cars were operable.

"Who ever did this was very quick and stealthlike with their sabotage and no one was caught," says Pogrant.[160]

1998

JANUARY: MELBOURNE, FLORIDA

Mayor John A. Buckley issued a proclamation declaring January, the twenty-fifth anniversary of the *Roe v. Wade* decision, to be "a month of prayer to end abortion in the City of Melbourne." The pronouncement followed a midnight City Council vote on the statement.[161]

JANUARY: WASHINGTON, D.C.

The Clinic Access Project of the Feminist Majority Foundation sent a memo to abortion clinics across the country following the receipt of a hoax bomb by a Louisville, Kentucky, health facility the month before. "Do not open any package that is not expected or that has an unrecognized return address," the memo warned, adding that in case of doubt about a letter or packet's contents, "call the cops."[162]

JANUARY 15: PITTSBURGH, PENNSYLVANIA

A thirteen-year battle with fugitive anti-abortion fanatic Joan Andrews Bell ended in the courtroom of Judge Raymond Novak. Andrews Bell had been on the run since April 1990, when she lost her appeal of a trespassing conviction and failed to show up for sentencing. She was captured in Bayonne, New Jersey, and was returned to Pittsburgh to face the judge she had fled from nearly eight years earlier.

Andrews Bell's bizarre saga began on May 10, 1985, when she and another protestor invaded Pittsburgh's Women's Health Services (WHS). According to

WHS archives, the pair went into Exam Room 6, locked the door and barricaded themselves by positioning examination tables against the entrance. The police had to cut the lock off the door to force it open. At a trial on November 12, 1985, the two were convicted of criminal mischief and trespassing.[163]

Andrews Bell was unable to appear before the judge for sentencing, however, because by the time the court date came around, she was incarcerated in Florida for a subsequent clinic invasion in that state. In 1988 Florida Governor Bob Martinez commuted her sentence upon condition that she return to Pittsburgh. On October 18, 1988, she went before Judge Novak and was ordered to serve three years' probation; she appealed and lost her bid on February 27, 1990. Novak then ordered Andrews Bell to report to the probation office on May 16 to begin her punishment. She did not, and a warrant for her arrest was issued.[164]

At her January 1998 sentencing Andrews Bell—who has been arrested more than two hundred times over the past twenty years—was offered a sentence of probation. She refused the offer and made a barely coherent statement to Novak about why she favored jail. "I think it's wrong to impose probation on anyone in a country that has legal child killing, to impose probation so they won't try to rescue babies. Only way you can affect me, put me in jail, five years, ten years, whatever. That would affect my residence, won't affect the way I think or how much I try to save babies through prayer or other means in jail, you know, or my being in jail which would be a helpless mode because I have to, you know, cooperate with a system that promotes child killing."[165]

Novak sentenced Andrews Bell to three- to twenty-three months in prison followed by three years probation. According to WHS director Mary Ellen Tunney, "When he announced her sentence Andrews Bell fell to the ground with her arms extended like Jesus Christ on the cross. It was interesting because the sheriff's deputies wouldn't let her do it. They folded her up really fast. She stayed in Allegheny County Jail for two months and then agreed to accept probation."[166]

JANUARY 28: CANADA

Ten years after the Supreme Court of Canada decriminalized abortion, the Canadian Abortion Rights Action League (CARAL) issued a report entitled *Access Granted: Too Often Denied*. Echoing the situation in the United States, the account found that a decade after legalization, "the pool of providers is shrinking, presenting a serious threat to abortion access in the years immediately ahead. This decline is mainly attributable to the 'graying' of current abortion providers; the lack of medical education and training in abortion procedures; and escalating harassment and violence by anti-choice organizations and individuals. . . . In every province anti-choice forces have waged an overt campaign of harassment and violence against providers and women seeking their help."[167]

The report also uncovered enormous disparities in access. "For rural or northern women, young and/or poor women, the last 10 years have offered little improvement in practical terms. One major regional variation is abundantly evident: Abortion access is more difficult in Atlantic Canada than elsewhere. Provincial health insurance funding is extremely uneven, particularly with respect to funding for abortions in private clinics."[168] Worse, the narrative highlights the fact that there are no providers whatsoever in Labrador, Prince Edward Island and Cape Breton.

"Despite fully-funded services in public hospitals, and clinics that will not see a woman go unserved, the distance from unserved remote areas is an enduring barrier for women outside metropolitan areas," *Access Granted* concludes. "Add to basic travel the cost of staying overnight in a big city, of arranging child care at home, of missing work or school, and the picture of economic inaccessibility becomes clearer."[169]

JANUARY 29: BIRMINGHAM, ALABAMA

Michelle Farley, former administrator at New Woman All Women Health Care, couldn't put her finger on it, but she knew something was wrong. "I felt unsettled on Wednesday the twenty-eighth," she says. "I could not get comfortable. I went to my favorite places to try and make myself feel better but I couldn't. Nothing was right and I could not make it right. I can't explain it. The morning of the twenty-ninth I was throwing up but I headed to work anyway. I was in the car and NPR told me it was 7:30. A few minutes later there was this massive kaboom. My brain tried to make it make sense. I thought it must have been a gunshot even though I knew it was too loud to be. When I turned the corner I saw smoke and thought, man, something has blown up."[170]

That "something" turned out to be New Woman All Women. As Farley pulled into the clinic's parking lot she saw glass everywhere but was reassured to see that a van belonging to off-duty police officer Robert "Sande" Sanderson, a part-time guard at the health center, was already there. "I thought, 'Oh good, Robert will take care of this,'" Farley recalls. "I got out of my car and took my keys, which was stupid because you could walk into the building through any of the blown out windows. In my haste, I left my purse on the seat, a mistake since the police would not let me retrieve it for several days. I then came up to the building. Robert would have been to my left but I didn't see him. He was covered with pine bark and dirt. I did see, on the sidewalk near the front door, someone else lying with a coat over them. I couldn't tell who it was and climbed inside the clinic through an open plate-glass window. My lamp was on but there was not a ceiling tile left in the front and the floor was awful. There was glass and dirt everywhere. I tried to call 911 but it was busy; I later learned that people for miles around were calling to report an explosion. Being inside the clinic was the strangest thing. People who had seen the explosion had come over and were inside the building. I had no idea what they were looking for or doing. I just wanted them to go away. They did not belong."[171]

Farley finally went back outdoors and this time noticed Sanderson on the ground. "I still had no conscious thought of him dying," she says, "but I also knew that blood does not come out of someone's mouth like it was coming out of Robert's. The blood looked as if someone was pumping it out of him. Right about the time that his condition started to register in me the police arrived and moved me across the street. A few minutes later an ambulance came and put a woman on a stretcher. Emily (Lyons, a nurse) always wore these hot pink scrubs and when I saw the color I knew it was Emily who had been hurt."[172]

Farley subsequently learned that thirty-five-year-old Robert Sanderson, a nine-year veteran of the Birmingham police force and a clinic employee for eight months, had died of injuries sustained in the bombing. As the story was pieced together she discovered that an incendiary device had been hidden in an overturned outdoor planter. When Sanderson tried to right the plant at 7:33 A.M., the nail-encased explosive sent him and nurse Emily Lyons hurtling through the air.[173]

"That morning was not real," Farley continues. "The police were putting up yellow tape, people evacuated from nearby University of Alabama–Birmingham dormitories and a day care center were sobbing, going to pieces, and I was in control, doing the Mother Hen routine and trying to make it better."[174] Within an hour police loaded all the eyewitnesses into a van and took them to the precinct. "Some university groundskeepers were there since they were witnesses as were several clinic staffers. Each of us was brought in individually to speak with the FBI, BATF and police," she adds.[175]

"We were at the police station three or four hours," says Lisa Hermes, a part-time counselor at two Birmingham clinics, including New Woman. "There were rumors that there had been later bombings at Summit Medical, another Birmingham provider, and at a clinic in Montgomery. The police did not know what was happening; they told us some of the rumors. I was flipped out, in shock. By the time I got back to the clinic from the police station I was shaking so bad a reporter dragged me over, sat me down and gave me something to eat and drink. Someone eventually came to pick me up and took me home. There were a ton of messages waiting for me. People I had not heard from for years had called wanting to make sure I was okay. A friend picked my nine-year-old daughter up from school and she got home and said she had to study for a spelling test. Honest to God, one of the words on her list was bomb. While I was trying to help her study the phone kept ringing; one of the morning shows and other media wanted to interview me. They called for days. I talked to some of them and had a friend come over to do interference for me. Still, on Friday all I could do was sit in a chair, stare and look at the newspaper. That night I watched the news. The minute the clinic came on I got really hot and dizzy and threw up. I was up all night. The next day, Saturday, I had to work at Summit. We had fifty patients that day because we were seeing women who had previously been scheduled at New Woman as well as our own patients. I was scared when I got there but was so focused on getting through the door I didn't even see the protestors. I later realized that there were more than the usual number and they were extremely rambunctious."[176]

BATF, the FBI and other law enforcers spent four days investigating the crime scene and on Sunday evening returned clinic access to staff. "On Saturday the thirtieth they'd brought me into the building because they needed me to tell them what was unusual," says Farley. "By this time the floors had been cleared but the ceiling tiles were coming down or were totally absent. The ones that did not fall from the bomb were broken and electrical fixtures were hanging. While I walked around I remember feeling dead, like I could barely put one foot in front of the other. I was having chills and it turned out I had bronchitis and pneumonia."[177]

Unfortunately, rest was a luxury Farley felt unable to afford. "When ATF was finished with the clinic, they left," she says. "We had no windows and were ripe for looting. Diane Derzis, the clinic owner, and most of the staff came in and we worked until 3:00 A.M. The windows had been measured Sunday afternoon and $10,000 worth of new glass was installed on Sunday night. I had been prepared to call a professional cleaning crew but by the time ATF finished there was not a speck of dust on the carpet. We all cleaned the front area. You picked a section and you started. There were people from activist groups like Refuse & Resist! and the Feminist Majority Foundation and several long-time providers like Susan Hill and Ann Rose who were here to help. We'd vacuum and clean and vacuum and clean."[178]

New Woman reopened a week after the bombing. "The first day was awful," Farley says, tears running down her face as she relives the experience. "I got out of my car and my knees were shaking. I felt as though I was going to fall apart right there. Diane Derzis met me and we walked in together. I don't think I could have made it without her. We tried so hard to be up, but Robert was dead and Emily was not here. We had a new nurse but she was not Emily. People were constantly disappearing that day and you'd find them on the steps boo-hooing because Emily had always handled everything."[179]

Emily Lyons, a registered nurse, had worked at New Woman since May 1994. While she was occasionally hassled by abortion foes, she spent little time concerning herself with them. "Every day I would go home and say so-and-so was at the clinic and guess what he said to me," says Lyons, "but we never thought anything like this would happen. Even when you shake packages for possible bombs you never expect anything like this to occur."[180]

Lyons has no memory of the explosion, but the thirteen operations she has had to repair the damage it caused are a constant reminder of how close to death she has come. Indeed, the bomb shot shrapnel into her abdomen, chest, face, hands, legs and neck. Her left eye was destroyed and her right badly damaged. "Bones were exposed in both legs and the doctors were afraid I'd lose my left one," she says. "Two of the three vessels of that leg were destroyed and they had to replace an artery. I also had a hole in my abdomen. My intestines had come out and they had to re-section my large intestine and take out ten inches of small intestine. When they removed the nails in my chest they left a crater two inches wide. Holes in my right hip and right knee had been left open and were packed with iodine-soaked gauze. It burns like fire when you put the packing in. It would not matter how many drugs I took, I felt it. The gauze was changed twice a day until June or July. I've also had surgery to remove nail heads in my fingers and hands, but I still have little dots of shrapnel all over, in my hands, pelvic area and legs."[181]

Lyons is remarkably calm, even good-humored and charming, as she reels off a litany of medical problems and enumerates the $1 million worth of surgeries she has had to correct them. Still nearly blind, she smiles often and laughs easily as she reflects on the experience. "The rage is not there very often," she admits, " although I felt it at the makeup counter this past weekend when I realized that I cannot put makeup on myself. I never learned to do it in the dark so my husband Jeffrey will have to do it for me."[182]

Still, she continues, the bombing has in some ways enhanced her life. "I've gained things and although they do not yet equal out, they are getting close. I've met so many neat people since this happened, Alex Sanger, the Reverend Howard Moody, Gloria Steinem. I was not involved politically before the bombing and I am shocked at myself, at who I'm now speaking to, but there was no thought about whether I would speak out. It's been an automatic reaction" to denounce anti-abortion violence.[183]

Indeed, since the bombing Lyons has addressed packed ballrooms at the conventions of groups including the National Abortion and Reproductive Rights Action League, Refuse & Resist!, Stand Up for Choice–Atlanta and the Planned Parenthood Federation of America. She has also testified before several state legislatures and starred in a TV commercial to support victorious United States Senate candidate Charles Schumer [D-NY] in 1998.

Although Lyons confesses to frustration due to optical limitations that make it impossible for her to read, sew and cook, she says that the support of her husband, two daughters and community has been essential to her recovery. "Jeffrey has been my lifeline," she says. "We've been married for five years and I've known him for twenty-three. On our honeymoon in New Orleans I went to a psychic and she told me that I'd met my soul mate. She was right."[184]

Follow-up note: Farley left her position at New Woman All Women in April 1999. She is no longer a provider.

Survivalist and Christian Identity movement supporter Eric Robert Rudolph, an army infantryman from August 1987 until January 1989—he was honorably discharged for nonspecific "conduct related" reasons—has been indicted for the clinic bombing as well as for the 1997 bombings at Atlanta's Northside Family Planning Clinic and The Other Side Lounge, a lesbian and gay night club. The 1996 Centennial Park explosion during the Olympic games has also been attributed to him.[185]

Two weeks after the bombing of New Woman All Women, FBI agents searched a storage facility traced to Rudolph. According to the *Birmingham News,* a lab analysis concluded that uniquely cut flooring nails used as shrapnel in the earlier Atlanta clinic bombing had come from a batch found in a shed rented by Rudolph in Marble, North Carolina.[186] A book entitled *How to Build Bombs of Mass Destruction* was also found in the locker. In addition, the FBI reports that the bombs used in the explosions were homemade antipersonnel devices; all were designed to maim or kill anyone coming into contact with them.[187]

Rudolph had not been seen since the January 29 explosion. Rumors that he is living in the Nantahala National Forest in western North Carolina have brought between eighty and two hundred FBI agents to the region at different times, but despite periodic stories about sightings, the suspect remains in hiding. Although Rudolph's ability to elude detection—despite the FBI's posting of a $1 million reward—worries clinics, they remain optimistic that he will eventually be apprehended. It took the FBI sixteen years to nail the Unabomber, they remind us, and 425 of the 460 people on the Most Wanted Fugitive roster have been captured since the list was created in 1950.[188]

JANUARY 31: MELBOURNE, FLORIDA

Twenty-one-year-old Amber Russo (a pseudonym) could not believe she was pregnant. Already the mother of a two-and-a-half-year-old-son, the single parent lived with her family and attended a vocational training program that would eventually license her as a medical assistant. "I went back and forth about my decision for weeks," she says, "and by the time I went to the clinic for an abortion I was thirteen weeks' pregnant. I was also one hundred percent sure that this was what I wanted. I remember the doctor giving me five mgs of Valium before I was brought in for surgery. The next thing I remember is saying 'ow, ow' during the abortion and holding my stomach. Then I remember being in aftercare. I vaguely remember being taken to the hospital."[189]

As it turned out, Amber's uterus had been perforated during the procedure and she was rushed to the hospital because of blood loss. "The risk might be one in 100,000 and I was that one," she says. "I don't know why there were complications. But I do know that it was no one's fault."[190]

The antis, however, saw it differently. "They followed us to the emergency room and the next day these two women—at the time I did not know they were antis—came to my room and asked if they could pray for me," Russo recalls. "My parents were visiting and I asked the women to come back. They returned fifteen minutes later and started to pray. They kept saying, 'please forgive Amber for her sins.' They left business cards and books, the gist of which were find Jesus or burn in hell, which my mom took home. But my mom also talked to them. She told the antis all about me, that I'd gone to Catholic school, because she thought they were just women who went room to room to provide company or prayer. The next day the priest who ran the Catholic school I'd attended, who had not known me, came and said he'd heard I needed prayer. I was under the influence of morphine, but I still thought it was strange."[191]

When Russo was released from the hospital several days later, she was startled to receive calls from the anti-abortionists. "Our number is unlisted so I don't know how they got it since none of us ever gave it to them," she says. "Then I started getting mail. All of the letters were sent to my dad since they'd gotten his car registration information. The first piece of mail hinted that we should consider getting legal help. The second letter urged us to sue. Other letters included lawyers' names and phone numbers. I later found out that Meredith Raney and another man had filed a complaint in my name with the state agency that handles medical malpractice. I called the agency and told the woman who answered the phone what had happened, that someone had filed a complaint using my name, and that the charges were not true. The antis have no way of knowing what happened to me at the clinic. I'm not sure if the complaint was dropped because of my call or if the state agency decided that there were no grounds for it but it never went forward."[192]

On February 11, when Amber returned to the clinic for a follow-up appointment, she noticed a sign in the waiting room advertising a "front desk" position. "They interviewed me and hired me on the spot," she boasts. "I was always pro-choice but I used to say I'd never have an abortion. Then the time came when I needed one. The antis make me so mad. They never cared about me. They just grabbed on to me because it was something they could use. If I had died they would've had a party. Since I started working at the clinic I've changed. Working here has toughened me up, not to kick someone's ass, but to stand up for myself and other women."[193]

FEBRUARY: BETTENDORF, IOWA

Planned Parenthood of Greater Iowa got the go-ahead to open a clinic in Bettendorf, at that time the largest metropolitan area in the United States without abortion services. The 320,000 people of the city had been stymied in their attempts to open a clinic by zoning regulations that barred the creation of such a facility. United States District Court Judge Charles Wolle struck down the zoning impediments in February, ruling them to be unfair road-blocks to abortion access.[194]

FEBRUARY: BRITISH COLUMBIA, CANADA

Nearly 150 healthcare workers in the Okanagan region received a letter from Kelowna Right to Life (KRTL), an affiliate of the British Columbia Pro-Life Society. The letter asked them to provide KRTL with the names of local abortion providers and physicians who refer women to clinics or doctors who provide that service. Shortly thereafter a nearly identical letter, signed by Nurses for Life, was sent to health workers in Vancouver.

"It now seems that the letters were copied word-for-word from originals supplied by a Texas anti-abortion group, Life Dynamics Inc.," wrote Will Offley in an article entitled "Cashing In On Terror."

> LDI has issued calls for supporters to send it home addresses and phone numbers of providers, photos, and vehicle license numbers, leading to serious concerns by providers that LDI is covertly working with the pro-murder wing of the anti-abortion movement. . . . . These letters are to be seen as a conscious

and systematic attempt to terrorize British Columbia providers into ceasing to perform abortions. When three doctors have been shot here and six providers (plus security guard Robert Sanderson) have been murdered in the U.S., the threat of publicizing one's name, address and picture is not a matter of minor harassment. . . . The letters are a clever tactic. They are genuinely intimidating, as intended. They carry a threat, but of an implied rather than explicit nature. This means that the writers will probably continue to escape criminal charges.[195]

Follow-up note: Workers at a Planned Parenthood in San Antonio, Texas, received an identical letter from Life Dynamics, Inc., addressed to American Health Care Professionals, within days of the mailing received by Okanagan health workers. Nine months later, in November 1998, staff at Planned Parenthood/Preterm Health Services of Greater Boston received a package printed to resemble an Express Mail envelope, with "Abortion Clinic Employee Alert" on the front cover. The following message greeted those who opened the packet: "Recently we've seen a large number of abortion clinic workers who say they want out of the abortion industry but feel like they are trapped. If this describes you, call or write Life Dynamics. We will not judge you, preach to you, or condemn you. Instead, we'll give you straight talk and practical answers. You have choices. If you want out, we can show you the way."[196]

Clinics throughout the United States and Canada reported receipt of the same materials.

FEBRUARY: LYNCHBURG, VIRGINIA

Philip "Flip" Benham, a Texas activist who had become the director of Operation Rescue National in 1994, was sentenced to six months in jail for criminal trespass. Benham had led 150 students from Jerry Falwell's Liberty University at a picket line in front of E. C. Glass High School. Screaming "Christians must remain at the gates of hell so that the King of Glory—Jesus— may enter in," the protestors held up five-foot-tall signs of bloody fetal parts. Benham told the students that he was presenting an "irrefutable contrast between the barbarism of abortion and the preciousness of life."[197] He also warned the teenagers that they would go to hell unless they returned prayer to the classroom.

"Violence of every sort is overwhelming our schools in spite of the vehement protestations of the Department of Education to the contrary," Benham wrote in an editorial in OR's June 1998 newsletter. "Our schools have become the most dangerous place for a young person to be. The answer is simple. God was violently expelled from our schools by a Supreme Court decision. He has been replaced with metal detectors, drugs, condoms, gangs, assault, rape, murder and violence of unprecedented order. When God is removed, violence always fills the void."[198]

Follow-up note: Lynchburg School superintendent James McCormick pointed out that E. C. Glass has no metal detectors and does not distribute condoms or have a gang problem. Surprisingly, Liberty University chancellor Jerry Falwell also disavowed the protest and offered to reimburse the Lynchburg police for overtime expenses incurred from the action.[199]

Benham was released from jail on May 5, 1998.

MARCH: CHICAGO, ILLINOIS

After twelve years of preparation, arguments began in *NOW v. Scheidler*, a class-action lawsuit that charged Operation Rescue, the Pro-Life Action League and four individuals with waging an anti-abortion conspiracy against clinics throughout the United States.

"When we walked into the courtroom it was incredible," says NWHO president Susan Hill. "The antis were all men in gray suits. Our side was all female with one exception. I realized that this was it: This was the story of gray men versus women who want something different. The antis packed the courtroom with priests and nuns. There were political statements everywhere. The judge would not allow buttons or signs, but you could see young women on our side, priests and nuns on the other. I was the first witness. I had lived through the twelve years it took for the case to reach trial, and had done this work for twelve years before that. I knew I could lay out what had been done and said and what I feared. I spent a few days on the stand, speaking about our clinics, about other clinics and about the theft of our fetuses from a medical lab near Chicago. I was sitting close to the jury and could feel them. I saw them react and felt they were open to the story.

"From where I sat it seemed as if Joe Scheidler was his own worst enemy. He has a malignant look to him and he never sat at the defendant's table. He stood against a wall with [codefendants] Murphy and Scholberg. He did not seem to want to connect with the jury. When he was called to testify he was arrogant, dismissive and sarcastic.

"During the trial, one of the Catholic priests, a guy who was very old and hunched over, began to speak to me. We'd talk every day. He said he prayed for me and I told him I hoped he'd pray for my safety. The next day he gave me a St. Christopher medal which he said I should keep with me. He said it would protect me. A number of other anti-choice people also came up to me after I testified and said, 'I'm sorry. You should never have had to go through that.' I realized that we'd made our case when Scheidler's people started to privately express sympathy with me. I thought if his supporters were doing this, we had a chance."[200]

Strong testimony from providers and former patients helped sway the jury, says Hill. But it was Congressman Henry Hyde [R-IL], a personal witness for Joseph Scheidler, who put the final nail in the antis' case. "The judge allowed Scheidler to bring in a character witness because he successfully argued that we had attacked his character," says Hill. "A few days before Hyde was scheduled to come in we were in the War Room, the place we used for strategy meetings. Our lawyers were wondering what they should ask Hyde. While they debated, I called Ron Fitzsimmons at the National Coalition of Abortion Providers because I vaguely remembered that Hyde had come out against clinic violence during congressional hearings on FACE. Ron faxed us Hyde's testimony, where he said that anyone guilty of anti-clinic violence should be punished under the RICO law. When Hyde came into the courtroom he talked like he was at a political rally. There were media everywhere. Then, as Hyde was cross-examined, it became clear that he did not know about Scheidler's arrest record. He had not prepared. When our lawyers read him his statements, where he had condemned the things we wanted condemned, the jury saw him boxed in by his own words. Throughout Hyde's testimony Scheidler stood against the wall, staring."[201]

APRIL 12: DENVER, COLORADO

Three anti-abortion protestors were arrested at St. John's Episcopal Cathedral for disrupting the church's annual Easter egg hunt; they were apprehended after yelling about "all the babies that weren't able to participate." Earlier in the day demonstrators had picketed the homes of two Denver physicians employed by Planned Parenthood of the Rocky Mountains.[202]

MAY 16: ORLANDO, FLORIDA

"I'd heard for years about other clinics getting hit with butyric acid," says Marion Ornstein, coadministrator of the Central Florida Women's Health Organization (CFWHO), "but the words 'butyric acid' didn't mean anything until I opened up that morning and there it was."[203]

According to Pat Davis, the organization's other coadministrator, vandals had drilled holes in the clinic's window frames and pumped large quantities of acid into the facility. "It was so caustic it took the wax up off the floor," she says. In addition, the acid splashed on to the wheels of the ultrasound machine, and it took more than six months for the smell to dissipate.[204]

Although the clinic moved to a new building on June 5, for the three weeks before the move staff and patients had to endure the nauseating odor. "We would go in in the morning wearing scrubs," says Ornstein. "You went into your house at night and immediately threw them into the wash. You would then take a long shower and wash your hair. For weeks the only thing staff wore was scrubs; because of the stench no one wanted to wear their real clothes inside."[205]

Despite the fact that the fire department had neutralized the acid on the morning of the attack, the center was forced to close for that day. Then, "every single morning until we left that site we washed the whole place with Lysol and floor cleaners. Whatever cleaners we could find, we tried," says Ornstein. "We put new charcoal filters in the air conditioner and washed everything you could wash. We put baking soda down over and over. Still, the day we were moving the chief of police came by and the first thing he said was, 'What's that smell in here?' During this whole period we did procedures as scheduled. Patients seemed to understand but of course it pissed them off that the antis had done this."[206]

Security at the CFWHO has been beefed up since the butyric attack. Cameras now operate twenty-four-hours a day, seven-days-a-week, and an armed guard is posted at the clinic's entrance at all times.

Two other Florida clinics were hit with butyric acid the same day that the CFWHO was attacked; during the next week clinics in ten additional Florida cities were similarly victimized. In Miami, health workers report that ninety children had to be rerouted to their day care center following a chemical blitz at a neighboring clinic.[207]

JUNE: EL PASO, TEXAS

When Marta Gutierrez (a pseudonym) came into Reproductive Services, she was seventeen weeks' pregnant and positive that she wanted an abortion. After going through counseling, staff inserted laminaria into her cervix to swell the entrance to the uterus and make the abortion easier. They instructed Gutierrez to return the next morning so that the procedure could be completed. She did not do so.

"We began to piece together what happened when another patient came in and relayed that she'd seen a woman walking toward the clinic," says Gerri Laster, executive administrator of Reproductive Services. "We were told that this woman had been pulled into a van. By the description of the vehicle we knew that she'd been accosted by Pentacostals for Life, a group that had been coming around for about six months. Until this incident they had screamed into our windows and sung religious songs really loudly. We later learned that Marta had been taken to a church where she was shown films of babies being torn apart, their limbs thrown in trash cans. They really scared her, not only with the films, but by telling her that she was going to be picked up by Immigration and deported back to Mexico because she was having an abortion. Around 3:00 o'clock the Pentacostals dropped Marta off near the clinic. She came inside because she didn't know what else to do but by this point she was so traumatized she was hysterical. She said that she no longer wanted the abortion so we removed the laminaria. After we spoke to her, we called the FBI and they came and talked to her. They were great. The Pentacostals were questioned and we have not seen them here since."[208]

JUNE: ORLANDO, FLORIDA

Operation Rescue teamed up with the American Family Association, Focus on the Family and the Southern Baptist Convention for a week-long protest at Walt Disney World. The religious groups met to protest Gay Days, the annual early June gathering of gay men and lesbians at Orlando's Disney theme parks.

Anti-abortion zealot Meredith Raney, representing Christians for Life, told *Florida Today* that the groups were targeting "the triple gates of Hell: The killing of unborn little boys and girls in their mothers' wombs, child pornography, and the sin of sodomy being promoted by Disney World as a legitimate lifestyle."[209] Although most of the protests were slated for Disney, local women's clinics and bookstores were also picketed.

The Southern Baptists had announced their boycott of Disney in 1997, but this was their first foray into street-level activism. They went along with the plan to picket outside Disney because of Disney CEO Michael Eisner's support of the liberal People for the American Way and his endorsement of policies to end discrimination based on sexual orientation and HIV status.

Letters to the right-wing faithful from the organizations sponsoring the protest urged them to travel to Florida to counter "Disney's radical, homosexual agenda" and lambasted the company's policy of extending domestic partnership benefits to unmarried and same-sex couples. But despite invitations to thousands of conservatives and fundamentalist Christians, the protest fizzled. Fewer demonstrators than anticipated showed up and, for the most part, people attending Gay Days had no clue that rabid adversaries were lurking outside the theme park's gates.

JULY 13: MELBOURNE, FLORIDA

From the deposition of protestor Meredith T. Raney in *Aware Woman Center for Choice, Inc. et al. v. Meredith T. Raney, et al.:*

ATTORNEY ROY LUCAS: Would it be fair to say that your pro-life activities have included interstate travel extensively?

RANEY: Certainly.

LUCAS: Did you go to the Dayton/Cincinnati area to picket the home of one of the physicians who works at the Aware Woman clinic from time to time?

RANEY: I went to Dayton and that was one of the things we did in Dayton, yes.

LUCAS: Have you done things inducing him to stop working at the clinic, as you have with other doctors?

RANEY: My purpose was just to put the truth out there and let the chips fall where they may.

LUCAS: That's the truth as you see it, right?

RANEY: It's the truth.

LUCAS: So you think the way you see the truth is the one and only truth?

RANEY: I don't know how to answer that question. The truth is the truth.

LUCAS: In your 10 years of activities around the clinic, how many patients have you sat down and counseled?

RANEY: Dozens.

LUCAS: Do you consider yourself a full-time provider of reproductive health care services?

RANEY: Yes.

LUCAS: Do you consider that you provide reproductive health care services at the Aware Woman Center for Choice facilities?

RANEY: Yes, that's one place.

LUCAS: What other places do you provide such services?

RANEY: Wherever the opportunity presents itself.

LUCAS: Do you have any kind of an office to provide counseling services?

RANEY: No.

LUCAS: Do you have any kind of license to provide counseling services?

RANEY: No.

LUCAS: Are you subject to any kind of oversight or regulation in the counseling services that you claim to provide?

RANEY: Just by the Holy Spirit.

LUCAS: I have seen on your letterhead the initials WLAC. What do these initials stand for?

RANEY: Women's Legal Action Coalition.

LUCAS: How was that name derived and by whom?

RANEY: I made it up.

LUCAS: Just yourself?

RANEY: Yes.

LUCAS: Now, there were no women involved in the organization, or was it an organization?

RANEY: It really wasn't an organization. It was just a slogan.

LUCAS: And there were no lawyers involved in it?

RANEY: No.

LUCAS: And it wasn't a coalition of organizations or people or anything like that?

RANEY: That's correct.

LUCAS: What kind of action was it involved in?

RANEY: The action was to help anyone that needed help who was a former or future patient of Aware Woman or any other abortion clinic for that matter.

LUCAS: Did you use the letterhead to write to people whose license plates you copied who had gone in and out of the clinic area?

RANEY: Yes.

LUCAS: What kind of punishment do you think there ought to be for a person having an abortion that you disapproved of if you were able to write your views into law?

RANEY: I believe it should be like any other murder.

LUCAS: You think it ought to be a capital offense?

RANEY: Yes.[210]

Patricia Baird-Windle: "When we deposed Meredith Raney he was ordered to produce hundreds of videotapes, phone records and bills, and daily log sheets of the antis' activities. Though we had seen him and his zealous crew running around with clipboards, tape recorders, video cameras and binoculars since at least 1989, we did not understand the overwhelming scope of all they had done. We could not have imagined the extent of it. We knew Raney had corresponded with patients because women had brought some of the letters to us. During the depositions, they delivered fourteen three- to four-inch-thick three-ring binders, each with three hundred to four hundred sheets containing lists of license plates they had tracked. Each page held the date, name of the observer or 'scribe,' and the license numbers and descriptions of the cars entering the parking lot. Here's an example: 'Red Chevy Malibu with male driver, female passenger. Man dressed in black, cursed us. Must be part of Satan Gang.' Many notations listed the arrival and departure of employees, noting if someone drove them to work or if they were accompanied. Some were ominous: 'Dr. Whitney is not wearing his bulletproof vest today.'

"Literally thousands of people and cars were listed for the nine-year period studied, 1990 to 1999. Our attorney referred to the information gathered as a 'blackmail database,' a truth born out by the letters that had been sent to patients. We learned that driver's license and auto tag data were obtained from the Florida Department of Motor Vehicles and from CompuServe [now WorldCom MCI] and through TML Services in Queens, New York. After seeing what the antis had done, Ted and I countersued Raney in 1998. Unfortunately, by that point it was too late to help us. Raney's ten years of outrageous abuse had scared patients away and we had already lost twenty-five doctors. Yet Janet Reno and the Department of Justice did not find these tactics worth fighting. The Federal Driver's Privacy Protection Act may afford some protection, but as in Canada, the plates can be tracked by anti-friendly police and by licensed investigators."[211]

SUMMER: SAN CLEMENTE, CALIFORNIA

Survivor Summer '98, a camp for adolescents between the ages of fourteen and eighteen, brought twenty-five mostly home-schooled evangelical Christians together for classes in political activism. Largely the sons and daughter of Operation Rescue leaders and former leaders, participants sported T-shirts explaining their political position on abortion: "If you were born after 1973, you're a survivor! One third of our generation has been killed before birth."[212]

According to the *Los Angeles Times*, a typical day at the camp involved listening to speakers address subjects such as sexual purity or fetal pain. Then came hands-on activism: picketing abortion clinics, demonstrating against Democratic gubernatorial candidate (and victor in the November 1998 race) Gray Davis's Los Angeles headquarters, or "street ministering" at area beaches.[213]

Subsequent Survivor Summers were organized in 1999 and 2000.

AUGUST 25: MELBOURNE, FLORIDA

At a City Council hearing on "appropriate zoning for abortion clinics," anti-abortion legislators took a new tack in attempting to defeat providers. Anti-choice vice-mayor John Carroll disingenuously stressed that, "We are not trying to outlaw abortion, but are trying to prevent abortion clinics from being located in neighborhoods." According to minutes from that meeting, Carroll listed numerous activities that had occurred at the Melbourne clinic—arrests, assaults, bomb scares and obstruction of traffic among them—and argued that these activities pose a danger to people living nearby. Rather than cracking down on those who cause the danger by engaging in illegal protest, however, he insisted that clinics should be banned from residential areas. In making his claim he recalled an incident in which a suspicious device was detonated by the bomb squad without the neighborhood being evacuated. "Children who exited a school bus during this time were walking nearby," he said. "The State Attorney's office also believes there is a problem. . . . I was in attendance during a court case when a State Attorney repeatedly referred to the pro-lifers in the neighborhood as a terrorist element. Today, there is a buffer zone between the abortion clinic and certain activities. It would be a good idea to provide a minimal buffer between the abortion clinic and a neighborhood."[214]

Anti-abortion council member Steven Beltz, an active supporter of the Christian Coalition, concurred: "This is an opportunity to protect citizens. . . . Abortion clinics have rights. But so do citizens and we cannot neglect one over the other."[215]

Nonsense, Melbourne city attorney Paul Gougelman argued. "Courts, almost without exception, have construed local government attempts to zone abortion clinics as little more than attempts to stop a woman from getting an abortion. Thus, courts will almost automatically assume that a local government zoning plan for abortion clinics is suspect and little more than a veiled attempt to deprive someone of their fundamental constitutional rights."[216]

Gougelman's report to the City Council cited the attempts of two nearby cities, Cocoa Beach and Orlando, to restrict clinics through zoning regulations and pointed out that these losing efforts had cost their respective cities significant sums of money.[217]

FALL: LITTLE ROCK, ARKANSAS

Like most clinics, Little Rock Family Planning Services relies on an ad in the Yellow Pages to publicize its services. At a cost of $18,000 a year, clinic director Carolyn Izard tries to cram as much information into the listing as possible: the types of obstetrical and gynecological services offered, rates and regulatory limitations on the provision of surgery. Most important, Izard says, a Web address allows potential patients to "tour" the clinic and view the lab as well as the counseling, operating and recovery rooms before scheduling their appointments.

"We began listing our Web address in 1996," she says, "so I was shocked when the Southwestern Bell representative called me in the fall of 1998 and said that there had been a rules change. She said that because we were classified as 'sensitive advertising' we could no longer list our Web address. Actually, the rep gave me two choices, run the ad without the Internet address or pull it out entirely. The clinic had to have an ad so I reluctantly agreed to run it without the address."[218]

Izard contacted her attorney and was preparing to sue Southwestern Bell when the 1999 phone book came out; oddly, Little Rock Family Planning Services' listing contained their Web address (www.lrfps.com). Izard is currently monitoring the situation and will litigate if the phone company again tries to bar Web information from their ad.

FALL: BINGHAMTON, NEW YORK

Randall Terry, running for Congress against upstate incumbent Maurice Hinchley, unveiled his platform. Calling his campaign "You Pay for It," his electoral pledges included advocacy of: a constitutional amendment to repeal all property taxes; the elimination of the Internal Revenue Service and the abolition of the federal income tax; an end to mandatory Social Security payments; the "restoration of America's Judeo-Christian political heritage"; full legal protection for "pre-born babies"; and a renewed fight against "militant homosexuals who are trying to destroy the institution of marriage and seduce our sons and daughters." In addition, the campaign promised to fight for the elimination of public funding for Medicaid, Medicare, public education and all health and human services programs. "They call it compassion, but it's theft," he told supporters.[219]

Hinchley won the race despite the fact that his opponent raised more than a quarter of a million dollars, most of it from out-of-state donors.

OCTOBER 23: AMHERST, NEW YORK

Dr. Barnett (Bart) Slepian, his wife, Lynne, and their four sons had returned from Friday night services at their synagogue a little before 10:00 P.M. They had gone to the temple to say Kaddish, the Jewish prayer for the dead, in commemoration of the ninth anniversary of Bart's father's passing. After settling into their home, the obstetrician/gynecologist, his wife and one son went into the kitchen. The three other children went into the living room to watch TV. But the family's tranquility did not last long. Shortly after 10:00 P.M. a sniper's bullet entered the house through a partly draped kitchen window, hitting Dr. Slepian in the back and exiting through his chest. The bullet then bounced off a cabinet before ricocheting into the living room. Although Lynne Slepian and one son tried to revive the doctor, he was pronounced dead by physicians at the Millard Fillmore Suburban Hospital an hour later.[220]

The assault was not the first time snipers had attacked abortion providers in their homes. Vancouver gynecologist Garson Romalis nearly bled to death after a bullet shattered his femur in November 1994, and a year later, in November 1995, Dr. Hugh Short of Ancaster, Ontario, lost the use of his right arm after being hit by bullets. Then, in November 1997, the gunman struck twice: Winnipeg, Manitoba, gynecologist Jack Fainman was wounded while watching television and a never-identified Rochester, New York, doctor was hit while sitting beside his indoor swimming pool. All four men survived the attacks.

Law enforcers believe that the shootings were timed to coincide with Remembrance Day, a mid-November holiday to honor Canadian war veterans. Since the early 1990s, the day has been appropriated by anti-abortionists as "Remember the Unborn Children Day," and both American and Canadian providers have red-flagged the weeks surrounding the holiday. In fact, on the day of Slepian's murder, the National Abortion Federation (NAF) sent a fax to Slepian's workplace, Buffalo GYN Womenservices—and to private abortion providers in the Buffalo area—urging them to take extra precautions due to the pattern and timing of earlier shootings. The clinic faxed a copy of the letter to Dr. Slepian; Lynne Slepian passed it to local police.

According to the *Buffalo News,* the department's commanders never relayed NAF's warning to the officers assigned to patrol Slepian's neighborhood.[221] Other malfeasance also came to light in the days immediately following the slaying. Canadian police told the *Buffalo News* that they were not informed about the shooting until 4:00 A.M. even though there was suspicion that the killer might have entered Canada after the attack.[222] In addition, the dispatcher who took Lynne Slepian's 911 call told police respondents that a man was down but neglected to mention that he had been shot. As a result, the first officers to arrive on the scene were unaware that they should look for a killer fleeing the neighborhood.[223]

Despite the bungling, Lynne Slepian does not blame police for her husband's murder. Instead she blames anti-abortion activists and says that the rhetoric they spew encourages violence against providers nationwide. Indeed, when the Reverend Robert L. Schenck, a leader of 1992's "Spring of Life" and now a minister in Washington, D.C., sent roses to Slepian's private practice after the doctor's death, she was so outraged that she mailed them back. "He's a big hypocrite," Lynne Slepian told reporters. "This is the same man who called Bart a pig, who confronted him at a demonstration and who sat behind me in court humming 'Jesus Loves the Little Children' loud enough so I, but not the judge, could hear it. He was a thorn in my side."[224]

The *Buffalo News* echoed Slepian's outrage. Decrying the "fighting words" that incite anti-abortion violence, an October 26 editorial criticized the movement's often-volatile rhetoric. "This tragedy should give those in the anti-abortion movement pause to think about the climate they create when they throw around words like 'baby killer' and 'murderer' or tolerate those who do," editors wrote. "That kind of inflammatory rhetoric can only aid and abet the kind of extremist who hid behind Dr. Slepian's house Friday night and killed him in his home. Words have consequences. Anti-abortion forces ought to consider that reality."[225]

Precisely the point, countered the Reverend Donald Spitz and the Nuremberg Files' Neal Horsley. While most anti-abortion groups, from the Catholic church to the National Right to Life Committee, condemned the killing, Spitz, the head of Pro-Life Virginia, wasted no time in issuing a statement lauding Slepian's assassin. "We as Christians have a responsibility to protect the innocent from being murdered the same way we would want someone to protect us. Who ever shot the shot protected the children," he wrote.[226] Similarly, within hours of the murder, the Nuremberg Files Web site put a line through Slepian's name to indicate that he was no longer "a threat to unborn children," and remnants of New York State's Operation Rescue chapter announced "Operation Save America," a protest that would bring OR to Buffalo in April 1999.

Meanwhile, pro-choice forces responded to the murder with a mix of somber reflection and steely determination to keep the one remaining Buffalo-area clinic open. "The Slepian murder was the culmination of efforts to shut us down," says Buffalo GYN Womenservices director Marilynn Buckham, " but it did not work. We are resilient. No matter what, women will seek out abortion services. Even though we've come perilously close to having no providers in this area we will continue our work."[227]

Two and a half months after Slepian's death, the clinic already appeared to be functioning smoothly. Staff seemed calm, efficiently friendly, as they called patients from the waiting room. This ambiance was relatively new, Buckham admitted. Immediately after Slepian was shot, half of the clinic's staff—as well as its cleaning crew and snow-shoveling contractor—resigned. "Some of it was fear, some was that people had been thinking of leaving anyway. In the first weeks we were in shock, but we were very busy and terribly short-staffed. In addition to everything else we had to do we also had to interview new people," she adds.[228]

"On top of the trauma of Dr. Slepian's death we also had to plead and beg the agencies that manage Medicaid and the HMOs so that we could get paid,"

Buckham continues. Her tone is grim, and she sounds exhausted, as she speaks of negotiating with state agencies and licensing boards for permission to bring out-of-state physicians to Buffalo to perform abortions at GYN Womenservices. "Right after Bart died we got calls from doctors all over the country offering to help, and it was a bureaucratic nightmare to get the state to do the credentialing to enable them to work here. Many people were helpful and sped up the process but it was still very hard. The first three weeks after his death are a blur. There were press people all over the place and I had to concentrate on getting physicians to come in. I also had to do the paperwork so we could run a clinic. But I have to say, although we still can't believe that Bart is gone, we're doing quite well. The staff pulled through. Of course, we miss him. Bart was an excellent physician, a master clinician. He was very good with staff and had a good heart."[229]

Follow-up note: Within days of Slepian's murder, law enforcers announced that they were searching for James Charles Kopp as a material witness. Kopp, an itinerant handyman and anti-abortion extremist known to his colleagues as "Atomic Dog," has a long activist history. Involved with both OR and the Lambs of Christ, Kopp was jailed for blockading and for participating in lock-and-block protests in Georgia, New York, Vermont and West Virginia. Authorities say that his 1987 Chevrolet Cavalier was seen directly behind Slepian's home on the night of the murder, and Kopp himself was seen jogging in the neighborhood that morning. In addition, investigators have found records showing that Kopp crossed the United States–Canadian border at the time of the earlier sniper attacks on Canadian physicians.[230]

In early November 1998 the Justice Department announced the formation of a task force to investigate violence directed at doctors and clinics. A similar task force was convened following the July 1994 murder of Dr. John Bayard Britton and his escort James Barrett in Pensacola, Florida; that group found no evidence of a national anti-abortion conspiracy.[231] Providers are not optimistic. Patricia Baird-Windle notes that the 1994 task force interviewed only one clinic owner and wonders how the Department of Justice can understand extortion and sabotage against health centers in two countries without questioning the victims.

Like Eric Robert Rudolph, the man charged with the January 1998 bombing of New Woman All Women Health Care in Birmingham, James Kopp remains at large. No other suspects have been identified in the Slepian slaying.

OCTOBER 30: FT. WAYNE, INDIANA

When Raquel Sims, office manager at the Ft. Wayne Women's Health Organization, got word that five clinics, including an Indianapolis Planned

Parenthood, had received letters claiming to contain the potentially deadly anthrax bacteria, she immediately contacted law enforcement to determine how to protect her clinic. The response she received stunned her and her rage remains audible. "First I called the local office of the United States marshal and they said they had not heard about the letter. Then I called the local FBI office; they had not heard about it yet either. Then I called our doctor. My details were sketchy, but I knew that there was a scare that had come through the mail. I should not have been the one to inform the FBI and the marshals. They should have immediately called to inform me."[232]

Days after more than three dozen people in Indiana, Kansas, Kentucky and Tennessee were exposed to a brown powder, tests revealed the threat to be a hoax. Nonetheless, clinics across the United States and Canada, already on red alert following the murder of Dr. Barnett Slepian one week earlier, were terrified that the letters—purporting to contain a biological weapon that can cause a life-threatening form of pneumonia if its spores are inhaled—might be an easy way to effect an across-the-board slaughter of clinic workers. As a precaution, employees and patients at the clinics that received the letters were stripped and scrubbed down by emergency crews after the small envelopes were unwittingly opened. Some were also treated with antibiotics to deter against possible infection while the powdery substance was tested and identified.[233]

HALLOWEEN WEEKEND: FARGO, NORTH DAKOTA

"Eight days after Dr. Slepian's murder we came into the Fargo Women's Health Organization to find graffiti all over everything," says director Kim Horab. "There were upside-down peace signs and serpents and the front door said, 'I'm gonna suck your brains out. Beware.' They wrote, 'Satisfy your killer needs' on the back door, and the ground-floor windows, signs and surveillance warnings were painted over. They also used red paint to look like blood dripping on our benches and outdoor carpet. The police were very slow to respond and treated it like a Halloween prank. I took two rolls of pictures to document the damage. The police took three photos."[234] No one was apprehended.

NOVEMBER 7: SYRACUSE, NEW YORK

Operation Rescue founder Randall Terry declared personal bankruptcy in an effort to avoid paying fines to the National Organization for Women and Planned Parenthood. He owed the groups a total of $1.6 million. "I cannot in good conscience permit the National Organization of [sic] Women, Planned

Parenthood and others who have profited from abortion to harass my wife and family, and possibly get money from me to continue their crusade against unborn life," he told the Associated Press. "Hence, I have filed a Chapter 7 petition to discharge my debts to those who would use my money to promote the killing of the unborn."[235]

Bankruptcy lawyers say that Terry can be forced to pay the damages if the courts find that he caused property destruction to either group, or assaulted or slandered organizational staff. To date, there has been no ruling on this matter.

NOVEMBER 9: FARGO, NORTH DAKOTA

Less than two weeks after finding menacing graffiti on their building, staff at the Fargo Women's Health Organization discovered their offices covered with fluorescent paint. Obscenities, as well as phrases like "an eye for an eye" and "your doctor is dead and in hell," were found on the clinic's walls and windows and on the fence surrounding the property.[236]

NOVEMBER 10: WASHINGTON, D.C.

Attorney General Janet Reno announced a $500,000 award for information leading to the capture of Dr. Barnett Slepian's murderer. She also announced the formation of a National Clinic Violence Task Force to supplement the work of local law enforcement authorities. The group was charged with coordinating information and examining possible links between attacks on abortion facilities and clinic staff. Bill Lann Lee of the Civil Rights Division of the Department of Justice was named as task force head. Representatives of the FBI, BATF, United States Marshals Service and the Postal Service were also named to the investigative body.[237]

MID-NOVEMBER: BUFFALO, NEW YORK

Industrial historian Elena Schweitzer (a pseudonym), an active member of Buffalo United for Choice (BUC), was at a meeting in Pittsburgh when she heard that an upstate New York doctor had been killed by a sniper. "I called a friend and was told that it was Dr. Slepian. I left the conference immediately. As soon as I got back home, I attended a candlelight vigil and was interviewed by a TV station and several newspapers. About three weeks later, in mid-November, a woman I knew from BUC called and told me that I had been added to the Nuremberg Files list. Since then I've talked to the marshals and local police but it seems as if the feds are not taking it seriously. They never even notified me that I was on the list."[238]

Since being placed on the roster, Schweitzer has experienced several petty acts of vandalism at her home; for several weeks she also received a barrage of hang-up calls. "For weeks after I saw the Nuremberg Web site I couldn't sleep," she says. "Then something happened. On December 10 there was a memorial service for Bart. There was supposed to be an officer protecting me, but there was not. During the service I realized this is not two weeks, like the Spring of Life. This is forever."[239]

Follow-up note: Schweitzer says that she and her family now keep their home curtains drawn and try to remain alert to what is going on around them. Still, there are limits to her ability to be vigilant. "I recently had a book come out which I am trying to promote," she says. "We always have security at book signings, but it is hard to try and hide and also promote a book."[240]

1999

JANUARY 4: MELBOURNE, FLORIDA

After years of effort to get the antis to stop using information gleaned from motor vehicle records, the Aware Woman Center for Choice sued sixteen anti-abortion extremists as well as CompuServe and TML Information Services. According to legal papers filed by AWCC lawyers, both TML and CompuServe had for years provided information to Meredith Raney without investigating his credentials or ascertaining if he was a bona fide investigator. The suit sought thousands of dollars in compensatory damages. It was eventually dropped before the charges could be examined because Aware Woman was too financially strapped to pursue it.[241]

WINTER: GEORGIA

A Georgia clinic received the following letter:

> I hope that the following experience will help you know that what you are doing is important. Two years ago my daughter-in-law told me she needed to go two states away to see a doctor. I was frantic and insisted on knowing what was wrong with her. Quietly, she told me that she was pregnant again. They already had two children and her youngest has Cerebral Palsy. I asked her if there were complications and she then dropped the bomb that she was going to an abortion clinic. I thought she was crazy. I am the only person in the family who was anti-abortion, not pro-life, but anti-abortion. Why on earth would

she pick me? She said that she trusted me to comfort her and help her make any difficult decisions logically. She stated that she understood my beliefs, but needed me to just give of myself unselfishly this one time. Against my better judgment, that night we left my house at midnight and headed for St. Louis. We had a wonderful trip of laughter, tears, and great conversation and by the time we arrived, I was convinced that she knew what she was doing. I still did not believe in abortion, but I believed in her. When we arrived at the clinic I saw something I didn't expect—protestors.

I still agreed with them but I decided I would protect her. We got out of the car and she took my hand, held her head up, and walked right through the center of them. One woman shouted at her and said "Why are you killing your baby?" I wanted to slug her. My daughter-in-law just turned around and said "I am making the choice that is right for me. God bless you!" I was amazed. I had never seen such courage. Her strength is an inspiration to me. I am now a pro-choice grandma.[242]

SPRING: MELBOURNE, FLORIDA

Patricia Baird-Windle: "A contingent of my family met with me and said they were begging me to quit working as an abortion provider. They were scared of the danger. This was followed by planned, coordinated phone calls asking me if I was talking to a buyer yet. My husband wanted to retire. My legendary energy was gone. I knew Aware Woman in Melbourne would need to find a new place to rent or buy because the highway we were on was widening. Still, it was my sister's diagnosis that May—she has ALS, Lou Gehrig's disease—that was the final straw for me. I knew I couldn't help her and run two clinics. We sold the Aware Woman Centers for Choice effective July 1, 1999. I had never intended partial retirement. For more than three years, the clinics had lost large amounts of money. I paid the debts out of the sale of the property and out of our retirement fund. I now have to sell our home. Call this forced retirement."[243]

SUMMER: NATIONAL

The National Abortion and Reproductive Rights Action League (NARAL) began a nationwide campaign to amend the bankruptcy code to ensure that judgments issued in court cases resulting from clinic violence are not dischargeable in bankruptcy proceedings. The group cited Randall Terry's bankruptcy claims as the impetus for their efforts. They are also pressuring lawmakers for stricter enforcement of laws preventing the fraudulent transfer of assets to avoid liability.[244]

OCTOBER 19–21: WASHINGTON, D.C.

The United States Senate passed the Partial Birth Abortion Ban Act by a vote of 63 to 34. According to a position paper released by NCAP in early October:

> Let's assume that new legislation could be drafted that could actually outlaw this particular abortion procedure. What would be accomplished? What would change in the clinics? The answer is: Absolutely nothing. Not one abortion would be prevented in this country. That is because some women with unwanted pregnancies will still need and will still seek out abortion services—and some will do so late in their second trimester of pregnancy. And, to serve that need, our doctors have other (perhaps less medically preferable) procedures available to help these women terminate their pregnancies. This is not a startling revelation. Even some leaders of the "pro-life" movement know this to be the case. For example: Mr. Mark Crutcher, president of Life Dynamics in Denton, Texas, has stated publicly that the partial birth abortion proposals are a scam. Similarly, Ms. Colleen Parro, director of the Republican National Coalition for Life, told *Life Talk Video Magazine* that this legislation "doesn't stop any abortions."[245]

2000

JANUARY: NATIONAL

According to the National Abortion Federation, there were eight arsons—double the 1998 number—against clinics during 1999. Phony anthrax letters were received by more than three dozen health centers, and there was a slight increase in the number of bomb scares received during the year.[246] In addition, seventy anti-choice measures were enacted by state legislatures in 1999, up from sixty-two in 1998 and fourteen in 1996.[247]

2001

According to NAF, during the year 2000 there were 2 arsons, 20 bomb threats, 7,855 picket lines, 50 invasions, 16 instances of stalking, 4 blockades, 9 death threats, 1 attempted murder and 944 harassing telephone calls and received pieces of hate mail at U.S. clinics.[248]

CHAPTER EIGHT

Of Champions and Challenges

On July 11, 2000, Dr. Garson Romalis of Vancouver, British Columbia, won the dubious distinction of becoming the first North American abortion provider to survive two attempts on his life. The first, in 1994, occurred when a sniper fired into his kitchen as he ate breakfast. The then-fifty-seven-year-old gynecologist was wounded in the leg. Six years later he was stabbed in the back as he entered his office one summer morning. In neither incident was the assailant apprehended.

Clearly, the violence continues. On January 3, 2000, Ohio clinic owner Debi Jackson spotted a suspicious package in the mail and called the bomb squad. She also notified Cincinnati Planned Parenthood, urging security specialists there to peruse health center grounds—and incoming mail—for anything unusual. Thanks to her vigilance, staff found a packet that had been sent by anti-abortionists.

Both packages contained shrapnel bombs. Although they were detonated by police, causing no injury to personnel or clients, the bombs could have killed or maimed less eagle-eyed workers.

Other incidents have also been reported. In the spring of 2000, police intercepted two men with a large cache of explosives intended for Dr. Damon Stutes's Reno, Nevada, clinic. In other places, butyric acid and anthrax attacks, menacing behavior, fires and sabotage remain daily threats.

These occurrences beg the question: Is there anything providers and their organizations can do to temper the violence? What about pro-choice activists and groups like the Feminist Majority Foundation (FMF) and National

Organization for Women (NOW)? Can government and law enforcement do anything to diffuse the climate of hatred?

GOVERNMENT COMPLICITY:
UNRAVELING THE BUREAUCRATIC RED TAPE

"After David Gunn was murdered (in March 1993), we went to state and federal law enforcement and said, 'We're waiting for the next murder. It will happen.' They just looked at us," says Ellie Smeal, president of the Feminist Majority Foundation. "You start to worry about your perceptions when you get that reaction, but we believe that both the public and law enforcement are in massive denial about the threat to providers and others. We knew in 1993 that David's murder was not an isolated event, that there was and is a right-wing political movement that hates abortion and is anti-Semitic, anti-gay, anti-Black and anti-woman. They say they want to establish a Christian theocracy in the United States. It's hard to think that there is a terrorist movement working against us, but more people have begun to open their eyes since the Oklahoma City bombing, the Matthew Shepard murder and the abortion doctor murders."[1]

Although appalling, it is not surprising that it took twenty-one years, from 1973 when the Supreme Court legalized abortion, until 1994, for the United States government to enact a law with prosecutorial teeth to punish anti-abortion lawlessness. The Freedom of Access to Clinic Entrances (FACE) Act was signed in May 1994, making it a federal crime to "engage in violent or obstructive conduct intended to interfere with people seeking or providing reproductive health services."[2]

The act has had a positive, if markedly limited, impact; most moderately targeted clinics report fewer illegal incidents since FACE was passed. Furthermore, FACE had caused the pool of anti-abortionists willing to demonstrate at clinics or engage in civil disobedience to shrink. Nonetheless, problems with the act's enforcement require attention. For one, regulatory agencies in many areas of the country still refuse to coordinate tasks and formulate litigation and enforcement strategies. To date, there have been no repercussions for their intransigence, although in some locales individual staffers have personally—albeit privately—apologized for their agency's lack of effort.

In addition, seven years after its passage, FACE remains unevenly enforced. Carla Eckhardt, clinical services director of the National Abortion Federation (NAF), reports that, "When a clinic in Knoxville got a letter claiming to contain anthrax, the director called the FBI and got a recording saying that all the agents were out to lunch. There was no beeper or other number to call in case of emergency. Nothing. They were simply out to lunch. One and a half hours passed between the clinic getting the letter and the FBI showing up at their offices. By contrast, when a clinic in Indianapolis got a similar letter, the FBI arrived immediately and scrubbed the staff down. They acted with appropriate urgency."[3]

What's more, says Ellie Smeal, the Civil Rights Division of the Department of Justice, the unit charged with overseeing FACE violations, gives abortion violence short shrift because it is also responsible for investigating police brutality and hate crimes. Regardless of reason, the facts remain stark: between May 1994 and September 1998, only forty-six cases were prosecuted under the act.[4] "We believe we need a unit dedicated to monitoring and prosecuting nothing but anti-abortion violence," Smeal concludes.[5]

Patricia Baird-Windle goes even further, calling on law enforcement to use restraint of trade laws, interstate commerce regulations and anti-racketeering protections to stop the extremists once and for all. "I'm asking for a decisive move on the part of the Department of Justice," she says, "a shift in business as usual. To date, whenever FACE has been invoked it's been used in a watered-down way, with weak civil, rather than criminal, charges brought against the individuals and groups that travel from state to state conspiring and conducting 'rescues.' After a July 1998 blockade in Dayton, Ohio, for example, DOJ wimped out and allowed the protestors to sign an agreement that they would not conduct blockades in Dayton again. The stipulation did not even slap their hands for disrupting the clinic. This type of cop-out cannot be allowed to continue."[6]

THE PRO-CHOICE COMMUNITY: OPERATING BEHIND BLINDERS

With the exception of the Feminist Majority Foundation, national pro-choice groups have been reluctant to aggressively counter or even study anti-abortion activity. Instead, they have confined their efforts to lobbying against abortion restrictions and to working to elect pro-choice candidates to local, state and national office. It is as if they have succumbed to magical thinking, hoping against hope that if they ignore the violence it will vanish.

Ron Fitzsimmons has seen this strategy up close. A lobbyist for the National Abortion Rights Action League (NARAL; renamed the National Abortion and Reproductive Rights Action League in 1994) from 1980 to 1983, he says that, "In the early 1980s, the National Abortion Federation was a quiet little medical organization that was never proactive. NARAL was totally focused on the legality of abortion. I don't remember hearing about the violence; it was tangential to what we were doing. The Hatch Amendment [which would have permanently prohibited taxpayer-funded abortion and removed federal court jurisdiction in overturning state anti-abortion laws] passed the Judiciary Committee on my first day on the job. That's what we were fighting. I was told by a NARAL board member not to ask clinic people to testify before Congress. I'm a grass-rootsy person. I saw the value of bringing clinic staff in to testify about the law's potential impact on them and their patients. NARAL felt that because the clinics had a vested interest, their testimony was tainted. They kept themselves separate from the clinics, as if they operated in different worlds. No one was speaking to the clinics then. They had no presence on Capitol Hill."[7] In the nearly twenty years since Fitzsimmons left NARAL, little has changed in terms of how the group relates to service providers.

NOW has done only slightly better. After a decade of firebombing and arson, three members of The November Gang, a provider support group, met with NOW president Patricia Ireland in early 1990. Their goal was to encourage NOW's increased involvement in efforts to stem the violence. As a result of the meeting, Ireland began to work with the Washington Area Clinic Defense Task Force (WACDTF), organizing a national conference on the worsening climate at women's health centers. Those attending the autumn 1990 event found the meeting instructive; nonetheless, it did not lead NOW to sustained, long-term activity to protect clinics. (The group did, however, provide massive funding for the *NOW v. Scheidler* lawsuit that was decided in 1998. The case proved that there has been an extortion and conspiracy campaign against clinics.)

PROVIDERS: RECTIFYING PAST ERRORS

But national organizations are not the only ones to shoulder blame for paying too little attention to the violence. In fact, despite a rash of bombings and fires beginning in the early 1980s, it took more than a decade for most providers to demand action to stop the terror. This head-in-the-sand approach meant that clinics, NARAL, NAF and feminist organizations did not do much of anything quell the increasing disruptions.

do not know why NAF did not get involved in fighting the violence early Carla Eckhardt, NAF's clinical services director, "if they thought they what it took, if they thought other groups were doing enough, or if they defined themselves as an exclusively educational organization, but whatever the reason, it was not the right response."[8]

Clarion calls to NAF—repeatedly voiced by birth control pioneer Bill Baird and Patricia Baird-Windle (the two are not related), among others—went unheeded, and even when the group finally did get involved, most providers felt their efforts inadequate. "As I tried to educate the media about the violence and harassment, I found that the NAF surveys of clinic violence, which they started doing in 1977, were seriously incomplete," says Baird-Windle. "They poll NAF members only, or about one-quarter of the provider population. Likewise, the Feminist Majority Foundation's annual surveys, done since 1993, count only the most violent activities, missing the constant, daily torment that whittles away at women's right to privacy and our right to work."[9]

Indeed, in the face of organizational and governmental reticence, violence flourished. And as it did, clinic after clinic donned the veneer of defiant stoicism. Workers demonstrated superhuman strength, telling reporters that they were coping despite the attacks against them, as if by keeping a stiff upper lip they could ward off future incidents. In hindsight, many providers now believe that this posture has lessened community support and increased their isolation. "We felt as if we couldn't say we needed help," says Peg Johnston, executive director of Southern Tier Women's Services in Vestal, New York.[10] Whether facing an impending eviction or coming in to find hundreds of blockaders in the doorway, staff felt that to reveal fear was to admit weakness.

"For years we've pretended that everything is fine," adds former clinic director Charlotte Taft, "that the violence hasn't affected us. We've protected the public from seeing our suffering after attacks."[11] Predictably, most people do not see defending the clinics as their responsibility. Likewise, they do not rally in support of abortion doctors or other threatened medical workers. After all, if clinics have things under control, why should folks pitch in to ensure that services are offered?

Clearly, a comprehensive history of the full spectrum of anti-abortion tactics and strategies must be compiled. Still, differences abound over how to use this data; in fact, providers disagree over whether clinics are best served by confronting the antis or if ignoring them is the better approach. Debates on the subject are heated and vary depending on the extent of targeting at a particular health center and whether that targeting is ongoing or seemingly over.

Nonetheless, in those places where the antis trace car ownership from vehicle license plates and then berate patients for their choices, clinic staff feel that turning the other cheek is both personally and politically dangerous. Similarly, they argue that the ongoing threat of sniper and other attacks requires their continued vigilance. Whether through (unevenly enforced) injunctions, (unevenly enforced) legislation, or creative, grass-roots events or mobilizations— or a completely new set of strategies—they hold that an active offense is the best defense against anti-abortion tyranny.

CLINICS IN THE TWENTY-FIRST CENTURY: ADJUSTING TO POLITICAL AND SOCIAL CHANGE

Providers, prompted by recognition that the topography of abortion has shifted since *Roe v. Wade* was decided nearly thirty years ago, are creating new approaches to service delivery and constantly adapting to new technologies and scientific advances.

An untitled, internal report written in 1999 by the National Coalition of Abortion Providers outlines the challenges:

> The congressional debate over the legality of abortion peaked in 1983 when the United States Senate defeated a Constitutional Amendment overturning the Roe decision. In the ensuing years, the horrors of illegal abortion became a distant memory and the public's attention began turning towards the more complex moral issues associated with the procedure. Unfortunately, supporters of Roe remained relatively silent on the morality of abortion and opponents of Roe were anxious to fill that void. While we continued to argue for "choice," they talked about "life" and urged women not to "kill their babies." While we vowed to "never go back" to the old days, the anti-abortion movement spoke of fetal pain, "sex selection abortions," minors obtaining abortions without their parent's knowledge, and, ultimately, "partial birth abortions." The result has been that while more than one million women a year have abortions in this country, the procedure itself is highly stigmatized. Women will travel hundreds of miles to avoid being seen walking into their local clinic. Most people are uncomfortable talking about the issue, and if they do, it is often in judgmental or uninformed terms. Even some supporters of abortion rights are quick to describe it as a "necessary evil," a "bad thing," or a "tragedy."[12]

Providers know that abortion engenders mixed emotions in women terminating unwanted pregnancies: feelings of empowerment, relief and resolve often mingle with feelings of sadness and loss. They also know that the current political climate has stifled positive sentiments, as if it is somehow wrong to acknowledge the consolation the procedure can offer.

A VISION FOR SLOWING THE VIOLENCE

So what can be done?

Without the uniform imposition of legal constraints on anti-abortion terrorists, medium to heavily targeted clinics will continue to be financially and emotionally burdened by violence. Replacing doctors frightened off by coercion; making repairs when the antis bomb, flood, torch or vandalize facilities; moving from site to site when leases are not renewed or canceled; purchasing ever more costly fire and liability insurance; and hiring lawyers to secure injunctions and fight false complaints and nuisance lawsuits: these tasks are tremendously burdensome to clinic owners and other providers.

While improved relationships between clinics and law enforcement in some cities—Buffalo, Knoxville, Mobile and Pittsburgh, among them—have enabled clinic principals to focus on expanding and improving existing services, the stuff on the "inside" rather than the rancor on the "outside," health centers in places including Fargo, Ft. Wayne, Melbourne, Milwaukee, Pensacola, Redding and Wichita have not had this option. Year after year providers in these areas find themselves returning to court to fight meritless lawsuits and get injunctions enforced and lawbreakers arrested. Mired in holding their ground rather than expanding their vision, they feel frustrated and betrayed.

"Providers never intended to be warriors," says Baird-Windle. "It was never part of our job description. We certainly never intended to moonlight as combatants or deal with a war outside our doors. Since *Roe,* providers have succeeded in keeping clinics open during chaos and ugly pressure. We also established the National Coalition of Abortion Providers. But we must do more. The one visit we arranged with the Department of Justice should have been followed by an orchestrated campaign to get the agency to investigate and learn about the pattern of violence and the conspiracy against us. Instead, we retreated. I have spent twenty years of my life trying to convince my fellow providers to organize efforts to show the media and public what is happening to us. We must now look beyond our own denial and wishful thinking. There is currently a lull in anti activity, true, but we must stop hoping that the antis will go away, and prepare ourselves so that we can come to the assistance of our injured colleagues. We need to put forward an aggressive effort to present our case and stop suffering alone and in silence."[13]

Education, she continues, is key to increasing public awareness of the problem. To that end, in 1996 Baird-Windle and a team of sociologists began a comprehensive study of the tactics and strategies used against providers. The survey will ultimately poll every targeted clinic in North America and will serve to document what the antis call "termite tactics," the insidious acts of intentional sabotage and harassment—torment to torture—designed to impair or stop clinics from functioning.

Also essential is the exchange of ideas between clinics. Since less than one-third of the abortion providers in North America attend NCAP and NAF meetings, the Internet can serve as a mighty unifier, allowing strategic information, ideas and organizing materials to be gathered and discussed.

But information alone, however central, is just one component of what is needed to defend reproductive freedom and reclaim pro-choice turf. "The soldiers on the abortion battlefield must no longer be solely responsible for paying for the war," concludes Baird-Windle. "Providers should not have to foot the bill for obscene amounts of security, constant repairs and increased insurance premiums. We need an Abortion Services Protection Fund, money raised by the pro-choice philanthropic community, so that providers have something to draw on when major violence strikes or sustained targeting depletes us. Foundations tend to award money to groups working to keep abortion legal. This leaves the providers of abortion, the key link in the chain, to fend for themselves. It seems to me that they are putting things in the wrong order because without providers, choice is an empty right and legal abortion is meaningless."[14]

"Clinics need the gift of a rapid response team to help them heal their wounds, followed by long range help," Baird-Windle continues. "I envision 100 influential people stepping forward and pledging to learn about the violence and disseminating that information."[15]

In addition, a cadre of public lobbyists—regular folks whom Baird-Windle calls "champions"—must be developed. This group could exert considerable pressure on insurance carriers, urging them not to drop clinics as clients when adversity strikes; their existence would lift a gigantic weight off providers' shoulders and enlarge the population of people taking responsibility for what happens at women's health centers. Likewise, a consortium of pro-choice investors and funders would benefit clinics unable to secure conventional mortgages or loans for expanded services. Such donors might also consider funding a think tank exclusively geared to stopping anti-abortion violence and religiously inspired hatred; they might also provide low-interest loans or grants and recuperation awards to staff worn down by attacks.

"My vision," concludes Baird-Windle, "calls for a cadre of our own, people who will champion providers as the major agents of social change they have proven themselves to be. People, some of them women who've had life-sustaining abortions or who know women for whom abortion has been life-saving, understand the enormous contribution providers have made to society as a whole and to individual women across the United States and in Canada. Although it is true that people who come to our defense are often harassed by the antis, I am positive that the courage of those speaking out will cost them less than their fear. I also believe that religious leaders of all persuasions have a role to play. I'm not talking about small statements uttered the day after a tragedy. I believe that religious leaders must show that they do not identify with those who tacitly or explicitly support the violence. They must be clear. This is not about the morality of abortion. We can disagree about that. This is about stopping the shootings, stabbings, murders and other forms of violence. But that's not all. Years back, the media championed woman suffrage and civil rights. I challenge today's media—editors, reporters and publishers—to, first, cover the full story. I also challenge pro-choice activists and organizations to defend us. As I see it, they have been hypocritical and cowardly in failing to assert our value and worth. Finally, my major challenge goes to the Department of Justice, the FBI and state and local law enforcement agencies. Give us that to which we are entitled: equality under the law and equal protection. I urge you not to capitulate, or let others capitulate, to religious bias or a religious agenda that interferes with our rights as health providers, or with women's rights to control their own bodies and futures. I believe that a few federal cases under RICO would cause the anti-abortion movement to dry up. In concert with an Abortion Services Protection Fund and a rapid response team of concerned individuals, the antis would quickly realize the futility of violence."[16]

As many second-wave feminists remind us, abortion is fundamental to women's equality. But as long as providers are forced to deal with full-time extremists who stalk them and their children, picket their homes and the venues they frequent, periodically drop bombs on their clinics and fire shots through their windows, they will be too bogged down defending themselves to formulate solutions to the violence that plagues them.

That providers continue in their chosen field despite the targeting is testament to their powerful resolve to help women who need them. Despite fears about personal safety and the safety of loved ones, thousands of courageous people throughout the United States and Canada each day counsel women, give solace to them and their partners and abort unwanted pregnancies. Their dedication and determination mark them as heroes. It is time for the two nations that have benefited to show their gratitude.

Interviews

JULY 1998 TO MAY 2000

Kathy Spillar
Feminist Majority Foundation
Los Angeles, CA
July 20, 1998; in person

Carol Downer, Esq.
Los Angeles, CA
July 23, 1998; in person

Dr. Damon Stutes
West End Women's Medical Group
Reno, NV
July 23, 1998; in person

Eileen Schnitzer
Penny Bertsch
Shauna Heckert
Women's Health Specialists
Chico and Sacramento, CA
July 27, 28, 29, 1998; in person

Dido Hasper
Women's Health Specialists
Chico, CA
July 30, 1998; by telephone

Carye Ortman
Tim Schuck
Lovejoy SurgiCenter
Portland, OR
August 4, 1998; in person

Allene Klass
Lovejoy SurgiCenter
Portland, OR
August 4 and 10, 1998; in person

Dr. Mark Nichols
Lois Bachus
Planned Parenthood of the Columbia/Willamette
Inc.
Portland, OR
August 5, 1998; in person

Elena Hawley
Student
Portland, OR
August 6, 1998; in person

Dr. W. A. Peter Bours
Joan Moss
Bours Health Center
Portland, OR
August 6 and 10, 1998; in person

Dr. Elizabeth Newhall
Everywoman's Health Center
Portland, OR
August 11, 1998; in person

Jeanne Canon
Bours Health Center
Forest Grove, OR
August 11, 1998; by telephone

Detective Dave Famous
Criminal Investigation Unit
Portland, OR
August 12, 1998; in person

Laura Blue
All Women's Medical Center
Portland, OR
August 12, 1998; in person

Dee Larson
Margaret Voboril
Lovejoy SurgiCenter
Portland, OR
August 12, 1998; in person

Dr. Jim Newhall
Downtown Women's Medical Center
Portland, OR
August 13, 1998; in person

Tom Burghardt
Bay Area Coalition to Oppose Operation Rescue
(BACOOR)
San Francisco, CA
August 25, 1998; in person

Jude Hanzo
(formerly) All Women's Medical Center
Portland, OR
September 7, 1998; by telephone

Roy Lucas, Esq.
Melbourne, FL
September 9, 1998; in person

Lee Kirkpatrick
Lisa Sanford
Roni Windle
Aware Woman Center for Choice
Melbourne, FL
September 11, 1998; in person
Also Roni Windle: November 11, 1999; by
telephone

Ted Windle
Aware Woman Center for Choice
Melbourne, FL
September 12, 1998 and June 10 1999; in person

"Janet Williams" (pseudonym)
"Amber Russo" (pseudonym)
Aware Woman Center for Choice
Melbourne, FL
September 14, 1998; in person

"Lilia Jones" (pseudonym)
Daughter of former clinic staffer
unnamed central Florida location
September 15, 1998; in person

Alexandra Aitken
Southern Tier Women's Center
Vestal, NY
September 21, 1998; by telephone

Dr. Brian Finkel
Metro Phoenix Women's Center
Phoenix, AZ
September 21, 1998; by telephone

Gail Frances
Cygma Health Center, Kensington, MD
Annandale Women and Family Center, Alexandria,
VA
September 22, 1998; by telephone

Susan England, Esq.
Orlando, FL
September 22, 1998; by telephone

Pam O'Leary
Center for Choice II
Toledo, OH
September 23, 1998; by telephone

Jennifer Vriens
(formerly) Delaware Women's Health Organization
Wilmington, DE
September 23, 1998; by telephone

Mary Lou Greenberg
Refuse & Resist!
New York, NY
September 24, 1998, and July 9, 1999; in person

Bill Baird
Joni Scott
Pro-Choice League
Huntington, NY
September 25, 1998; in person

Carol Dunn
Center for Choice II
Toledo, OH
September 28, 1998 and September 15, 1999; by
telephone

Peg Johnston
Southern Tier Women's Center
Vestal, NY
September 28, 1998; by telephone

Allison Hile
Hope Clinic
Granite City, IL
September 29, 1998; by telephone

Susan Hill
National Women's Health Organization
Raleigh, NC
October 1 and 2, 1998; in person
September 1, 1999; in person

Lorraine Maguire
Charleston Women's Medical Clinic
Charleston, SC
October 3 and 4, 1998; in person

Shelley Maguire
Charleston, SC
October 3, 1998; in person

Dr. William Lynn
Beaufort, SC
October 5, 1998; in person

Deborah Walsh
Family Reproductive Health
Charlotte, NC
October 6 and 7, 1998; in person

Hannah Branch
Family Reproductive Health
Charlotte, NC
October 7, 1998; in person

Tina Welsh
Women's Health Center
Duluth, MN
October 13, 1998, and October 11, 1999; by
telephone

Cathy Conner
(formerly) Delaware Women's Health Organization
October 14, 1998; by telephone

Roger Evans, Esq.
Planned Parenthood Federation of America
New York, NY
October 15, 1998; in person

Pat Davis
National Women's Health Organization of Central
Florida
Orlando, FL
October 16, 1998; by telephone

Beverly Whipple
A Woman's Choice, Yakima, WA
Cedar River Clinic, Renton, WA
October 16, 1998; by telephone

Sherri Finik
Reproductive Services
Tulsa, OK
October 20, 1998; by telephone

Will Offley
Unaffiliated activist
Vancouver, British Columbia, Canada
October 21, 1998; by telephone

Suzette Caton
Hillcrest Clinic
Norfolk, VA
October 22, 1998; by telephone

Ron Fitzsimmons
Ilse Knecht
National Coalition of Abortion Providers
Alexandria, VA
October 26, 1998; in person
Also Ron Fitzsimmons: July 12, 1999, in person;
May 26, 2000, via e-mail

Catholics for a Free Choice Library staff
Washington, D.C.
October 27, 1998; in person

Marjorie Brahms Signer
Religious Coalition for Reproductive Choice
Washington, D.C.
October 27, 1998; in person

Lauren Sabina Kneisley
Mike Doughney
Biblical America Resistance Front
Burtonsville, MD
October 28, 1998; in person

Eleanor Smeal
Feminist Majority Foundation
Arlington, VA
October 30, 1998; in person

Alice Cohan
Feminist Majority Foundation
Arlington, VA
November 3, 1998; by telephone

Kim Horab
Fargo Women's Health Organization
Fargo, ND
November 4, 1998; by telephone

Ruth Arick
Clinic consultant
Unnamed city in Florida
November 5, 1998; by telephone

Sally Burgess
Hope Clinic
Granite City, IL
November 6, 1998; by telephone

Marion Ornstein
Women's Health Organization of Central Florida
Orlando, FL
November 9, 1998; by telephone

"Katrina Douglas" (pseudonym)
Clinic for Women
Indianapolis, IN
November 9, 1998; by telephone

"Joan Linwood" (pseudonym)
Women's Clinic
Fort Lauderdale, FL
November 10, 1998; by telephone

"Carlyne Smith" (pseudonym)
unnamed south Florida clinic
November 10, 1998; by telephone

Marilyn Chrisman Eldridge
Nova Health Systems
San Antonio, TX
November 10, 1998, and
October 25, 1999; by telephone

Shelley Oram
Charlotte Taft
IMAGINE
Glorieta, NM
November 11, 1998; by telephone

Phyllis Chesler, Ph.D.
Psychologist and author
Brooklyn, NY
November 11, 1998; in person

Tammy Sobieski
Women's Health Centers
Daytona and Orlando, FL
November 13, 1998; by telephone

Jeannie Baron
Claire Keyes
Kathy Lynds
Nancy Gallagher
Allegheny Reproductive Health Center
Pittsburgh, PA
Baron and Keyes: November 16, 1998; in person
Lynds and Gallagher: November 17, 1998; in person

Mary Ellen Tunney
Dr. Tom Allen
Patty Madden
Sandie Matthews
Women's Health Services
Pittsburgh, PA
November 18, 1998; in person

Rachel Atkins
Vermont Women's Health Center
Burlington, VT
November 23, 1998; by telephone

Diane Straus
(formerly) Cherry Hill Women's Health
Organization
Cherry Hill, NJ
November 23, 1998; by telephone

Bob Rowell
South Jersey Clinic Defense Coalition
Cherry Hill, NJ
November 27, 1998; by telephone

Nicki Nichols Gamble
Alice Verhoeven
Planned Parenthood League of Massachusetts
Boston, MA
Nichols Gamble: November 30, 1998; in person
Verhoeven: November 30 and December 1, 1998; in
person

Dr. Mitchell Creinin
The University of Pittsburgh Medical School
Pittsburgh, PA
December 4, 1998; by telephone

Ann Baker
National Center for the Pro Choice Majority
Hightstown, NJ
December 7, 1998, and
October 11, 1999; in person

Renee Chelian
Northland Family Planning Centers
Clinton Township, MI
Southfield, MI
Westland, MI
December 8 and 9, 1998; by telephone

Ann Garzia
Atlanta Women's Medical Center
Atlanta, GA
December 8, 1998; by telephone

Anita Kuennen
Blue Mountain Clinic
Missoula, MT
December 9, 1998; by telephone

Raquel Sims
Ft. Wayne Women's Health Organization
Ft. Wayne, IN
December 9, 1998; by telephone

Carolyn Izard
Little Rock Family Planning Service
Little Rock, AK
December 9, 1998; by telephone

Diane Pogrant
Summit Women's Health Organization
Milwaukee, WI
December 11, 1998; by telephone

Sharon Lau
National Abortion Federation
Washington, D.C.
December 14, 1998; in person

Carla Eckhardt
National Abortion Federation
Washington, D.C.
December 15, 1998; in person

Rev. Susan Beem-Beery
Dr. John Beery
Alexandria, VA
December 16, 1998; in person
Also John Beery: November 12, 1999; by telephone

Rabbi Bonnie Margulis
Religious Coalition for Reproductive Choice
Washington, D.C.
December 17, 1998; in person

Dr. "James Schwartz" (pseudonym)
Owner of an unnamed New Jersey clinic
December 21, 1998; by telephone

Rachel Strauber
Planned Parenthood Federation of America
New York, NY
December 23, 1998; in person

Margaret Alvis Gifford
Alternatives of Tampa
Tampa, FL
December 28, 1998; by telephone

Rabbi Balfour Brickner
Stephen Wise Free Synagogue
New York, NY
December 28, 1998; by telephone

"Lena Rabinski" (pseudonym)
Unnamed clinic in central Florida
December 28, 1998; by telephone

"Susannah Davis" (pseudonym)
All Women's Health Center
St. Petersburg, FL
December 28, 1998; by telephone

Daniel McGuire
Religious Consultation on Population, Reproductive
Health and Ethics
Milwaukee, WI
December 28, 1998; by telephone

Ann Rose
Ann Rose & Associates
Abortion Clinics Online
Atlanta, GA
December 29, 1998; by telephone

Marilyn Cohen
Emma Goldman Clinic
Iowa City, IA
December 29, 1998; by telephone

The Reverend Bruce Buchanan
Carol Adams
First Presbyterian Church
Dallas, TX
December 29, 1998; by telephone

Barbara Doane
Sarasota Woman's Health Center
Sarasota, FL
December 31, 1998; by telephone

"Elena Schweitzer" (pseudonym)
Cathy McGuire
Buffalo United for Choice
Buffalo, NY
January 4, 1999; in person

Helen Dalley
Pro-Choice Network of Western New York
Tonawanda, NY
January 5, 1999; in person

Marilynn Buckham
Buffalo GYN Womenservices
Buffalo, NY
January 5, 1999; in person

The Reverend David Selzer
Religious Coalition for Reproductive Choice
Church of the Good Shepherd
Buffalo, NY
January 6, 1999; in person

Susan Ward
Buffalo GYN Womenservices
Buffalo, NY
January 6, 1999; in person

Ellie Dorritie
Worker's World Party/Buffalo United for Choice
Buffalo, NY
January 7, 1999; in person

Glenn A. Murray, Esq.
Attorney, Buffalo United for Choice
Buffalo, NY
January 7, 1999; by telephone

The Reverend Tom Davis
Vero Beach, FL
January 11, 1999; by telephone

The Reverend Stephen Mather
First Presbyterian Church of Anaheim
Anaheim, CA
January 11, 1999; by telephone

The Reverend Walter Carlson
United Methodist Church
Pana, IL
January 11, 1999; by telephone

Nancy Boothe
Feminist Women's Health Center
Atlanta, GA
January 12, 1999; by telephone

Dr. Henry Morgentaler
Morgentaler Clinics
Toronto, Ontario, Canada
January 13, 1999; by telephone

Jeanne Singletary
Sandy Sheldon
Pensacola Medical Services
Pensacola, FL
January 15, 1999; in person

Linda Taggart
Community Healthcare Center
Pensacola, FL
January 15 and 16, 1999; in person

Bill Caplinger
Clinic Defender
Pensacola, FL
January 16, 1999; in person

Dallas Blanchard
University of Western Florida
Pensacola, FL
January 17, 1999; in person

Michelle Farley
(formerly) New Woman All Women Health Care
Birmingham, AL
January 19 and 23, 1999; in person

Emily Lyons, R.N.
(Formerly) New Woman All Women Health Care
Birmingham, AL
January 19, 1999; in person

Lisa Hermes
Summit Medical Center
Birmingham, AL
January 20, 1999; in person

Michele Wilson
University of Alabama
Birmingham, AL
January 20, 1999; in person

Gloria Gray
Dr. Louis Payne
West Alabama Women's Center
Tuscaloosa, AL
January 22, 1999; in person

Patricia Mitchell
Ginger Highfill
Center for Choice
Mobile, AL
January 25, 1999; in person

Hallie Joyce
Religious Coalition for Reproductive Choice
Pensacola, FL
January 26, 1999; in person

Keri Taggart
Community Healthcare Center
Pensacola, FL
January 26, 1999; in person

Jeri Rasmussen
Midwest Health Center for Women
Minneapolis, MN
February 1, 1999; by telephone

The Reverend Don Smith
The Reverend Carl Horton
Westminster Presbyterian Church
Lincoln, NE
February 1, 1999; by telephone

Dr. LeRoy (Lee) Carhart
Abortion and Contraception Clinic of Nebraska
Bellevue, NE
February 1 and October 13, 1999;
by telephone

The Reverend Linda Morgan Clark
Oklahoma affiliate,
Religious Coalition for Reproductive Choice
Tulsa, OK
February 2, 1999; by telephone

Dr. Susan Wicklund
Fargo Women's Health Organization and
(formerly) Mountain Country Women's Clinic
Fargo, ND and (formerly) Bozeman, MT
February 3, 1999; by telephone

Mary Kelly McColl
Planned Parenthood of Idaho
Boise, ID
February 3, 1999; by telephone

Amy Hagstrom Miller
Westside Women's Medical Pavilion
New York, NY
February 4, 1999; in person

Sonja Mitchell
student at an unnamed New England college
February 5, 1999; by telephone

John Nugent
Planned Parenthood of Spokane and Whitman
Counties
Spokane, WA
February 9, 1999; by telephone

Bill Morlin
Spokesman Review
Spokane, WA
February 9, 1999; by telephone

Tod Windle
(formerly) Aware Woman Center for Choice
West Palm Beach, FL
February 9, 1999; by telephone

Jennifer Boulanger
Allentown Women's Center
Allentown, PA
February 11, 1999; by telephone

The Reverend Howard Moody
Judson Memorial Church
New York, NY
February 12, 1999; by telephone

The Reverend George Gardner
College Hill United Methodist Church
Wichita, KS
February 15, 1999; in person

Julie Sheppard
Dena Vogler
Dr. George Tiller
Women's Health Care Services
Wichita, KS
February 15, 1999; in person

Linda Diamond-Stoner
Fran Belden
Cathy Reavis
Women's Health Care Services
Wichita, KS
February 16, 1999; in person

Peggy (Jarman) Bowman
Olympia, WA
(formerly) Women's Health Care Services
Wichita, KS
February 16, 1999; by telephone

Dr. Glenna Halvorson-Boyd
Fairmount Center/Dallas
Office of Curtis Boyd, MD/PC
Albuquerque, NM
February 18, 1999; by telephone

Lisa Gerard
Fairmount Center
Dallas, TX
February 19, 1999; by telephone

Judy Reiner
(formerly) Planned Parenthood of Houston and
Southeast Texas
Houston, TX
February 19, 1999 and September 16, 1999; by
telephone

Dr. James Armstrong
Kalispell, MT
February 22, 1999; by telephone

Roberta Geidner Antoniotti
Planned Parenthood of Maryland
Baltimore, MD
February 24, 1999; by telephone

Lynne Randall
(formerly) Feminist Women's Health Center
Atlanta, GA
March 4, 1999; by telephone

Susan E. Davis
(formerly) Committee for Abortion Rights and
Against Sterilization Abuse
New York, NY
June 22, 1999; by telephone

"Natalie Collins" (pseudonym)
(formerly) staffed an unnamed Texas clinic
Brooklyn, New York
July 6, 1999; in person

Sara Love, Esq.
Feminist Majority Foundation
Arlington, VA
July 13, 1999; in person

Jim Sedlak
American Life League
Stafford, VA
July 14, 1999; by telephone

Susan Nenney
Planned Parenthood of Houston and Southeast
Texas
Houston, TX
September 15, 1999; by telephone

Frances Kissling
Catholics for a Free Choice
Washington, D.C.
September 28, 1999; in person

Gerri Laster
Reproductive Services
El Paso, TX
October 25, 1999; by telephone

Anne Bower
(formerly) *The Body Politic*
Binghamton, NY
November 14, 1999; by telephone

Gina Shaw
Washington, D.C.
November 22, 1999; by telephone

The Reverend Andrew McDonald
Westminster Presbyterian Church
Lincoln, NE
May 22, 2000; by telephone

Linda Turley, Esq.
Law Offices of Turley and Stutz
Dallas, TX
May 22, 2000; by telephone

Cities Experiencing Blockades: 1988–1993[*]

ALABAMA
Birmingham
Huntsville
Mobile
Montgomery

ALASKA
Anchorage

ARIZONA
Phoenix
Tucson

CALIFORNIA
Chico
Concord
Cypress
Daly City
Fairfax
Fremont
Fresno
Hayward
Long Beach
Los Angeles
Los Gatos
Monterey
Oakland
Redding
Redwood City
Rosemead
Sacramento
San Bernadino
San Diego
San Francisco
San Jose
San Marcos
San Rafael
Santa Ana
Santa Cruz
Santa Rosa
Sunnyvale
Tustin
Ventura
Walnut Creek

COLORADO
Aurora
Boulder
Colorado Springs
Denver

CONNECTICUT
Bridgeport

---

* Information courtesy of the National Center for the Pro Choice Majority.
The years 1988 to 1993 represent the period in which blockades were the tactic of choice for most militant anti-abortion activists. Once President Clinton signed the FACE Act in May 1994, making it a crime to "injure, intimidate, or interfere with providers of reproductive health services or their patients," the tactic became less popular.

Danbury
Hartford
Stamford
West Hartford

DELAWARE
Dover
Wilmington

DISTRICT OF COLUMBIA

FLORIDA
Boca Raton
Coral Springs
Fort Lauderdale
Fort Myers
Jacksonville
Lakeland
Mary Esther
Melbourne
Miami
Oakland Park
Orlando
Pensacola
Pompano Beach
Port St. Lucie
Sarasota
St. Petersburg
Tallahassee
Tampa
Venice
West Palm Beach

GEORGIA
Atlanta
Chamblee

IDAHO
Boise
Coeur d'Alene

ILLINOIS
Aurora
Champaign
Chicago
Elgin
Granite City
Lake Forest
Lincolnwood
Peoria
Rockford
Westmont

INDIANA
Fort Wayne
Indianapolis
Merrillville
South Bend

IOWA
Des Moines
Iowa City

KANSAS
Kansas City
Lawrence
Overland Park
Shawnee
Topeka
Wichita

KENTUCKY
Lexington
Louisville

LOUISIANA
Baton Rouge
Metaire
New Orleans
Shreveport

MARYLAND
Annapolis
Baltimore
College Park
Glen Burnie
Kensington
Pasadena
Suitland

MASSACHUSETTS
Boston
Brighton
Brookline
Hyannis
New Bedford
Springfield
Worcester

MICHIGAN
Ann Arbor
Detroit
Farmington Hills
Flint
Grand Rapids
Kalamazoo
Lansing

Lathrop Village
Livonia
Niles
Oak Park
Pittsfield
Sterling Heights
Ypsilanti

MINNESOTA

Duluth
Minneapolis
St. Paul

MISSISSIPPI

Jackson

MISSOURI

Columbia
Kansas City
Springfield
St. Louis

MONTANA

Billings
Helena
Missoula

NEBRASKA

Lincoln
Omaha

NEVADA

Las Vegas
Reno

NEW HAMPSHIRE

Concord
Portsmouth

NEW JERSEY

Atlantic City
Bordentown
Cherry Hill
Englewood
Howell
Irvington
Montclair
Morristown
Shrewsbury
Trenton/Hamilton Township
Willingboro
Woodbridge

NEW MEXICO

Albuquerque
Santa Fe

NEW YORK

Albany
Amherst
Binghamton
Blooming Grove
Buffalo
Coram
Deer Park
Dobbs Ferry
Greenburgh
Hicksville
Levittown
Lindenhurst
Malone
Monsey
New York City—four boroughs
Rochester
Schenectady
Syracuse
Utica
White Plains

NORTH CAROLINA

Asheville
Chapel Hill
Charlotte
Greensboro
Raleigh
Wake Forest

NORTH DAKOTA

Fargo

OHIO

Akron
Cincinnati
Cleveland
Columbus
Dayton
Toledo
Youngstown

OKLAHOMA

Oklahoma City

OREGON

Ashland
Forest Grove
Portland

PENNSYLVANIA
Allentown
Chester
Harrisburg
Paoli
Philadelphia
Pittsburgh
Reading
Yardley
York

RHODE ISLAND
Cranston
Providence

SOUTH CAROLINA
Charleston
Columbia
Greenville

SOUTH DAKOTA
Sioux Falls

TENNESSEE
Bristol
Chattanooga
Knoxville
Nashville

TEXAS
Austin
Corpus Christi
Dallas
Houston

Lufkin
San Antonio

VERMONT
Burlington
Rutland

VIRGINIA
Alexandria
Charlottesville
Falls Church
Lynchburg
Manasses
Norfolk
Richmond
Roanoke
Virginia Beach

WASHINGTON
Bellevue
Renton
Seattle
Spokane
Tacoma
Yakima

WEST VIRGINIA
Charleston

WISCONSIN
Appleton
Madison
Milwaukee

NOTE: Five states experienced no blockades or "rescues" during the specified period: Arkansas, Hawaii, Maine, Utah and Wyoming.

Pro-Choice Organizations in the United States and Canada

U.S. REPRODUCTIVE HEALTH ADVOCATES

American Association of University Women
1111 16th Street NW
Washington, D.C. 20036
202-785-7793
info@aauw.org
www.aauw.org

American Civil Liberties Union
Reproductive Freedom Project
125 Broad Street, 18th floor
New York, NY 10004
212-549-2633
rfp@aclu.org
www.aclu.org

Americans for Religious Liberty
P.O. Box 6656
Silver Spring, MD 20916
301-598-2447
arlinc@erols.com

Americans United
518 C Street NE
Washington, D.C. 20002
202-466-3234
americansunited@au.org
www.au.org

Catholics for a Free Choice
1436 U Street NW, Suite 301
Washington, D.C. 20009
202-986-6093
cffc@igc.org
www.cath4choice.org

Center for Constitutional Rights
666 Broadway, 7th floor
New York, NY 10012
212-614-6464
ccr@igc.apc.org

Center for Democratic Renewal
P.O. Box 50469
Atlanta, GA 30302
404-221-0025
cdr@igc.apc.org

Center for Reproductive Law and Policy
120 Wall Street
New York, NY 10005
212-514-5534
info@crlp.org
www.crlp.org

Civil Liberties and Public Policy Program
Hampshire College
Amherst, MA 01002-5001
413-559-5645
clpp@hamp.hampshire.edu
hamp.hampshire.edu/~clpp

Emily's List
805 15th Street NW, Suite 400
Washington, D.C. 20005
202-326-1400
www.emilyslist.org

Feminist Majority Foundation
1600 Wilson Blvd., Suite 801
Arlington, VA 22209
703-522-2214
femmaj@feminist.org
www.feminist.org

Alan Guttmacher Institute
120 Wall Street
New York, NY 10005
212-248-1111
info@agi-usa.org
www.agi-usa.org

Alan Guttmacher Institute
1120 Connecticut Avenue NW, Suite 460
Washington, D.C. 20036
202-296-4012
policyinfo@.agi-usa.org
www.agi-usa.org

Human Rights Campaign Fund
919 18th Street NW, Suite 800
Washington, D.C. 20006
202-628-4160
hrc@hrc.org
www.hrc.org

Institute for First Amendment Studies
P.O. Box 589
Great Barrington, MA 01230
413-274-0012
ifas@berkshire.net
www.ifas.org

International Planned Parenthood Federation
120 Wall Street, 9th Floor
New York, NY 10005
212-248-6400
info@ippfwhr.org
www.ippf.org

Lambda Legal Defense and Education Fund
120 Wall Street, Suite 1500
New York, NY 10005
212-809-8585
lambda@lambdalegal.org
www.lambdalegal.org

Medical Students for Choice
2041 Bancroft Way, Suite 201
Berkeley, CA 94704
510-540-1195
msfc@ms4c.org
www.ms4c.org

National Abortion and Reproductive Rights
Action League
1156 15th Street NW, Suite 700
Washington, D.C. 20005
202-973-3000
naral@naral.org
www.naral.org/home.html

National Abortion Federation
1755 Massachusetts Avenue NW, Suite 600
Washington, D.C. 20036
202-667-5881
naf@prochoice.org
www.prochoice.org

National Association of Nurse Practitioners in
Women's Health
503 Capitol Court NE, Suite 300
Washington, D.C. 20002
202-543-9693
npwhdc@aol.com
www.npwh.org

National Center for the Pro Choice Majority
P.O. Box 1315
Hightstown, NJ 08520
609-443-8780
www.prochoicemajority.org

National Coalition of Abortion Providers
206 King Street
Alexandria, VA 22314
703-684-0055
www.ncap.com

National Network of Abortion Funds
c/o CLPP
Hampshire College
Amherst, MA 01002-5001
413-559-5645
clpp@hamp.hampshire.edu
hamp.hampshire.edu/~clpp/nnaf

National Organization for Women
733 15th Street NW, Second Floor
Washington, D.C. 20005
202-331-0066
now@now.org
www.now.org

NOW Legal Defense and Education Fund
395 Hudson Street
New York, NY 10014
212-925-6635
www.nowldef.org

People for the American Way
2000 M Street NW
Washington, D.C. 20036
202-467-4999
pfaw@pfaw.org
www.pfaw.org

Physicians for Reproductive Choice and Health
1780 Broadway, 10th Floor
New York, NY 10019
212-765-2322
PRCH@aol.com
www.PRCH.org

Planned Parenthood Federation of America
810 Seventh Avenue
New York, NY 10019
212-541-7800
communications@ppfa.org
www.plannedparenthood.org

Political Research Associates
1310 Broadway, Suite 201
Somerville, MA 02144
617-666-5300
publiceye@igc.apc.org
www.publiceye.org/pra

Pro Choice League
P.O. Box 324
Huntington, NY 11743
516-673-6871
bbaird322@aol.com

Pro Choice Resource Center
16 Willett Avenue
Port Chester, NY 10573-4326
914-690-0938
914-934-0148
info@prochoiceresource.org
www.prochoiceresource.org

Refuse & Resist!
305 Madison Avenue, Suite 1166
New York, NY 10165
212-385-9303
refuse@calyx.com
www.calyx.com/~refuse

Religious Coalition for Reproductive Choice
1025 Vermont Avenue, Suite 1130
Washington, D.C. 20005
202-628-7700
info@rcrc.org
www.rcrc.org

Voters for Choice Education Fund
1010 Wisconsin Avenue, Suite 410
Washington, D.C. 20007
202-944-5080
vfc@ibm.net
www.voters4choice.org

Women's Campaign Fund
734 15th Street NW, Suite 500
Washington, D.C. 20008
202-393-8164
womenscampaignfund@erols.com
www.wcfonline.org

Zero Population Growth
1400 16th Street NW, Suite 320
Washington, D.C. 20036
202-332-2200
info@zpg.org
www.zpg.org

CANADIAN REPRODUCTIVE HEALTH ADVOCATES

Canadian Abortion Rights Action League
Association Canadienne Pour Le Droit A L'avorte-
ment (ACDA)
1 Nicholas Street, Suite 726
Ottawa, Ontario K1N 7B7
613-789-9956 (call for information about organizing
in other provinces)
caral@caral.ca
www.caral.ca

Childbirth by Choice Trust
344 Bloor Street West, Suite 502
Toronto, Ontario M5S 3A7
416-961-7812

Planned Parenthood Federation of Canada
1 Nicholas Street, Suite 430
Ottawa, Ontario K1N 7B7
613-241-4474
admin@ppfa.ca
www.ppfc.ca

Abortion in the United States and Canada

A Time Line of Major Events

1966

Formation of the National Right to Life Committee by the United States Catholic Conference's Family Life Bureau.

1967

April 6: Activist Bill Baird is arrested for "indecent exposure of obscene objects" at Boston University. The charges stemmed from a talk during which Baird handed a can of contraceptive foam to a nineteen-year-old student.

1969

September: The California Supreme Court ruled that the state law banning abortion was unconstitutional; the shift mandated that all abortions be performed in a hospital.

1970

March 1: New York state legalized abortions performed by licensed medical doctors before the twenty-fourth week of pregnancy. The surgery did not have to be performed in a hospital.

1972

March 22: The Supreme Court decided *Baird v. Eisenstadt*, a case stemming from Bill Baird's 1967 arrest in Boston. The decision made it legal to sell contraceptives to unmarried people.

1973

January 22: The Supreme Court decided *Roe v. Wade*, finding that state laws which made abortion illegal violated the due process clause of the Fourteenth Amendment. Decision making about first-trimester abortions was left to a woman and her doctor; states were allowed to restrict abortions performed in subsequent months to those needed to protect women's health.

1975

Summer: Six women were arrested in Rockville, Maryland, at the first anti-abortion sit-in in U.S. history.

1976

July 1: By a vote of 6 to 3, the Supreme Court invalidated provisions of a Missouri statute that: required a married woman to obtain the consent of her husband before having an abortion; required a doctor to preserve the life and health of a fetus at every stage of a pregnancy; and prohibited the use of saline amniocentesis as a method of abortion. By a 5 to 4 vote, the Court invalidated a state requirement that an unmarried minor get the written consent of one parent before having an abortion. The *Planned Parenthood v. Danforth* decision upheld a requirement that all women sign a written consent form before abortion surgery. In addition, the Justices upheld a statistical reporting requirement for clinics.

September: The Hyde Amendment, cutting off Medicaid funding for the abortions of most poor women, passed Congress.

1977

February 18: A flammable liquid was thrown into a receptionists face at the Concerned Women's Clinic in Cleveland, Ohio. The assailant also set fire to the clinic's interior.

June 20: The Supreme Court, in *Poelker v. Doe,* upheld the refusal of a public hospital to provide publicly funded abortions for women in non life–threatening situations.

October 3: Rosaura Jimenez, a twenty-seven-year-old single mother, died following an illegal abortion. Jimenez was a Medicaid recipient who resorted to a back-alley procedure because her medical insurance would not pay for the surgery.

1979

January 9: By a vote of 6 to 3, the Supreme Court invalidated as unconstitutionally vague a Pennsylvania statute that required doctors, under threat of criminal penalties, to use the method and "degree of care" most likely to preserve the life and health of a fetus if the physician had "sufficient reason to believe a fetus was viable," that is, able to live outside the womb. The case was called *Colautti v. Franklin.* In a second 1979 case, *Bellotti v. Baird,* the Court invalidated a Massachusetts law that required a minor to get the consent of both parents before obtaining an abortion. The Bellotti decision was issued on July 2.

February 15: Peter Burkin, a twenty-one-year-old abortion foe, stormed into a non-profit clinic owned by Bill Baird with a flaming two-foot torch and threatened "to cleanse Bill Baird's soul by fire."

Judie and Paul Brown formed the American Life League.

1980

June 30: By a 5 to 4 vote, the Supreme Court upheld the Hyde Amendment, a law that since 1976 has prohibited the use of federal funds for abortion surgery unless the procedure is needed to preserve the life of the pregnant woman. The amendment has since been expanded so that Medicaid now covers the cost of abortions for women whose pregnancies are the result of rape or incest.

Joseph Scheidler formed the Pro-Life Action League, a national group.

1982

January 23: The Hope Clinic for Women in Granite City, Illinois, was gutted by fire.

May: Two Florida clinics, the St. Petersburg Women's Health Center and the Sarasota Women's Health Center, were set on fire by Don Benny Anderson.

August 12: Abortion provider Dr. Hector Zevallos and his wife, Rosalee Jean, owners of the Hope Clinic for Women in Granite City, Illinois, were kidnapped by the Army of God and held in an abandoned ammunition bunker for eight days.

1983

May 26: Joseph Grace set fire to the Hillcrest Clinic in Norfolk, Virginia.

June 15: In *City of Akron v. Akron Center for Reproductive Health,* the Supreme Court invalidated a city ordinance that: required physicians to give anti-abortion information—including the "fact" that the unborn child is a human life from the moment of conception—to patients; required a twenty-four-hour waiting period following these lectures; mandated that all second- and third-trimester abortions be performed in a hospital; required minors to get parental consent before abortion surgery; and required physicians to dispose of fetal remains in an unspecified "humane and sanitary manner." A second case, *Planned Parenthood Association of Kansas City v. Ashcroft,* invalidated a similar Missouri law.

1984

American Portrait Films released *The Silent Scream.*

June 25: The Ladies Center in Pensacola, Florida, was firebombed for the first time.

October 7: The Catholic Statement on Pluralism and Abortion was published in the *New York Times*.

November: A 225-pound canister bomb destroyed a Wheaton, Maryland, clinic.

December: FBI director William Webster announced that abortion clinic bombings did not conform to the FBI definition of terrorism.

December 25: The Ladies Center in Pensacola, Florida, and the private offices of two abortion doctors, were firebombed.

1985

January 1: Washington, D.C.'s Hillcrest Women's SurgiCenter was bombed.

Joseph Scheidler's book, *99 Ways to Stop Abortion*, was published.

1986

Winter: Mail carriers intercepted four letter bombs en route to three abortion clinics in Portland, Oregon.

June: The National Women's Health Organization filed suit against Joseph Scheidler and several of his associates for conspiring and racketeering against NWHO clinics across the United States.

Fall: Evangelical Christian Randall Terry founded Operation Rescue.

Fall: Boulder, Colorado, passed the first citywide "buffer zone ordinance" to separate anti-abortion protestors from patients at local clinics.

1987

November: Randall Terry organized test-run "rescues" in Cherry Hill, New Jersey, and Philadelphia, Pennsylvania.

1988

January 28: The Canadian Supreme Court struck down that country's abortion laws as an infringement on a woman's "right to life, liberty and security of the person."

February 2: The U.S. Department of Health and Human Services promulgated regulations prohibiting federally funded health and family planning clinics from doing abortion counseling or making referrals to providers.

May: Operation Rescue organized its first large-scale "rescue" in New York City; 1,600 people were arrested.

July 18–22: Operation Rescue converged on Atlanta, Georgia, during the Democratic National Convention; 1,235 protestors were arrested.

1989

Anti-abortion violence and disruptions for the year:

bombings/arson and attempted bombing and arson:	9
invasions, assault and battery, vandalism, death threats, stalking and burglary:	66
hate mail, harassing phone calls and bomb threats:	51
arrests at blockades:	12,358
number of blockades:	201
incidents of picketing:	72

1990

Anti-abortion violence and disruptions for the year:

bombings and arsons, or bombing/arson attempts:	11
invasions, assault and battery, vandalism, death threats, stalking and burglary:	60
hate mail, harassing phone calls and bomb threats:	32
arrests at blockades:	1,363
number of blockades:	34
incidents of picketing:	45

June: Rachel Vargas, an eight-year employee of Reproductive Services in Corpus Christi, Texas, was excommunicated from the Catholic church because of her work.

July: Elva Bustamante, director of the New Women's Clinic in Corpus Christi, Texas, was excommunicated by the Catholic church.

September: Former Detroit gang member Matt Trewhella founded Missionaries to the Pre-Born.

1991

Anti-abortion violence and disruptions for the year:

murder or attempted murder:	2
bombings, arsons and attempted bombings and arsons:	9

invasions, assault and battery, vandalism,
death threats, burglary and stalking: 83
hate mail, harassing phone calls and
bomb threats: 157
arrests at blockades: 3,885
number of blockades: 41
incidents of picketing: 292

February: Lovejoy SurgiCenter in Portland, Oregon, won an $8.2 million judgment against anti-abortion activists. To date, virtually nothing has been collected.

July: Operation Rescue launched a seven-week "Summer of Mercy" in Wichita, Kansas; 1,734 people were arrested over the course of the summer.

1992
Anti-abortion violence and disruptions for the year:
bombings, arsons and attempted bombings
and arsons: 19
invasions, assault and battery, vandalism,
death threats, burglary and stalking: 164
hate mail, harassing phone calls and
bomb threats: 481
arrests at blockades: 2,580
number of blockades: 83
incidents of picketing: 2,898

Law enforcers discovered *The Army of God Manual,* a how-to guide for violent anti-abortion activity.

Mark Crutcher, a Texas marketing consultant, formed Life Dynamics, Inc., to offer hands-on instruction in initiating malpractice lawsuits against abortion providers.

April 21–May 2: Operation Rescue organized the "Spring of Life" in Buffalo, New York.

June 29: By a vote of 7 to 2, the Supreme Court upheld provisions of a Pennsylvania law that: required a doctor to provide patients with anti-abortion materials, including pictures of fetuses at various developmental stages; imposed a twenty-four-hour waiting period following these lectures; imposed one-parent consent—or judicial bypass—for all minors seeking abortions; and mandated a plethora of reporting requirements.

August: Houston-area clinics initiated a lawsuit claiming that anti-abortion activists engaged in tortious interference with their right to do business. The

lawsuit was filed immediately before that year's Republican National Convention; area clinics won the case and were awarded $1.1 million in damages. Despite the court victory, only a few thousand dollars was ever collected.

Fall: Operation Rescue distributed 140,000 anti-Clinton brochures to voters.

1993
Anti-abortion violence and disruptions for the year:
murders or attempted murders: 2
bombings, arsons or attempted bombings
or arsons: 13
invasions, assault and battery, vandalism,
death threats, burglary and stalking: 415
hate mail, harassing phone calls, and
bomb threats: 650
arrests at blockades: 1,236
number of blockades: 66
incidents of picketing: 2,279

Life Dynamics mailed an anti-abortion "comic book" to 30,000 medical students, leading to the formation of Medical Students for Choice.

January 10: The IMPACT Team arrived in Melbourne, Florida, for a four-month campaign against the Aware Woman Center for Choice and other central Florida clinics.

March: *The Brockhoeft Report,* written by incarcerated clinic bomber John Brockhoeft, published its inaugural issue.

March 10: Abortion provider Dr. David Gunn was assassinated in Pensacola, Florida, by anti-abortion zealot Michael Griffin.

March 23: The Freedom of Access to Clinic Entrances Act (FACE) was introduced into the United States Senate.

July: Operation Rescue sponsored "Cities of Refuge" protests in ten cities across the United States.

July: Anti-abortion activist Paul Hill released a statement declaring support for violence as a tactic to end abortion. The statement was signed by dozens of "pro-life" leaders.

August 19: Dr. George Tiller, owner of Women's Health Care Services in Wichita, Kansas, was shot in both arms by Oregon anti-abortion activist Rachelle

"Shelley" Shannon. His injuries were not life threatening.

August 21: Dr. George Wayne Patterson, owner of Pensacola Medical Services and an abortion provider, was shot to death in Mobile, Alabama. Although the pro-choice community remains skeptical, his death was categorized as a bungled robbery by law enforcement.

1994

Anti-abortion violence and disruptions for the year:

murders or attempted murders:	12
bombings, arsons or attempted bombings or arsons:	12
invasions, assault and battery, vandalism, death threats, burglary and stalking:	135
hate mail, harassing phone calls and bomb threats:	395
arrests at blockades:	217
number of blockades:	25
incidents of picketing:	1,407

February: The FBI announced that it would investigate death threats received by abortion providers in Florida, Indiana, Kansas and Wisconsin.

Spring: The Department of Justice gave United States Marshals protection to clinics in eleven cities across the country in the aftermath of Dr. Gunn's murder and the wounding of Dr. George Tiller.

May 26: President Bill Clinton signed the Freedom of Access to Clinic Entrances Act (FACE) into law. The Act makes it a crime to use force of the threat of force to "injure, intimidate, or interfere with providers of reproductive health services or their patients."

June 30: In *Madsen v. Women's Health Center,* the Supreme Court upheld provisions of a Florida injunction that created a thirty-six-foot buffer zone outside the entrance of a reproductive health clinic and that prohibited protestors from making noise that could be heard by patients inside the facility.

July: Operation Rescue members traveled to Little Rock, Arkansas, for the "Summer of Justice." Smaller than earlier national events, the three-day protest resulted in twenty-six arrests.

July 29: Anti-abortion fanatic Paul Hill shot and killed Dr. John Bayard Britton and his escort, Colonel James Barrett, in Pensacola, Florida. Hill also wounded Barrett's wife, Jane.

August: Former roofer Andrew Burnett formed the American Coalition of Life Activists.

September: Convicted clinic firebomber the Reverend Michael Bray published *A Time to Kill,* a scholarly defense of violence against abortion providers.

October: The Ku Klux Klan picketed the Pensacola, Florida, clinic where Dr. Britton and Col. Barrett were shot to protest the presence of United States Marshals.

November 7: Ninety clinic owners and employees met with the Department of Justice for their first—and to date only—meeting with that agency.

November 8: Dr. Garson Romalis of Vancouver, Canada, was shot in both legs by a sniper hiding behind his house.

December 30: Two clinic receptionists, Shannon Lowney and Leeann Nichols, were shot to death in Brookline, Massachusetts, by John Salvi III.

1995

Anti-abortion violence and disruptions for the year:

murders or attempted murder at clinics:	1
bombing, arsons and attempted bombings and arsons:	15
invasions, assault and battery, vandalism, death threats, burglary and stalking:	142
hate mail, harassing phone calls, and bomb threats:	296
arrests at blockades:	54
number of blockades:	5
incidents of picketing:	1,356

January 21: The American Coalition of Life Activists released the "Deadly Dozen" list at a press conference in Portland, Oregon. The poster listed twelve providers dubbed "Guilty of Crimes Against Humanity" and offered a $5,000 reward for "information leading to the arrest, conviction, and revocation of license to practice medicine" for those named.

Spring: The American Coalition of Life Activists kicked off its Stigmatize, Harangue, Agitate, Mortify and Expose—SHAME—Campaign in Portland, Oregon.

November 11: Canadian abortion provider Dr. Hugh Short was left permanently disabled by a sniper who fired into his home while he was watching television. The bullet shattered his right elbow.

1996

Anti-abortion violence and disruptions for the year:

murders and attempted murders: 1

bombings and arsons and attempted
bombings and arsons: 5

invasions, assault and battery, vandalism,
death threats, burglary and stalking: 101

hate mail, harassing phone calls and
bomb threats: 618

arrests at blockades: 65

number of blockades: 7

incidents of picketing: 3,932

January: The Reverend Michael Bray organized the first—now annual—White Rose banquet to honor anti-abortion zealots including John Brockhoeft, Shelley Shannon, Paul Hill and Michael Griffin.

1997

Anti-abortion violence and disruptions for the year:

murder and attempted murders: 1

bombings, arsons and attempted bombings
and arsons: 13

invasion, assault and battery, vandalism,
death threats, burglary and stalking: 150

hate mail, harassing calls, and
bomb threats: 2,059

arrests at blockades: 29

number of blockades: 25

incidents of picketing: 7,827

January: The Nuremberg Files, a Website asking readers to "visualize abortionists on trial" for their "crimes against humanity" was posted on the World Wide Web for the first time. More than 200 individual clinic workers were named on the Files.

November: Canadian provider Dr. Jack Fainman was wounded by a sniper while watching television in his home. A second, never-identified doctor in Rochester, New York, was also shot.

1998

Anti-abortion violence and disruptions for the year:

murders and attempted murder: 3

bombings/arson and attempted bombing
and arson: 9

invasions, assault and battery, vandalism,
death threats, stalking and burglary: 100

hate mail, harassing phone calls and
bomb threats: 946

arrests at blockades: 16

number of blockades: 2

incidents of picketing: 8,402

letters received purporting to contain anthrax: 19

January 29: A bomb was left in front of New Woman All Woman Health Care in Birmingham, Alabama. The device killed security guard Robert "Sande" Sanderson and seriously injured nurse Emily Lyons. Eric Robert Rudolph has been charged with the attack, but remains at large.

February: A Portland, Oregon, jury found the Nuremberg Files and the Deadly Dozen poster to be "true threats" not protected by the First Amendment.

October 23: Dr. Barnett Slepian was shot and killed by a sniper while standing in his Amherst, New York, kitchen. His assailant, believed to be James Kopp, remains at large.

1999

Anti-abortion violence and disruptions for the year:

murder and attempted murder: 0

bombings/arson and attempted bombing
and arson: 10

invasions, assault and battery, vandalism,
death threats, stalking and burglary: 95

hate mail, harassing phone calls and
bomb threats: 1,685

arrests at blockades: 5

number of blockades: 3

incidents of picketing: 8,727

received letters purporting to contain anthrax: 36

June 2: A California clinic sustained $100,000 in damage from an arson attempt.

October: A federal jury convicted Marvin Uphoff of setting fire to a Sioux Fall, South Dakota, Planned Parenthood. Uphoff had previously been convicted of vandalizing the clinic and had been ordered not to picket the facility. The clinic was the sole abortion provider in the state.

2000

Anti-abortion violence and disruption statistics, January 1 to September 1:

murder and attempted murder: 0

bombings/arsons and attempted bombing
and arson: 5

invasions, assault & battery, vandalism,
death threats, stalking and burglary: 36

hate mail, harassing phone calls and
bomb threats: 175

arrests at blockades: 0

number of blockades: 3

incidents of picketing: 2,984

June 28: The United States Supreme Court, in *Hill v. Colorado,* ruled that an eight-foot bubble zone separating patients and staff from protestors is not an "unreasonable violation of free speech" protected by the First Amendment.

July 11: Dr. Garson Romalis of Vancouver, British Columbia, was stabbed on his way into his office. The incident marked him as the first person to sustain two attempts on his life by anti-abortionists.

September: The Food and Drug Administration approved Mifepristone, the first chemical alternative to surgical abortion. Called Mifeprex, the drug must be provided by or under the supervision of a physician who can accurately assess the duration of the pregnancy, who can diagnose ectopic pregnancies and who has the ability to provide surgical intervention or refer the patient to other physicians if surgery becomes necessary. Within twenty-four hours of Mifeprex' approval, a Catholic priest drove to a Rockville, Illinois, clinic and took an ax to the facility. He was caught on videotape and apprehended.

Overall statistics on clinic violence and disruption, 1977–September 2000, compiled by the National Abortion Federation:

7 murders

17 attempted murders

40 bombings

163 arsons

80 attempted bombings or arson attacks

368 invasions

882 incidents of vandalism

115 incidents of assault & battery

332 death threats

3 kidnappings

60 burglaries

420 incidents of stalking

8,246 harassing phone calls and received pieces of hate mail

526 bomb threats

40, 687 incidents of picketing

679 blockades

33, 830 arrests at clinics

NOTES

CHAPTER 1

1. Stanley K. Henshaw, "Abortion Incidence and Services in the U.S., 1995-1996," *Family Planning Perspectives,* November-December 1998, p. 268.
2. Barbara Vobejda, "Study Finds Fewer Facilities Offering Abortion," *The Washington Post,* December 11, 1998.
3. "Who Decides? A State by State Review of Abortion and Reproductive Rights" (Washington, D.C.: NARAL, 1999), pp. 254-255.
4. Susan Dudley, Ph.D., "Teenage Women, Abortion and the Law" (Washington, D.C.: NAF Fact Sheet, 1996), www.prochoice.org.
5. "The Adolescent Right to Confidential Care When Considering Abortion," Policy Statement of the American Academy of Pediatrics, May 1996, www.aap.org.
6. "Who Decides?" p. xiv.
7. Ibid., p. xv.
8. Rosemary Candelario and Catherine Rich, "Barriers to Abortion Access," *Update: Medical Students for Choice,* September 1998, p. 1.
9. *Conscience,* The Newsjournal of Catholics for a Free Choice (Washington, D.C.), Winter 1997/1998, p 5.
10. Henshaw, "Abortion Incidence," p. 268.
11. Candelario and Rich, "Barriers to Abortion Access," p.4
12. Jennifer Baumgardner, "Immaculate Conception," *The Nation,* January 25, 1999, p. 2.
13. Candelario and Rich, "Barriers to Abortion Access," p. 4.
14. In-person interview with Eileen Schnitger, July 27, 1998.
15. Marlene Gerber Fried, "Legal But . . . Framing the Ethics of Abortion Rights," *Resist* Newsletter (Boston: MA), April 1998, p. 5.
16. www.all.org.
17. Ibid.
18. Telephone interview with Jim Sedlak, July 14, 1999.
19. Personal correspondence between Patricia Baird-Windle and Eleanor Bader, June 17, 2000.
20. www.orn.org.
21. www.fwhc.org/ritewing.htm.
22. http://spiritone.com/~lifeadvo.
23. www.execpc.com/~restore/mtp/mtp.
24. www.thelambsofchrist.com.
25. Ibid.
26. Skipp Porteous, "Nuremberg Files Project Menaces Doctors," www.berkshire.net/~ifas/fw/9603/Nuremberg.html.
27. www.oicj.org.
28. T. W. Adorno (with Else Frankel-Brunswick, Daniel J. Levinson, and R. Nevitt Sanford), *The Authoritarian Personality* (New York, NY: Harper & Row, 1950), www.psrg.lcs.mit.edu.
29. Erich Fromm, *Escape from Freedom* (New York, NY: Avon Books, 1941), p. 246.

30. Ibid., p. 177.
31. Ibid.
32. In-person interview with Dr. John Beery, December 16, 1998.
33. Telephone interview with Dr. John Beery, November 12, 1999.
34. In-person interview with Dr. Phyllis Chesler, November 11, 1998.
35. Ibid.
36. Ibid.
37. In-person interview with Susan Hill, October 2, 1998.
38. In-person interview with Shauna Heckert, July 27, 1998.
39. Ibid.
40. Jane E. Brody, "Researchers Unravel the Motives of Stalkers," *New York Times,* August 25, 1998.
41. www.rcpsych.ac.uk/public/help/welcome/htm.
42. In-person interview with Eileen Schnitger, July 27, 1998.
43. In-person interview with Mary Lou Greenberg, July 6, 1999.

CHAPTER 2

1. Lawrence Lader, *Abortion II: Making the Revolution* (Boston, MA: Beacon Press, 1973), p. 6.
2. Ibid., pp. 6-7.
3. Ibid., p. 5.
4. Cynthia Gorney, *Articles of Faith: A Frontline History of the Abortion Wars* (New York, NY: Simon and Schuster, 1998), p. 48.
5. Ibid., pp. 49-51.
6. www.bowdoin.edu/~sbodurt2/court/cases/griswold.html.
7. Archives of Catholics for a Free Choice, Washington, D.C.
8. Lader, *Abortion II: Making the Revolution,* p. 28.
9. Ibid.
10. Ibid., p. 33.
11. In-person interview with Bill Baird, September 25, 1998.
12. "He'll Defy the Law to Teach Birth Control in the Slums," *Long Island Press* (New York), April 18, 1965.
13. In-person interview with Bill Baird, September 25, 1998.
14. Ibid.
15. Ibid.
16. Ibid.
17. Ibid.
18. "Court Rules Singles Can Get Birth Control," *New York Post,* March 22, 1972.
19. Arlene Carmen and Howard Moody, *Abortion Counseling and Social Change: From Illegal Act to Medical Practice* (New York, NY: Judson Press, 1973), pp. 30-31.
20. Telephone interview with the Reverend Howard Moody, February 12, 1999.
21. Ibid.
22. Ibid.
23. Ibid.
24. Telephone interview with Dr. Henry Morgentaler, January 13, 1999.
25. Ibid.
26. Ibid.
27. Ibid.

28. Lader, *Abortion II: Making the Revolution,* pp. 4-5

29. In-person interview with Carol Downer, Esq., July 23, 1998.

30. Ibid.

31. Ibid.

32. Ibid.

33. Ibid.

34. Ibid.

35. Ibid.

36. Ibid.

37. Ibid.

38. Lader, *Abortion II,* p. 93.

39. Kathryn Cullen-DuPont, *Encyclopedia of Women's History in America* (New York, NY: Facts On File, 1996), p. 144.

40. Lader, *Abortion II,* pp. 110-111.

41. Ibid., p. 28.

42. Ibid., p. 113.

43. Ibid., p. 113.

44. Ibid., p. 114.

45. Tanya Melich, *The Republican War Against Women: An Insider's Report From Behind the Lines* (New York, NY: Bantam Books, 1996), p. 15.

46. Lader, *Abortion II,* p. 162.

47. Bill Baird, "The Prison Diary of Bill Baird," *Boston Globe Sunday Magazine,* June 14, 1970.

48. Ibid.

49. Ibid.

50. Gorney, *Articles of Faith,* p. 97.

51. Lader, *Abortion II: Making the Revolution,* p. 117.

52. Baird, "Prison Diary."

53. "Threat Forced Baird to Move, Wife Testifies," *Newsday* (New York), June 25, 1974.

54. Doug Smith, Bob Keeler and Jim O'Neill, "Suffolk Police Say Baird's Talk Endangered Welfare of Infant," *Newsday,* August 7, 1971.

55. "Threats Forced Baird to Move, Wife Testifies," *Newsday,* June 25, 1974.

56. Melich, *The Republican War Against Women,* pp. 28-29.

57. Lader, *Abortion II,* p. 163.

58. Ibid.

59. www.religioustolerance.org.

CHAPTER 3

1. Connie Paige, *The Right to Lifers* (New York, NY: Summit Books, 1983), p. 60.

2. Ibid., p. 71.

3. Cynthia Gorney, *Articles of Faith: A Frontline History of the Abortion Wars* (New York, NY: Simon and Schuster, 1998), p.190.

4. Paige, *The Right to Lifers,* p. 110.

5. Ibid., pp. 156-157.

6. Mary Lou Greenberg, "Women Are Not Incubators," a pamphlet published by RCP Publications, 1989 (Chicago, IL), p.15.

7. *Conscience,* The Newsjournal of Catholics for a Free Choice (Washington, D.C.), Winter 1997/1998, p. 5.

8. Telephone interview with Marilyn Chrisman Eldridge, October 25, 1999.
9. *Conscience,* p. 5.
10. Telephone interview with Dr. Henry Morgentaler, January 13, 1999.
11. Ibid.
12. Ibid.
13. Ibid.
14. Telephone interview with Gail Frances, September 22, 1998.
15. Ibid.
16. David McNamee, "Member of the Wedding," *Capital Region* (Washington, D.C.), May 1987.
17. Telephone interview with Dido Hasper, July 30, 1998.
18. Ibid.
19. Ibid.
20. Ibid.
21. "Feminist Health Center Wins Suit Against Doctors," *The Sacramento Bee* (California), May 17, 1983.
22. Bill Miller, "Abortion Clinic Set in Redding," *Record Searchlight* (Redding, CA), August 6, 1983.
23. www.naral.org/publications/facts/sup_97.html.
24. Gorney, *Articles of Faith,* p. 248.
25. www.naral.org/publications/facts/sup_97.html.
26. Tanya Melich, *The Republican War Against Women: An Insider's Report from Behind the Lines* (New York: Bantam Books, 1996), p. 63.
27. In-person conversation between Patricia Baird-Windle and Eleanor Bader, June 7, 1999.
28. Ibid.
29. Glen Macnow, "Cocoa Beach Sets Abortion Clinic Rules," *Florida Today,* July 22, 1977.
30. In-person conversation between Patricia Baird-Windle and Eleanor Bader, June 7, 1999.
31. Ibid., June 8, 1999.
32. "We Must Not Forget Rosaura Jimenez, 1950-1977," www.naral.org/publications/newslet_win97.html.
33. In-person interview with Susan Hill, September 1, 1999.
34. Ibid.
35. Ibid.
36. Gorney, *Articles of Faith,* p. 261.
37. In-person interview with Ann Baker, October 12, 1999.
38. Joni Scott, "From Hate Rhetoric to Hate Crimes: A Link Acknowledged Too Late," *The Humanist,* January/February 1999, p. 2.
39. Ibid.
40. Ibid.
41. Ibid.
42. Unpublished writing of Patricia Baird-Windle, August 2000.
43. Sandra Matuska, "Abortion Clinic Draws Fire," *The Morning Call* (Allentown, PA), September 14, 1978.
44. "The Clinic: A Brief Chronology," *Valley Monthly Magazine* (Lehigh Valley, PA), January 1979.
45. "Abortion Clinic Loses Zoning Permit," *Globe-Times* (Allentown, PA), March 23, 1970.
46. www.all.org.
47. Scott, "From Hate Rhetoric to Hate Crimes," p. 3.

48. In-person conversation between Patricia Baird-Windle and Eleanor Bader, November 4, 1999.
49. Telephone interview with Margaret Alvis Gifford, December 28, 1999.
50. Ibid.
51. www.catholicity.com.
52. Lee Epstein and Joseph F. Kobylka, *The Supreme Court and Legal Change: Abortion and the Death Penalty* (Chapel Hill, NC: University of North Carolina Press, 1992), p. 231.
53. Melich, *The Republican War Against Women,* p. 131.
54. Ibid., p. 132.
55. Ibid., p. 131.
56. Ibid., p. 148.
57. Ibid., p. 151.
58. Ibid., pp. 221-222.

CHAPTER 4

1. Sara Diamond, *Roads to Dominion: Right-Wing Movements and Political Power in the U.S.* (New York, NY: The Guilford Press, 1995), p. 233.
2. Ibid., p. 235.
3. James Risen and Judy L. Thomas, *Wrath of Angels: The American Abortion War* (New York, NY: Basic Books, 1998), p. 114.
4. Lori Sharn, "City, Abortion Clinic Settle Dispute," *Florida Today,* September 22, 1981.
5. "Lindgren Seeks to Block List Gathered by Anti-Abortionists," *Fargo Forum* (North Dakota), undated clipping.
6. Telephone interview with Allison Hile, September 29, 1998.
7. Ibid.
8. Ibid.
9. Ibid.
10. Ibid.
11. "A Right to Life Kidnapping?" *Newsweek,* August 30, 1982.
12. Telephone interview with Alison Hile, September 29, 1998.
13. Ibid.
14. Ibid.
15. In-person interview with Susan Hill, September 1, 1999.
16. In-person conversation between Patricia Baird-Windle and Eleanor Bader, November 4, 1999.
17. In-person interview with Alice Verhoeven, November 30, 1998.
18. Ibid.
19. *Reports,* #54, Planned Parenthood League of Massachusetts, September 1983.
20. *Reports,* #60, Planned Parenthood League of Massachusetts, September 1984.
21. In-person interview with Nicki Nichols Gamble, November 30, 1998.
22. Richard N. Ostling, "The Nun vs. the Archbishop," *Time,* March 21, 1983.
23. www.naral.org/publications/facts/sup_97.html.
24. Terry Uau Dell, "Feminist Center Wins a Round in Legal Battle; DA, State to Appeal," *Chico Enterprise Record* (California), November 3, 1988.
25. "FWHC Charges Dropped Again," *Chico News and Review* (California), February 2, 1989.
26. Telephone interview with Dr. Henry Morgentaler, January 13, 1999.

27. "Chronology of Court Cases: Dr. Morgentaler and Others," Childbirth by Choice Trust, Toronto, Canada.
28. Ibid.
29. Telephone interview with Dr. Henry Morgentaler, January 13, 1999.
30. Ibid.
31. Telephone interview with Beverly Whipple, October 16, 1998.
32. Ibid.
33. Ibid.
34. Ibid.
35. "Everett FWHC: 1983-1996, A Chronology," *Voices for Choice,* FWHC Newsletter (Everett, Washington), Summer 1996.
36. Ibid.
37. *NCAP News* (Washington, D.C.), November 12, 1996.
38. Brian Duffy, "Abortion Clinic Rules Fuel Father's Rage: He Talks with Fists," *The Miami Herald,* November 17, 1983.
39. Telephone interview with "Joan Linwood" (pseudonym), November 10, 1998.
40. Ibid.
41. Ibid.
42. Ibid.
43. "The Facts Speak Louder Than Words: The Planned Parenthood Critique of the *Silent Scream,*" www.plannedparenthood.org.abt/silentscream.HTM.
44. In-person interview with Deborah Walsh, October 6, 1998.
45. Telephone interview with Carol Dunn, September 28, 1998.
46. Ibid.
47. Ibid.
48. Ibid.
49. Michael Bray, "Postcard from the Edge: Marjorie Reed Out, Others In," *Life Advocate,* Magazine (Portland, OR), September/October 1997.
50. In-person interview with Susan Hill, September 1, 1999.
51. Telephone interview with Carol Dunn, September 28, 1998.
52. Telephone interview with Suzette Caton, October 22, 1998.
53. In-person interview with Linda Taggart, January 15, 1999.
54. Ibid.
55. Ibid.
56. Tanya Melich, *The Republican War Against Women: An Insider's Report From Behind the Lines* (New York, NY: Bantam Books, 1996), p. 175.
57. Barbara Ferraro, Patricia Hussey with Jane O'Reilly, *No Turning Back: Two Nuns Battle with the Vatican Over Women's Right to Choose* (New York, NY: Poseidon Press, 1990), p. 218.
58. *Conscience,* The Newsjournal of Catholics for a Free Choice (Washington, D.C.), Winter 1997/1998, p. 9.
59. Ibid.
60. Ferraro, Hussey with O'Reilly, *No Turning Back,* pp. 331-332.
61. *Conscience.*
62. Telephone interview with Alexandra Aitken, September 21, 1998.
63. Telephone interview with Peg Johnston, September 28, 1998.
64. Telephone interview with Alexandra Aitken, September 21, 1998.
65. Ibid.
66. Telephone interview with Gail Frances, September 22, 1998.
67. Ibid.

68. Telephone interview with Sherri Finik, October 20, 1998.
69. Ibid.
70. Ibid.
71. "Clinic Workers Disagree with FBI, Call Bombings Terrorism," *Fargo Forum* (North Dakota), December 6, 1984.
72. "Getting Priorities Straight on Clinic Attacks," *Minneapolis Star and Tribune* (Minnesota), December 12, 1984.
73. Archive of the Community Healthcare Center of Pensacola, Pensacola, Florida.
74. In-person interview with Linda Taggart, January 15, 1999.
75. Bill Dingwall, "Christmas Bomb Raid Rocks Abortion Clinics," *Pensacola News Journal* (Florida), December 26, 1984.
76. Ibid.
77. Dallas Blanchard and Terry Prewitt, *Religious Tolerance and Abortion* (Gainesville, FL: University Press of Florida, 1993), p. 51.
78. Craig Pittman, "Bombed Out Doctor to Leave Pensacola," *Pensacola News Journal,* December 29, 1985.
79. "One Year After Bombing, Issue Waxes Hot Here," *Pensacola News Journal,* October 8, 1985.
80. Blanchard and Prewitt, *Religious Tolerance and Abortion,* p. 45.
81. Ibid., p.46.
82. Ibid.
83. Ibid., p. 131.
84. Barbara Janesh, "Psychologists: Defendants Obsessed," *Pensacola News Journal,* April 21, 1985.
85. Ginny Graybiel, "Insanity Defense Takes Beating in Bombing Trial," *Pensacola News Journal,* April 24, 1985.
86. Barbara Janesh, "Clinic Bombers Avoid Further Prosecution," *Pensacola News Journal,* July 10, 1985.

CHAPTER 5

1. Gavin Quill, "Conversation with Randall Terry," December 1991, http://forerunner.com/forerunner/XO430_conversation_with_Ra.html.
2. Ibid.
3. "Randall Terry: A 20th Century Hero," http://forerunner.com/forerunner/XO779/_1988_-_ Randall Terry.html.
4. Quill, "Conversation with Randall Terry."
5. Randall Terry, *Accessory to Murder: The Enemies, Allies and Accomplices to the Death of Our Culture* (Brentwood, TN: Wolgemuth and Hyatt Publishers, 1990), p. 192.
6. http://apocalypse.berkshire.net/~ifas/fw/9806/majority.html.
7. Kevin Sherlock, *Abortion Buster's Manual* (California: Operation Rescue of California, 1985), p. 2.
8. Ibid., Chapter Three, page 9.
9. Ibid., Chapter Three, page 10.
10. Ibid., Chapter Three, page 1.
11. In-person interview with Deborah Walsh, October 6, 1998.
12. Ibid.
13. Ibid.
14. Archive of the Community Healthcare Center of Pensacola, Inc., Pensacola, Florida.

15. Telephone interview with Charlotte Taft, November 11, 1998.
16. Ibid.
17. Ibid.
18. Ibid.
19. Joseph Scheidler, *Closed: 99 Ways to Stop Abortion* (Westchester, IL: Crossway Press, 1985), p. 38.
20. Ibid., pp. 74-75.
21. Ibid., p. 157.
22. Ibid., p 181.
23. Ibid., p. 305.
24. Ibid., Forward, p. 14.
25. Telephone interview with Suzette Caton, October 22, 1998.
26. Ibid.
27. Telephone interview with Cathy Conner, October 14, 1998.
28. Telephone interview with Charlotte Taft, November 11, 1998.
29. Ibid.
30. Telephone interview with Cathy Conner, October 14, 1998.
31. Ibid.
32. Archive of All Women's Health Center, Portland, Oregon.
33. Dr. Warren M. Hern, "A Special Report to Jo Ann Harris, Criminal Division, U.S. Department of Justice," January 6, 1995.
34. Ibid.
35. Charlie Brennan, "Abortion Clinic Falls Victim to Phony Service Calls," *Rocky Mountain News* (Colorado), January 3, 1985.
36. *The Campaign Report,* vol. 1, no. 18, January 13, 1986, The 80% Majority Campaign (Hightstown, NJ).
37. "Planned Parenthood Exec Excommunicated," *The Daily News* (New York, New York), January 22, 1986.
38. "Wave of Controversy Jarring to RI Catholic Community," *The Boston Globe,* January 23, 1986.
39. Ibid.
40. In-person interview with Laura Blue, August 12, 1998.
41. Ginny Graybiel, "Pro-Lifer Gets House Arrest," *Pensacola News Journal* (Florida), July 3, 1986.
42. Margaret Fifield and Bill Dingwall, "Pensacola Warrant Lands Scheidler in Denver Jail," *Pensacola News Journal,* June 13, 1986.
43. In-person interview with Susan Hill, October 2, 1998.
44. Ibid.
45. www.prolifeaction.org/background_of_now_v.htm.
46. In-person interview with Sara Love, Esq., July 13, 1999.
47. Ibid.
48. Archive of the Feminist Majority Foundation, (Arlington, VA). Document was an exhibit at the RICO Trial.
49. Ibid.
50. "Anti-Abortion Conspiracy Cracked Today in Chicago Federal District Court," Press release of the National Women's Health Organization, April 20, 1998.
51. Mike Robinson, "Judge Fines Anti-Abortion Leaders," Associated Press, July 17, 1999.
52. In-person interview with Dr. George Tiller, February 15, 1999.
53. Ibid.

54. James Risen and Judy L. Thomas, *Wrath of Angels: The American Abortion War* (New York, NY: Basic Books, 1998), p. 247.
55. Ibid., p. 255.
56. Ibid., p. 267.
57. Ibid., p. 268.
58. Ibid., p. 269.
59. Hern, "A Special Report to Jo Ann Harris."
60. Archive of the Planned Parenthood League of Massachusetts, Boston, Massachusetts.
61. Archive of the National Women's Health Organization, headquartered in Raleigh, North Carolina
62. Telephone interview with Cathy Conner, October 14, 1998.
63. Ibid.
64. Ibid.
65. Ibid.
66. Ibid.
67. Telephone interview with Bob Rowell, November 27, 1998.
68. Telephone interview with Sherri Finik, October 20, 1998.
69. Ibid.
70. Ibid.
71. Archive of the National Women's Health Organization, headquartered in Raleigh, North Carolina.
72. Archive of All Women's Health Services, Portland, Oregon.
73. Archive of the National Center for the Pro Choice Majority, Hightstown, New Jersey.
74. www.law.nyu.edu/lawyeringprogram/visualtour/regular/lsa2.html.
75. http://report.kff.org/repro/db2/1992/09/a920928.21.
76. Archive of the National Women's Health Organization, headquartered in Raleigh, North Carolina.
77. Hern, "A Special Report to Jo Ann Harris."
78. Ibid.
79. Archive of All Women's Health Services, Portland, Oregon.
80. Michael L. Atchinson and Cindy West, "Explosives Found Near Clinic," *Pensacola News Journal,* May 8, 1988.
81. Allison Smith and Cindy West, "Investigator Probes Possible Bomb Accomplice," *Pensacola News Journal,* May 9, 1988.
82. Ginny Graybiel, "Kentucky Abortion Foe Indicted." *Pensacola News Journal,* May 27, 1988.
83. "Clinic Bomber to Be Released," *Pensacola News Journal,* January 19, 1995.
84. Ginny Graybiel, "Abortion Foe to Enter Bomb Plea," *Pensacola News Journal,* July 27, 1988.
85. Graybiel, "Kentucky Abortion Foe Indicted."
86. Tanya Melich, *The Republican War Against Women: An Insider's Report From Behind the Lines* (New York, NY: Bantam Books, 1996), p. 226.
87. Ibid., p. 219.
88. Cindi Lash, "Abortion Protesters Face Liens on Property," *Pittsburgh Press* (Pennsylvania), October 18, 1989.
89. Michael A. Fuoco and Linda Wilson Fuoco, "Judge Faults Police Tactics at Abortion Protest Scene, *Pittsburgh Post Gazette,* April 26, 1990.
90. Janet Williams and Dan Donovan, "Cohill: Why Are Prisoners at Mayview?" *Pittsburgh Press,* June 22, 1989.
91. Telephone interview with Lynne Randall, March 4, 1999.
92. Ibid.

93. Telephone interview with Ann Garzia, December 8, 1998.

94. Ibid.

95. Marian Faux, *Crusaders: Voices from the Abortion Front* (Secaucus, NJ: Carol Publishing Group, Birch Lane Press, 1990).

96. Ibid., p. 44.

97. Ibid., p. 145.

98. "A Police View of the Sit-In," *Pittsburgh Press,* August 10, 1988.

99. Telephone interview with Jennifer Vriens, September 23, 1998.

100. Mary Lou Greenberg, "Another American Tragedy: The Death of Becky Bell," *On the Issues* Magazine (Forest Hills, NY), Winter 1990.

101. *Closed: 99 Ways to Stop Abortion,* The Operation's Manual of Anti-Abortion Organizing, a monograph prepared for use by Crown Council in the Bubble Zone Trials, *R. v. Lewis,* held in British Columbia Provincial Court, undated.

102. Michael A. Fuoco, "City Safety Officials Ready for Anti-Abortion Protest," *Pittsburgh Post Gazette* (Pennsylvania), April 27, 1988.

103. Telephone interview with Dr. Glenna Halvorson-Boyd, February 18, 1999.

104. Ibid.

105. Ibid.

106. Ibid.

107. Ibid.

108. *Pro-Choice Network of Western New York, Buffalo GYN Womenservices, Erie Medical Center, and Doctors Paul Davis, Shalom Press and Barnett Slepian v. Project Rescue New York, Operation Rescue* and 50 named individuals.

109. Dan Herbeck, Jane Kwiatkowski and Michael Beebe, "Five Leaders of Protest Face Arrest," *Buffalo News* (New York), April 28, 1992.

110. Telephone interview with Glenn A. Murray, Esq., January 7, 1999.

111. "Bus Bill Is $7283 for Spring of Life," *Buffalo News,* May 13, 1992.

112. Telephone interview with Jennifer Vriens, September 23, 1998.

113. In-person interview with Susan Hill, September 1, 1999.

114. Telephone interview with Lisa Gerard, February 19, 1999.

115. Ibid.

116. Ibid.

117. In-person interview with Tim Shuck, August 4, 1998.

118. Ibid.

119. Ibid.

120. www.naral.org/publications/facts/sup_97.html.

121. Telephone interview with Jennifer Vriens, September 23, 1998.

122. Telephone interview with Marilyn Chrisman Eldridge, November 10, 1998.

123. In-person interview with Susan Hill, September 1, 1999.

124. In-person interview with Deborah Walsh, October 6, 1998.

125. Ibid.

126. Ibid.

127. Ibid.

128. Ibid.

129. Ibid.

130. Ibid.

131. Ibid.

132. *Conscience,* The Newsjournal of Catholics for a Free Choice (Washington, D.C.), Winter 1997/1998, p. 9.

133. Ibid.
134. Hern, "A Special Report to Jo Ann Harris."
135. Telephone interview with Diane Straus, November 23, 1998.
136. Ibid.
137. Ibid.
138. Ibid.
139. Telephone interview with "Lena Rabinski" (pseudonym), December 28, 1998.
140. Ibid.
141. In-person conversation between Patricia Baird-Windle and Eleanor Bader, June 9, 1999.
142. Fuoco, "City Safety Officials Ready for Anti-Abortion Protest."
143. Telephone interview with Diane Straus, November 23, 1998.
144. John Mecklin, "Tort Abort," *Phoenix New Times* (Arizona), December 8-14, 1994.
145. Telephone interview with Dr. Brian Finkel, September 21, 1998.
146. Mecklin, "Tort Abort."
147. Telephone interview with Dr. Brian Finkel, September 21, 1998.
148. Archive of the Planned Parenthood Federation of America, New York, New York.
149. Tom Vercellotti, "Lock and Block Tactic Is Spreading Among Groups Protesting Abortion," *Pittsburgh Press,* June 25, 1989.
150. William Mausteller, "Police, Abortion Protesters Face Off in Filmed Struggle at East Liberty Site," *Pittsburgh Press,* June 18, 1989.
151. Joe Smydo, "Abortion Protesters Still in Jail," *Pittsburgh Press,* June 19, 1989.
152. Michael A. Fuoco, "Protesters Remain Defiant as 20 Are Released," *Pittsburgh Post Gazette,* June 22, 1989.
153. Cindi Lash, "Abortion Foes Free on Bond After Giving Names," *Pittsburgh Press,* June 29, 1989.
154. In-person interview with Susan Hill, September 1, 1999.
155. Bob Caylor, "Abortion Doctor Followed From Indy by Anti-Abortionists," *Post Gazette* (Ft. Wayne, IN), August 30, 1989.
156. In-person interview with Claire Keyes, November 16, 1998.
157. Ibid.
158. Ibid.
159. Ibid.
160. Ibid.
161. Ibid.
162. Ibid.
163. In-person conversation between Patricia Baird-Windle and Eleanor Bader, November 4, 1999.
164. Phil Fairbanks, "Radical Fringe's Violent Bond Born in Confinement," *The Buffalo News* (New York), November 8, 1998.
165. Telephone interview with Carol Dunn, September 28, 1998.
166. In-person interview with Sandie Matthews, November 18, 1998.
167. Ibid.
168. Ibid.
169. Archive of Women's Health Services, Pittsburgh, Pennsylvania.
170. Telephone interview with the Reverend Walter Carlson, January 11, 1999.
171. Ibid.
172. Ibid.
173. Ibid.

174. Kathryn Cullen-DuPont, *The Encyclopedia of Women's History in America* (New York, NY: Facts On File, 1996), p. 160.

175. Telephone interview with Rachel Atkins, November 23, 1998.

176. Diane Derby, "Protesters Jailed for Contempt," *Burlington Free Press* (Vermont), October 26, 1989.

177. In-person conversation between Patricia Baird-Windle and Eleanor Bader, November 5, 1999.

178. *Conscience,* p. 10.

CHAPTER 6

1. Skipp Porteous, "The Christian Coalition: An Introduction," http://mother.qrd.org/qrd/www/FTR.christco.html.

2. Ibid.

3. Ibid.

4. www.berkshire.net/~ifas.

5. Ibid.

6. Michael Bray, *A Time to Kill* (Portland, OR: Advocates for Life Publications, 1994), p. 18.

7. Randall Terry, *Accessory to Murder: The Enemies, Allies and Accomplices to the Death of Our Culture* (Brentwood, TN: Wolgemuth and Hyatt Publishers, 1990), p. 20.

8. Ibid., p. 118.

9. Ibid., p. 119.

10. Ibid., p. 206.

11. www.naral.org/federal/court/court.html.

12. In-person conversation between Patricia Baird-Windle and Eleanor Bader, November 5, 1999.

13. Maryclaire Dale, "Out of State Protesters Arrested at Clinic," *Sunday Gazette Mail* (Charleston, West Virginia), January 7, 1990.

14. Frank Hutchins, "Candlelight Vigil Planned Near Jail," *The Daily Mail* (Charleston, West Virginia) January 11, 1990.

15. Jennifer Bundy, "Injunction Limits Protests at Women's Health Center," *The Daily Mail* (Charleston, West Virginia) February 3, 1990.

16. Brian Bonner, "Keith Tucci Fights Back," *St. Paul Pioneer Press Dispatch* (Minnesota), September 5, 1991.

17. Kurt Chandler, "Leader: We Believe in Higher Laws Than 'Thou Shalt Not Trespass,'" *Minneapolis Star Tribune* (Minnesota), April 18, 1993.

18. Bonner, "Tucci Fights Back."

19. *Conscience,* The Newsjournal of Catholics for a Free Choice (Washington, D.C.), Winter 1997/1998, p. 10.

20. Archive of All Women's Health Services, Portland, Oregon.

21. Telephone interview with Rachel Atkins, November 23, 1998.

22. Ibid.

23. Ibid.

24. "Clinic Invaders," *The Charleston Gazette* (West Virginia), June 9, 1990.

25. In-person interview with Claire Keyes, November 16, 1998.

26. Ibid.

27. Ibid.

28. Ari L. Goldman, "Director of Abortion Clinic Excommunicated in Texas," *New York Times,* June 6, 1990.
29. Ibid.
30. Jesse Trevino, "Bishop Gracida's Threats on Abortion Out of Place," *The Austin-American Statesman* (Texas), July 15, 1990.
31. "Abortion Center Workers Cut from Church in Texas," *The Catholic Messenger* (Staten Island, NY), July 5, 1990.
32. "Corpus Cristi Sheriff Announces Support for Rescuers," *The Wanderer* (St. Paul, MN), February 8, 1990.
33. Telephone interview with "Susannah Davis" (pseudonym), December 28, 1998.
34. Ibid.
35. Archive of Catholics for a Free Choice, Washington, D.C.
36. "Corpus Christi Bishop Excommunicates Third Person Over Abortions," *El Paso Times* (Texas), November 10, 1990.
37. Archive of All Women's Health Services, Portland, Oregon.
38. John Goetz, "Missionaries' Leader Calls for Armed Militias," Planned Parenthood Federation of America Newsletter, vol. 1, no. 2, August 1994.
39. Shirley E. Perlman, "Conscience Clause for Cops Urged," *Newsday* (New York), September 24, 1990.
40. In-person interview with Patty Madden, November 18, 1998.
41. In-person interview with Mary EllenTunney, November 18, 1998.
42. In-person interview with Patty Madden, November 18, 1998.
43. Archive of the National Center for the Pro Choice Majority, Hightstown, New Jersey.
44. www.naral.org/federal/court/court.html.
45. Telephone interview with Gerri Laster, October 25, 1999.
46. Ibid.
47. *Lovejoy SurgiCenter Inc. v. The Advocates for Life, Inc. et al.*
48. In-person interview with Allene Klass, August 4, 1998.
49. In-person interview with DeborahWalsh, October 6, 1998.
50. Ibid.
51. Betsy Gerboth, "Lambs Leader Has Simple, Unshakable Stand on Abortion," *Fargo Forum* (North Dakota), July 19, 1991, p. A1.
52. Deanne Hilgers, "Lambs Pricking at Consciences and City Coffers," *Fargo Forum,* June 20, 1991.
53. Telephone interview with Dr. Glenna Halvorson-Boyd, February 18, 1999.
54. In-person interview with Penny Bertsch, July 27, 1998.
55. Ibid.
56. Ibid.
57. Ibid.
58. Ibid.
59. Denny Walsh, "Prosecutors Say Suspect Is Serial Arsonist," *The Sacramento Bee* (California), October 5, 1997.
60. Telephone interview with Dr. Glenna Halvorson-Boyd, February 18, 1999.
61. Steve Terrell, "Protesters Exonerated of Charges," *The New Mexican* (Santa Fe, NM), September 5, 1991.
62. Archive of Women's Health Care Services, Wichita, Kansas.
63. In-person interview with the Reverend George Gardner, February 15, 1999.
64. In-person interview with Dr. George Tiller, February 15, 1999.
65. In-person interview with Cathy Reavis, February 16, 1999.

66. Telephone interview with Peggy Bowman, February 16, 1999.

67. Judy Lundstrom Thomas, "A Battle of Wills," *Wichita Eagle* (Kansas), July 31, 1991.

68. Jim Lynn, "Abortion Protests Cost Soars," *Wichita Eagle,* September 13, 1991.

69. In-person interview with the Reverend George Gardner, February 15, 1999.

70. Nicki Flynn, "Protesters Could Tie Up City Court," *Wichita Eagle,* August 1, 1991.

71. Jennifer Comes, "City Hits Protesters With Higher Fines," *Wichita Eagle,* October 23, 1991.

72. In-person interview with the Reverend George Gardner, February 15, 1999.

73. Ibid.

74. Telephone interview with Dr. LeRoy Carhart, February 1, 1999.

75. Ibid., October 13, 1999.

76. Ibid., February 1, 1999.

77. Ibid.

78. Ibid., October 13, 1999.

79. Ibid., February 1, 1999.

80. Ibid., October 13, 1999.

81. Dan Herbeck, "Robert Schenck Lashes Out at Brother's Fine," *Buffalo News* (New York), September 29, 1992.

82. Dan Herbeck, "Pro-Life Pastor Tells Judge He Can't Pay $20,000 Fine," *Buffalo News* (New York), January 30, 1993.

83. Telephone interview with Glenn A. Murray, Esq., January 7, 1999.

84. Ibid.

85. Judy Lundstrom Thomas, "Protest Picture Marked by Increased Hostility," *Wichita Eagle* (Kansas), October 6, 1991.

86. Archive of the Planned Parenthood League of Massachusetts, Boston, Massachusetts.

87. In-person interview with Nicki Nichols Gamble, November 30, 1998.

88. Ibid.

89. Ibid.

90. Telephone interview with Dr. Susan Wicklund, February 3, 1999.

91. Ibid.

92. Ibid.

93. Telephone interview with Sonja Mitchell, February 5, 1999.

94. Telephone interview with Dr. Susan Wicklund, February 3, 1999.

95. Ibid.

96. Telephone interview with Sonja Mitchell, February 5, 1999.

97. Ibid.

98. Ibid.

99. *Fargo Women's Health Organization, Doctors George Miks and Susan Wicklund, and Jane Bovard, administrator v. The Lambs of Christ, Focus on Fargo, Help and Caring Ministries* and six named individuals.

100. In-person interview with Susan Hill, September 1, 1999.

101. *NCAP News* (Washington, D.C.), November 11, 1991.

102. *NCAP News,* January 1992.

103. "Shelley Shannon: A Soldier in the Army of God," www.bodypolitic.org.

104. *Army of God Manual,* pp. 10-11. Neither author nor publisher of this underground manual are listed on the document. The only identifier is the Army of God. At this time, law enforcers are uncertain if the Army of God is an actual organization, or whether it simply represents a loose affiliation of like-minded individuals and groups.

105. Ibid., p. 12.

106. Ibid., p. 13.

107. Ibid., pp. 14-15.
108. Ibid., p. 15.
109. Ibid., p. 16.
110. Ibid., pp. 20-23.
111. Ibid., p. 34.
112. Ibid., p. 42.
113. Ibid., p. 56.
114. Ibid., p. 57.
115. Ibid., Appendix, p. 36.
116. Ibid., Epilogue, pp. 1-3.
117. *NCAP News,* January 1992.
118. Christopher John Farley, "Malpractice as a Weapon," *Time,* March 13, 1995.
119. Will Offley, "Texas Tactics Come North—Kelowna Right to Life and Life Dynamics Inc.," 1998, unpublished paper.
120. www.naral.org/federal/court/court.html.
121. Rhonda Copelon, "From Rhetoric to Reality: The Challenge of Casey," *Reflections After Casey: Women Look at the Status of Reproductive Rights in America* (New York, NY: Center for Constitutional Rights, 1993).
122. Personal files of Patricia Baird-Windle.
123. In-person interview with Sandy Sheldon, January 15, 1999.
124. Ibid.
125. In-person interview with "Elena Schweitzer" (pseudonym), January 4, 1999.
126. "Facing a Future Without Choice—A Report on Reproductive Liberty in America," National Commission on America Without Roe (Washington, D.C.: NARAL Foundation, 1992).
127. In-person interview with "Elena Schweitzer," January 4, 1999.
128. In-person interview with Cathy Maguire, January 4, 1999.
129. In-person interview with "Elena Schweitzer," January 4, 1999.
130. Ibid.
131. In-person interview with Susan Ward, January 6, 1999.
132. Kevin Collison, "Griffin Calls Arcara Ruling on Abortion Protest Stupid," *Buffalo News* (New York), undated clipping.
133. In-person interview with Deborah Walsh, October 7, 1998.
134. Ibid.
135. Ibid.
136. Ibid.
137. Ibid.
138. Timothy Clifford and Wendell Jamieson, "Protester Shoves Fetus at Clinton," *Newsday* (New York), July 15, 1992.
139. Telephone interview with Jeri Rasmussen, February 1, 1999.
140. Mike Dooley, "Pro-Life Activists Hassle Doctor," *News Journal* (Ft. Wayne, IN), August 13, 1992.
141. Telephone interview with Judy Reiner, September 16, 1999.
142. Ibid.
143. Ibid.
144. Ibid.
145. Ibid.
146. Ibid.
147. Ibid.
148. Telephone interview with Susan Nenney, September 15, 1999.

149. Ibid.

150. Ibid.

151. Tanya Melich, *The Republican War Against Women: An Insider's Report From Behind the Lines* (New York, NY: Bantam Books, 1996), p. 263.

152. In-person conversation between Patricia Baird-Windle and Eleanor Bader, June 8, 1999.

153. Personal files of Patricia Baird-Windle.

154. Frederick Clarkson, *Eternal Hostility: The Struggle Between Theocracy and Democracy* (Monroe, ME: Common Courage Press, 1997), p. 7.

155. In-person conversation between Patricia Baird-Windle and Eleanor Bader, June 8, 1999.

156. *Norman T. Tompkins, MD and Carolyn Tompkins v. Thomas Cyr, et al;* 995 *Federal Supplement,* p. 671.

157. Ibid.

158. Ibid., p. 672.

159. Ibid., p. 673.

160. Ibid., p. 686.

161. Ibid., p. 674.

162. In-person interview with Patricia Mitchell, January 25, 1999.

163. S. K. Bardwell, "Poisonous Acid Poured at Four Women's Clinics," *Houston Chronicle* (Texas), July 9, 1998.

164. In-person interview with Patricia Mitchell, January 25, 1999.

165. Kathy Kemp, "Markley Forgoes Violent Ways, He Offers No Apologies for Clinic Violence," *Birmingham News-Post Herald* (Alabama), January 21, 1995.

166. In-person interview with Patricia Mitchell, January 25, 1999.

167. Parker Holmes, "Trosch Clings to His Beliefs," *Mobile Register* (Alabama), August 22, 1993.

168. In-person interview with Patricia Mitchell, January 25, 1999.

169. Parker Holmes, "Priest Says Killing Abortion Mds Justifiable Homicide," *Mobile Register,* August 15, 1993.

170. Laura Goldberg, "Priest Scolded Over Ad," *USA Today,* August 18, 1993.

171. Archive of the Center for Choice, Mobile, Alabama.

172. Ibid.

173. In-person interview with Patricia Mitchell, January 25, 1999.

174. Telephone interview with the Reverend Bruce Buchanan, December 29, 1998.

175. Ibid.

176. Ibid.

177. Telephone interview with Carol Adams, December 29, 1998.

178. Archive of First Presbyterian Church of Dallas, Texas.

179. The Reverend Bruce A. Buchanan, "Out of the Stewpot," *National Christian Reporter* (Dallas, TX), October 3, 1993.

180. Archive of the First Presbyterian Church of Dallas, Texas.

181. Telephone interview with Dr. Susan Wicklund, February 3, 1999.

182. Ibid.

183. Ibid.

184. Ibid.

185. Ibid.

186. In-person interview with Lorraine Maguire, October 3, 1998.

187. Ibid.

188. Ibid.

189. In-person interview with Shelley Maguire, October 3, 1998.

190. In-person interview with Lorraine Maguire, October 3, 1998.

191. Ibid.

192. Ibid.

193. Ibid.

194. Ibid.

195. Ibid.

196. Richard Green, Jr., "Security for Stalking Trial Tight," *The Post and Courier* (Charleston, SC), February 13, 1994.

197. David W. MacDougall, "Stalker Receives Probation," *The Post and Courier* (Charleston, SC), February 18, 1994.

198. Telephone interview with Charlotte Taft, November 11, 1998.

199. Ibid.

200. Offley, "Texas Tactics Come North."

201. Personal files of Patricia Baird-Windle.

202. Ibid.

203. *Conscience*, p. 11.

204. Offley, "Texas Tactics Come North."

205. Ibid.

206. "More Sleazy Tactics Revealed from 'Project Choice' Survey," *Clinic Support Update*, NAF (Washington, D.C.), October 20, 1993.

207. Telephone interview with Tina Welsh, October 13, 1998.

208. Ibid., October 11, 1999.

209. Ibid., October 13, 1998.

210. Ibid.

211. Ibid.

212. Ibid.

213. Ibid.

214. Ibid.

215. Ibid.

216. Ibid.

217. Ibid.

218. Ibid.

219. Paul Gray, "Camp for Crusaders," *Time*, April 19, 1993, p. 40.

220. Ibid.

221. In-person conversation between Patricia Baird-Windle and Eleanor Bader, June 8, 1999.

222. Ibid.

223. Ibid., June 10, 1999.

224. Ibid., June 8, 1999.

225. Ibid.

226. Telephone interview with Marilyn Chrisman Eldridge, November 10, 1998.

227. Ibid.

228. In-person interview with "Janet Williams" (pseudonym), September 14, 1998.

229. In-person conversation between Patricia Baird-Windle and Eleanor Bader, June 8, 1999.

230. In-person interview with Lisa Sanford, September 11, 1998.

231. Ibid.

232. Ibid.

233. Archive of the National Center for the Pro Choice Majority, Hightstown, New Jersey.

234. Personal files of Patricia Baird-Windle.

235. Archive of the National Coalition of Abortion Providers, Washington, D.C.

236. In-person interview with Jeanne Singletary, January 15, 1999.

237. Ibid.

238. In-person interview with Linda Taggart, January 16, 1999.

239. Ibid.

240. Ibid.

241. "Doctor Fatally Shot," *Pensacola News Journal,* March 11, 1993.

242. Ibid.

243. Ginny Graybiel, "Defendant Shows Conflicting Personalities," *Pensacola News Journal,* February 20, 1994.

244. Ginny Graybiel, "Griffin's Guilty," *Pensacola News Journal,* March 6, 1994.

245. In-person conversation between Patricia Baird-Windle and Eleanor Bader, June 8, 1999.

246. Telephone interview with Sally Burgess, November 6, 1998.

247. Judy Lundstrom Thomas, "Wichita Losing Two Catalysts in Struggle Over Abortion," *Wichita Eagle* (Kansas), August 1, 1993.

248. Telephone interview with Jeri Rasmussen, February 1, 1999.

249. Helen R. Franco, "Freedom of Access to Clinic Entrances Act of 1994: The FACE of Things to Come," *Nova Law Review* (Florida), vol. 19, 1995.

250. Kenneth R. Thomas, "Anti-Abortion Protests and Medical Clinic Blockades: Statutory and Constitutional Implications," *Congressional Research Service,* Library of Congress, April 16, 1993.

251. 18 U.S. Code 248 (FACE).

252. "Legal Action for Reproductive Rights: FACE," A Planned Parenthood Federation of America fact sheet.

253. In-person conversation between Patricia Baird-Windle and Eleanor Bader, June 9, 1999.

254. "But You Can't Say @#$%&! on the Air," *Clinic Support Update,* NAF (Washington, D.C.), April 15, 1993.

255. Ibid.

256. Telephone interview with Anita Kuennen, December 9, 1998.

257. Ibid.

258. Ibid.

259. Ibid.

260. Archive of the Blue Mountain Clinic, Missoula, Montana.

261. Telephone interview with Anita Kuennen, December 9, 1998.

262. Ibid.

263. Telephone interview with Tammy Sobieski, November 13, 1998.

264. In-person interview with Ted Windle, June 10, 1999.

265. Ibid.

266. Ibid.

267. In-person conversation between Patricia Baird-Windle and Eleanor Bader, June 10, 1999.

268. Personal files of Patricia Baird-Windle.

269. In-person interview with the Reverend Susan Beem-Beery, December 16, 1998.

270. "Chronology of Violence and Harassment," NAF fact sheet, undated.

271. Telephone interview with Jeri Rasmussen, February 1, 1999.

272. Personal correspondence between the Reverend Steven Mather and Eleanor Bader, received by Bader on February 12, 1999.

273. Robin Toner, "Twin Cities Gird for OR," *New York Times,* July 6, 1993.

274. Lesley Tritschler, "Former Minister Sees Himself as Prophet in Abortion Battle," *Pensacola News Journal,* August 29, 1993.

275. Jeff Magaw, "Clinics Plans to Provide Abortions on Hold," *Patriot News* (Muncie, Indiana), October 4, 1998.

276. In-person interview with Dr. George Tiller, February 15, 1999.

277. Ibid.

278. Telephone interview with Peggy Bowman, February 16, 1999.

279. Ibid.

280. In-person interview with Cathy Reavis, February 16, 1999.

281. Ibid.

282. Gail Randall, "Shannon Sentenced to 11 Years," *Wichita Eagle*, April 27, 1994.

283. Gail Randall and Judy Lundstrom Thomas, "Guilty and Unrepentant," *Wichita Eagle*, March 26, 1994.

284. Cindy West, "Shooting: Protest, Random Violence?" *Pensacola News Journal*, August 23, 1993.

285. Ginny Graybiel, "Slaying Closes Abortion Clinic," *Pensacola News Journal*, August 25, 1993.

286. In-person interview with Jeanne Singletary, January 15, 1999.

287. In-person interview with Sandy Sheldon, January 15, 1999.

288. Ibid.

289. In-person interview with Patricia Mitchell, January 25, 1999.

290. Ibid.

291. Telephone interview with "Carlyne Smith" (pseudonym), November 10, 1998.

292. Ibid.

293. In-person interview with Roni Windle, September 11, 1998.

294. Telephone interview with Dr. LeRoy Carhart, February 1, 1999.

295. Dan Herbeck, "Pro-Lifers Ordered to Pay Legal Fees," *Buffalo News*, October 2, 1993.

296. Telephone interview with Glenn A. Murray, Esq., January 7, 1999.

297. Lesley Stedman, "Abortion Foes Pause to Pray, Reflect on City Clinic's Rolls," *Journal Gazette* (Ft. Wayne, IN), October 4, 1993.

298. Laura-Lynn Powell, "Police Clerk Admits Leaking Addresses," *Orange County Register* (California), December 4, 1993.

299. 18 U.S. Code 2721-25.

300. In-person conversation between Patricia Baird-Windle and Eleanor Bader, November 5, 1999.

301. In-person conversation between Patricia Baird-Windle and Eleanor Bader, June 8, 1999.

302. Correspondence between Patricia Baird-Windle and Eleanor Bader, June 17, 2000.

303. Paul M. Barrett, "FBI Begins to Attack Abortion Clinic Violence, But with Less Vigor than Some Activists Want," *Wall Street Journal*, February 16, 1994.

304. "Antis Picket Provider Funeral," *Clinic Support Update*, NAF, March 16, 1994.

305. *NCAP News*, March 21, 1994.

306. Chronology of Violence and Harassment, NAF fact sheet.

307. Telephone interview with Dr. LeRoy Carhart, February 1, 1999.

308. Kristen Kolb, "Down on the Corporate Farm," *In These Times* Newsmagazine (Chicago, IL), March 7, 1999.

309. Michael Lasab Andra, "Reno Had Been Asked to Protect Clinic in Brookline," *Boston Herald*, March 31, 1994.

310. Archive of the National Women's Health Organization, headquartered in Raleigh, North Carolina.

311. In-person interview with Ted Windle, June 10, 1999.

312. Ibid.

313. In-person conversation between Patricia Baird-Windle and Eleanor Bader, June 9, 1999.

314. Tom Bates, "Godly Force," *The Oregonian* (Portland, OR), November 6, 1994.

315. Ibid.

316. Ibid.

317. *NCAP News,* July 1, 1994.

318. "First FACE Criminal Sentences are Maximum Allowable," *Clinic Support Update,* NAF, February 14, 1995.

319. In-person interview with Linda Taggart, January 16, 1999.

320. Ibid.

321. Personal files of Patricia Baird-Windle.

322. Ibid.

323. In-person conversation between Patricia Baird-Windle and Eleanor Bader, June 9, 1999.

324. *NCAP News,* July 26, 1994.

325. Telephone interview with Carolyn Izard, December 9, 1998.

326. Ibid.

327. In-person interview with Hallie Joyce, January 26, 1999.

328. In-person interview with Keri Taggart, January 26, 1999.

329. Ibid.

330. Ibid.

331. In-person interview with Linda Taggart, January 16, 1999.

332. Ibid.

333. Ibid.

334. Ibid.

335. Ginny Graybiel, "Hill Attorney: Dismiss Federal Charges," *Pensacola News Journal,* August 16, 1994.

336. Lesley Tritschler, "Suspect's File Cites Violence," *Pensacola News Journal,* July 30, 1994.

337. Cindy West, "Hill Says He Plotted Days Before Killing," *Florida Today,* December 4, 1994.

338. Ginny Graybiel, "Hill Receives Death Sentence for Murders," *Pensacola News Journal,* December 7, 1994.

339. In-person conversation between Patricia Baird-Windle and Eleanor Bader, June 9, 1999.

340. Joni Scott, "From Hate Rhetoric to Hate Crime: A Link Acknowledged Too Late," *The Humanist,* January/February 1999.

341. In-person conversation between Patricia Baird-Windle and Eleanor Bader, June 9, 1999.

342. Ibid.

343. News release, Planned Parenthood Federation of America, August 17, 1994.

344. "Rhode Island Bank Stands Firm in Face of Harassment," *Clinic Support Update,* NAF, September 2, 1994.

345. Michael Bray, *A Time to Kill* (Portland, OR: Advocates for Life Publications, 1994), p. 28.

346. Ibid., p. 41.

347. Ibid., pp. 116-117.

348. Ibid., p. 158.

349. Ibid., pp. 173-174.

350. Ibid., pp. 174-175.

351. Ibid., p.175.

352. Ibid., pp. 180-181.

353. "FACE-Less," *Journal Gazette* (Ft. Wayne, IN), September 24, 1994.

354. Archive of the Feminist Majority Foundation, Arlington, Virginia.

355. DuWayne Escobedo, "3 Klan to Pensacola to Protest U.S. Marshals at The Ladies Center," *Pensacola News Journal,* October 2, 1994.

356. Archive of the National Women's Health Organization, Raleigh, North Carolina.

357. Sara Diamond, *Roads to Dominion: Right-Wing Movements and Political Power in the U.S.* (New York, NY: The Guilford Press, 1995), p. 312.

358. In-person interview with Dr. Damon Stutes, July 23, 1998.

359. Ibid.

360. Ibid.

361. Ibid.

362. Ibid.

363. In-person conversation between Patricia Baird-Windle and Eleanor Bader, June 7, 1999.

364. Paul Nielson and Paul DeParrie, "Canadian Abortionist Shot," *Life Advocate* Magazine (Portland, OR), December 1994.

365. Phil Long, "Florida May Hold Clues to Shooting," *Miami Herald* (Florida), November 12, 1994.

366. "Terry Off to Jail Again, *Clinic Support Update*," NAF, November 17, 1994.

367. In-person conversation between Patricia Baird-Windle and Eleanor Bader, June 9, 1999.

368. Telephone interview with Anne Bower, November 14, 1999.

369. Alison Bass, "Physician Reported Calls Two Weeks Before Shootings," *Boston Globe* (Massachusetts), January 5, 1995.

370. Ibid.

371. Ibid.

372. In-person interview with Alice Verhoeven, December 1, 1998.

373. Ibid.

374. Ibid.

375. In-person interview with Nicki Nichols Gamble, November 30, 1998.

376. Katherine Webster, "Witness: Gun Toting Salvi Said: 'This Is What You Get,'" *The Standard-Times* (New Bedford, MA), February 16, 1994.

377. David Armstrong and Judy Rakowsky, "Police Find Gun Receipts in Bag at Clinic, Target NH Man," *Boston Globe,* December 31, 1994.

378. In-person interview with Nicki Nichols Gamble, November 30, 1998.

379. In-person interview with Alice Verhoeven, December 1, 1998.

380. Ibid.

381. Ibid.

382. In-person interview with Nicki Nichols Gamble, November 30, 1998.

383. Ibid.

384. Ibid.

385. Paula Childs, "Clinic Shooting Survivors Say Life Has Changed Forever," *Sunday Post Gazette* (Boston, MA), January 7, 1996.

386. Telephone interview with Renee Chelian, December 8, 1998.

387. Ibid.

388. Ibid.

389. Ibid.

390. Ibid.

391. "Conspiracy Link to Salvi Suspected," *The Orlando Sentinel* (Florida), January 6, 1995.

392. Laura LaFey, "Suspect Answers Charges," *Boston Globe,* January 3, 1995.

393. Telephone interview with Suzette Caton, October 22, 1998.

CHAPTER 7

1. "Casualties Mount in Battle Against Right to Choose," *USA Today,* October 27, 1998.

2. Barry Yeoman, "Art and States' Rights," *The Nation,* June 29, 1998.

3. Ibid.

4. Ibid.

5. Ibid.

6. Ibid.

7. "Radical GOP State Platforms—1996," http:apocalypse.berkshire.net/~ifas/fw/update.html.

8. www.msnbc.com/news/254736.asp.

9. Yeoman, "Art and States' Rights."

10. Telephone interview with Susan E. Davis, June 22, 1999.

11. Ellen Goodman, "Pro-Life? Show It," *Miami Herald* (Florida), January 9, 1995.

12. Telephone interview with Dr. "James Schwartz" (pseudonym), December 21, 1998.

13. Ibid.

14. Ibid.

15. Ibid.

16. Ibid.

17. Excerpts from "Dirge Without Music," by Edna St. Vincent Millay, *Collected Poems* by Edna St. Vincent Millay and Norma Millay Ellis (New York, NY: HarperCollins, 1928, 1955). Reprinted by permission of Elizabeth Barnett, Literary Executor.

18. *Greenville Women's Clinic, Charleston Women's Medical Clinic, Inc. and William Lynn, MD v. Douglas E. Bryant, Commissioner, David Beasley, Governor of South Carolina, and Charles M. London, Attorney General of South Carolina.* Filed 1995.

19. "Lorraine Maguire on 'Insects, Rodents and Debris,'" *The Body Politic* (Binghamton, NY), March/April 1999.

20. Ibid.

21. David Talbot, "Neighbors: Fight Filled Week with Parents Preceded Suspects' Murderous Rampage," *Boston Herald,* January 2, 1995.

22. John Ellemont, "Videotapes Show Salvi at Brookline Vigils," *Boston Globe,* February 22, 1996.

23. Scott A. Campbell, "Boss Describes Suspect as 'A Very Odd Character,'" *Boston Herald,* December 21, 1994.

24. Daniel Golden and Brian McGrory, "NH Man Held in Brookline Deaths After VA Facility Hit," *Boston Globe,* January 1, 1995.

25. Nancy Roberts, "Abortion Foes Rally for Suspect," Associated Press, January 1, 1995.

26. Bill Hutchinson, "What Went Wrong with John Salvi III?" *Boston Herald,* January 8, 1995.

27. Ibid.

28. James L. Franklin, "Salvi Pleads Not Guilty to Charges," *Boston Globe,* January 7, 1995.

29. *NCAP News* (Washington, D.C.), January 1995.

30. "Women's Rights? Or Hoodlums' Rights?" *New York Times,* March 11, 1995.

31. Ibid.

32. *Planned Parenthood of the Columbia/Willamette, Inc. et al v. The American Coalition of Life Activists, et al.* Filed 1995, U.S. District Court for the District of Oregon, 41 Federal Supplement. 2d 1130 (D. Or. 1999).

33. In-person interview with Dr. Elizabeth Newhall, August 11, 1998.

34. Ibid.

35. Sam Howe Verhovek, "Creators of Anti-Abortion Web Site Told to Pay Millions," *New York Times,* February 3, 1999.

36. Order and Permanent Injunction, U.S. District Court for the District of Oregon, *Planned Parenthood of the Columbia/Willamette, Inc. et al. v. The American Coalition of Life Activists, et al.* Filed 1995.

37. In-person interview with Dr. James Newhall, August 13, 1998.

38. In-person interview with Susan Hill, October 1, 1998.

39. Ibid.
40. Ibid.
41. In-person conversation with Susan Hill, September 1, 1999.
42. Mark Hamblett, "Salvi's Parents Warn Others," *Patriot Ledger* (Plymouth, MA), January 28/ 29, 1995.
43. Personal files of Patricia Baird-Windle.
44. Ginny Graybiel, "Gunn's Gain Burt's Land as Suit Ends," *Pensacola News Journal,* July 4, 1996.
45. Ibid.
46. "No Longer Pro-Violence to Fight Abortion," *Times-Union* (Jacksonville, FL), March 2, 1994.
47. Personal files of Patricia Baird-Windle.
48. Skipp Porteous, "Terry Calls for a Christian Nation," www.apocalypse.berkshire.net/ifas/fw/ 9509/terry.htm.
49. Ibid.
50. Telephone interview with Jude Hanzo, September 7, 1998.
51. Archive of All Women's Health Services, Portland, Oregon.
52. Telephone interview with Jude Hanzo, September 7, 1998.
53. Ibid.
54. Ibid.
55. Ibid.
56. Tamar Lewin, "Study on Late Term Abortion Finds Procedure Is Little Used," *New York Times,* December 11, 1998.
57. "Partial Birth Abortion Procedures," fact sheet prepared by New York State NARAL.
58. Lewin, "Study on Late Term Abortion."
59. Jennifer Gonnerman, "Inside Operation Rescue," *Village Voice* (New York, NY), February 11, 1997.
60. Telephone interview with Carol Adams, December 29, 1998.
61. Gayle Reaves, "Operation Rescue Items Sold to Foe," *Dallas Morning News* (Texas), May 2, 1995.
62. Personal files of Patricia Baird-Windle.
63. Ibid.
64. Archive of the Planned Parenthood League of Massachusetts, Boston, Massachusetts.
65. Telephone interview with Sally Burgess, November 6, 1998.
66. Ibid.
67. Telephone interview with Ann Rose, December 29, 1998.
68. Personal files of Patricia Baird-Windle.
69. Michael Bray, "Tale of Two Armies—and Their Manuals," *Life Advocate* Magazine (Portland, OR), November 1995.
70. "Another Abortion Provider Shot," *Pro-Choice News,* Canadian Abortion Rights Action League, Fall 1995.
71. Adrian Humphreys, "Shooting Meant to Kill Three Abortion Doctors," *The Hamilton Spectator* (Hamilton, Ontario), November 15, 1997.
72. Telephone interview with Anita Kuennen, December 9, 1998.
73. www.nytaxpayers.org/candidates.
74. Ibid.
75. Amanda Ripley, "Terrorists and Saints," *Washington City Paper* (Washington, D.C.), February 5, 1999.
76. Ibid.

77. Ibid.
78. DuWayne Escobedo and Winnie Hur, "Reno: No Abortion Violence Conspiracy," *Pensacola News Journal*, January 26, 1996.
79. Archive of the National Center for the Pro Choice Majority, Hightstown, New Jersey.
80. In-person interview with Nicki Nichols Gamble, November 30, 1998.
81. Dirk Johnson, "NE Bishop Threatens Excommunication for Dissenters," *New York Times*, March 26, 1996.
82. Bob Reeves, "Prochoice Viewpoint Attracts Flak," *Lincoln Journal Star* (Nebraska), September 12, 1996.
83. www.thonline.com/th/news/032397/national/515.20/htm.
84. News release, Catholics for a Free Choice, Washington, D.C.
85. Personal files of Patricia Baird-Windle.
86. In-person conversation between Patricia Baird-Windle and Eleanor Bader, November 5, 1999.
87. Archive of the Planned Parenthood League of Massachusetts, Boston, Massachusetts.
88. In-person conversation between Patricia Baird-Windle and Eleanor Bader, November 5, 1999.
89. www.s-tcom/daily/05-96/05-16-96/2 excom.htm.
90. In-person conversation between Patricia Baird-Windle and Eleanor Bader, November 6, 1999.
91. James Hitchcock, "The Strange Political Career of Father Drinan," *Catholic World Report* (San Francisco, CA), July, 1996.
92. Ibid.
93. Ibid.
94. In-person interview with Frances Kissling, September 28, 1999.
95. Ann Sheridan, "Father Drinan Recants," *HLI Reports*, a publication of Human Life International (Front Royal, VA), July 1997, p. 5.
96. Telephone interview with Anita Kuennen, December 9, 1998.
97. Telephone interview with Bill Morlin, February 9, 1999.
98. Ibid.
99. Telephone interview with John Nugent, February 9, 1999.
100. Ibid.
101. Bill Morlin, "Spokane Bombers Get Lifer Terms," *Spokesman-Review* (Spokane, WA), November 5, 1997.
102. Telephone interview with John Nugent, February 9, 1999.
103. Letter in personal files of Patricia Baird-Windle.
104. Ibid.
105. Telephone interview with Jeri Rasmussen, February 1, 1999.
106. Ibid.
107. *Conscience,* The Newsjournal of Catholics for a Free Choice, Winter 1997/1998 (Washington, D.C.), p. 11.
108. Peter L. Canellos and Jordana Hart, "Violent Actions Fueled by Deep Personal Woes, Fears," *Boston Globe,* November 30, 1996.
109. *Violence Against Reproductive Health Care Centers,* report compiled by the Feminist Majority Foundation, Planned Parenthood Federation of America, the National Abortion Federation and the National Center for Women and Policing, 1997.
110. Telephone interview with Diane Pogrant, December 11, 1998.
111. Ibid.

112. Edie Gross, "Copycat Incident in Lake Clarke Shores?" *Palm Beach Post* (Florida), December 26, 1996.
113. Personal files of Lorraine Maguire.
114. *Planned Parenthood of the Columbia/Willamette, et al. v. The American Coalition of Life Activists, et al.* Filed 1995.
115. Telephone interview with the Reverend Carl Horton, February 1, 1999.
116. Telephone interview with the Reverend Don Smith, February 1, 1999.
117. Ibid.
118. Telephone interview with the Reverend Carl Horton, February 1, 1999.
119. Ibid.
120. Telephone interview with Sherri Finik, October 20, 1998.
121. "Shock, Uncertainty in Wake of Bombings," *Atlanta Constitution* (Georgia), January 17, 1997.
122. Rust Bynum, "Six Injured as Bombs Hit Abortion Clinic," *Miami Herald,* January 17, 1997.
123. Telephone interview with Sherri Finik, October 20, 1998.
124. Ibid.
125. Ibid.
126. "Sentencing Postponed for Oklahoma Couple," Associated Press, January 23, 1998.
127. Telephone interview with Sherri Finik, October 20, 1998.
128. Dan Herbeck, "Judge Urges Parties to Settle Abortion Demonstration Issues," *Buffalo News* (New York), April 2, 1998.
129. Claire McCurdy, "Phony Planned Parenthood Web Site Enjoined," *Speak Out,* the newsletter of the Pro-choice Network of Western New York, Summer 1997.
130. Ibid.
131. Ashbel S. Green, "Reward Offered in Clinic Arson Case," *The Oregonian* (Portland), August 3, 1998.
132. In-person interview with Carye Ortman, August 4, 1998.
133. Ibid.
134. Ibid.
135. Telephone interview with Diane Pogrant, December 11, 1998.
136. Personal files of Patricia Baird-Windle.
137. In-person interview with Lois Bachus, August 5, 1998.
138. Telephone interview with "Katrina Douglas" (pseudonym), November 9, 1998.
139. Ibid.
140. *Who Decides? A State by State Review of Abortion and Reproductive Rights* (Washington, D.C.: NARAL, 1999).
141. *NCAP News,* July 23, 1997.
142. In-person interview with Gloria Gray, January 22, 1999.
143. In-person interview with Dr. Louis Payne, January 22, 1999.
144. Ibid.
145. In-person interview with Gloria Gray, January 22, 1999.
146. Ibid.
147. *Violence Against Reproductive Health Care Centers.*
148. In-person interview with Lorraine Maguirre, October 3, 1998.
149. Telephone interview with Carolyn Izard, December 9, 1998.
150. Ibid.
151. Bass and Howes, *America's Health Held Hostage: How Politics Is Paralyzing Medical Advances,* report prepared for NARAL, 1997.
152. Ibid.

153. Ibid.
154. Legal brief of Christopher F. Sapp, Esq., *Meredith Trotter Raney Jr. v. The Aware Woman Center for Choice, Inc. and Patricia B. Windle and Edward W. Windle*, p. 5.
155. Legal Brief of Spurgeon Roy Lucas, Esq., *Raney v. Aware Woman et al.*, p. 7.
156. *Who Decides? A State by State Review of Abortion and Reproductive Rights.*
157. Telephone interview with "Katrina Douglas," November 9, 1998.
158. "Doctor Shot: Was It Anti-Choice Attack?" *Pro-Choice News,* Canadian Abortion Rights Action League, Winter 1998.
159. Telephone interview with Diane Pogrant, December 11, 1998.
160. Ibid.
161. Laurin Sellers, "Melbourne Mayor: Pray, Fast, To End Abortion," *Orlando Sentinel* (Florida), January 15, 1998.
162. Archive of the Feminist Majority Foundation, Arlington, Virginia.
163. Archive of Women's Health Services, Pittsburgh, Pennsylvania.
164. Ibid.
165. Ibid.
166. In-person interview with Mary Ellen Tunney, November 18, 1998.
167. Nancy Bowes, Varda Burstyn and Andrea Knight, *Access Granted, Too Often Denied: A Special Report to Celebrate the 10th Anniversary of the Decriminalization of Abortion,* Canadian Abortion Rights Action League, January 28, 1998, p. 5.
168. Ibid., p. 4.
169. Ibid., p. 35.
170. In-person interview with Michelle Farley, January 23, 1999.
171. Ibid.
172. Ibid.
173. Carol Robinson, "Toppled Plant Baited Abortion Clinic Bomb," *Birmingham News* (Alabama), March 8, 1998.
174. In-person interview with Michelle Farley, January 23, 1999.
175. Ibid.
176. In-person interview with Lisa Hermes, January 20, 1999.
177. In-person interview with Michelle Farley, January 23, 1999.
178. Ibid.
179. Ibid.
180. In-person interview with Emily Lyons, January 19, 1999.
181. Ibid.
182. Ibid.
183. Ibid.
184. Ibid.
185. http://CNN.com/US/9802/clinic.bombing.folo/index/html.
186. Carol Robinson, "Nails in Rudolph Shed Linked to Atlanta Bombs," *Birmingham News,* undated clipping.
187. Edward Walsh, "FBI Increases Reward for Bombing Suspect," *Washington Post,* May 6, 1998.
188. "10 Most Wanted Fugitives," *Birmingham Post Herald* (Alabama), July 15, 1998.
189. In-person interview with "Amber Russo" (pseudonym), September 14, 1998.
190. Ibid.
191. Ibid.
192. Ibid.
193. Ibid.
194. Roger Munns, "Judge: Zoning Blocked Clinic," Associated Press, February 12, 1998.

195. Will Offley, "Cashing in on Terror," *International Viewpoint,* no. 303, 1998 (London, England), p. 15.

196. Archive of the Planned Parenthood League of Massachusetts, Boston, Massachusetts.

197. www.2lifecoalition.com/lci.

198. www.orn.org/june98/htm.

199. "Liberty U Students Invade Public High Schools in Lynchburg, Va.," newsletter of Americans United for Separation of Church and State (Washington, D.C.), summer 1998.

200. In-person interview with Susan Hill, September 1, 1999.

201. Ibid.

202. *Hotspots,* Planned Parenthood Federation of America (New York, NY), May 1, 1998.

203. Telephone interview with Marion Ornstein, November 9, 1998.

204. Telephone interview with Pat Davis, October 16, 1998.

205. Telephone interview with Marion Ornstein, November 9, 1998.

206. Ibid.

207. *NCAP News,* May 29, 1998.

208. Telephone interview with Gerri Laster, October 25, 1999.

209. Frank Oliveri, "OR Targets Gay Days Gathering," *Florida Today,* June 5, 1998.

210. *Aware Woman Center for Choice, et al. v. Meredith T. Raney, et al.* Filed in U.S. District Court, Middle District of Florida, Orlando District, November 1998.

211. In-person conversation between Patricia Baird-Windle and Eleanor Bader, November 5, 1999.

212. Jeff Gottlieb, "Teens Give New Life to Operation Rescue," *Los Angeles Times,* October 12, 1998.

213. Ibid.

214. Minutes, Melbourne City Council meeting, August 25, 1998; personal files of Patricia Baird-Windle.

215. Ibid.

216. Paul Gougelman, "Report on the Legality of Using Zoning Powers Relative to Abortion Clinics," August 10, 1998; unpublished report submitted to the Melbourne, FL City Council.

217. Ibid.

218. Telephone interview with Carolyn Izard, December 9, 1998.

219. Annette Fuentes, "Campaigning for a Christian Nation," *In These Times* Newsmagazine (Chicago, IL), October 4, 1998.

220. David Rohde, "Quiet, Affluent Town Is Stunned by Sniper Slaying of One of Its Doctors," *New York Times,* October 26, 1998.

221. Dan Herbeck, Patrick Lakamp and Lou Michel, "Police Under Fire," *Buffalo News,* October 28, 1998.

222. Ibid.

223. Ibid.

224. Gene Warner, "Slepian Widow Sends Flowers Back, Calls Rev. Schenck a 'Hypocrite,'" *Buffalo News,* November 2, 1998.

225. "An Attack on the Community," *Buffalo News,* October 26, 1998.

226. Rohde, "Quiet, Affluent Town Is Stunned by Sniper Slaying of One of Its Doctors."

227. In-person interview with Marilynn Buckham, January 5, 1999.

228. Ibid.

229. Ibid.

230. Blaine Harden and Roberto Suro, "Abortion Foe Sought for Questioning in Shootings," *Washington Post,* November 5, 1998.

231. Michael J. Sniffen, "Feds Probing Anti-Abortion Web Site," Associated Press, November 5, 1998.

232. Telephone interview with Raquel Sims, December 9, 1998.

233. John Kelly, "Clinic Victims Wait While Authorities Test Substance," Associated Press, October 30, 1998.

234. Telephone interview with Kim Horab, November 4, 1998.

235. "Terry Files for Bankruptcy to Avoid Paying Clinics," *Buffalo News,* November 8, 1998.

236. Sarah Coomber, "Vandals Deface Fargo Abortion Facility," *Fargo Forum* (North Dakota), November 10, 1998.

237. David Johnston, "US Expands Investigation into Violence at Abortion Clinics," *New York Times,* November 10, 1998.

238. In-person interview with "Elena Schweitzer," January 4, 1999.

239. Ibid.

240. Ibid.

241. Personal files of Patricia Baird-Windle.

242. "Patient Story of the Month," *NCAP News,* March 11, 1999.

243. In-person conversation between Patricia Baird-Windle and Eleanor Bader, November 5, 1999.

244. "Enforce Clinic Protection Laws to Their Fullest Potential," www.naral.org/publications/facts/1999/enforce.html.

245. *NCAP Newsletter,* October 24, 1999.

246. "1999 Year End Analysis of Violence and Disruption Against Reproductive Health Care Clinics," National Abortion Federation (Washington, D.C.), January 19, 2000.

247. "Texas and Michigan Lead 1999 Assault on Reproductive Freedom and Choice," NARAL press release, January 13, 2000, www.naral.org/mediaresources/press.

248. "NAF Violence and Disruption Statistics," National Abortion Federation, Washington, D.C., Dec. 31, 2000.

CHAPTER 8

1. In-person interview with Ellie Smeal, October 30, 1998.

2. "Abstracts of GAO Reports and Testimony," FY 99, p. 3, www.gao.gov/alndexfy99/abstracts/gg99002.htm.

3. In-person interview with Carla Eckhardt, December 15, 1998.

4. "Abstracts of GAO Reports and Testimony."

5. In-person interview with Ellie Smeal, October 30, 1998.

6. Unpublished writing of Patricia Baird-Windle, August 2000.

7. In-person interview with Ron Fitzsimmons, July 12, 1999.

8. In-person interview with Carla Eckhardt, December 15, 1999.

9. In-person conversation between Patricia Baird-Windle and Eleanor Bader, November 4, 1999.

10. Telephone interview with Peg Johnston, September 28, 1998.

11. Telephone interview with Charlotte Taft, November 11, 1998.

12. Untitled/unpublished paper prepared by the National Coalition of Abortion Providers, 1999.

13. Unpublished writing of Patricia Baird-Windle, July 2000.

14. Ibid.

15. E-mail correspondence between Patricia Baird-Windle and Eleanor Bader, November 30, 2000.

16. Unpublished writing of Patricia Baird-Windle, July 2000.

INDEX

A

abortion, history of legalization, 22, 33, 35, 37
abortion ambivalence, 92
Abortion and Contraception Clinic of Nebraska, 160, 223, 226–227
abortion and medical societies, 46
Abortion Buster's Manual, 87, 89–90
Abortion Clinics On-Line, 269
abortion providers before *Roe v. Wade*, 22, 29–30, 33
abortion services
    and advertising, 46–47, 166–167
    after *Roe v. Wade*, 1
    availability nationwide, 3
    Medicaid, 2, 58–59, 290
    restrictions, 2, 3, 53
    societal threats to access, 3–4
Abortion Services Protection Fund, 330, 331
Accessory to Murder, 142
ACLA
    collects data for Nuremberg Files, 282–283
    founded, 228–229
    launches SHAME Campaign, 265–266
    meets in Portland, 259
    pickets Hope Clinic for Women, 268–269
    publishes *A Time to Kill*, 237
    publishes Nuremberg Files, 9–10
    sued by Planned Parenthood, 259–260
Acquino, Eduardo (M.D.), 148, 149
Adams, Carol, 188, 266
Adorno, Theodor Wiesengrund, 11, 13
advertising, 46–47, 166–167, 313–314
Advocates for Life Ministries, 9, 108, 153–154
Affiliated Medical Services, 229
Agrawal, Anjana (Anu), 245
Ahmanson, Howard, 140
Alan Guttmacher Institute, 2, 3–4, 266
Alexander, Clay, 183
Allegheny Reproductive Health Center, 128–129, 131–132, 147–148
Allentown Women's Center, 55–56
Allied Business PAC, 140
All Women's Health Center, 149
All Women's Health Services, 96, 98–99, 110, 146
All Women's Medical Services, 150
Alternatives of Tampa, 57–58
American Academy of Pediatrics, 2
American Center for Law and Justice, 162, 287
American Coalition of Life Activists. *See* ACLA
American Family Association, 309
American Law Institute, 22

American Life League, 6, 57, 108, 253
American Public Health Association, 2
Anderson, Don Benny, 64, 66, 101
Andrews, Richard Thomas, 156–157, 211–212, 213
anthrax threats, 318
anti-abortion activists, personality traits, 11–13
anti-abortion activity, costs to taxpayers
    Buffalo, 176
    El Paso, 153
    Fargo, 155
    Little Rock, 231
    Pittsburgh, 111–112
    Wichita, 159
anti-abortion activity, effects on
    clinic workers (*See* violence and effects on clinic workers)
    feminism, 14, 33
Arcara, Richard, 117, 162, 176, 223
Arena, John, 113, 272
Arick, Ruth, 208
Armstrong, Carl, 75
Army of God, 65, 167
Army of God Manual, 141, 167–170
arson. *See* fires
Assemblies of God, 85
Assignment Life, 85
Atkins, Rachel, 136, 146
Atlanta Feminist Women's Health Center , 112
Atlanta Women's Medical Center, 112
authoritarian personality, 11
Aware Woman Center for Choice
    awarded judgment, 63
    blockaded by OR, 126
    bomb scares, xvii, 66, 281
    at Cocoa Beach, 50–51
    first protestors, 49
    founded, 47–50
    lawsuit over patient harassment, 320
    and *Madsen* case, 211, 225, 230–231
    Melbourne clinic loses lease, 49–50
    Melbourne issues anti-abortion proclamation, 296
    patients receive letters from WLAC, 172, 262–263, 264
    performs first abortion, 52
    physician resigns after harassment, 274–275
    picketed by Klu Klux Klan, 239
    Port St. Lucie clinic loses lease, 182, 224–225
    target of IMPACT Team, xv–xvii, 181, 200–202
    telephone harassment, 52

vandalism, 52
wanted posters, 143, 144
zoning board dispute, 50–51
AWCC. *See* Aware Woman Center for Choice

B

Bachus, Lois, 290
Bagenholm, Bo (M.D.), 85
Baird, Bill
  arrested and jailed, 25–26, 36
  clinic firebombed, 57
  employment at Emko, 24
  initiates Plan Van, 25
  organizes after Cleveland firebombing, 55
  prison diary, 34–35, 36
Baird v. Eisenstadt, 21
Baird-Windle, Patricia
  on clinic violence and the pro-choice commu-
    nity, 326–327
  death threat, 235–236
  decision in *Madsen*, 230–231
  on FACE enforcement, 325
  and Florida protests, 132
  founding member of November Gang, 136–
    137
  initiates national survey of providers, 329–330
  and loss of police protection, 275
  meets with U.S. Attorney in Florida, 276–277
  on NCAP meeting with Department of Justice,
    242
  organizes Connection Conference, 243
  proposes Abortion Services Protection Fund,
    330–331
  on Raney deposition, 311–312
  receives letter from DOJ, 279–280
  retires, 320
  and right to work laws, 274–275
  Supreme Court agrees to hear case, 225
  testifies in RICO suit, 100
  writes to DOJ, 289
Baird-Windle, Patricia, and IMPACT Team
  events during IMPACT training, 200–202
  on IMPACT and the media, xi–xii
  notified IMPACT coming to Melbourne, 181
  target of IMPACT, xv–xvii
Baker, Ann, 54
Baker, Jeffrey, 10
Bakker, Jim, 89
Balagher, Pat, 117
Barbee, Charles, 278–279
Barnes, Helen (M.D.), 261
Barnes & Noble, 8, 176
Barrett, James, 141, 232–233
Barrett, June, 232, 234
Barringer, Felicity, xiv–xv
Bauman, Bob, 59–60
Beaver, Gerald, 154–155
Beem-Barry, Rev. Susan, 215–216
Belew, Harley, 178
Bell, Joan Andrews, 95, 99, 296–297

Bell, Rebecca Suzanne, 114
Benham, Rev. Philip "Flip"
  arrives in Melbourne for IMPACT Team, 181
  denounced for church service disruption, 188
  endorses Phillips for president, 271
  named in Tompkins lawsuit, 184
  and OR/OSA activities, 8
  pressures Florida resident physicians, 274–275
  sentenced, 305–306
Berry, John, 12
Berry, Robert, 278–279
Bertsch, Penny, 156–157
Beseda, Curtis, 72–73
Biblical Action League, 82
Billings, Rev. Robert, 41, 59
birth control legalized, 23
birth control pill, approved, 21
Birthright opens in Cocoa Beach, FL, 52
Blackmun, Harry, 167
Blanchard, Dallas, 85
Blinded by the Might, 253
Blinn, Richard, 181, 184
blockades
  Affiliated Medical Services, 229
  Allegheny Reproductive Health Center, 128–
    129
  All Women's Health Center, 149
  Atlanta Feminist Women's Health Center, 112
  Atlanta Women's Medical Center, 112
  AWCC, 126
  Buffalo clinics, 174–175
  Charleston Women's Health Center, 144
  Cherry Hill Women's Center, 124–125
  Delaware Women's Health Organization, 114,
    119–120
  Dr. Boyd, Santa Fe, 157
  Knoxville Volunteer Medical Clinic, 121–122
  Little Rock Family Planning Services, 293
  Reproductive Services of El Paso, 152–153
  Toronto Medical Services, 114
  Women's Health Care Services, 158–159
Blue Mountain Clinic, 211–212
Bodigheimer, Edward, 276–277
Body of Christ, The, 148
bombings
  attempts at Ohio clinics, 323
  Dr. Bo Bagenholm's office, 85
  Dr. William Permenter's office, 85
  Hillcrest Clinic, 78
  The Ladies Center, 78–79, 84
  letter bombs, at Portland clinics, 98–99
  New Woman All Women Health Care, 298–
    299
  Northside Family Planning, 285
  Planned Parenthood, Chico, 156
  Planned Parenthood, Spokane, 278–279
  Reproductive Services of Tulsa, 285
  scare, at AWCC, xvii, 66
  scare, at West Palm AWCC, 281
  Wheaton, MD clinic, 81

Bonner, Brian, 145
Bottom Feeder, 194
Boulder Abortion Clinic, 96, 109–110, 124
Bovard, Jane, 240
Bower, Anne, 243–244
Bowman, Peggy, 158, 219
Boyd, Curtis (M.D.), 115, 116, 155, 157
Bray, Jayne, 10, 273
Bray, Michael
    on *Army of God Manual*, 270–271
    bombs Wheaton clinic, 81
    corresponded with Joseph Scheidler, 101
    jailed for bombing, 78
    pens *A Time to Kill*, 141
    present at Reed sentencing, 77
    publishes (with Andrew Burnett) *A Time to
        Kill*, 236–237
    sentenced, 82
    signer of Defensive Action, 218
    sponsors White Rose banquet, 272
Bright, Bill, 41
British Columbia Pro-Life Society, 304
Britton, John Bayard (M.D.), 232–233
Brockhoeft, John
    convicted of arson in Cincinnati, 111
    jailed, 110
    MTPB raises money, 150
    at White Rose Banquet, 272
    writes *The Brockhoeft Report*, 204–205
Brockhoeft Report, The, 204–205
Brown, Judie, 6, 57, 271
Brown, Paul, 6, 57
Brownesville Assembly of God, 208
Bruskewitz, Bishop Fabian, 273–274, 276
Bryn, Robert, 36–37
Bucci, Richard, 287
Buchanan, Rev. Bruce, 187–189
Buckham, Marilynn, 316–317
Buffalo GYN Womanservices, 116–117, 176, 316–
    317
Buffalo United for Choice, 173–174
buffer zone ordinances
    Buffalo, 117 (*See also* Schenck)
    Charleston, 144
    first, in Boulder, 104
    Melbourne, 211 (*See also* Madsen)
    Pensacola, 234
Burgess, Sally, 268–269
Burkin, Peter, 57
Burnett, Andrew
    elected to PLAN Leadership Council, 108
    founds Advocates for Life Ministries, 9
    founds American Coalition of Life Activists,
        228–229
    and Lovejoy judgment, 153–154
    publishes (with Michael Bray) *A Time to Kill*,
        237
    signer of Defensive Action, 218
Burt, John
    begins anti-abortion activism, 78

corresponded with Joseph Scheidler, 101
and John Brockhoeft, 110–111
and Michael Griffin, 208
and Our Father's House protestor, 84
sued by SPLC, 263
Bush, George, 79, 139
Bustamante, Elva, 149–150
Buxton, C. Lee (M.D.), 23

C

California Republican Assembly, 140. *See also*
    Republican Party and abortion
Call to Action, 273–274
Calos, Rev. Steve, 174–175
Campaign Life, 114
Campaign Report, The, 97
Campbell, Bill, 285
Canada repeals abortion laws, 70
Canadian Abortion Rights Action League, 271,
    297–298
Canady, Charles, 266
Candelario, Rosemary, 4
Capitol Area Christian News, 236
Cappell, Butch, 153
Carhart, LeRoy (M.D.), 160–162, 223, 242
Carlson, Rev. Walter, 135
Carmen, Arlene, 28
Carter, Jimmy, 61
Catholics for a Free Choice, 45, 79, 274
Caton, Suzette, 249–250
Center for Choice, Mobile, 184–187, 221
Center for Choice, Toledo, 75, 77–78
Center for Choice II, 133
Center for Reproductive and Sexual Health, 28
Center for Reproductive Law and Policy, 256, 275
Central Florida Women's Health Organization,
    307–308
Central Health Center for Women, 167
Charity Chapel, 207–208
Charleston Women's Health Center, 144, 191,
    292–293
Charleston Women's Medical Clinic, 256–257
Chelian, Renee, 184–185, 242, 247–249
Chen, Pamela, 277
Cherry Hill Women's Center, 106, 124–125, 127
Chesler, Phyllis, 13
Chico Feminist Women's Health Center, 45–46, 69
Child Custody Protection Act, 2, 5
Choices Women's Medical Center, 208
Chrisman, Rev. Myron "Chris", 42, 120
Christian Action Group, 10
Christian Coalition, 139–140, 252
Christian Identity movement, 278, 302
Christian Manifesto, 87
Christian Pro-Life Foundation, 252
Christians for Life, 274
Church of Pierce Creek, 103
church service disruptions, 175, 284, 307
*City of Akron v. Akron Center for Reproductive
    Health*, 68, 257

Cleary, Kevin, 128
Clergymen's Consultation Service on Abortion, 27–28
Clinic Access Project, 296
clinic advertising. *See* advertising
clinic blockades. *See* blockades
clinic bombings. *See* bombings
clinic damage, costs of
    Boulder Abortion Clinic, 110
    Center for Choice, Mobile, 185
    Florida clinics, 85
    Lovejoy SurgiCenter, 288
    national overview, 210
    New Woman All Women Health Care, 300
    Planned Parenthood, Spokane, 279
    Redding Feminist Women's Health Center, 156
    Reproductive Services of Tulsa, 286
    West Alabama Women's Center, 291
    West End Women's Medical Group, 240–241
    Women's Health Services, 151–152
clinic fires. *See* fires
clinic invasions. *See* invasions
clinic judgments
    Aware Woman Center for Choice, 63
    Delaware Women's Health Organization, 102
    Houston clinics, 179
    The Ladies Center, 263
    Lovejoy SurgiCenter, 153–154
    Planned Parenthood Federation, 180
    Planned Parenthood of the Columbia/Willamette, 260
    Summit Women's Health Organization, 102
clinic protection laws, 128. *See also* FACE
clinic shootings. *See* shootings
clinic stabbings, 281, 323
Clinic Support Update, 196, 211
clinic telephone harassment. *See* telephone harassment
clinic zoning regulations, 50–51, 56, 304, 312–313
clinics, state regulation of, 296
clinics lose leases
    AWCC, Melbourne, 49–50
    AWCC of Port St. Lucie, 182, 224–225
    Center for Choice, Toledo, 76
    Long Island Gynecological Associates, 258–259
    Reproductive Services of Tulsa, 83
    South Florida, 222
    Summit Women's Health Organization, 100
    Women's Health Center, 196–197
Clinton, Bill
    and fetal tissue research, 293–294
    presented with fetus during campaign, 178
    repeals gag rule, 109
    sends letter to NCAP, 226
    signs FACE Act, 142, 210
    vetoes "partial birth abortion" bill, 266
Clinton, Hillary Rodham, 278
Closed: 99 Ways to Stop Abortion, 7, 87

Coar, David, 102
Codispoti, Sharon, 73
Coleman, John (M.D.), 226
Committee for Survival of a Free Congress, 41
Commonwealth Clinic, 272
Community Healthcare Center of Pensacola. *See* The Ladies Center
Concerned Women's Clinic, 54
Congressional letter to FBI, 205–206
Connections Conference, 243–244
Conner, Cathy
    clinic invaded, 95, 105
    harassment, 96
    resigns after harassment, 15
    testifies in RICO suit, 100
Conservative Caucus, 41
Constitution Party. *See* U.S. Taxpayer's Party
Cooke, Terence Cardinal, 28, 36
Coors Foundation, 41
Copelon, Rhonda, 172
Crabb, Winston (M.D.), 283–285
Crane, David, 9–10, 228, 259
Creator's Rights Party, 283
crisis pregnancy centers
    congressional hearing, 93
    Fargo Women's Help Organization, 109
    Life Enterprises Unlimited, 186
    Melbourne, Florida, 214
    Pittsburgh Word and Worship Fellowship, 145
    Problem Pregnancy Center, 104
    Problem Pregnancy, Inc., 67
    and Randy Terry, 103
    The White Rose, 91–92
    and Yellow Page advertising, 167
Crist, Robert (M.D.), 216, 259
Crossroads, 6
Crusaders: Voices from the Abortion Front, 113
Crutcher, Mark, 171
Cyr, Thomas, 182–184

D

D'Alemberte, Talbot "Sandy," 225
Dallas First Presbyterian Church, 187–189
Dallas Pro-Life Action Network, 182
Davis, Pat, 307–308
Davis, Paul (M.D.), 117
Davis, Susan E., 254
"Deadly Dozen", 259
death threats received
    Baird-Windle, Patricia, 235–236
    Boyd, Dr. Curtis, 116, 155
    Gamble, Nicki Nichols, 247
    Halvorson-Boyd, Glenna, 116
    Houston physicians, 179
    Jackson Women's Health Organization, 261
    Long Island clinics, 258
    Maguire, Lorraine, 192
    Mitchell, Patricia, 186
    Newhall, Dr. James, 260–261
    Planned Parenthood Brookline doctor, 244

Rasmussen, Jeri, 280
Tompkins, Dr., 183
Windle, Roni, 222
Defensive Action, 218
Delaware Women's Health Organization, 102, 105, 114, 119–120
Democratic National Convention, Atlanta, 112–113
De Moss, Art, 41
DeParrie, Paul C., 153–154, 218, 265, 266
Department of Justice, 241–242, 261, 280, 317
Derzis, Diane, 300
DeVos, Richard, 40–41
Diamond, Sara, 240
Dillon, Denis, 57, 151
Disney World, 309
Dobson, Ed, 253
Doctors for the Right to Choose, 128
Dodds, Michael, 228
Donlan, Larry, 283
Downer, Carol, 30, 32–33
Downtown Women's Center, 260
Dreste, Tim, 209
Drinan, Father Robert, 277
Drury, Joan, 198
Drzymala, Rev. Darren, 162
Duke, David, 139
Dunn, Carol, 75, 77–78, 133

E

Eckhardt, Carla, 324–325, 326–327
"800 Club, The," 171
Eighty Percent Majority Campaign. See National Center for the Pro Choice Majority
Eldridge, Marilyn Chrisman, xiv, 42, 120, 202
Elim Bible College, 88
Elizabeth Bagshaw Clinic (Canada), 242
Emko Pharmaceuticals, 24
England, Susan, 225, 276
Erie Medical Center, 116, 117

F

FACE
    effects of, 324
    enacted, 210–211
    enforced against Cathy Rider, 193–194
    first prosecution, 229
    and Paul Hill, 229–230
    and police enforcement, 238–239
    signed into law, 142
Fainman, Jack (M.D.), 295
Fairmont Clinic, 115–116, 118–119
Falwell, Jerry, 59, 61, 89, 305–306
Family Protection Act, 62
Family Reproductive Health, 177
Fargo-Moorhead Women's Help and Caring Connection, 109
Fargo Women's Health Organization
    and crisis pregnancy center advertising case, 109

    injunction, 166
    Lambs of Christ summer blockades, 155
    opens, 63
    sends letter to Department of Justice, 240
    vandalized, 318, 319
Farley, Guy, Jr., 59
Farley, Michelle, 15, 298–299, 300–301
Faux, Marian, 112
FBI
    and Cleveland firebombing, 55
    and clinic death threats, 225–226
    denies "domestic terrorism", 83
    and FACE, 229–230, 324–325
    investigates Birmingham bombings, 302
    investigates Pentacostals for Life, 309
Federal Bureau of Investigation. See FBI
Federal Drivers' Privacy Protection Act, 224
Feminist Majority Foundation
    assists Buffalo organizing, 174
    assists Houston organizing, 180
    assists Little Rock clinic, 231
    assists organizing during IMPACT Training, 201–202
    assists with South Florida clinic fundraiser, 222
    sends letter on FACE prosecutions, 239
    sends warning letter about fake bombs, 296
Feminist Women's Health Center, 71–73
Ferraro, Barbara, 80
fetus funerals, 117–118, 223
Finik, Sherri, 82–83, 106–108, 285–286
Finkbine, Sherri, 22–23
Finkel, Brian (M.D.), 127–128
fires
    Allegheny Reproductive Health Center, 131–132
    All Women's Health Center, 149
    Blue Mountain Clinic, 211–212
    Center for Choice, Toledo, 76
    Commonwealth Clinic, 272
    Concerned Women's Clinic, 54
    Fairmont Clinic, 115, 116
    Feminist Women's Health Center, 72
    Fort Meyers, FL, 126
    Ft. Wayne Women's Health Organization, 54
    Hempstead, NY, 57
    Hope Clinic for Women, 63
    Lovejoy SurgiCenter, 288
    Margaret Sanger Center, 111
    Mountain Country Women's Center, 190
    NWHO at Fairfield, 77
    Ocala, FL, 125
    Planned Parenthood of Lancaster, 218
    Planned Parenthood of Minnesota, Inc., 236
    Redding Feminist Women's Health Center, 156–157
    Reproductive Health Services, Corpus Christi, xiii, 202
    Reproductive Services of Tulsa, 285
    Toronto, 71
    West Alabama Women's Center, 291–292

Wheaton, MD, 81
Women's Health Care Services, 102
Fitzsimmons, Ron, 137, 154, 307, 325–326
Focus on Fargo, 166
Focus on the Family, 309
Forder, Kevin, 230, 233
Foreman, Joseph Lapsley, 10, 178, 211
Forerunner, The, 88, 214
Forish, Rev. Stephen T., 55–56
Frances, Gail, 44, 81–82
Frandsen, Deb, 271
Freedom of Access to Clinic Entrances Act. *See* FACE
Freedom of Choice Act, 195
Friedan, Betty, 20
Fromm, Erich, 11
Ft. Wayne Women's Health Organization
    anthrax hoax letters, 317–318
    bomb scares, 53
    fires, 54
    physician followed, 130
    physician had car keys stolen, 178

G

Gabriel, Mark, 201
gag rule, 109, 152
Gallagher, Chet, 181, 200
Gamble, Nicki Nichols
    on cost of litigation, 68
    on PPLM blockades, 163
    at PPLM shootings, 245–246
    on receiving death threat, 247
    staff ineligible for U.S. Marshal protection, 227
Gardner, Rev. George, 159–160
Gardner, Steve, 104
Gartner, Eve, 275
Garzia, Ann, 112
Gay Days, 309
Gerard, Lisa, 118–119
Gessell, Arnold, 33
Gey, Steve, 225
Gideon Project, The, 85
Gifford, Margaret Alvis, 57–58
Goldsby, Matthew, 13, 85, 86, 101
Gracida, Bishop Rene, 148, 149
Graff, Joshua, 272
grand jury and conspiracy investigation, 273
Gray, Gloria, 291–292
Greenberg, Mary Lou, 17
Greenville Women's Clinic, 256–257
Griffin, Jimmy, 174, 176
Griffin, Michael Frederick, 150, 207–208, 263
Griffin, Richard, 257–258
Griswold, Estelle, 23
Griswold v. Connecticut, 21, 23
Gunn, David (M.D.), 141, 206

H

Hackmeyer, Paul (M.D.), 226
Hale, Margi, 144–145

Halvorson-Boyd, Glenna, 115, 116, 157
Hanzo, Jude, 14–15, 265–266
harassment of patients
    All Women's Health Services, 110
    All Women's Medical Services, 150
    Aware Woman Center for Choice, 172, 262–263, 264
    Boulder Abortion Clinic, 124
    Center for Choice, Mobile, 185
    Charleston Women's Health Center, 191
    Fairmont Clinic, 118
    Fargo Women's Health Organization, 166
    Reproductive Services of El Paso, 308–309
    South Florida unnamed clinic, 222
    Vermont Women's Health Center, 136
harassment of providers
    All Women's Health Services employee, 96
    AWCC office manager, 182
    AWCC physician, 274
    Baird-Windle, Patricia, 143, 230–231
    Carhart, Dr., 160–162
    Carson, Walter, 135
    Chelian, Renee, 248
    Chrisman Eldridge, Marilyn, 120
    Dr. Coleman funeral, 226
    Conner, Cathy, 95, 96, 105–106
    Crist, Dr., 216
    Fairmont Clinic nurse, 115
    Frandsen, Deb, 271
    Ft. Wayne physician, 130
    Hanzo, Jude, 265–266
    Hope Clinic for Women, 209
    hospitalized Charleston doctor, 292–293
    Houston physicians, 179
    Klopfer, Dr., 178
    Maguire, Lorraine, 191, 192–193, 282
    Mather, Rev. Steve, 217
    Merritt Sanford, Lisa, 203–204
    Mullen, Sally, 271, 278
    Pogrant, Diane, 281, 295–296
    Rasmussen, Jeri, 178, 209, 216–217
    Reproductive Services of Tulsa, 107
    Rose, Ann, 269
    Ruangsamboon, Dr., 200
    Sheldon, Sandy, 173
    South Florida unnamed clinic, 222
    Summit Women's Health Organization, 289
    Walsh, Deborah, 91
    Wicklund, Dr., 164, 165–166, 190
    Welsh, Tina, 197
    Wichita doctor, 209
    Windle, Reid, 217
    Windle, Roni, 222
    Windle, Ted, 217
    Women's Medical Center, Omaha, 162
Harris v. McRae, 58
Hasper, Dido, 45–46, 100
Hatch Amendment, 326
Heckert, Shauna, 14
Help and Caring Ministries, 166

Henries, William Jennings Bryan (M.D.), 21
Heritage Foundation, 41
Hermes, Lisa, 299–300
Hern, Warren (M.D.)
    clinic fired at, 109–110
    clinic vandalized, 96
    on "deadly dozen" list, 259
    and first buffer zone law, 104
    on harassment of patients, 124
Hernandez, Antonio, 245
Hickey, James A. (Bishop), 55
Hickey, James Cardinal, 277
Hickey, James T., 148–149
Hile, Allison, 63–65
Hill, Paul
    begins picket of The Ladies Center, 229–230
    founds Defensive Action, 218
    murders Dr. Britton and Colonel Barrett, 232
    sends letter to White Rose Banquet, 273
    sentenced to die, 234
    on TV after Gunn assassination, 208–209
Hill, Susan
    amends anti-trust case, 118
    on the Army of God, 65–66
    on Chrisman funeral disruption, 120
    on cost of anti-abortion activity to feminism, 14
    discovers national scope of anti-abortion activism, 99–100
    on Fargo injunction, 166
    father's death, 130
    founding member of NCAP, 137
    at Ft. Wayne blockades, 129–130
    on *NOW v. Scheidler* trial, 306–307
    opens Mississippi clinic, 261–262
    sues Nurses Concerned for Life, 53
    testifies in RICO suit, 100
Hillcrest Clinic, 78, 94, 249–250
Hirsh, Michael, 104
Hodgson v. Minnesota, 143
Hoffman, Merle, 208
Hogan, Frank, 28
Holy Faith Rescue, 157
Hope Clinic for Women, 63, 209, 268–269
Horsley, Neal, 282–283
Horton, Rev. Carl, 283–285
Houston physician harassment, 179
Human Life Amendment, 41, 62
Human Life Bill, 62
Hussey, Patricia, 80
Hyde, Henry, 307
Hyde Amendment, 53, 290

I

I Believe in Life, 91
IMPACT Team
    announced, xiii–xv
    harasses AWCC workers, 203
    profile of members and activities, 200–202
    targets Aware Woman Center for Choice, xv–xvii
    targets Florida clinics, xiii–xiv, 181, 195
imprecatory prayer, 290
Indianapolis Clinic for Women, 295
Infant Roe, 36
informed consent, 3, 68, 295
injunctions
    Aware Woman Center for Choice, 211
    Buffalo, 117
    Charleston Women's Health Center, 144
    Detroit clinics, 248
    Fargo Women's Health Organization, 166
    First Presbyterian Church in Dallas, 189
    Hillcrest Clinic, 94
    Houston clinics, 178–179
    Jackson Women's Health Organization, 262
    Knoxville Volunteer Medical Clinic, 123
    Lovejoy SurgiCenter, 153
    Morgentaler clinics in Canada, 70
    Northern Virginia Women's Medical Center, 44–45
    Planned Parenthood League of Massachusetts, 68, 163
    Toledo Medical Services, 75
    Women's Health Care Services, 158–159
    Women's Health Center, 197
Institute of Mobilized Prophetic Activated Christian Training. *See* IMPACT Team
insurance coverage
    Allegheny Reproductive Health Center, 148
    Lovejoy SurgiCenter, 288–289
    Planned Parenthood, Spokane, 279
    Reproductive Services of Tulsa, 286
    West Alabama Women's Center, 292
intact dilation and evacuation, 3, 266, 322
International Socialist Organization, 174
invasions
    Abortion and Contraception Clinic of Nebraska, 223
    Buffalo clinics, 116–117
    Center for Choice, Toledo, 76
    Delaware Women's Health Organization, 95
    Fairmont Clinic, 115–116
    first, 29
    first after *Roe v. Wade*, 47
    Hillcrest Clinic, 94
    New Women's Clinic, Corpus Christi, 148–149
    Ob-Gyn Associates, 146–147
    Pittsburgh Women's Health Services, 296–297
    Vermont Women's Health Center, 136
    Western Carolina Medical Clinic, 154–155
    Women's Health Services, 133–134
Ireland, Patricia, 326
Izard, Carolyn, 231, 293, 313–314

J

Jackson, Calvin (M.D.), 281
Jackson, Debi, 323

Jackson Women's Health Organization, 261–262
Jakubczyk, John J., 127–128
Jancha, Rick, 276–277
Jankowski, John, 190
Jepsen, Dee, 59
"Jericho Walk," 265
Jimenez, Rosaura "Rosie", 53
Johns, Eric, 201
Johnston, Peg, 81, 327
Joyce, Hallie, 231–232
judicial bypass, 2
"justifiable" homicide, 141, 186, 218, 236–237

K

Kamin, Alan, 127
Karpan, Douglas (M.D.), 170
Kelly, Patrick, 158–159
Kelowna Right to Life, 304
Kennedy, Edward M., 210
Keyes, Claire, 130–132, 147
Killea, Lucy, 137
Kilpatrick, Rev. John, 208
Kissling, Frances, 274
Klass, Allene, 153–154
Klopfer, Ulrich George, 178
Klu Klux Klan, 239
Knoxville Volunteer Medical Clinic, 121–123
Kolb, Kristin, 227
Koop, C. Everett (M.D.), 61, 62
Kopp, James
    at 1988 Democratic Convention, 113
    at Allegheny blockade, 128–129
    eludes capture, 252
    as material witness in Slepian murder, 317
    placed on FBI most wanted list, 254
    protests at Vermont Women's Health Center, 146
    suspected in Romalis shooting, 243
    suspected in Short shooting, 271
Krol, John Cardinal, 79
Kuenen, Anita, 211–213

L

Lader, Lawrence (Larry), 22, 30, 33–34, 37
Ladies Center, The
    bombed, 78–79, 84
    double murder, 232–233
    invasions, 99
    picketed by Klu Klux Klan, 239
    receives judgment in Burt case, 263
    Santa Claus visit, 84
    site of massive picket, 91
Lambs of Christ
    blockade Center for Choice II, 133
    and Dr. Wicklund, 165
    Fargo injunction, 166
    invade Western Carolina Medical Center, 154–155
    leaders arrested in Houston, 179
    and personal hygiene, 155

Larson, Darold, 63
Laster, Gerri, 152–153, 308–309
Law, Bernard Cardinal, 254
Lea, Penny, 91, 104
Lee, Bill Lann, 319
Lewis, Clayton, 82
Liberty University, 305–306
Life Advocate Magazine, 9, 258
Life Amendment Political Action Committee, 41
Life Dynamics Inc., 171, 194, 195–196, 304–305
Life Dynamics Update, 171, 196
Life Enterprises Unlimited, 186
Linwood, Joan (pseudonym), 73
Lipscomb, Archbishop Oscar H., 186
litigation costs to clinic, 63, 68, 198
Little Rock Family Planning Services, 231, 293, 313–314
Long Island Gynecological Associates, 258–259
Love, Sara, 100
Lovejoy SurgiCenter, 98–99, 119, 153, 288
Lowney, Shannon, 141, 244–245, 256
Lucas, Roy, 11, 51, 294
Lyons, Emily, 300–302

M

Madden, Patty, 151–152
Madsen v. Women's Health Center, Inc, 225, 230–231
Maginnis, Patricia, 24
Maguire, Lorraine, 15, 190–194, 282, 292–293
Maher, Bishop Leo, 137
Mahoney, Pat, 179, 181
malpractice suits, 127–128, 171. *See also* Life Dynamics Inc.
Manfredonia, Nancy, 36
March for Women's Lives, 125
Margaret Sanger Center, 111
Markley, Father Ed, 185, 187
Martinez, Bob, 132, 297
Massachusetts Citizens for Life, 67
Mather, Rev. Steven, 217
Matthews, Sandie, 133–134
McAteer, Ed, 41
McCormack, Billy, 139
McGuire, Cathy, 174
McHugh, Bishop James, 277
McHugh, Rev. James, 23–24
McMillan, Roy, 10, 218, 262
McMurty, Roy, 70
Medicaid coverage for abortion services, 2, 58–59, 290
Medical Students for Choice, 194
Melich, Tanya, 34, 59, 111, 180
Merrell, Verne Jay, 278–279
Midwest Health Center for Women, 280
Miller, Monica Migliorino, 117–118, 290–291
Missionaries to the Pre-Born, 8, 150, 182
Missouri Militia, 209
Mitchell, James, 272
Mitchell, Patricia, 184–187

Mitchell, Sonja, 164, 165
Moody, Rev. Howard, 27, 29
Moore, Matthew, 64, 66
Moore, Wayne, 64, 66
Moral Majority, 59, 61, 89, 139
Morgentaler, Henry (M.D.), 29–30, 43–44, 70–71, 114
Mother Teresa, 93
motor vehicle records and anti activity, 172, 224, 262–263, 320. *See also* Federal Drivers' Privacy Protection Act
Mountain Country Women's Center, 189–190
Mullen, Sally, 271, 278
Murphy, Timothy, 100, 102
Murray, Brian, 245
Murray, Glenn A., 117, 162, 223

N

NAF, 116, 326–327
NARAL, 293–294, 320–321
Nathanson, Bernard (M.D.), 74
National Abortion and Reproductive Rights Action League. *See* NARAL
National Abortion Federation. *See* NAF
National Association for the Repeal of Abortion Laws, 33
National Center for the Pro Choice Majority, 54, 97–98
National Clinic Violence Task Force, 319
National Coalition of Abortion Providers. *See* NCAP
National Committee for a Human Life Amendment, 195
National Organization for Women, 7, 326
National Press Club Conference, xiv
National Right to Life Committee, 5
National Women's Health Organization (NWHO), 100, 117
NCAP
    abortion report released in 1999, 328
    and Community Development Block Grants, 154
    founded, 137
    meets with Department of Justice, 241–242
    organizes congressional hearing, 93
Nenney, Susan, 180
Newhall, Elizabeth (M.D.), 259
Newhall, James (M.D.), 259, 260–261
New Right, 39, 40–41, 62
New Woman All Women Health Care, 298–301
New Women's Clinic, Corpus Christi, 148–149
New York Times, xiv, 79, 258–259, 260
Nichols, Leanne, 141, 245, 256
Nixon, Richard, 36, 227
Northern Virginia Women's Medical Center, 44–45
Northern Virginia Women's Medical Center v. County of Fairfax, 44–45
Northland Family Planning, Detroit, 247
Northside Family Planning, 285

Nova Health Systems, 82
November Gang, 136–137, 326
NOW. *See* National Organization for Women
NOW v. Scheidler, 100–102, 306–307
Nuremberg Files
    appear on Internet, 282–283
    and Planned Parenthood lawsuit, 259–260
    published by ACLA, 9–10
    and Slepian murder, 316
Nurses Concerned for Life, 53
Nurses for Life, 304

O

Ob-Gyn Associates, 146–147
O'Connor, John Cardinal, 277
O'Connor, Sandra Day, 62
Office of International Criminal Justice, Inc., 10
Officers for Life, 149
Offley, Will, 196
Ohio v. Akron Center for Reproductive Health, 143
O'Neill, Eileen, 178–179
One Nation Under God, 40
Operation Goliath, 214
Operation John the Baptist, 182
Operation Rescue
    announces IMPACT Team training, 195
    changes name to Operation Save America, 176
    first brochure, 108
    first rescues, 103
    judgment in Houston lawsuit, 179
    leaders arrested in Houston, 179
    mission, 7–8
    mounts Cites of Refuge campaign, 218
    and new agenda as OSA, 253
    and Operation John the Baptist, 182
    organizes Wichita blockades, 157–160
    pickets First Presbyterian in Dallas, 187–189
    property purchased at auction, 266
    protests at Disney World, 309
    Tucci assumes leadership, 145
    urges votes against Clinton, 182
Operation Rescue blockades
    at 1988 Democratic Convention, 112–113
    Allegheny Reproductive Health center, 128–129
    All Women's Health Center, 149
    AWCC, 126
    Buffalo clinics, 174–175
    Canada, 114
    Cherry Hill Women's Center, 124–125
    Delaware Women's Health Organization, 114
    Dr. Boyd's Office, Santa Fe, 157
    Knoxville Volunteer Medical, 121–122
    Little Rock Family Planning, 231
    Wichita clinics, 157–159
Operation Rescue National. *See* Operation Rescue
Operation Save America, 176, 253. *See also* Operation Rescue
OR. *See* Operation Rescue
Orleans Women's Clinic, 281

Ornstein, Marion, 307–308
O'Rourke, Father Joseph Francis, 45
Ortman, Carye, 17, 288–289
OSA. *See* Operation Save America
Ostrowski, William, 223
Our Father's House, 84, 110

P

parental consent laws, 2, 114, 171
Parnham, John, 208
"partial birth abortion." *See* intact dilation and
    evacuation
Partners in Vision, 63
Pastoral Plan for Pro-Life Activities, 39–40
patient harassment. *See* harassment of patients
Patrick, Deval, 279–280
Patrick, Kathy, xvii, 202, 225
Patterson, George Wayne (M.D.), 141, 220–221
Payne, Louis (M.D.), 291
Pensacola Medical Services, 141, 206–208
Pentacostals for Life, 309
People for the American Way, 252
Permenter, William (M.D.), 85
Phillips, Howard, 271
Phineas Priesthood, 278–279
Phoenix Women's Center, 127–128
Pittsburgh Response Team, 131
Pittsburgh Women's Health Services, 296–297
Pittsburgh Word and Worship Fellowship, 145
PLAN, 108
Planned Parenthood
    Brookline, 244
    Chico, 156
    Cincinnati, 323
    Federation, 180
    of Houston and Southeast Texas, 179
    Lancaster, 218
    League of Massachusetts, 67–68, 163, 244–
        245
    of Minnesota, Inc., 236
    Portland, 98–99
    San Antonio, 305
    Spokane, 278, 279
    Texas, 42
Planned Parenthood of Southeastern Pennsylvania v.
    Casey, 171, 257
Planned Parenthood of the Columbia/Willamette v.
    The American Coalition of Life Activists, 259–
    260
Plan Van, 25
Pogrant, Diane, 281, 295–296
police, at mass demonstrations, 112, 113–114,
    121–123
police, enforcing clinic protection laws
    Allentown Women's Center, 56
    Buffalo GYN Womanservices, 176
    Center for Choice, Mobile, 187–189
    Cherry Hill Women's Center, 125
    Hillcrest Clinic, 94
    Hope Clinic for Women, 268–269

    Houston, 179
    New Jersey, 256
    PPLM, 163, 247
    Vermont Women's Health Center, 146
    Women's Health Center, 199
police, failing to respond to clinics
    Allegheny Reproductive Health Center, 130–
        131
    Aware Woman Center for Choice, 215
    Center for Choice II, 133
    Charleston Women's Health Center, 145
    Cherry Hill Women's Center, 124–125
    Corpus Christi, 148–149
    Delaware Women's Health Organization, 120
    Ft. Wayne Women's Health Organization, 54
    Hope Clinic for Women, 63
    Midwest Health Center for Women, 280
    Northern Virginia Women's Medical Center,
        44
    Redding Feminist Women's Health Center,
        156
    Reproductive Services of El Paso, 152–153
police, involvement in anti-abortion activity, 90–
    91, 149, 181, 284
police, and Slepian murder, 315
police lose stabbing suspect, 281
Policemen for Life, 284
post-traumatic stress disorder, 15
PPLM. *See* Planned Parenthood League of Massa-
    chusetts
Press, Shalom (M.D.), 117, 174–175
Preterm Health Services, 245–246
Prewitt, Terry, 85
Price, Bill, 196
Problem Pregnancy Center, 104
Problem Pregnancy Inc., 67
Pro-Choice Action League, 219
pro-choice community ignores clinic violence, 325–
    326
Pro-Choice Network of Western New York, 117
"Project Choice: The Abortion Provider--A Self
    Analysis," 195–196
Project Rescue Western New York, 116–117
Pro-Life Action League, 6–7, 58, 93
Pro-Life Action Network. *See* PLAN
Pro-Life Virginia, 258
Pyrdum, Carl, Jr., 113

R

Rabinski, Lena, 125–126
Racketeer Influenced Corrupt Organizations Act.
    See RICO
Ramey, Cathy, 228
Randall, Father John, 98
Randall, Lynne, 100, 112
Raney, Meredith Trotter, Jr.
    admits WLAC is fictitious, 172–173, 205
    deposed, 11
    deposition excerpts, 310–311
    files complaint against AWCC, 303

files FACE lawsuit against AWCC, 294
files first lawsuit against AWCC, 143
first protest at AWCC, 132
loses AWCC malpractice lawsuit, 270
sends letter to Dr. Rodriguez, 267–268
sends WLAC letter to AWCC patients, 172, 262–263
targets Dr. Whitney in letters, 269–270
traces AWCC patients through motor vehicle department, 205
WLAC prompts state inspections of AWCC, 267
WLAC sends letter to patients, 172
Rasmussen, Jeri, 178, 209, 216–217, 280
Ratigan, Brian, 278–279
Reagan, Ronald, 61, 64, 79, 115
Reavis, Cathy, 158, 220
Reconstructionists, 140
Redding Feminist Women's Health Center, 156–157
Redmond, Eugene (M.D.), 294
Reed, Marjorie, 75, 77, 132
Reiner, Judy, 179, 180
Religious Leaders for Choice, 159
Religious Violence and Abortion, 85
Reno, Janet, 227, 244, 319
Reproductive Services, Texas, 42–43
Reproductive Services of Corpus Christi, 202
Reproductive Services of El Paso, 152–153, 308–309
Reproductive Services of Tulsa, 82–83, 106–108, 285, 286
Republican Party, influence of Christian right, 240
Republican Party and abortion
1976 platform supports abortion ban, 47
1980 platform guided by Moral Majority, 59
1984 platform supports Human Life Amendment, 79
1988 Convention plank and delegate profile, 111
Houston blockades during convention, 178–179
lures Democratic Catholic voters, 34
Rescue America, 10, 179
Rescue the Heartland, 283–284
rescues and costs to cities, 111–112
Reynolds, James, 242, 280
RICO, 7, 100–102, 306–307
Rider, Cathy, 191–194
Risen, James, 62, 103
Ritter, Father Bruce, 93
Roberts, Dotti, 73
Robertson, Pat, 109, 139, 159, 162
Rock for Life, 6
Rodriguez, Lino B. (M.D.), 267–268
Rodriguez, Pablo (M.D.), 236
Roe v. Wade, 19, 37
Rogers, Jay, 88, 214
Romalis, Garson (M.D.), 242–243, 323
Roman Catholic Church

anti-abortion legislation, 39–40, 42
and Brookline shootings, 254
and Call to Action, 273–274
on Catholics for a Free Choice *New York Times* ad, 80
and City Bank of Rhode Island, 236
creates National Right to Life Committee, 23–24
denounces Father Trosch, 186
efforts to reverse New York State abortion laws, 36–37
excommunicates clinic director, 98, 148, 150
excommunicates physician, 148
forbids abortion in their hospitals, 43
hires public relations firm, 145–146
hospital mergers as threats to access, 4
Minnesota Bishop lobbies state legislature, 197
protests Allentown Women's Center opening, 55
rebukes Archbishop Weakland, 124
retired bishop warns against voting for Clinton, 280–281
and Santa Fe blockades, 157
urges Candidate Killea to reverse position on abortion, 137
withdraws contribution to Duluth United Way, 199
Rose, Ann, 269
Ross, Michael
convicted of threatening Dr. Wicklund, 190
sends threatening letters, 211–212, 271, 277–278
sentenced, 213
Routh Street Women's Clinic, 91–92, 194
Rowell, Bob, 106
Ruangsamboon, Monthree (M.D.), 200, 203
Rudolph, Eric Robert, 252, 254, 285, 302
Rushdoony, Rousas John, 140

S

Salvi, John, III
background, 257–258
captured, 249–250
commits suicide, 281
convicted of murder, 275
and Donald Spitz, 258
found competent to stand trial, 268
murders clinic workers, 244–246
pleads not guilty, 258
trial begins, 273
Sanderson, Robert "Sande," 298–299
Sanford, Lisa Merritt, 203–204
Sauer, Jane, 245
Scaife, Richard Mellon, 41
Scalia, Antonin, 228
Schaeffer, Francis, 61, 87
Scheidler, Joseph
at 1984 NAF convention, 116
announces publication of his book, 93
arranges for fetus theft, 117–118

arrested for trespass at Delaware Women's
    Health Organization, 105
arrested in Denver, 99
conduct during RICO trial, 306–307
elected to PLAN Leadership Council, 108
endorses Phillips for president, 271
founds Pro-Life Action League, 6–7, 58
meets President Reagan, 61
NOW v. Scheidler (RICO trial), 100–102,
    306–307
at OR blockade in Canada, 114
at rally in Dallas, 95
and Randy Terry, 103
Schenck, Rev. Paul Chaim, 162
Schenck, Rev. Robert, 178, 315–316
Schenck v. Pro-Choice Network, 287
Schnitger, Eileen, 4, 17
Scholberg, Andrew, 100, 102
Schweitz, Bishop Roger, 197
Scott, Daniel, 183
Sedlak, Jim, 6
Seron, Richard J., 245
SHAME, 265–266
Shannon, Rachelle "Shelley"
    at 1988 Democratic Convention, 113
    AOG Manual unearthed in backyard, 167
    found guilty of shooting Dr. Tiller, 220
    knitting auctioned at White Rose Banquet, 272
    and Lovejoy judgment, 153–154
    mails *The Brockhoeft Report*, 205
    MTPB raises money, 150
    shoots Dr. Tiller, 219
Sheldon, Lou, 182
Sheldon, Sandy, 15, 173
Sherlock, Kevin, 87
Shield of Roses, 102
Shields, Kenneth, 81, 82
shootings
    Barrett, James, 232–233
    Barrett, June, 232–233
    Boulder Abortion Clinic, 109–110
    Britton, Dr., 232–233
    Central Health Center for Women, 167
    Fainman, Dr., 295
    Gunn, Dr., 206–207
    Hackmeyer, Dr., 226
    Hillcrest Clinic, 249–250
    Karpan, Dr., 170
    The Ladies Center, 232–233
    Lowney, Shannon, 244–245, 256
    Nichols, Leanne, 245, 256
    Patterson, Dr., 141, 220–221
    Reproductive Services of Tulsa, 286
    Romalis, Dr., 242–243
    Short, Dr. Hugh, 271
    Slepian, Dr., 314–315
    Tiller, Dr., 219
Short, Hugh (M.D.), 271
Shuck, Tim, 119
Silent Scream, The, 74–75

Simmons, James, 85, 86
Simmons, Kathren, 13, 85, 86
Sims, Raquel, 317–318
Singletary, Jeanne, 206, 221
Slepian, Barnett (M.D.)
    and Buffalo injunction, 117
    confronted by Rev. Paul Schenck, 162
    letter to editor, 235
    murdered, 314–315
    reward offered to solve murder, 319
Slepian, Lynne, 314–315
Slovenic, Joe, 181
Smeal, Eleanor "Ellie," xiv, xvi, 132, 324, 325
Smith, Rev. Don, 283
Snydle, Frank (M.D.), 143, 200
Sobieski, Tammy, 213–214
Sons of Thunder, 34
Sorrentino, Ann, 98
Southern Baptist Convention, 309
Southern Poverty Law Center. *See* SPLC
Southern Tier Women's Services, 80
South Florida unnamed clinic, 222
Spencer, Robert (M.D.), 30
Spillar, Kathy, xiv, xv, 201–202
Spinks, Thomas, 81, 82
Spitz, Rev. Donald, 10, 258, 272, 316
SPLC, 263
spousal consent, 47, 171
Spring of Life, 117, 174
St. John the Baptisting, 217
Stigmatize, Harangue, Agitate, Mortify and Expose
    (SHAME) Campaign, 265–266
Stop Planned Parenthood (STOPP), 6
Stover, Dawn, 228
Straus, Diane, 124–125, 127
Strauss, Diane, 100
Stutes, Damon (M.D.), 15, 240–241
Summer of Mercy, 157–160
Summit Women's Health Organization
    clinic administrator property vandalized, 281
    loses lease, 100
    staff picketed at restaurant, 289
    vandalism, 295–296
    wins RICO judgment, 102
Supreme Court and abortion
    Baird v. Eisenstadt, 21
    *City of Akron v. Akron Center for Reproductive
        Health*, 68, 257
    Griswold v. Connecticut, 21, 23
    Harris v. McRae, 58–59
    Hodgson v. Minnesota, 143
    Madsen v. Women's Health Center, Inc, 230
    *Northern Virginia Women's Medical Center v.
        County of Fairfax*, 44
    Ohio v. Akron Center for Reproductive Health,
        143
    *Planned Parenthood of Southeastern Pennsylva-
        nia v. Casey*, 171, 257
    Roe v. Wade, 19, 37
    Rust v. Sullivan (Title X funds), 152

Webster v. Reproductive Health Services, 119
Survivor Summer, 312
Swaggert, Jimmy, 89
Sweet Home United Methodist Church, 174–175
Sweigert, Karen (M.D.), 259

T

Taft, Charlotte, 91, 95–96, 194, 327
Taggart, Linda
  on Britton shooting, 233
  Christmas Eve bombing, 84
  on Gunn shooting, 207
  Ladies Center bombed for the first time, 78–79
  and Paul Hill, 229
  permanently injured in invasion, 99
  testifies in RICO suit, 100
Teen Savvy Conference, 187–189
telephone harassment, 52, 96, 171, 201. *See also*
  "The 800 Club"
"termite tactics", 330
Terry, Cindy, 80
Terry, Randall "Randy"
  at 1988 Democratic Convention, 113
  announces Buffalo blockades, 173–174
  arrives in Melbourne for IMPACT Team, 181
  begins activism in Binghamton, 103
  begins serving Atlanta sentence, 136
  on birth control, 8
  candidate for Congress, 314
  contact with Joseph Scheidler, 103
  at crisis pregnancy center, 103
  declares bankruptcy, 318–319
  elected to PLAN Leadership Council, 108
  endorses Phillips for president, 271
  first invasion, 88
  first OR "rescue", 103
  first pickets, 80
  during IMPACT training, xvi–xvii, 202
  jailed in Wichita, 159
  mission, 9
  named in RICO suit, 100
  organizes Operation Rescue, 88
  quotes from *Accessory to Murder*, 142
  reason for founding OR, 7–8
  receives award, 264
  serves sentence in federal prison, 243
  at Wichita blockades, 158
Therapeutic Abortion Committees, 31, 43
Thomas, July L., 62, 103
Thorburn, Father Timothy J., 274
Tiller, George (M.D.), 102–103, 158, 218–219
Time to Kill, A, 141, 237–238
Toledo Medical Services, 75
Tomanek, Oldrich, 91, 93, 183–184
Tompkins, Carolyn, 93, 183
Tompkins, Norman (M.D.), 93, 183–184
Toronto Medical Services, 114
Traditional Values Coalition, 182
Treshman, Donald, 10, 128, 290
Trewhella, Matt, 8, 10, 150, 211, 218

Trosch, Father David, 10, 185–187, 218
Tucci, Keith
  arrives in Melbourne for IMPACT Team, 181
  assumes head of OR, 145
  and Connections Conference, 243
  jailed in Wichita, 159
  letter exhorting followers, 152
  purchases house across from AWCC, 214
  at RICO trial, 101
  at Sweet Home Church during OR blockades,
    175
Tunney, Mary Ellen, 297
Turley, Linda, 184

U

United States Marshals, 159, 227, 233, 234–235
unsolved crimes
  fake bomb, AWCC at West Palm, 281
  fire, Dr. Carhart, 160–162
  fire, Fairmont Clinic, 115–116
  fire, Florida clinic, 125–126
  fire, Lovejoy SurgiCenter, 288
  fire, Omaha garage, 162
  fire, Reproductive Services, Corpus Christi,
    202
  fire, West Alabama Women's Center, 291–292
  shooting, Central Health Center for Women,
    167
  shooting, Dr. Fainman, 295
  shooting, Dr. Hackmeyer, 226
  shooting, Dr. Karpan, 170
  shooting, Dr. Patterson, 220–221
  shooting, Dr. Romalis, 242–243
  shooting, Dr. Short, 242–243
  shooting, Dr. Slepian, 317
  vandalism, Abortion and Contraception Clinic
    of Nebraska, 227
  vandalism, Fargo Women's Health Organiza-
    tion, 318
  vandalism, Summit Women's Health Organi-
    zation, 295–296
U.S. Taxpayer's Party, 264, 271–272

V

vandalism. *See also* fires
  Abortion and Contraception Clinic of
    Nebraska, 226–227
  Allegheny Reproductive Health Center, 132,
    147–148
  Boulder Abortion Clinic, 96
  Center for Choice, Mobile, 184
  Cherry Hill Women's Center, 127
  Fairmont Clinic, 115
  Fargo Women's Health Organization, 318,
    319
  Florida clinics, 307–308
  The Ladies Center, 79
  Mountain Country Women's Center, 190
  outlined in *Closed: 99 Ways to Stop Abortion*,
    93–94

Reproductive Services of El Paso, 152
Reproductive Services of Tulsa, 107
Ruangsamboon, Dr., 200
Southern Tier Women's Services, 81
Summit Women's Health Organization, 281
West End Women's Medical Group, 240
The Women's Center, 74
Women's Health Care Services, 162
Women's Health Center, 197
Women's Health Services, 151–152
Vargas, Rachel, 148
Vaughn, Bishop Austin, 103
Verhoeven, Alice, 67, 244–245, 246
Vermont Save a Baby, 146
Vermont Women's Health Center, 136, 146
Viguerie, Richard, 41
violence and effects on clinic workers
    anthrax hoax letters, 318
    Baird-Windle, Patricia, 208
    Buckham, Marilynn, 316–317
    Central Florida Women's Health Organiza-
        tion, 308
    Chelian, Renee, 247–249
    Florida doctors, 85
    Hermes, Lisa, 300
    Hile, Allison on Zevallos kidnapping, 65
    Keyes, Clair, 131
    Lyons, Emily, 301
    Maryland, 82
    Newhall, Dr. Elizabeth, 259
    overview, 15–17
    Reavis, Cathy, 220
    Redding Feminist Women's Health Center,
        156
    Taggart, Linda, 233
    Verhoeven, Alice and PPLM staff, 246
    Walsh, Deborah, 75, 176–177
    Wicklund, Dr., 164, 190
VitaMed, 117–118
Volunteer Medical Clinic, 75, 91
Vriens, Jennifer, 100, 118, 120
Vuitch, Milan (M.D.), 33

W

waiting periods, 3, 171, 295
Walsh, Deborah
    and anti police officer, 90–91
    assaulted, 75
    and clinic invasion in NC, 154–155
    files federal lawsuit, 123
    injured at Knoxville blockade, 121–122
    and protestors, 176–177
Walton, Rus, 40
wanted posters
    "Deadly Dozen", 259
    Evans, Dr., 144
    Florida physicians, 181
    Sheldon, Sandy, 173
    Snydle, Dr., 143
    Wicklund, Dr., 164

Ward, Susan, 175
Washington Area Clinic Defense Task Force, 326
Watson, Gordon, 10
Weakland, Archbishop Rembert, 123–124
Welsh, Tina, 196–200
Weslin, Father Norman
    at 1988 Democratic Convention, 113
    arrested in Fargo, 155
    at Center for Choice II blockade, 133
    founder, Lambs of Christ, 9
    and plannedparenthood.com, 287
West Alabama Women's Center, 291–292
West Coast Sisters, 31–32
West End Women's Medical Group, 240–241
Western Carolina Medical Clinic, 154–155
Westminster Presbyterian Church, 283–285
Weyrich, Paul, 41, 253
What Ever Happened to the Human Race?, 61
Wheaton, MD clinic, 81–82
Whipple, Beverly, 71–72
White, Jeff, 10
White Rose, The, 91–92
White Rose Banquet, 272–273
Whitney, Randall "Randy", 50, 52, 269–270
Why Life?, 6
Wichita doctor harassed, 209
Wicklund, Susan (M.D.), 163–166, 189–190, 212
Wiggins, Kaye, 13, 85, 86
Wilson, F. Scott, 73–74
Windle, Patricia Baird. See Baird-Windle, Patricia.
Windle, Reid, 57, 217
Windle, Roni, 222
Windle, Ted, xv, 217, 227–228
WLAC, 172–173, 262–263, 264
Women and Children Resources Act, 5
Women's Center, The, 73–74
Women's Health Care Services, 102–103, 158–
    159, 162
Women's Health Care Specialists, 4
Women's Health Center (Canada), 242
Women's Health Center, Minnesota, 196–197,
    198, 199
Women's Health Center, Orlando, 213–214
Women's Health Services, 133–134, 151, 151–152,
    196
Women's Legal Action Coalition. See WLAC
Women's Medical Center, Omaha, 162
Women's Medical Center, Texas, 170

Y

Yellow Page Publisher's Association, 166–167
Yeo, Rev. Eleanor, 100
Yeoman, Barry, 253–254

Z

Zevallos, Hector (M.D.), 64–65
Zevallos, Rosalee Jean, 64–65
zoning regulations. See clinic zoning regulations